Property of:
    Elaine Wechsler

FERRUCCIO
BUSONI

FERRUCCIO BUSONI
Drawing from memory by RAFFAELLO BUSONI
1925

FERRUCCIO BUSONI

A BIOGRAPHY

By

EDWARD J. DENT

EULENBURG BOOKS

LONDON

This edition first published in 1974 by
Ernst Eulenburg Ltd
48 Great Marlborough Street, London w1v 2bn

This reprint has been authorised by the
Oxford University Press

isbn 0 903873 02 8 paperback
0 903873 15 x hardback

**Printed and bound in England by
Caligraving Ltd, Thetford, Norfolk.**

Alla

SIGNORA

GERDA BUSONI

ed ai suoi figli

BENVENUTO

e

RAFFAELLO

PREFACE

WHEN I was first entrusted with the task of writing the life of Ferruccio Busoni I imagined that the greater part of my book would be devoted to a study of his compositions. Biographical material, so far as I could judge from what had previously been written about him, was scanty and of minor interest. Dr. Hugo Leichtentritt's little book (*Ferruccio Busoni*, Leipzig, Breitkopf & Härtel, 1916) gives a useful outline and a concise guide to his works; Gisela Selden-Goth's (*F. B.*, Vienna, E. P. Tal, 1922) paints an interesting portrait in a rather ecstatic style; Siegfried Nadel's (*F. B.*, Breitkopf & Härtel, 1931) is valuable mainly as a supplement to Leichtentritt. Busoni was very unwilling to talk about his early life; even his own sons knew very little about it, and the reader of this book will soon discover the reason. Had he lived longer in the enjoyment of sound health, it is quite probable that he might have written his own autobiography. He began to do so in 1909, but carried it no farther than his sixth year; various memoranda, however, exist in his handwriting which suggest that he in later life had some idea of continuing it. It was not until after his death that more copious materials for the story of his life became available, so copious indeed, that when I came to examine them I soon saw that they were sufficient for an entire book. My chief difficulty, in fact, has been that of selection and arrangement.

The reader must therefore not expect to find here any detailed analysis or criticism of Busoni's compositions, nor any elaborate discussion of his pianoforte-playing. To treat either of these subjects at all adequately would have required a second volume at least as long as this one, with extensive musical illustrations and written in a strictly technical style. My chief aim in this book has been to tell the story of Busoni's career and to present

his many-sided personality as far as possible in his own
words.

A very large number of Busoni's letters have been preserved, as well as many letters of his parents and friends.
Programmes and press-cuttings were also available in
large quantities, going back as far as the début of Busoni's
mother in 1847, though unfortunately far from complete.
During Busoni's early life these were collected and arranged by his father; in later years they were put in order
by the kindness of Fräulein Agnes Krziwik. I have
quoted few of Busoni's letters in their entirety or even at
any great length, as there is some likelihood of a selection
from them being published separately; but I have drawn
upon them perpetually for information. Various relatives
and friends of Busoni have supplied me with personal
recollections of great interest, and I have naturally made
use of my own memories of Busoni during a friendship
of over twenty years. I have most carefully avoided any
temptation to treat his life after the manner of a novel, and
I hope I can safely say that there is no statement in this
book for which I cannot produce positive evidence. The
various conversations recorded are taken word for word
from letters or from other authentic sources.

For personal recollections I am naturally indebted first
and foremost to Signora Gerda Busoni. Since I first
began work on this book in 1926 I have profited continuously by her generous help and wise counsel. Busoni's
cousins, Signor Orfeo Busoni and the late Signora
Ersilia Grusovin-Zilli, kindly supplied me with many
details, especially about Busoni's parents and his early life.
Signor Emilio Anzoletti, Mr. and Mrs. Frederick Delius,
Herr Egon Petri, and Monsieur I. Philipp have given me
much valuable information, and I am further indebted
to Miss Maud Allan, Professor Felice Boghen, Signor
Bonucci, Signor Alfredo Casella, Mrs. Cottlow, Herr
H. W. Draber, Mr. Frederick Jacobi, Professor Fritz
Kreisler, Miss Rosamond Ley, Mr. W. J. L. Pearson,
the late Mr. Percy Pitt, Frau Dr. Prelinger (*née* Mayer),

Preface

Monsieur Leonhard Tauber, Dr. Francesco Vatielli, Dr. William Wallace, and Herr Michael von Zadora.

Signora Busoni placed all her own letters from Busoni at my disposal and also collected a large number of his letters to other people; further correspondents have sent me letters directly. Besides those of Signora Busoni, I have utilized letters to Dr. Volkmar Andreae, Signor Emilio Anzoletti, Monsieur Émile R. Blanchet, the late Marchese Silvio della Valle di Casanova, Professor Robert Freund, Frau Gericke, Professor Philipp Jarnach, Fraulein Margarete Klinckerfuss, the late Herr Otto von Kapff, the late Mrs. Lanier, Baroness Jella Oppenheimer, Monsieur I. Philipp, Frau Dr. Prelinger, Herr Egon Petri and his parents, Herr Hans Reinhart, Dr. Alicja Simon, Herr Leopold Stolz, Professor José Vianna da Motta, and the late Professor Martin Wegelius. To all these (or their representatives) I express my grateful thanks.

I have to thank also the physician who attended Busoni during his last illness for a detailed description of it and for many touching reminiscences.

For portraits I am indebted to Signor Raffaello Busoni, Messrs. Elliot & Fry, Mr. Edmond X. Kapp, Mr. Sydney Loeb, and the various photographers named in the list of illustrations. I have to thank Messrs. J. M. Dent & Sons for kind permission to quote a letter of Wagner from a translation published by them.

I owe a very special debt of gratitude to Dr. Friedrich Schnapp. The list of Busoni's repertory and the catalogue of his compositions printed as appendices are entirely his work. He has constantly supplied me with minor information, verified references, and corrected my errors with an industry and accuracy for which the epithet 'German' is the only adequate word. Without his help I could never have written this book; there came a moment when I felt forced to refuse it, or the book would have remained unfinished at my death. I thank him most sincerely, not only for his labours but also for his unending patience and kindness.

Preface

Lastly, I must thank Mrs. Creighton, Miss Rosamond Ley, Mr. Lawrence Haward, and Dr. Anton Mayer for reading my manuscript and giving me the benefit of much valuable advice and criticism.

Busoni used often to tease me for my academic habit of saying that one must look at things 'from a historical point of view'. The last time that I went to see him—it was in April 1922, before his illness had become serious—he suddenly called out, by way of friendly greeting, 'My dear Dent, how pleased you will be when I am dead and gone, for then you will be able to look at *me* from a historical point of view.' Needless to say, no answer was expected; after this disconcerting remark Busoni, as always, covered up his tracks with his characteristic roar and rumble of explosive laughter.

E. J. D.

CAMBRIDGE,
October 1932.

x

CONTENTS

ILLUSTRATIONS

xiii

B·

Illustrations

Illustrations

CHAPTER I

CHILDHOOD

TRAVELLERS in Italy know Empoli, if they know it at all, only as a railway-junction where they change trains for Siena on the journey from Florence or Pisa. It is a town of little historical or artistic interest. It lies on the south bank of the Arno, almost half-way between Pisa and Florence, in a fertile agricultural district; its only pictur- esque feature is the arcaded market square, on the east side of which stands the cathedral with its characteristic Tuscan façade of black and white marble. Half a century ago Empoli was so untouched by modern developments as to be still without gas-light. It had then some seven thousand inhabitants; its chief industries were tanning and the manufacture of sulphur matches, its chief claim to a tourist's notice the curious 'flight of the ass' which annu- ally enlivened the festival of Corpus Domini. Every year on this day a young ass brought from Florence was taken to the top of the cathedral tower. A towel was put round his neck and a man went through a pretence of shaving him; after that he was adorned with a pair of gilt wings and made to slide down a rope to the foot of the Palazzo Ghibellino. This curious custom, which survived until 1861, commemorated an incident in 1397, when the citizens of Empoli were besieging the neighbouring town of San Miniato. The besieged, confident in their walls, mockingly said that the Empolesi could no more storm them than they could make an ass fly. But the Empolesi did succeed in storming San Miniato, and having done so proceeded to show that they could make an ass fly too. Empoli has never produced any famous poets, and the 'flying ass', as Ferruccio Busoni remarked, was its nearest acquaintance with Pegasus.

In the days before railways existed the river Arno was an important highway of traffic between Florence and the

I

seaport of Leghorn. To own a barge was a source of considerable prosperity; several of the well-to-do families in Empoli at this day are descended from barge-owners of the eighteenth century. One of these barge-owners, who lived not at Empoli but at Spicchio, a little village on the north bank of the Arno inhabited mainly by bargemen, bore the name of Busoni. His family is said to have come originally from Corsica. He amassed a good fortune, but as he died of a contagious disease, the local authorities, to whom plague was too familiar a terror not to be dreaded, ordered his house and property to be burned, with the result that his widow and her three sons were left in destitution. They migrated to Empoli, where the sons became makers of felt hats and appear to have done fairly well in their business. The second son, Giovanni Battista, married Anna Bini, the daughter of a market-gardener, and had by her six sons and three daughters. He died after a long illness in 1860, and his wife did not long survive him. Once again the Busoni family found themselves in difficult circumstances. Giovanni Battista's third son, Alfonso, who was not more than ten years old when his father died, had to devote himself to the maintenance of his younger brothers. The second son was already married; the eldest, Ferdinando, although undoubtedly the most remarkable member of the family, was by no means the man to undertake such a responsibility.

Ferdinando Busoni, who was born on June 24, 1834, was strangely different from the rest of the family. His brothers settled down to be prosperous tradesmen in Empoli or the neighbourhood; Ferdinando, however, had no inclination for the humdrum life of a provincial town. His father had intended him to be a hat-maker, but he neglected his work and hid himself in corners to read the literary classics and practise the clarinet. He had a passion for horses and dogs, and the Italian's love of ostentation without the Italian's capacity for hard work. From childhood he was capricious and self-willed, hot-tempered and impatient. His general education seems to

2

have been irregular; but he had the Tuscan's facility for literary expression, as well as his full share of the Tuscan genius for bitter speech. He was naturally gifted for music, but never received a systematic training in it. As a boy he learned to play the clarinet, and on this instrument he eventually came to develop a singular technical skill. His teacher at Empoli was Gaetano Fabiani, the director of the town band, but as he was perpetually quarrelling with him (and with all the other musicians in the town as well) he left Empoli when he was about twenty, having escaped military service by the system of payment, and joined the Banda Carini at Leghorn. It was natural enough that he should be ill at ease in his native town. Perhaps he overrated his own abilities; more probably his fellow-musicians underrated them and were at the same time jealous of them. But in any case Ferdinando Busoni was a man who made enemies wherever he went.

Italy was at that period the country in which clarinet-playing had been developed to the highest degree of accomplishment. Ernesto Cavallini (1807–73), who for a long time was first clarinet in the orchestra of La Scala at Milan, was regarded as 'the Paganini of the clarinet'. Whether Ferdinando Busoni was ever a pupil of his has not been ascertained; Cavallini went to Russia in 1852 and remained there for fifteen years, but it is possible that Ferdinando may have studied under him or at least heard him as a youth. He undoubtedly modelled his style on Cavallini, and Cavallini's operatic fantasias formed his chief repertory. Ferdinando was first clarinet in the Banda Municipale at Novara and professor of the instrument at the Istituto Musicale for five months in 1862, but resigned in September of that year on grounds of ill-health. There may well have been other reasons besides ill-health for his resignation, but from what is known of him in later life there can be no doubt that the reason alleged was only too well established.

For the rest of his active life Ferdinando adopted the career of a travelling virtuoso. It suited his nomadic temperament and his peculiar artistic outlook as well; his lack of conventional musicianship made him unfitted for a permanent post in an orchestra, and his quarrelsome temper injured him the less when he never stayed more than a few days in one place. He was a poor sight-reader and his sense of rhythm was erratic, but his performance on the clarinet was everywhere considered quite extraordinary; his son described it as combining the virtuosity of a violinist with the beauty and sensitiveness of the old Italian *bel canto*.

We hear of him at Milan in 1863; in June 1864 he was at Bologna, where he was made an honorary member of the famous Accademia Filarmonica, and on April 12, 1865, he played at Trieste. As partner at his second concert, in May, he had a young local pianist, Signorina Anna Weiss. Ferdinando was an imposing figure, strikingly handsome in the style of his day, with a luxuriant brown beard and a somewhat theatrically romantic appearance. He was alleged to have had innumerable love-affairs with ladies of the Italian aristocracy. Anna fell in love with him at first sight. She was no longer in her first youth, being over thirty, and she was none too happy at home. She had had many suitors, but her father had considered none of them good enough for her. The moment came at last when she made her own choice.

Her father, Josef Ferdinand Weiss, was of Bavarian stock, but born and educated at Laibach (Ljubljana), where his father was a painter and gilder of some skill. Josef, who was born in 1799, had a decent schooling, but was cast on his own resources by his father at the age of thirteen. He went to sea, and at the age of about thirty established himself at Trieste, where he was employed by a firm of grain merchants in Hamburg, Alexander and Christian Schröder, whom he served continuously for sixty years. 'Weisserle', as the partners called him, was much beloved by his employers, and must have started in their business with a position of some responsibility and dignity, for he married a young lady of good Italian family,

4

Carolina de Candido, who came from Friuli, the country lying at the foot of the Venetian Alps. They had three children, a son and two daughters. The son showed promise of talent as a painter, but became mentally deranged at the age of twenty and lived in an asylum until his death at the age of forty-eight. Anna was born on January 13, 1833; her younger sister Mina married a Signor Grusovin about 1855 and died of consumption in 1870, leaving two daughters, Ersilia and Carolina, of whom the younger is still living.

Anna had been brought up with considerable strictness. From the time that he settled at Trieste, if not before, 'Sor Giuseppe' Weiss had become completely Italian. The family, like every Italian family in Trieste, spoke the local dialect, differing little from that of Venice. Anna evidently had a good literary education. She wrote Italian fluently and correctly, expressing herself always in well-turned sentences, if with a somewhat conventional phraseology; she knew French well, and her favourite authors were Chateaubriand and Lamartine. She was equally familiar with German, but she never spoke it if she could possibly avoid doing so, and probably never wrote it. When she did speak German she affected a pedantic accuracy of pronunciation. Throughout her life she certainly had the greatest difficulty in reading German script. The Weiss family indeed had nothing German about them but their name, and their circle of friends was almost exclusively Italian.

Anna's musical gifts had manifested themselves at an early age, and she was given every opportunity of cultivating them. She made her first public appearance as a pianist at the age of fourteen, playing a fantasia of Thalberg at a school concert in February 1847. Her teacher at that time was a man named La Font; she was also studying counterpoint with Scaramelli. She played again in May, presenting a fantasia this time of her own composition, and her audience was quite enraptured not only by the delicacy and precision of her execution, but still more by her fairy-like appearance and the ecstatic devotion with which the child threw herself into the expression of her music. About 1848 she began to take lessons from a Hungarian pianist, Ferdinand Carl Lickl, under whom she made still more rapid progress; her teacher for composition was Luigi Ricci. Ricci was a Neapolitan, famous as the composer, or rather joint composer with his brother Vittorio, of the once widely popular comic opera *Crispino e la Comare*, produced in 1850 at Trieste, where Luigi Ricci had been director of music at the cathedral since 1835. A *Sanctus* with orchestra, composed by Anna Weiss, was performed at the cathedral on Easter Sunday, 1851.

She played frequently at charity concerts in Trieste during the next few years and became quite a local celebrity. She is always described in the newspapers as an amateur; her father no doubt considered it out of the question for a young lady of her social position to become a professional player. It may be noted, too, that music in Trieste was in those days very largely dependent on amateur talent, and it is clear from the programmes given that the amateurs of Trieste, both Italian and German, possessed a notably high general standard of ability. A naval bandmaster by name Sawerthal had organized an orchestra, and Anna frequently played concertos to its accompaniment. Her repertory, however, does not seem to have been large; Mozart's Concerto in D minor and Weber's in E flat were her stock pieces with orchestra, and her solos seldom went beyond the operatic fantasias of Thalberg and Liszt. In 1855 she gave three concerts in Vienna. Even in Vienna pianoforte recitals were at that time unknown and concert programmes were of a type which one would hardly encounter to-day except at such places as Nice or Monte Carlo—an easy classical trio to begin with, followed by a string of showy solo pieces. Such were Anna's programmes at Vienna. The critics praised her precision of style and her delicacy of expression; with true Viennese gallantry they made the most of her good looks.

6

She was beautiful indeed, but seems to have been hardly conscious of either her beauty or her popularity. At home she was much in request as a teacher for young ladies, no doubt largely on account of her unimpeachable personal character. Brought up by an adoring mother whose adoration she returned with passionate intensity, she was profoundly religious, and seemed to live entirely in a world of artistic sentiment and devotional aspiration—a world reflected only too accurately in the favourite music of her age. It was a world not so much of culture as of refinement, and refinement was perhaps the main characteristic of Anna's personality; we see it not only in her music, but in her letters and in her literary tastes. It was a characteristic utterly lacking in the man who was to be her husband. Her father, 'Sor Giuseppe', had no romantic illusions about him. He saw at once that Ferdinando Busoni was the type of man who sought popular applause ('ricercatore di facili glorie' is his son's description of him), had no great love of hard work and was only too ready to let himself be supported by the labour of others. He turned him out of the house and set his face sternly against the marriage; but Anna insisted, and married they were within a few weeks.

After marriage Ferdinando added his wife's surname to his own, thinking, apparently, that the double name of Weiss-Busoni sounded more distinguished. They toured together giving concerts at various places, and towards the end of March 1866 they were in Rome, where Anna played in the presence of Liszt. Her confinement was close at hand, and Ferdinando, realizing the situation, hurried her off to his native town. At Empoli, in a little house occupied by his sisters on the Campaccio, as it was then called (now Piazza Vittorio Emmanuele), an unpaved open space which served as a horse-market, she gave birth with desperate effort to a son on the morning of Easter Sunday, April 1. It was just a week after her concert at Rome. Ferdinando, who 'like Tristram Shandy's father', as the son remarked later, believed that a child's name

7

could exercise an influence on its future, had him chris-
tened after various illustrious Tuscans—Ferruccio Dante
Michelangiolo Benvenuto. His godfathers were Gaetano
Fabiani, the bandmaster, with whom Ferdinando must
have made peace again, and Ettore Chiarugi, a lawyer;
his godmother was his aunt, Raffaella Busoni. In after
life Ferruccio, feeling that all these names involved too
formidable a responsibility, dropped those of the three
great artists and kept the first alone.

As soon as Anna was fit to travel the Busonis returned
to their wandering concert life. The child was sent with
his nurse to the grandfather at Trieste. The Busoni
grandparents had been dead for some years. Giuseppe
Weiss was a widower, and although inclined to be somewhat of a tyrant to his daughters, had himself submitted
completely to the tyranny of his housekeeper, who was at
the same time his mistress. He had a great affection for
his grandson, and was at heart a genuinely kindly man, but
Ferruccio, mainly owing to the ill-will of Matilde the
housekeeper, formed (as he afterwards admitted) an
entirely false conception of his grandfather in these days
of his childhood. Fortunately he was taken care of to a
great extent by his aunt, Mina Grusovin, and her two
little girls Ersilia and Carolina, who adored their cousin
and remained devotedly attached to him as long as he lived.

Ferdinando now began to seek fame farther afield. In
February 1868 he was at Laibach; in March at Trieste,
and again in June. It was probably on the occasion of this
visit that he and his wife took Ferruccio back into their
own charge. They played at Venice in July; during the
summer months they toured the health resorts of southern
Styria. But Ferdinando's real goal was Paris. To any one
of Latin race Paris is always the natural centre of the world,
and the Paris of Rossini, Meyerbeer, and Offenbach was
still a musical centre of first-rate importance. In October
they were at Stuttgart, playing to an almost empty hall;
about a month later they crossed the frontier to Nancy
and reached Paris in December.

Their first appearance in Paris was at a New Year's Eve entertainment in the house of M. Kugelmann, the proprietor of *Le Gaulois*. His receptions were the meeting-place of all that was famous in literature and the arts. 'Kugelmann is the father of the young writers,' said *La Presse Musicale*; 'it is he that hath said: Suffer little journalists to come unto me.' There was music, of course; Nicolini sang and so did Tamberlik, delighting the audience with the first performance of Gounod's immortal *Méditation*. 'A German clarinet-player, Monsieur Busonei [*sic*], created a striking impression and was vigorously applauded. Let Monsieur Pasdeloup take notice: a great virtuoso came into the world the other night at the house of Kugelmann.'

It was a good beginning, for it brought Ferdinando a number of engagements in private houses. Anna did not always accompany him; some other lady, perhaps the hostess herself, took the pianoforte part of Weber's *Duo* or Cavallini's Fantasia on *Il Trovatore* while the romantically handsome Italian sighed forth his insinuating melodies and caressed the air with fluttering arpeggios. Their public concerts, at which Anna was the more important figure of the two, were acclaimed with unquestioning admiration. Marriage and motherhood had wrought something of a change in Anna's personality; she had developed a new force and fire in her playing and Paris provided audiences before whom she could show her powers in music of more serious import. 'Mme Weiss-Busoni was beyond all praise. Under her steely touch the pianoforte sings, shudders, and becomes a complete orchestra in itself. In the Quintet of Schumann she showed a loftiness of style and a brilliance of execution which one would never have believed possible from the fingers of a mere woman.'[1]

After their third concert, in May, they were described as 'decidedly the heroes of this musical season, which is now at its last gasp'. Ferdinando resolved to make Paris

[1] *L'Art musical*, Paris, 8 April 1869.

his home. Anna had a busy life between practising for her concerts and looking after Ferruccio, who had reached the most delightful age of childhood and was developing rapidly both in body and in mind. It was a happy moment for Anna—one of the few moments of happiness that she ever enjoyed after she was married. Her letters to her niece Ersilia Grusovin at Trieste are full of a young mother's enthusiasm.

'Ferruccio remembers you all: how Carolina let him have her chair and her doll, and how Aunt Mina gave him nice rusks to dip in the coffee. You see what a memory the little rascal has! He sings several little songs and says his prayers to the Holy Mother morning and evening all by himself. He talks Italian[1] quite nicely and is the admiration of everybody for his precocious intelligence.

'He gives me plenty to do; he is as lively as can be, and has to be watched continually. This is the most dangerous age. He jumps and dances and gets up on to the chairs; he is a regular *moto perpetuo* and often makes my hair stand on end for fright. You can imagine how between the music of my own pianoforte and the "music" of that little imp I often do not know where I am! He is very big and strong for his age and uncommonly clever. You should see him at the pianoforte and how prettily he puts those dear little hands on the keyboard. He tries to imitate me, lifts his head and says "What a lovely thing Daddy's playing!" Ferruccio plays scales *glissés* [*sic*]. He makes himself understood charmingly in French, and in the street everybody stops to look at him; you hear the ladies say "Isn't he lovely? isn't he charming? what a beautiful head!" May God make him good and studious! then he will be a consolation to me.'

No wonder the ladies of Paris admired the little boy with pink cheeks, blue eyes, and golden curls. As time went on his musical abilities became more evident. A year later, in January 1870, Anna is happy to report that Ferruccio shows great love of his studies.

'He sits at the pianoforte like an angel, and holds his violin as if he had been practising for three years. He has a little toy flute too, on which he accompanies my pieces, and it is astonishing how he feels the expression of the movement. He is all music and when he

[1] 'Lingua pura'—i.e. pure Italian, as opposed to the dialect of Trieste.

hears a beautiful melody he dances and jumps for joy and is quite beside himself. How you would laugh if you saw him!'

Anna was always full of religious aspirations, and Ferdinando, on the rare occasions when he wrote a letter, was even more prolix of pious counsels. His health was causing Anna some anxiety. He was a chronic dyspeptic and often sleepless with pain. Like many chronic dyspeptics, he had little faith in doctors. He tried one remedy after another, but would never submit to a plain and regular regime. The remedies in which he most fervently believed were the prayers of Ersilia and the lighting of candles to his favourite Madonna at Trieste. His health, however, did not improve, nor did his temper.

Rumours of impending war led the Busonis to leave Paris in the spring of 1870. Ferdinand Strakosch had offered them a concert tour in Norway and Sweden, and some Italian papers asserted that they played in England, but it may be taken as certain that they visited none of these countries. Anna was beginning to be nervous about Ferruccio's health, for he was easily liable to childish ailments, and she had a horror of northern climates. Besides that, nothing would ever induce her, throughout the whole course of her life, to set foot on a ship and cross the sea, even for the shortest distance.

They went first to Trieste, leaving Ferruccio with the nieces while they gave concerts at Gorizia and other places in the neighbourhood, but Anna could not bear to be parted from him for long and soon fetched him away again. Ferdinando was in constant pain; Anna too was ill and depressed, but forced herself to play. In the summer they went to Abano near Padua, where Ferdinando tried the mud-baths, but with little success; they had better luck with their concerts. They thought of going to Recoaro, to combine concert-giving with taking the waters. Ferruccio was thin, but healthy, and benefiting by days spent in the open air. The music lessons perhaps were pursued with less insistent assiduity. But Anna, and still more Ferdinando, with his acute Italian foresight, had

11

made up their minds that Ferruccio was to be 'a consolation' to them—in other words, that he was to be the bread-winner of the family and the support of their old age. There was no doubt about his parents being Italians.

It must have been in the following spring (1871) that Ferdinando and Anna decided to separate for a time, not from any incompatibility of temperament but simply on account of domestic difficulties. Ferdinando no doubt felt that the old wandering life with his clarinet was preferable to residence at Trieste, where his father-in-law, instead of supporting him as a father-in-law should, refused to have anything to do with him. Anna could return to live with old Weiss—this at least would be an economy—and earn money by teaching young ladies the pianoforte. Anna accepted the situation, but it was one which for her was painful in the extreme. She was devoted to her father, with an Italian daughter's habit of blind and unquestioning obedience. Old Weiss was kind-hearted enough, but self-willed to the point of obstinacy, and lost no opportunity of reminding her that she was paying the penalty for having chosen her own husband. Matilde the servant was complete mistress of the house; not only was she grossly disrespectful to Anna, but did her best to make trouble between father and daughter. Even little Ferruccio became pretty clearly aware of the situation and, as soon as he was able to write a letter by himself, made pitiful complaint to his father about it. For the first year or so Ferdinando was not very far off, and returned every now and then to give a concert and see his wife and child at Trieste. But he was away for the whole of the year 1872, and Anna felt the separation very bitterly.

Ferruccio's first letter is dated February 28, 1870, but it was evidently written with the guiding hand of his mother; the expressions of thanks for music, promises of industry, and pious phrases are not those of a small boy. As soon as he could write at all his mother dictated his letters to his father; the first letter which he says he has written all by himself is dated August 11, 1872. The following letter, dated January 22, 1872, gives a good idea of Anna's literary style and of the amount of work the child was expected to do, though it is hardly possible to represent in English the quaint formality of the Italian.

'After I came out of school I had my pianoforte lesson with my dear Mamma, which lasted a full hour; then I wrote my school exercise; after that I thought I would dedicate a small part of the evening to you, thinking that it will not be displeasing to you to read my writing. I rejoice in your musical triumphs and re-echo the general applause. The other day Mamma, being very much pleased with me in regard to my studies, desired to reward me, and presented me with Czerny's *Method for the Pianoforte*, as well as a little piece for four hands and one for two. I have an hour's lesson on the pianoforte every day with Mamma, and I take assiduous lessons on the violin. I hope to do credit to myself in my studies and thus to endear myself the more to my beloved parents.'

Ferruccio's education was the one thing which kept Anna at Trieste. Her own thoughts come out clearly in the letters which she wrote to Ferdinando herself.

'I too am tired enough of this sort of life, but how can one make a change after the experiences which we went through on our travels? One can do little with empty pockets and the inevitable expenses of three people. Besides, how could we distract our dear Ferruccio from his lessons, which he learns with so much love and diligence? My suggestion is that when you are in Florence you should try (if Princess Margherita is there) to get me given the title of chamber pianist to her, and perhaps with some influence you could obtain some little pension for me or an assured position; in that case I should be ready enough to make up my mind to change my country and never come back again to this home of mine where I too have suffered so much.'

She goes on to complain of the enforced separation and then adds the characteristic remark:

'taking all this into consideration, the Most Holy Virgin would do well to make me win some small sum[1] with which, as I said, I might take other steps to provide for our future and for that of our beloved Ferruccio.'

Ferruccio seems to have been fairly happy and keenly

[1] i.e. in the lottery.

interested in his lessons. He attended a day-school, but we hear nothing of any other children as his friends and playmates. The two cousins were almost grown up by now, and since their mother's death would be a good deal occupied with domestic cares. Ferruccio probably spent most of his time with his mother, and she certainly grudged every moment that he spent in other company as long as she lived. His favourite playmate seems to have been his dog; a devotion to dogs was one of the few characteristics which Ferruccio Busoni shared with Richard Wagner. 'Fede' is the first whose name has been recorded; Ferruccio writes regretfully of her fidelity and intelligence in a letter of October 21, 1872. She had died; but Papa had written from Empoli to say that he had bought Ferruccio a new dog, and he was much excited at the prospect of becoming its owner.

The winter dragged on; Ferdinando did not come back, and they missed him more and more. They spent a lonely Christmas—no one asked them out; 'Nonno' (Grandpapa) gave Ferruccio a napoleon, but Anna's young lady pupils did nothing for them. It was probably about this time that Ferruccio wrote the letter (undated) to his father complaining of the offensive behaviour of his grandfather's maidservants. New Year came, and still Ferdinando remained away; how different it was, wrote Anna, from the happy New Year that they had spent twelve months before at Monfalcone!

It must have been early in 1873 (not, as Ferruccio in his fragment of an autobiography suggests, in the autumn of the previous year) that an episode took place, the story of which Ferruccio shall tell in his own words.

'I shall never forget one evening—it must have been in the autumn of 1872—when we were living alone at Trieste, my mother and I. On that memorable evening she thought of taking me to a mechanical theatre, which was a little way out of the town, as Trieste was in those days, at the corner of Via del Torrente and Corsia Stadion.[1] In this theatre, or rather hut, little scenes were

---

[1] Now called Teatro Fenice. Via Stadion is now Via Cesare Battisti.

14

acted by puppets which had an interior mechanism, needing no help
of visible strings. One scene made a great impression on me—when
one of the puppets drank a bottle of wine; you saw the contents of
the bottle diminishing, as the liquid passed into the mouth of the
puppet until the bottle was empty.

'After the performance we went homewards, almost in silence.
We had nothing to talk about and nothing to look forward to; we
were in that state of melancholy indifference which is habitual
among poorer Italian families, especially when they have enjoyed
some unaccustomed pleasure and their thoughts go back to the
monotony of the daily round. We had walked some twenty yards,
when suddenly a gentleman stood in our way. He had a commanding presence, a big beard with two points, and high boots which came
up to his knees. He was leading a very elegant and obedient poodle
on a steel chain, as if it were a wild beast, and the man's whole
appearance suggested a lion-tamer or the ring-master of a circus.

'My mother greeted him with some emotion and embarrassment;
the gentleman embraced me and called me "Ferruccio", repeating
the name rapidly in a hoarse and excited voice. From that, and from
the awakening of memories which portraits and descriptions had
kept alive, I knew that it was my father. He had come back on the
spur of the moment, and the surprise led me to anticipate all sorts
of delightful things. On my mother's lips there was a tiny smile, half
affectionate, half uncertain; my heart was beating like a small
hurricane—it was the counterpart of that smile, the invisible
counterpart, but perhaps all the more violent for being so.

'From that evening onwards my life underwent a complete
change.'

CHAPTER II

THE FORD OF WAILING

FERDINANDO'S first act was to take his wife and child away from the grandfather—'that old ruffian of a father of yours' (*quell'assassino di tuo padre*), as he amiably called him. He took a couple of rooms in the Via Geppa, opposite the Turkish Consulate, a fact which Ferruccio noted the more carefully because the consul had a small daughter of about eight or nine with whom Ferruccio started his first flirtation, though it does not appear to have gone farther than an exchange of affectionate glances from one balcony to the other.

Ferdinando, indifferent though his own musicianship might be, was shrewd enough to see that his son's talent for music was something out of the common and decided to take charge of the boy's musical education himself. Anna should by rights have been an ideal teacher for him, with her own thorough training, her long practical experience as a music-mistress, and her unfailing patience and gentleness. Ferdinando probably thought her too gentle; besides, with a husband at home, there would be other domestic duties to claim her attention.

'My father knew little about the pianoforte and was erratic in rhythm,' writes Ferruccio in the fragment of autobiography, 'so he made up for these shortcomings with an indescribable combination of energy, severity and pedantry. For four hours a day he would sit by me at the pianoforte, with an eye on every note and every finger. There was no escape and no interruption except for his explosions of temper, which were violent in the extreme. A box on the ears would be followed by copious tears, accompanied by reproaches, threats and terrifying prophecies, after which the scene would end in a great display of paternal emotion, assurances that it was all for my good, and so on to a final reconciliation—the whole story beginning again the next day.'

Within the year Ferruccio was presented to the public as

16

a pianist. He appeared with his parents at a concert of the Schiller-Verein on November 24, 1873, playing the first movement of Mozart's Sonata in C major, Schumann's *Povero Orfanello* and *Marcia del Soldato*, and Clementi's fourth Sonatina (in F major). He was then about seven and a half. On March 26, 1874, he gave a concert of his own, assisted by his parents, at which he played two fugues of Handel in C major, Schumann's *Knecht Ruprecht*, and a Theme with Variations by Hummel.

He was a composer as well as a pianist, and from these earliest years to the end of his life he never wavered in the conviction that composition was his truest form of self-expression. His earliest attempts were copied out, or possibly written down for him, by his father. As might be expected, they are entirely childish in material and expression, but they show a clear and well-defined sense of musical form—the best promise for the future. They show too how his ear must have been perpetually haunted by the sound of his father's clarinet, for some of them have slow sustained melodies, rather after the manner of Concone's vocal studies, with every now and then a wayward flourish such as a clarinet-player might have introduced. And one of the little pieces seems to suggest that Gounod's *Méditation* was in Ferdinando's repertory. It might well be, for he had heard Tamberlik sing it on the night of his own first appearance in Paris. Was that Ferruccio's first introduction to Bach? One thing is certain—it was his father who gave him his first understanding of Bach's music; and it was with an elegy in the manner of Bach that he afterwards commemorated his father's death.

In the last year of his life (August 1923) Busoni recalled these early lessons, when writing an epilogue to his complete edition of Bach's Clavier Works.

'I have to thank my father for the good fortune that he kept me strictly to the study of Bach in my childhood, and that in a time and in a country in which the master was rated little higher than a Carl Czerny. My father was a simple virtuoso on the clarinet, who liked

17

to play fantasias on *Il Trovatore* and the *Carnival of Venice*; he
was a man of incomplete musical education, an Italian and a culti-
vator of the *bel canto*. How did such a man in his ambition for his
son's career come to hit upon the one very thing that was right? I
can only compare it to a mysterious revelation. He educated me in
this way to be a "German" musician and showed me the path
which I never entirely deserted, though at the same time I never
cast off the Latin qualities given to me by nature.'

Ferdinando's volcanic temperament required other out-
lets besides the music-lessons. He was always quarrelling
with his neighbours and made matters worse by complaining openly and loudly of their treatment of him. An
Italian who is universally disliked is fairly certain, sooner
or later, to have it said of him that he has the evil eye; and
when once that malignant report has been set on foot
there is no escape from it. Trieste branded Ferdinando
as a *jettatore*. He was none too faithful as a husband, and
like all unfaithful husbands he was furiously jealous of his
wife; he would not allow her to go out to give lessons
without sending one of the nieces to chaperone her.
Violent scenes were frequent at home, ending by Ferdinando throwing himself on his knees before Anna, invoking
the Madonna and all the Saints and imploring her forgiveness. Anna forgave everything. But with her it was
never a case of *tout comprendre c'est tout pardonner*; she
was quite unable to understand and could only bear her
burdens with Christian resignation.

Fortunately the volcano was not always in eruption.
Ferdinando would disappear for a concert-tour, taking
the poodle 'Nanni' with him, much to Ferruccio's regret,
and there would be a few weeks' peace. Ferruccio had
begun to go to school at the age of six and his mother saw
to it that his general education was not neglected. In 1874
he was learning both German and Latin; in his letters to
his father he often mentions that he has done well in
Latin, as his father attached great importance to that
subject. Anna seems to have been a very strict disciplin-
arian, for she would not allow him to miss his weekly

violin lesson from Professor Cappelletti even to go to his
cousin Ersilia's birthday party!

The following fragment of a letter probably dates from
this time:

'Another thing I forgot to tell you. In geography I have
finished Cosmography and we have gone on to the shapes of the
earth and the seas. In German 4 tenses of the verb to have and
have finished the verb to be. Natural History we have finished the
different parts of man and have gone on to domestic animals. Cat
I have copied out in full.

'Next time you come home I shall let you hear by heart a beautiful poem of Zaiotti the President of the Tribunal who is now dead
this poem is called "Il Ritorno del crociato" (the Crusader's return).
This next time talk to me a little more about Nanni and please do
not tell me lies because I love her very much and if you have given
her away just tell me straight out I like that better than when you
say you have not.

                              Good-bye your
                              loving (only-begotten) son FERRUCCIO.'

Nanni was not given away. She came back to Trieste safe
and sound, for Ferruccio was again asking for news of her
when he wrote to his mother from Vienna in the autumn
of 1875.

On January 8, 1875, he played a prelude and fugue of
Bach, Rameau's Gavotte with Variations, and Hummel's
Rondo mignon; he also played in Haydn's D major Trio,
somewhat to the horror of the local critics, who protested
against the introduction of music so unpleasing, complicated, and abstruse. In May, at the age of nine, he
had played (his father conducting) Mozart's Concerto in
C minor at the Schiller-Verein 'with much precision and
delicacy of detail', as he recorded in after-life; the observation points more to Anna's instruction than to Ferdinando's. In the autumn of 1875, after a final farewell
concert, at which Ferruccio played compositions of his
own, Ferdinando, thinking the time had come to present
him to a more distinguished audience, took the boy to
Vienna. It was understood that Ferruccio was to pursue

his studies at the Vienna Conservatoire. Anna was left at Trieste; she had to earn money to support the family.

'After two years more'—Ferruccio is alluding to his father's spectacular return to Trieste in 1873—' he considered me mature and marvellous enough to take me to Vienna as pianist, composer and improviser, shielded under the sonorous name of Ferruccio Benvenuto Weiss-Busoni; not forgetting to bring his clarinet with him too, but otherwise provided with hardly means enough to make his way, and without knowing a single word of German.

'We went to the Hotel Erzherzog Carl—the hotel for princes and celebrities—and were lucky enough to meet Rubinstein. My father managed to have me introduced to him and to "get me heard" (*"farmi sentire"*), as he was pleased to express it. I can still hear that terrifying *"fagli sentire"* ("let him hear you")! He never met anybody at a café or in the street without telling him all about "my son". And he would end by bringing the stranger back to the hotel, bursting in and dragging the new acquaintance along with him and shouting at me those dreadful words "Fagli sentire!" The stranger was always described as a most distinguished gentleman—until my father came to know him better. The acquaintance generally resulted in his becoming "that fool" or "that disreputable fellow" or something else of the sort. If he accommodated my father with a small loan of money he might revert to being "a thoroughly good man", for the state of the exchequer was then, and always was, the weak point of my father's administration.'

Here the autobiography breaks off. It was written early in 1909, and Ferdinando was still alive; Ferruccio concludes the sketch with these regretful words:

'All through my childhood and all through my youth I had to suffer from this state of affairs, and as far as my father was concerned it never ended and indeed has not come to an end yet.'

Ferruccio was entered as a pupil at the Conservatoire, and the idea was that he should study there for five years; but he soon came to the conclusion himself that his teachers there took very little trouble about him, and that if it were not for his lessons with his father, he would go backwards instead of forwards. Ferdinando seems to have been in good health at this time, and as a natural consequence in better humour. The most important result of this winter

in Vienna was the friendship established with the Gomperz
family, who at that time were the centre of artistic and
intellectual life there. Theodor Gomperz was a distinguished philosopher; his brother Julius, also a well-known
man of letters, married Caroline Bettelheim, a girl born
in very humble circumstances who had risen to fame as a
contralto singer at the Opera. After her marriage she
retired from both stage and concert-room and never sang
in public except for charity. Besides Theodor and Julius
Gomperz there were two sisters, Josephine (Frau von
Wertheimstein) and Sophie (Baroness Todesco). The
three ladies took Ferruccio completely under their protection. Julius and Caroline, being childless, even proposed
to adopt him as their own son, but his parents could not
be persuaded to part with him. Baroness Todesco provided him with a tutor for German and general subjects,
besides contributing freely towards his other expenses.
Frau von Wertheimstein was no less large-hearted, and
for many years to come Ferruccio was assisted by their
generosity. He derived perhaps still more precious benefits from their genuine personal affection, their wise
counsels, and their constant thoughtfulness for his interests.

Vienna opened Ferruccio's eyes to a new world, and he
began to develop rapidly. He was taken to operas and
concerts; he bought himself the scores of Mozart's operas
and Beethoven's *Missa Solemnis*; he was perpetually composing, and although not receiving very systematic instruction was attempting such forms as fugues, quartets,
and overtures. He heard Brahms play; thought little of
him as a pianist, but liked his music. His own favourite
model in composition was Cherubini. He felt music as
an Italian. 'Music is performed here by the yard,' he
wrote to his mother, 'just like shopkeepers measuring out
cloth—always counting *eins, zwei, drei, vier*, and that's
all.' Hellmesberger had suggested that he should study
composition at the Conservatoire, but his father considered
that he was too young. Counterpoint seems to have come
to him by natural instinct. 'I am starting to arrange my

Overture for orchestra and it will soon be finished, I hope;
we got a gentleman to come who knows Counterpoint and
he said that all the parts were well fitted and well written.
As soon as it is finished I will send it you for four hands
and in score.'

A concert for Ferruccio had been planned as far back
as November, but for some reason it did not take place
until February 8, 1876. He played in Haydn's D major
Trio, and his solos were a Rondo of Mozart, Hummel's
Theme and Variations, and five pieces of his own. His
playing still had the attractiveness of childhood. One of
the critics called him the 'Tom Thumb of pianists' and
said he was 'the most delightful duodecimo edition of
Liszt, Rubinstein, Brahms, or any other long-haired composing virtuoso'. All agreed as to his remarkable ability
as a pianist; on his compositions opinions were divided.
Hanslick found them surprisingly serious; that worthy
pedant had naturally taken it for granted that an Italian
boy would have no ideas beyond dance music and recollections of tawdry operas. The learned Ambros examined
him, and pronounced that he had excellent ideas, but just
played with them like a child and threw them away. It
was true enough; Ferruccio had ideas, but he had had no
proper training in composition. The harmonization of a
melody given him by Ambros, here printed, will show at
once how totally un-German was his instinctive outlook
on music:

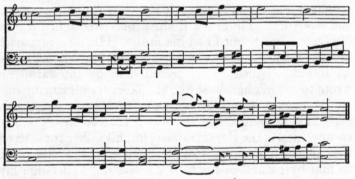

One thing on which practically all were firmly agreed
was that both his undoubted ability as a player and his
disputed ability as a composer would soon be utterly
ruined if he continued to play at public concerts. Ferdinando was never much inclined to take good advice, and
advice of this kind was the very last that he had any intention of following.

Ferruccio had thoroughly enjoyed his life at Vienna;
every day had brought him new interests, while Baroness
Todesco's generous hospitality knew no bounds. None
the less the strain of so much excitement was too much for
him, and he fell ill after his concert. His father took him
back to Trieste, where, ill or well, nothing could keep him
from composition. A fragment of a diary dated March 8,
1876, gives an amusing picture of his mornings. Half
asleep, he hears his mother talking German to the maid;
he calls 'Mamma' impatiently and demands his tea.
Mamma helps him on with his jacket, and brings in tea
and Nanni the poodle, who jumps on to his bed to say
good-morning. As soon as the tea is finished he calls for
pencil and music-paper, starts writing a fugue and dresses
bit by bit in the intervals of waiting for inspiration. The
cathedral clock strikes eleven; he has been three hours
over his fugue and toilet; he goes to the pianoforte to play
the fugue over, while the maid who comes in to do the
room—she is a Viennese, accustomed to the music of
Strauss—stops her ears, makes a face and runs away
(*prende la fuga*).

In June the family went to Gmunden in the Salzkam-
mergut. Ferruccio had need of fresh air and quieter
surroundings. Frau von Gomperz-Bettelheim recommended Habert, the *Regens Chori* of the cathedral, as a
teacher of counterpoint, and Goldmark was expected to
give further help and advice. Ferruccio went for long
walks and composed perpetually. But the summer was
not to be wasted in convalescence and composition, for
lodgings had to be paid for. The Queen of Hanover
and the Archduchess Elizabeth were at Gmunden, the

23

Emperor and Empress at Ischl; the opportunity of playing before so much royalty was not to be missed.

When they returned to Vienna in the autumn, staying once more at the Erzherzog Carl—Ferdinando knew how important it was, especially at Vienna, for a celebrity to live up to a certain social standard—Anna came with them too. Ferruccio gave no concert this winter; Ferdinando must have yielded to the advice of the critics, the more so as he could count on the generosity of Frau von Gomperz-Bettelheim and her sisters-in-law. Ferruccio was becoming known as a second Mozart (so his mother wrote) and was making rapid progress both with music and with general education. In March 1877 Liszt came to Vienna for the celebration of the fiftieth anniversary of Beethoven's death. Ferruccio heard him play the Concerto in E flat, but was bitterly disappointed with his performance. Liszt was then sixty-six and had long retired from playing in public;[1] Ferruccio, accustomed to the fiery style of Rubinstein, found his interpretation cold and un-inspiring. There was a supper-party after the concert at which Caroline Gomperz-Bettelheim sat next to Liszt; they were intimate friends, and she seized the opportunity of talking to him about her little Italian protégé. Liszt at once wrote to Anna, asking her to bring the boy to see him. One morning Ferruccio and his mother went to the rooms of Eduard von Liszt[2] in the Schottenhof, where Ferruccio played to the master. No account of the meeting has survived. Doubtless both Ferdinando and Ferruccio wrote a full account of it to their friend Luigi Cimoso at Trieste, but unfortunately all the letters written to Cimoso have been lost. This young man, a pianist and teacher, came of a family of musicians who had been close friends of Anna for many years. Luigi was devotedly attached to Ferruccio, and his long letters to Ferdinando—otherwise full of humour, with many ironic observations on local

[1] Liszt had also injured his left hand, and had to play the Concerto without using his forefinger at all.
[2] Liszt's cousin, with whom he stayed when in Vienna.

musicians—show that he felt an almost motherly responsibility towards the boy; he may well have feared that Ferdinando was not always the most thoughtful of fathers. Indeed the second winter in Vienna brought a graver illness to Ferruccio. He caught diphtheria in May, and although another summer at Gmunden restored him to health, he was still none too strong when the family went back to Vienna in the autumn of 1877. Diphtheria left his throat subject to perpetual catarrhs, and he was so sensitive to changes of temperature that he was seldom allowed to leave the house, if a letter of Anna is to be believed. But she was evidently exaggerating, for Ferruccio had given a concert, at which he had played Bach's Chromatic Fantasia and Fugue, and he had also attended the Conservatoire, where he had been much annoyed by the amorous advances of the girl pupils, whom he described in a letter to Ersilia as *masnade sbacciuchianti*—'kiss-snatching bands of brigands'!

The doctor ordered him away from Vienna; but the problem was, where to go next. Cimoso said that Trieste was hopeless—'poor Sarasate' had played to empty benches there. He suggested Munich. Ferdinando was more inclined for Italy. Cimoso thought it a good idea; perhaps Ferruccio could be presented to Queen Margherita and obtain a pension from the King. In any case he must take plenty of cod-liver oil and seltzer-water. Anna tried the cod-liver oil; but she was evidently not a very good sick-nurse. She had little faith in the Vienna doctor and begged Ersilia to ask the advice of their old doctor at Trieste. But, as before, the method in which she had the most complete confidence of all was the lighting of a candle by Ersilia to her favourite Madonna. It was in February 1878, if not earlier, that the Viennese doctor had advised the Busonis to take Ferruccio away; yet in May they were still there. At first perhaps Ferruccio was not well enough to travel; as the months passed it seems that the real difficulty was the one which pursued them everywhere—Ferdinando's habit of getting into debt. The situation was desperate; Ferdinando's only idea was that Luigi Cimoso should try to get money for him out of the parents of his own pupils. Cimoso very naturally refused, and passed the request on to Grusovin, Anna's brother-in-law, the father of Ersilia and Carolina. Ferdinando seems to have replied with indignation. Cimoso, always tactful, did his best to prevent a quarrel. Of course, it was those abominable Viennese who were to blame for everything. 'In fact I must admit that there are no more scoundrelly scoundrels (*carogne più carogne*) in the whole civilized world than those scoundrels of Viennese that you have met, if after all that reception which they gave you, and after flattering you in every possible way, they leave you in the lurch just at the very moment when anybody with a heart ought to be only too happy to help you as quickly as possible!'

This no doubt was exactly what Ferdinando thought. He was always running up debts at the hotel—no wonder, for it was the most expensive in Vienna—and could not leave until he had paid them. He did not leave until July. The Baroness Sophie Todesco, at any rate, was 'a person with a heart'; she came to the rescue, and the Busoni family, after giving concerts at Baden (near Vienna) in August and at Vöslau in September, made their way to Graz.

Ferdinando had a great belief in testimonials, and lost no opportunity of collecting letters from eminent musicians in praise of his son. He enlisted the support of Franz von Suppé, the composer of comic operas, and the court pianist Rudolf Willmers. Liszt was not quite so amenable to his desires, and Ferdinando seems to have written him a somewhat indiscreet letter. Liszt replied from Rome that he was sorry that his sincere praise of Ferruccio's talent had been misunderstood, and assured him that he had never said an unfavourable word about him. But he refused to take any steps about securing a pension for him, and added that he systematically refused to give testimonials. Rubinstein wrote a testimonial which was more in the nature of good advice to Ferruccio's father:

26

'Le jeune Ferruccio Busoni a un talent très remarquable autant pour l'exécution que pour la composition—à mon avis il devrait travailler sérieusement la musique, et avoir les moyens de ne pas devoir jouer en publique [*sic*] pour gagner de quoi vivre—une éducation intellectuelle soignée et l'étude assidu de son art feront qu'un jour il fera honeur [*sic*] à son pays come [*sic*] illustre musicien.

ANT. RUBINSTEIN.

Viene [*sic*] le 6 Fevrier 1878.'[1]

At Baden Ferdinando (or was it Ferruccio himself?) took care to get the letters of Rubinstein and others printed in the papers, and as soon as they reached Graz in October Ferruccio was interviewed and well talked about in the Press before his first concert. The moving spirit in all this propaganda was Wilhelm Kienzl, at that time a young man of twenty-two, who set seriously to work to provide for Ferruccio's education and future. Graz was a provincial town, but it was one in which music was taken seriously; it was no place for Cavallini's Fantasia on the *Trovatore* and Thalberg's *morceaux de salon*. With the help of Dr. von Hausegger, a leading critic, Kienzl managed to arouse the interest of Graz for Ferruccio both as pianist and as composer.

A concert in November brought him a letter from an unknown admirer who desired to make his acquaintance. Ferruccio was in no hurry. He had to prepare for another concert the following Saturday, and the admirer must wait till Sunday to present his compliments in person. On Sunday afternoon Ferruccio was busy, but he might call on Sunday morning. Ferruccio at twelve might have been a business man of forty, to judge from his method of making appointments. The admirer called, and a friendship began which lasted for the whole of Ferruccio's life. Otto von Kapff had come from Königsberg, the most Prussian of Prussian cities;

[1] 'The young Ferruccio Busoni has a very remarkable talent both for performance and for composition. In my opinion he ought to work seriously at music and not be forced to play in public to earn a living. A careful intellectual education and the assiduous study of his art will enable him one day to do honour to his country as a distinguished musician.

Vienna, 6 February 1878.   Ant. Rubinstein.'

27

but his sympathies were with the south, and he eventually became in most of his habits a typical Viennese. His in-born Prussianism came out only in his rigid sense of honour; misfortune overtook him in later life, but he lived for years in poverty without ever having owed a farthing and without having ever asked help from any one. When he heard Ferruccio play at Graz he was not much over twenty. By occupation he was a journalist, by inclination a poet, and by temperament a romantic senti-mentalist who modelled his appearance on King Ludwig II of Bavaria. His face was fat and puffy, with small eyes and large loose lips. His outward appearance was, however, somewhat variable; one day he would be photographed in a fur-trimmed coat and a profusion of jewellery, another day as a sort of Caliban with hair and beard that looked as if they had never encountered brush and comb in their whole existence. Ferruccio accepted his devotion as a matter of course. He was flattered at having a grown-up friend of his own and was quite prepared to meet him on equal terms. Kapff sent him poems; he set them to music —when they were suitable. If they were not, he told the poet so—politely, but as one artist to another. Kapff seems to have feared that his letters might appear too sentimental; Ferruccio, no doubt reading with an Italian eye for fine phrases, was delighted with them, but replied in language more business-like. Kapff offered romantic adoration; Ferruccio realized at twelve years old that a virtuoso can make good use of a press-agent and general factotum.

At Graz Ferruccio went to school, where he continued his Latin, physics, and chemistry. He was now becoming fairly fluent in German, but German script was still troublesome to him, and when he wrote German letters he made frequent mistakes in grammar and syntax. He ap-pears to have had no friends of his own age, and hardly ever associated with other children. He was always with his parents or other grown-up people. At Vienna he had started a friendship with a girl of about his own age,

28

Paula Flamm, the daughter of wealthy parents. Frau Flamm was one of his kindly benefactors; she had no son of her own, and was very ready to be a second mother to Ferruccio. Paula was learning the pianoforte with a view to becoming a public player, so she and Ferruccio met as professional colleagues rather than as children. She was a lively and frequent letter-writer, but Ferruccio was a disappointing correspondent; an occasional post-card was the most that he would send her. He was neither lazy nor selfish in character; on the contrary, every one who met him was struck by his singularly affectionate nature. But his upbringing made him self-centred. He already knew that he possessed musical ability of no common order. His parents early on instilled into him that it was his duty to support them, and even as a child of twelve he was completely aware of all their financial difficulties and prepared to share the burden of them. 'I never had a childhood,' he said in after-life. But there was no settling down yet to 'une éducation intellectuelle soignée'.

The Busonis stayed at Graz into November. Ferruccio had so much success with his two concerts that he was asked to play at a commemoration of Schubert—it was fifty years since he had died. But Graz evidently did not suit Ferruccio's health, and probably it did not suit Ferdinando's purse either. Luigi Cimoso suggested Naples, thinking more of the boy than of his father. Trieste at any rate was more hopeless than ever. Relations between the German and Italian elements were becoming more strained. Cimoso neither had nor desired to have anything to do with the Schiller-Verein, at which Ferruccio had given his first concert; Ferdinando, he wrote, was much too Italian to have any chance in that quarter. 'You know even better than I do that the Triestines love concerts about as much as dogs love a beating.'

Early in December they were at Klagenfurt, where they gave two concerts. On these occasions Ferruccio was expected to improvise on a theme supplied by some member of the audience, but the themes were not always

29

to Ferruccio's taste. 'I was given *three* themes', he wrote to Kapff, 'by one and the same gentleman, each stupider than the others. I chose the best and improvised badly on it. It is as if you were given a stupid subject for a poem and had to make a good poem out of it. The thing is impossible.' Ferruccio, like Mozart at the same age, was an outspoken critic, but he was equally critical of his own performances. From Klagenfurt they went on to Bozen, Trent, Arco, and Rovereto. The tour was unexpectedly successful; at Trent Ferruccio played three times in a fortnight, and to full houses, in spite of severe frost and very slippery streets. After the scraps of Wagner offered at Graz and the Carinthian folk-songs handed in at Klagenfurt Ferruccio must have rejoiced when a Professor Bazzicotti gave him the following spirited tune of Rossini on which to improvise at his concert at Trent on December 19, 1878:

Ferruccio treated it as a theme for variations. With Anna he played Schumann's Variations for two pianofortes, and one can imagine with what a clutch of emotion she must have read afterwards in *La Voce Cattolica* that 'mother and son seemed to play with but one single soul'.

In January 1879 they played at Bozen, in March at Klagenfurt. Ferdinando must have felt well satisfied with the results, to judge from a poem which he composed to celebrate Ferruccio's birthday on April 1. It exhibits the author's characteristic blend of grandiloquence and common sense.

> April fiorisca a Te ghirlande e doni,
> Vanto glorioso dei Diversi Suoni.
> Salute il ciel ti dia e freschi Allori,
> Denaro in quantità e Sommi Onori.

Garlands and gifts may April shower on thee,
Most glorious boast of various Harmony!
Heaven grant thee health and laurels ever new,
The crown of fame and heaps of money too.

Ferruccio's letters to Otto von Kapff give a clearer picture of the situation. Ferdinando had expected to arrange a third concert at Klagenfurt on their return, but according to his version of the story he was left in the lurch by some local aristocrat who had guaranteed him against loss, and the concert was a financial failure. He refused to attempt another, and the old story repeated itself—Ferdinando making more and more enemies and sinking deeper and deeper into debt. Ferruccio was still suffering from the strain of this erratic life and his health went from bad to worse. The strain was aggravated by the boy's consciousness that he himself was the only member of the family who had a real sense of their responsibilities and the only one who made a serious attempt to grapple with them. Ferruccio insists that his illness is in no way due to the effort and excitement of concerts—concerts never have any ill effect on him, he says; it was all due to a chill brought on after doing gymnastic exercises in his room—a treatment recommended by some one to his father.

Ill or well, he went on composing, even when he was too weak to play the pianoforte for more than half an hour. In the Tyrol he had composed a whole Mass for four voices in the style of the sixteenth century; after that two big works for two pianofortes, a solo for his father's clarinet, and miscellaneous pianoforte solos. At Klagenfurt he started on a setting of Uhland's ballad *Des Sängers Fluch*, for solo voice and orchestra.

In these letters to Kapff he is perpetually concerned about his education. 'Rubinstein advises me *very decidedly* not to go to a Conservatoire—at any rate not to that of Vienna.' His ideal was Leipzig, but he feared the climate would be too severe for him. In any case, if he went to the Leipzig Conservatoire, could he pursue his general

31

education there—'Geography, mathematics, and other school subjects?' Kapff evidently had some acquaintance with Leipzig and hoped much from the influence—if it could be secured—of Frau Elise Polko, a lady well known in those days as a poetess, a musical critic, and authoress of romantic and sentimental novels about the lives of great composers. So Ferruccio prepares an autobiography for Frau Polko's information—how he has played to the Emperor of Brazil and the Queen of Hanover and all the rest, has been examined by Liszt, Rubinstein, Brahms, and Goldmark, has given fifty to sixty concerts beginning at the age of seven, would have given more but for the time devoted to studies, has learned a large amount of harmony and counterpoint all by himself and has composed altogether about 150 works, of which some fifty or sixty are good and fit for publication. 'I don't tell you all this from vanity, but merely so that your sketch may be a fairly complete biography.'

He was annoyed at having to spend most of his birthday in bed, but nothing could stop him from composing for two or three hours a morning at least, scoring his ballad at the rate of six or even seven pages a day. And he had received the birthday presents which always pleased him most—books, to the extent of twenty-eight volumes: Hackländer, Auerbach, Jules Verne, Hauff, and a book on music in French by Colomb. He gives his order of preference too: first Hackländer (of whose novels there were twenty volumes), then Verne, and after him Hauff. But business matters must not be neglected. He discusses the idea of a tour with a violinist called Dugremont, who was a Brazilian boy-prodigy of his own age, but thinks it will not be of much use to him: Dugremont's terms are not very satisfactory, and he is not sure that he would have the position due to him as a solo pianist. He suggests another concert at Graz; is there a good contralto who could sing *Des Sängers Fluch*, which is now complete? They might leave their luggage at Graz as security for the hotel proprietor, and then come back, pay their debts with their profits and go to Italy, where they feel certain of success. He has a complete programme ready—'the celebrated Quartet of Schumann' (the pianoforte quartet), Mendelssohn's *Variations sérieuses*, an improvisation, of course, a new work of his own for two pianofortes (with his mother), and to end up with, the Finale of the *Waldstein* Sonata. And Kapff might arrange for friends to go round and sell tickets privately beforehand.

In spite of all these very practical suggestions the concert at Graz did not take place. The Busonis were rescued by the kindness of Kienzl, who collected money for them, and after May had reduced them to the lowest depths of despair, they were able to move in June to Cilli, a picturesque little old town founded by the Romans in the mountains to the south of Marburg. Glad indeed they were to leave Klagenfurt, where they felt themselves surrounded by enemies. But Ferruccio, at any rate, left one friend behind there—whom he was to find again after forty years.

Klagenfurt left an impression on Ferruccio's memory which he never forgot, as the following episode will show. In 1912 he was at Hamburg for the production of his opera *Die Brautwahl*. After a morning's rehearsal he went with friends to a restaurant. Conversation turned on some musician who had failed to fulfil the promise of his youth; he was a conductor in some remote provincial town, some one thought—it might be Klagenfurt. Klagenfurt! The name made the company laugh; it stood for the far end of the world, and probably most of them had no very clear idea where Klagenfurt was. Busoni, who had been sitting with his head in his hands, lost in meditation, suddenly looked up as if he had seen a ghost.

'Klagenfurt!' he said, almost with a groan—'Klagenfurt! who spoke of Klagenfurt?'

The others fell silent, hardly knowing whether to laugh or to shudder; they looked at Busoni and waited for the next prophetic word.

'Klagenfurt!' He prolonged the syllables, as if to suggest what they mean—'the ford of wailing'.

33

'Did you ever play there?'

'Did I ever play there? Klagenfurt! It brings back all my childhood!'

He seemed as if in a trance.

'There's a dragon there.'

Most of the others thought he must be going mad. One guest, however, had been to Klagenfurt, and remembered the 'Lindwurm'—a huge dragon in green slate, set up in the sixteenth century to commemorate a plague. An ordinary mortal having seen the dragon too, contact was restored; the company felt themselves on safe ground again, and Busoni for a moment lifted the curtain of memory. The sentences came out slow and detached.

'I was there with my parents; I was twelve years old; I was a wonder-child, and everything turned on me. We were in a hotel there and had to stay for three months, because we had no money and could not pay the bill.'

The vision faded, the curtain fell, and the company broke up.

CHAPTER III

THE AWKWARD AGE

THE summer of 1879 was uneventful. Concerts were given in the numerous watering-places of the neighbourhood of Cilli, and the financial situation, thanks mainly to Frau von Wertheimstein, seems to have been reasonably satisfactory. Negotiations were carried on for concert tours in Germany and Sweden, but Ferdinando thought Sweden dangerous for Ferruccio's health. Ferruccio and Kapff seem to have borne most of the burden of attending to these affairs. No doubt Ferdinando found it a convenience that his son could write German as well as compose music; and the faithful Kapff's devotion was quite useful too. Ferruccio's German was indeed making considerable progress, and the romantic environment of Cilli, coupled with the two dozen volumes of German literature, stimulated him to begin writing a German novel himself. It did not progress beyond a first introduction of the chief characters. The scene was laid in Cilli in the year 1237, a period in which, as the author observes, 'people were still simple and pious, and there was a general freedom from restraint such as nowadays we can unfortunately no longer enjoy'.

Romanticism makes its appearance in his music, too, for he set not only Uhland, but Heine as well, and Chamisso's *Tragische Geschichte*—'höchst schwärmerisch und für feinfühlende Damen' (highly sentimental and for ladies of refined feelings). They stayed on at Cilli into November; Ferdinando always had a difficulty in leaving places. Ferruccio was quite clear about his own desires. He did not wish to go on tour again; his health was not equal to it, and he was bent upon obtaining a really sound education, both in general subjects and in music. He had learned a certain amount of music from his father, but both he and his father knew clearly by this time that he had need

35

of more systematic teaching. From his mother he seems to have had only pianoforte lessons. Ferdinando was not easy to please in the matter of teachers for his son. He had tried several, but with each teacher the same thing happened: a few trial lessons were given, and then 'ik nehmen mio bambino wieder weg' ('I take my child away again'), as Ferdinando used to say in his grotesque mixture of Italian and broken German. It is possible too that Ferdinando was not always able to pay the teachers' fees.

Meanwhile Kienzl kept up interest in Ferruccio by long reviews of his published compositions in the *Grazer Tagespost*. On November 23 Ferruccio conducted his own *Stabat Mater* for soli, chorus, and stringed orchestra at Graz, Kapff providing a puff preliminary. It cannot be said that the performance was a success. Kienzl wrote quite frankly that the work had no logical sense of construction; the necessary harmonies were sometimes given to the strings instead of to the voices, so that the singers found it extremely difficult to sing. In the final fugue there was a complete breakdown. But the concert fulfilled its function; it showed the musical public of Graz that Ferruccio possesssed unusual natural talent for composition, and, at the same time, that he was urgently in need of thorough and systematic tuition. A committee was formed to take the responsibility of Ferruccio's education; it was announced in the papers that the Busoni family were settling definitely in Graz, that Anna would give pianoforte lessons and that Ferdinando would also take elementary pupils for the same instrument. The ideal teacher for Ferruccio was on the spot, and Kienzl had already secured his interest in the boy; he had even provided him with a theme from one of his own works on which to extemporize at a concert.

The teacher in question was Dr. Wilhelm Mayer. Kienzl himself had been his pupil and well knew his singular capabilities as an educator of musicians. Mayer, who was born in 1834 at Prague, was the son of a lawyer and had once intended to follow the same sort of career.

He took his degree in law and held various posts in the Austro-Hungarian civil service, but in 1861 decided to devote himself entirely to music and settled down at Graz. For a few years he conducted concerts there, but eventually found his true vocation in teaching. As a composer (under the pseudonym of W. A. Rémy) he belonged to the later romantic school, with a certain leaning towards the illustrative style, although he cordially detested the music of Wagner and had little sympathy for that of Brahms. He was one of those composers whose charm of personality and highly finished craftsmanship deserve the respect and win the affection of a limited circle of friends, but who have not the force and vitality to become known and remembered by a wider public. Outspoken in his opinions, and perhaps not always tactful in his relations with other musicians, he felt ill at ease in the Austrian capital; he preferred the provincial life of Graz and eventually came to find his chief satisfaction in the distinguished careers of those who came to Graz to be his pupils, among whom he numbered Wilhelm Kienzl, Felix von Weingartner, Ferruccio Busoni, and E. N. von Reznicek. He died on January 23, 1898.

Ferruccio felt at home with him the moment he came into the house, for there were Italian pictures on the walls, copies made in Italy by Mayer's father-in-law. While Ferruccio stared at the pictures, Dr. Mayer, corpulent and apoplectic, listened to Ferdinando's torrent of talk and wondered what was to be made of the pale-faced boy with the mop of brown-gold hair, long nose, and large yet strangely resolute mouth. The usual infant prodigy, he supposed—dressed like a child and talking like a grown man—he knew the type, conceited and unwilling to do any serious work.

Dr. Mayer soon discovered that Ferruccio was far from being what he had expected. Ferruccio was quite well aware of his own musical talents, but he was never in the least degree vain or envious of others. He regarded his gifts as a bird might regard its wings—as something

37

perfectly natural and normal. He never boasted of what he had already achieved; he was far too intensely concentrated on the future. Mayer was astonished to find how much he knew, but he insisted none the less on his going through every detail of his prescribed course of instruction. It generally required two years; Ferruccio mastered it in fifteen months. When he left Graz in April 1881 he took with him a book of 430 folio pages written out in his own hand with every elegance of Italian calligraphy—a complete treatise on composition, beginning with the first rudiments of music and proceeding through harmony, counterpoint, and fugue to instrumentation and composition in all forms. But Mayer, for all his German thoroughness, was no dry pedant. *Möglichst vielseitige Bildung macht den Künstler* (the widest possible culture makes the artist) was the motto written at the foot of the table of contents. The history of music was taught as well as the contemporary practice, not as a separate subject, but as a source of musical illustration to all other branches. Ferruccio's book was full of examples from medieval and Renaissance music. Mayer's methods were in general what might naturally be expected in those days; his history was based on Burney, Hawkins, and Ambros, his counterpoint on Cherubini, and his orchestration on Berlioz. Orchestration indeed takes up about half the book; the copious illustrations include examples from Brahms and Gounod. Wagner is occasionally cited, but generally as a warning against what not to do.

But there was a personal note too about Mayer's teaching which left a memorable impression on his pupils. He was himself a man of wide culture, and had a happy way of illuminating music which appealed vividly to the young and eager mind. It was Mayer who first made Ferruccio realize the genius of Mozart.

'When he mentioned Mozart's name, his thoughtful face assumed an expression of almost fatherly confidence and happiness, while his eyes betrayed a deep inward amazement. It was perhaps Rémy's greatest achievement, at any rate the most fruitful achievement for his pupils, that he stamped the picture of Mozart so profoundly upon our minds.'[1]

After Mozart Bach was his next great hero. He never tired of analysing and explaining the *Forty-eight Preludes and Fugues*. The first four preludes he called 'the four elements—water, fire, earth, and air'; the theme of the fugue in C sharp major was 'the butterfly' alighting on a flower, taking its sip of honey and then flying off in a zigzag. The great Fugue in B flat minor of Book II he compared to Cologne Cathedral for the 'Gothic perforated work' of its broken counterpoint; the subject of the two-part fugue in E minor, he said, shot up like a rocket, fell slowly to earth and left a bad smell behind in its final diminished seventh.

The fifteen months with Dr. Mayer must have been one of the happiest periods of Ferruccio's life in spite of the extreme poverty in which he and his parents were living. They had rooms in a small hotel in the outer suburbs of Graz; in the winter Ferruccio often had to write his exercises for Dr. Mayer in bed, as they could not afford a fire. But he was constantly in the house of his teacher, and became an intimate friend of the family. Mayer's wife was a second mother to him, and he struck up a lasting friendship with Mayer's daughter Melanie, a girl a few years older than himself. There was no long summer holiday in the year 1880. He had a fortnight free of lessons in August, but had so much holiday task to do for Dr. Mayer that he never played the pianoforte at all. He stayed in Graz in spite of the heat, and went to the opera, which had opened for the autumn with *Fidelio*, *La Juive*, and *Guillaume Tell*. Graz was an inspiring centre of music in those days.

At the end of his course in March 1881, after Dr. Mayer had presented him with a long and elaborate certificate signed and sealed with all possible formality, Ferruccio's committee arranged a farewell concert for him in April. He played Schumann's Concerto and Beethoven's

[1] Ferruccio Busoni, *Von der Einheit der Musik*, Berlin, 1922.

Sonata Op. 111; then followed a group of his own compositions—a String Quartet in C minor (Op. 56), a Prelude and Fugue for pianoforte solo (Op. 57) and a setting of Psalm lxvii in German for chorus and orchestra. For the summer Ferruccio and his mother went back to Trieste. Ferdinando seems to have gone the round of the Styrian baths with his clarinet. His clarinet-playing was no longer what it had been in the Paris days; when he played at Pisa in 1872 a local critic told him only too plainly that he played out of tune as well as out of time, that he had no gradation of tone between a *pianissimo* and an *arrabbiato*,[1] that his low notes were ugly and guttural, and that he took breath in the middle of phrases. No doubt his dyspepsia had affected his breath-control as well as his willingness to practise; he was gradually sinking into a chronic state of ill-temper and depression.

Anna and Ferruccio went to live with 'Nonno' again, but had to pay him for their board and lodging; Anna gave pianoforte lessons again, but money was short, and Ferruccio mentions that they could not afford to go to the theatre. What little could be saved had of course to be sent to Ferdinando. Ferruccio was practising the pianoforte, composing a *Requiem*, and filling up his spare time with drawing architectural views of Trieste. He had all his life a passion for drawing, especially for architectural drawing, and said that at one time painting had as great an attraction for him as music, but that after he had definitely decided to become a musician he dropped painting as he could not afford to risk splitting up his life. From his earliest boyhood he knew quite clearly what he wanted to do, and even in those periods when his life became more complicated and his aims appeared to be confused, he never lost the inward sense of direction towards a definite end.

His letters to his father, written almost every other day, give detailed accounts of the progress of the *Requiem*, not omitting comparisons with Berlioz and Verdi; for Verdi's

[1] 'A mad dog *fortissimo*.'

Requiem he had no very great admiration and says that his
trumpets in the *Tuba mirum* suggest a battle-field. Mayer
had evidently stirred up his interest in Berlioz. He was
always borrowing books from Mayer, and it is amusing
to note that among them must have been *Les Grotesques
de la Musique*, which he quotes with evident delight.
Trieste was not without its musical grotesques; there was
a composer called Bianchini who discussed music with
Ferruccio and showed him compositions of his own which
Ferruccio analysed with a mordant wit for the entertainment of his father. But Ferdinando did not want parodies
of musical analysis; what he wanted, and always wanted,
was money. That could not always be sent; Ferruccio did
the best he could for him by arranging clarinet solos for
him to play—Schumann's *Abendlied*, transposed into a key
with fewer flats, Ernst's *Elegy*, &c. Ferdinando was always
asking for a prelude of Bach, which puzzled Ferruccio;
he probably wanted either Gounod's *Méditation* or that
Ferruccio should arrange another prelude for him in the
same style.

After a concert at Trieste in October the Busonis went
to Italy. In November and December he gave two concerts at Milan. As usual, an improvisation was an item of
every concert. Italians do not go much to concerts, and
Ferruccio played to thin and depressed audiences on
gloomy winter afternoons. The concert-halls were, as they
often are still, badly warmed and badly lighted. The critics
commented on his pale and haggard appearance, like a
Byronic hero from a novel of George Sand, and found that
his programmes contained too many fugues. In January
they were at Bergamo; here Ferruccio played for the first
time his suite *La Festa del Villaggio*, which he repeated
at Milan. At Bologna in March his father joined him;
Ferdinando had learned a new piece, the *Gnomenklänge*
of Bärmann, which was to figure in his repertory for a
considerable time. Five concerts were given at Bologna,
and at the end of March the Accademia Filarmonica
conferred on Ferruccio its diploma for composition and for

pianoforte-playing. No composer since Mozart had been admitted a member of that famous Academy at so youthful an age.

In April they went to Empoli, where Ferruccio was presented with a gold medal and any number of sonnets. The programme of their second concert, at which the presentation of the medal took place, along with a bouquet and a poem for Anna as well, may be printed here:

Scherzo nell'Opera *Don Pasquale* . .	Cavallini.
FERDINANDO and ANNA BUSONI	
Marcia Nuziale	Mendelssohn-Liszt.
FERRUCCIO BUSONI	
'Casta Diva'	Cavallini.
FERDINANDO and ANNA BUSONI	
Improvvisazione	
FERRUCCIO BUSONI	
Fantasia sul *Trovatore*	Cavallini
FERDINANDO and ANNA BUSONI	
Canzone Veneziana	Liszt.
Carneval di Venezia	Fumagalli.
FERRUCCIO BUSONI	

They played at Pisa in May. Ferdinando had evidently forgotten his quarrel with the critic of ten years before—possibly he was dead and gone. With his usual pomposity he was walking round the hall collecting themes for Ferruccio's improvisation when he came up to a certain Signor Carassali, who was famous throughout Pisa for being totally unmusical and making no secret of the fact. Ferdinando was not aware of this, and insisted on Carassali's writing down a theme, in spite of his embarrassed excuses which finally ended in a plain statement of his unmusicality, to the immense amusement of the audience.

The earlier part of the summer was spent at San Giusto near Empoli, where one of Ferdinando's brothers had a villa. It was a novel and touching experience to the Busoni aunt and cousins to listen to Anna and Ferruccio playing duets and see them follow up the duets with close and prolonged embraces. In August there was

opened an exhibition of musical instruments at Arezzo,
in connexion with the celebrations of the millenary of
Guido Monaco, and through the kindness of Luigi Mancinelli, then living at Bologna, Ferruccio was employed
for three weeks during September to play daily on the
pianofortes exhibited. A performance of Boito's *Mefistofele* was conducted by Mancinelli, and this gave Ferruccio the opportunity of making friends with the composer.
Both Boito and Mancinelli at once realized Ferruccio's
exceptional gifts, and after he had given more concerts at
Bologna in the winter, they secured him a performance of
his new cantata *Il Sabato del Villaggio*, a setting of Leopardi's famous poem. It was given in the Teatro Comunale on March 2, 1883; Mancinelli conducted. *Il Sabato
del Villaggio* was a very skilfully written work, but it was
criticized at the time for its treatment of the poem, which
was much cut up and distributed between different voices,
with frequent repetitions of words; Leopardi's lines were
too contemplative and philosophical to bear handling in
such a style. Boito, whom one would have expected to be
the first to take a poet's view rather than a composer's,
praised its 'admirable exuberance of rhythm' and its un-
ceasing flow of melody. He urged Ferruccio to go on
setting Leopardi to music, for he felt that Leopardi's
profoundly thoughtful humanity was just what he wanted
to give wings to his inspiration. 'If I am a severe critic
of Ferruccio's music, the fault is his own; the admiration
which he aroused in me at Arezzo was great; I expect
great things of him, and I am sure he will give me them.'

When Ferruccio returned to Trieste in the spring of
1883 he was welcomed as a local celebrity of whom the
town might be justly proud. In the autumn, after a few
concerts at Laibach and Graz, he went again with his
father to Vienna. Vienna did not receive him this time
with much cordiality. He was no longer a child prodigy
and was judged as a young man. At twelve he had appeared to have the mind of a grown-up person; at seventeen he had the mentality of the 'awkward age'.

43

At first all seemed to be going well. The very day of their arrival at Vienna (October 10) he went to see Gutmann the publisher about the possibility of getting his Suite for orchestra performed at one of the Philharmonic Concerts. The programmes had not yet been made up, but there was no time to be lost. He went off the next day to see Richter, who was living at Döbling, a remote suburb. Richter was not at home, and Ferruccio called six times before he was able to see him. Richter's reception of him was chilly, but he at least allowed Ferruccio to play the Suite to him—that was something unusual—and after the Prelude exclaimed 'Bravo! if all the movements are like that I'll perform it at once.' An *allegro fugato* took him very much by surprise; the Minuet he found prolix and advised Ferruccio to cut it out. Ferruccio considered the question and finally took Richter's advice.

The parts, Richter said, must be ready by November 13. The Suite would then be tried over before the committee, without whose consent Richter could do nothing. If the Suite was well received in Vienna, he would play it at his London concerts. 'He went on to say', adds Ferruccio in his letter to his mother, 'that the young Italian and English composers are now doing much better work than the young Germans, who are ruining themselves by imitating Wagner.' The Italians and the English were represented by Sgambati and Stanford. Ferruccio heard a symphony of Sgambati, but thought it merely bizarre and eccentric. Stanford's early Serenade, which Richter conducted at Vienna, brought nothing new, but its finished craftsmanship, its elegance and grace, were qualities which Ferruccio at once recognized and appreciated. He wrote a long notice of it in the Trieste newspaper *L'Indipendente*.

Ferruccio was in high hopes. Hanslick had been very polite and encouraging, had given him a letter to Richter, and had advised him to make an appearance as a pianist. Ferruccio went to see his old friends the Flamms and played them his new Preludes.

The Flamms were enthusiastic over the Preludes, but

a week or so later Ferruccio was surprised to receive a tactful and motherly letter from Frau Flamm telling him that her husband had forbidden him to come to the house any more. Ferruccio's conduct had always been absolutely blameless, she admitted, but her husband's will was law. Paula was growing up, and Viennese parents did not wish to take any risks. Paula afterwards married Wilhelm Gericke, the well-known conductor.

Ferruccio had plenty of other calls to pay. He went to the Conservatoire to see Hellmesberger.

'Hellmesberger received me with his famous smile on the edge of his lips, always *chic*, always elegant and well groomed, with many pretty speeches and a something or other that gave me no confidence in him. He told me to come and see him again one morning; I shall carry out his instructions. Door was with him and on seeing me made a very nasty sneering face. They were chatting together while a girl pupil was playing, and every now and then they looked up and beat time for her with their feet.'

A characteristic Viennese picture. Hellmesberger was to try his Quartet, but as programmes were already made up there was little chance of its performance. Rosa Papir, the contralto, had promised to sing at his concert, but Ferruccio, knowing the ways of singers, was doubtful as to whether the promise would be kept.

There was an almost stormy interview with Baroness Todesco. She had been astonished at his enormous progress, but in view of the severity of the Viennese critics advised him to put off his concert until he had perfected himself under Leschetizky. The name of Leschetizky seems to have goaded Ferruccio to fury. He replied to the Baroness that he did not consider himself perfect, but that neither she nor her sister had had a proper opportunity of hearing him; that he knew his own shortcomings and that they would remedy themselves in the course of his artistic and physical development, since he was quite capable of observing them for himself; that he was quite ready to face Viennese criticism, that his style of playing could not possibly call for serious blame, and that any

45

E

small observations which might be made on it would be a help to him. The Baroness felt that it was no use arguing, and agreed to give him 100 florins a month. The underlying reason of Ferruccio's impatience with the Baroness was his knowledge that she was very much under the influence of her companion, whom he detested. The companion had a father and a brother, who both posed as pianists. The father had heard Chopin play, which gave him an immense prestige in Viennese society; he was too old to perform now, but occasionally in drawing-rooms would play one or two of the easy pieces of Chopin, or a few easy bars from the difficult ones, and say that that was exactly the way in which Chopin played them himself. The son had been obliged by neuralgia to abandon music for diplomacy; in society he assumed the part of a severe critic, but when asked to play excused himself as being out of practice. The Baroness was inclined to pay more attention to them than they deserved, and her kindly nature imagined that as they were not professional musicians they could not possibly be envious.

By November 25 Ferruccio had received notice from the Philharmonic committee that the Suite was to be tried. On November 30 he gave his own concert, which brought him a profit of 400 florins. But neither Hanslick, Brahms, nor Richter came to hear him. The only important musician present was Leschetizky, who much to Ferruccio's surprise expressed himself as highly pleased with his style and technique. The programme included Beethoven's Sonata Op. 111, Bach's *Italian Concerto*, Schumann's *Études symphoniques*, Chopin's *Andante Spianato* and *Polonaise Brillante*, and Liszt's transcription from Mendelssohn's *Midsummer Night's Dream*, besides several works of his own—Variations and Scherzo for pianoforte, violin and violoncello, a Serenade for violoncello and pianoforte, and two *Études* for pianoforte solo. Ferruccio had already started on his career of big programmes.

The trial of the Suite was put off to January (1884). Brahms took some interest in it and said that he would go to the trial. By January the trial had been put off till the next month or later. Meanwhile Ferruccio was preparing for two more concerts of his own and hearing a number of other concerts and operas. His letters often have the amusing quality of Mozart's from Italy at about the same age.

'Pose is the order of the day. There is a pianist here called Fried-heim, a pupil of Liszt, with long hair and a face that looks half severe, half bored. When he plays he comes forward and bows in such a way that his hair covers up all his face; then he throws his head back to tidy his mane. Then he sits down with a great deal of fuss, and looks round waiting till the audience is quiet; at last he seizes the keys "as a wild beast seizes his prey", to quote Hanslick. But the loveliest thing is to see him during the *Tuttis* of the orchestra. There he has room to show off all his tricks. He examines his nails, considers the audience, thrusts his hands into his hair, and does other silly things. . . .

'. . . There is music everywhere, and too much of it. The wars of the Wagnerians and anti-Wagnerians are not over yet. Brahms too has his party; and the *Slavs* and *Germans* are continually fighting. So the world goes on like cats and dogs: eternal unrest, without which the world would not exist . . .'

He had another talk with the Baroness in the hopes of paying a visit to Leipzig to see publishers. She returned to the idea of Leschetizky, and finally arranged to let Hanslick hear him in private, as Ferruccio resented the criticisms of the companion. The companion had had the impertinence to say that he thumped, and the still more atrocious impertinence to say that she had noticed the same fault in his mother's playing years ago. But it was no use to quarrel with the Baroness. His finances depended on her; and besides, she was far too good-natured to allow him to quarrel. 'Life teaches one to become a bit of a Jesuit,' he observed.

Rubinstein arrived in March, and at his first concert played more than thirty pieces, including a Sonata of Schumann and two of Beethoven. One can see whose example Ferruccio set himself to follow. Ferruccio called

47

on him, and found him fairly amiable, 'not more so than is correct for celebrities'. He did not play privately to Hanslick; that was put off too. But he determined to secure Hanslick's favour by playing a Sonata of Brahms at his third concert; Brahms was 'the only cheese to catch that mouse'. Hanslick came to the second concert, and criticized it with some coolness. But the Baroness came, and having heard him play in public had no more doubts.

It was the end of March. Richter informed him that it was now too late to try over the Suite, and that he would do his best for him next season. After some quarrelling Ferdinando and Ferruccio decided to spend the summer at Frohnleiten, a watering-place a little way north of Graz.

The winter in Vienna had brought disappointments, but Ferruccio determined to make the best of them. At any rate he had met several people who would be useful to him, if his concerts had not been altogether successful. He certainly had not been idle. In addition to practising for his concerts he had been steadily composing and had even made time to take a course of drawing lessons at the Academy. He had also written articles for *L'Indipendente* of Trieste about music in Vienna under the anagram of 'Bruno Fioresucci', in which he showed a sound critical sense and a literary style which made straight for the point without wasting time on flowers of rhetoric—an unusual style for an Italian journalist.

In April he went to Trieste for a short visit, saddened by the death of Luigi Cimoso in a lunatic asylum, worn out by the strain of supporting his two sisters and his invalid brother. Cimoso had been his best and truest friend; his tragic fate haunted Ferruccio's dreams for long afterwards. In June he joined his father at Frohnleiten, where they took two rooms in the Villa Audolensky. Life with Ferdinando was none too agreeable. His dyspepsia had been growing steadily worse. At Vienna he hardly ever left the hotel and refused to take exercise of any kind, much resenting Ferruccio's sensible advice. He seems to have spent his days chiefly in acting as valet to his son.

Cimoso's last letter to him, written in October 1883, had
told him some plain truths. Ferdinando, he wrote, ought
to have settled down somewhere with his wife to earn a
regular living until Ferruccio was old enough to earn his
own. If he had done this years ago he would have been
spared many troubles.

'I must allow myself to tell you that Ferruccio would have
achieved and would in the future achieve much more if you had been
more amiable towards your audiences, to other artists, and to all
people whom one cannot afford to disregard in such a career. At
Trieste they say that your concert was deliberately boycotted by the
public and the shareholders of the theatre on account of what you
said about them at the hotel and elsewhere. I heard the same thing
about your visits to Vienna, Milan, and Arezzo.'

Ferdinando's temper was not likely to be improved by
reading a letter of this sort.

The one consolation of Frohnleiten was that the Mayers
were there. Ferruccio was being made to undergo an
elaborate cold-water-cure; it was severe and unpleasant,
but in later years he often said that it had made a new man
of him. After the morning douches he had to go for a
quick walk, and on these walks Melanie Mayer was his
inseparable companion. It was a severe test of friendship
from her point of view, for Ferruccio's pace was rapid
and the midday sun was in full summer force. He had too
a sense of humour which her refinement found embarrassing. She tried in vain to interest him in natural history,
but he had in those days no eyes for such things, not even
for landscape. Human beings were all that he cared about,
and those too in an unconventional way. He was very
much of an *enfant terrible* and would horrify Melanie by
giving comic imitations of other visitors who were only a
few paces in front of them. Once they met an old woman
with a basket of potatoes, and Ferruccio, pretending he
had never seen such things before, asked her all sorts of
ludicrous questions. Graz was a place where a high standard of propriety was maintained—it is still a favourite
residence of retired civil servants—and the mere fact of his

going about anywhere with Melanie caused something of
a scandal.

Graz would indeed have been scandalized if it had
known that Ferruccio was trying to induce Melanie to
read Boccaccio in Italian. Their talk seems to have been
mostly about books. Ferruccio was always a voracious
reader, and even at seventeen keenly critical and apprecia-
tive of literary craftsmanship. At Vienna he had read a
good deal of Dickens as well as *Vanity Fair*. Of more
modern authors he seems to have preferred Turgeniev and
Anatole France. About this time he read Schopenhauer
with deep and careful attention. But his real enthusiasm
was for the Italian classics. Nobody but an Italian, he told
Melanie, could properly appreciate the perfection of
Boccaccio and of Manzoni's *Promessi Sposi*; when these
books were translated into other languages they became
trivial. 'I have often wondered', he said to her, 'why
Italian literature never shows the light-hearted cheerfulness which is characteristic of our nation in all other arts.
The heavy Germans are much more inclined to trivialities
in their writing than we are. On the other hand, to read
Dante, Alfieri, Leopardi, or Guerrazzi is even more of a
scientific than an artistic pleasure.' Leopardi was evidently
his favourite poet; in the course of the summer he wrote a
long letter in Italian verse to his uncle Alfonso at Empoli
to ask him to send them some of his wine; the style shows
distinct reminiscences of Leopardi.

Melanie was like a sister to him, and her intellectual
upbringing enabled her to understand him perhaps better
than he did himself. His own education had given him
a premature and excessive development of intellect; his
emotional life had not run parallel with it and was only
just beginning to unfold. In music Bach was at this time
his favourite composer; he loved and admired Mozart,
but his own mind ran in other directions. Beethoven,
Schumann, and Chopin he was only gradually learning to
understand; for Liszt he had no appreciation whatever.
He knew himself that he suffered from being too intel-

lectually critical as regards both music and human beings; he had a horror of giving way to his emotions. Though he was at all ages immensely attractive to women, his own attitude to them was always critical, especially in adolescence. 'No woman has ever made an intellectual appeal to me,' he said; 'I always feel them to be inferiors.' It must be remembered that his experience of women at this time was limited to those of Italy and Austria.

In spite of his indifference to landscape the romantic surroundings of Frohnleiten were not without their influence. Ferruccio, who in later life professed an utter want of sympathy for German *Lieder*, set a poem of Neidhard von Reuenthal—'an ugly name made up of envy (*Neid*) and remorse (*Reue*)'—which he treated as a suite of dances, minuet, bourrée, and gigue, 'all in the severe contrapuntal style of those times'. No wonder the songs (he set another by Walther von der Vogelweide) were unfavourably received when they were sung at Vienna.

Vienna held out hopes; the Philharmonic committee wrote to him in August promising to consider him as a pianist and asking him to send the Suite. In September he went to Vienna alone, intending to stay with the Wertheimsteins at Döbling for a fortnight. He saw Richter at once. Richter said that the Suite would be tried at the first rehearsal of new works, but once more the trial was put off from week to week. He tried to see Hellmesberger, but Hellmesberger was protected by a barricade of young lady pupils. Young Rosé was more friendly and promised to try his Quartet. He seems to have called on Richter nearly every day about the Suite; it is hardly surprising that Richter was generally 'not at home'. Wherever he went he was told that the acceptance of his work depended on some one else, partly on the committee, partly on the orchestra. Ferruccio had not yet learned the full extent of Viennese evasiveness. On September 21 he heard from members of the committee that his Suite would be tried and his concert-piece for pianoforte and orchestra too. At last, on October 4, the Suite was tried over. The rules of the society forbade the composer to be present, but Ferruccio managed to slip unnoticed into the gallery and heard his work played. The next day, at the theatre, he met Richter, who told him that everybody had been greatly struck with the Suite, that its contrapuntal skill and its instrumentation were perfectly wonderful, but that the orchestra refused to accept it. The orchestra had the right of voting on the programmes, and they rejected the Suite by a majority of one vote.

The fate of the Suite was a tragedy which embittered Ferruccio for years. It was not that he afterwards regarded that particular work as one of his outstanding compositions; but at that particular moment it was a matter of vital importance to him that it should meet with public success. It was to set the seal, he hoped, on his aspirations as a composer and prove openly to his patronesses that their benefactions had not been misplaced. He had often refused to follow their advice; they had trusted his judgement on himself, if somewhat unwillingly; he had need to give them convincing proof that he had been in the right. His own confidence in his powers was unshaken; the confidence of his friends might well suffer a disastrous shock. But Ferruccio's first thought, as always, was for his father, for after all, Ferdinando, despite all his tyrannical assertions of parental authority, was the one person who never for one moment lost faith in the genius of his son. He would be more distressed than Ferruccio himself. Ferruccio did his best to console him.

'Although I was and am still very much annoyed,' he wrote, 'yet I have tried to take the matter calmly and not feel discouraged, but maintain confidence in my talent and persevere. All that was humanly possible for the success of my plans was done—I have no cause to blame myself, I neglected nothing, left nothing undone. I worked hard, I went everywhere and waited in antechambers, I was my own copyist and my own porter. At any rate it was a satisfaction to hear my work, which the orchestra read to perfection, and I was especially glad to make sure that I had made no mistakes in my orchestral effects. To-day and to-morrow I shall have plenty to do with fetching the parts and score, packing my trunk and having a little talk with the Wertheimstein. I shall leave in a few days' time and will let you know the hour of my arrival. The one thing I beg of you is to receive me with good will and to be cheerful as if nothing had happened!'

Ferruccio swallowed his disappointment as best he could. Ferdinando told him to come back to Frohnleiten, but he was evidently more inclined to stay on in Vienna. His father was growing daily more peevish, and as soon as his son had shown any sign of managing his own affairs he had begun to suspect him of every possible folly and iniquity. It is clear from Ferruccio's almost daily letters that Ferdinando mistrusted everybody with whom Ferruccio came in contact, both men and women. He was also inclined to suspect that Ferruccio might be spending the Baroness's allowance on his own pleasures instead of sending at least half of it to his infirm and aged parent. Ferruccio went to Frohnleiten, but he did not stay long. When he returned to Vienna in November his father came with him. So did 'Mopsi', a new dog who had succeeded Nanni; and Mopsi, in Ferruccio's opinion, was a dog whose brain was bursting with the most wonderful ideas— if only nature had not condemned him to eternal silence. But Ferruccio had by now come to the conclusion that Vienna was a hopeless place for him. It was time, he felt, that he should think seriously about his future; at the Wertheimsteins' he had encountered a wise old gentleman who had seriously deplored his intention of devoting himself to music. A young man, he had said, should choose a sound profession which brings in a safe income, however small; why not, for instance, go into a carpenter's shop— or a sugar factory? After two recitals in December, Ferruccio said he was sick of both concerts and social functions. His songs had been condemned, his interpretation of the *Appassionata* had been condemned, and he had been advised to moderate his *forte* and *fortissimo*. One critic had headed his notice with the words 'A Musical Steeplechase'.

53

At last, after many uncomfortable interviews with Baroness Todesco, he was able in February (1885) to realize his ambition and visit Leipzig. Leipzig was in those days the centre of the musical world. The glory of Paris had faded after the war of 1870, the glory of Vienna was, on closer inspection, a tangle of intrigues, and Berlin, as a place of musical importance, had hardly begun to exist. Brahms, always ready to help a young musician, gave him an introduction to Reinecke. Ferruccio found Leipzig rather more provincial than he had expected, and Leipzig was amazed to hear of any musician coming out of Italy; Leipzig had never heard of any Italian pianist since Domenico Scarlatti. But Leipzig gave him a very cordial reception. Henri Petri and his partners played his Quartet. Marie Fillunger was to have sung his songs, but left him in the lurch at the last moment; luckily another singer was found who sang them to his satisfaction. Ferdinando went with him to Leipzig and to Berlin as well; he was not going to let Ferruccio travel alone. At Berlin, in the Singakademie, he played his new Variations on the C minor Prelude of Chopin—the only composition of his which shows the direct influence of Brahms. He was enchanted with Berlin as a city; it was so much cleaner, brighter, and altogether so much more alive than Vienna. On the return journey another concert was given at Leipzig, but his playing of the classics was not altogether to the taste of the critics. They had been delighted to find that his own compositions were quite German in style, but his interpretation of Bach, Handel, and Chopin was much too exuberant in rhythm to please them, his use of the pedal too free, and his general style wanting in depth of expression.

On April 1 Ferruccio had entered upon his twentieth year. Germany had criticized him with some severity, but for all that he felt that his last birthday had opened the gate to a new life.

CHAPTER IV

ESCAPE

FERRUCCIO refused to give a concert at Trieste, and decided to give no more concerts at Vienna. On May 14, 1885, he and his father settled down again at Frohnleiten, from where they hardly ever stirred until November 1886. They lived this time in the Villa Pabst; the Villa Audolensky, to their great regret, was no longer available. Melanie Mayer suggested that Ferruccio should appear there as a 'white lady'[1] and frighten the tenants away. Anna, except for two months at Frohnleiten in the summer of 1885, remained entirely at Trieste; she had been separated from husband and son almost without interruption since the autumn of 1883. There had been no definite breach between her and Ferdinando, but Melanie Mayer had noticed as far back as 1880 that they were none too happy together. Anna was now over fifty, and the trials of her married life had left their mark upon her. Solitude and poverty had thrown her more and more upon the consolations of religion. She began to grow anxious about Ferruccio. A change had taken place in him; that was evident from the style of his letters, which were often frank almost to the point of brutality. A photograph of himself which he had sent her from Berlin reduced her to a state of terror; was that dark, frowning, bearded man her son? He did his best to calm her fears. The Berlin photographer was to blame for a good deal; but in any case she must not be surprised if he had reached manhood and if his face showed the change of expression that inevitably accompanies maturity, especially after all that had happened to him in the last few years. She had asked about his religious observances; he told her frankly that he could no longer conform to her wishes. Ferruccio,

[1] Alluding to the ghost scene in Boieldieu's familiar comic opera *La Dame Blanche*.

55

like most young men, was surprised and hurt by that
sense of mistrust which overcomes parents exactly at the
moment when their sons are developing a serious sense
of responsibility. He had laboured for his parents, at first
almost unaware of the fact, since he was twelve; at twenty
he was more than ever determined to bear the burden of
providing for his mother's old age. Had it not been for
Ferdinando, Ferruccio might have solved the problem
more easily. But Anna's saintliness made it impossible
for her to say a word against her husband; and Italian
sons regard it as unthinkable to discuss their parents.

At first all went well at Frohnleiten. It was a relief to
Ferruccio to be by himself in the country. He spent his
days, as he told his mother, in practising, composing,
writing, thinking, and walking. For some months previously he had been planning the composition of an opera.
After reading Goetz's *Taming of the Shrew*, he asked
Kalbeck for an introduction to Brahms's friend, J. V. Widmann, who had written the libretto, and a long correspondence with Widmann followed. Widmann, not much inclined to provide a libretto for Ferruccio, whose abilities
were totally unknown to him, pleaded ill-health and over-
work. He also named his fee at once—1,000 marks after
the composer has read it: small alterations gratis. Ferruccio was not likely to be able to find £50 at a moment's
notice, which may well have been the reason why no
business was done with Widmann. But Widmann at any
rate gave him a number of suggestions in a very friendly
spirit. He entirely refused, however, to consider any
medieval German subject; after the *Rattenfänger von
Hameln* (Nessler) he had had enough of that period.
Keller's *Romeo and Julia auf dem Dorfe*, suggested to
Ferruccio by Wilbrandt,[1] he thought impracticable, owing
to the necessity of presenting hero and heroine at different
ages of their lives. Finally he told Ferruccio to look at
Alarcon's *El Niño de la Bola*; if it did not suit him as an
opera libretto, he would at any rate have read a master-

[1] A well-known writer of novels, and husband of a celebrated actress.

piece. But it was the moment when Ferruccio was just
entering into the spirit of German romanticism, and a
medieval German subject was what he really wanted. He
found it in *Das stille Dorf*, a fantastic short story in
Baumbach's *Sommermärchen*. Through Sacher-Masoch,
whom he had met in Berlin, he made the acquaintance of
a young poet named Soyaux, who undertook to make a
libretto out of it for him. The libretto, which was actually
written by Soyaux's wife, Frida Schanz, was given the
title of *Sigune*, and was sent to him at Frohnleiten in
October 1885. *Sigune* was an unlucky choice; it was
certainly romantic, but it was ill-adapted for the stage.
The opera was never completed, and such music as was
written down was afterwards utilized for other purposes.

Another occupation was the writing of musical articles
for the Trieste paper *L'Indipendente*. Under the anagram
of 'Bruno Fioresucci' he had contributed several letters
from Vienna in the spring of 1884, with amusing sketches
of Friedheim, Pachmann, and other pianists. Pachmann's
endearing mannerisms were as pronounced then as they
are now, and Ferruccio observed that his smiles and facial
contortions would have sufficed to explain the music to
a deaf-and-dumb institution! His experiences in Vienna
and Leipzig provided him with plenty of material. Hans
von Bülow's visit to Vienna with the Meiningen orchestra
had been the great event of the previous autumn, and
Ferruccio describes a very characteristic episode. After
Bülow's first concert the *Fremdenblatt* had severely, and
in Ferruccio's opinion unjustly, criticized his interpretation of Beethoven. Bülow apparently took no notice of it.
He gave his second concert, and for the third announced
a repetition of the *Egmont* Overture, as the last item of
the programme. After the previous piece, he came on to
the platform with a copy of the *Fremdenblatt* in his hand.
He made a sign for silence, shook his head expressively,
and then borrowed a programme from a lady sitting near.

'As I am a stranger (*ein Fremder*) here', he began, 'I feel it my
duty to return the amiability of the Viennese public by reading the

57

Fremdenblatt; and in fulfilling this duty I have discovered that its musical critic has been much disturbed by my interpretation of the overture to *Egmont*. I therefore think it better not to perform that work, as I had announced, and I shall substitute the *Academic Overture* of Brahms.'

After a moment of amazed silence, there were loud cries of '*Egmont, Egmont! we want Egmont!*' all over the hall. The few who called for Brahms were soon shouted down, and Bülow had to give way; but before he began *Egmont* he said to the audience scornfully, 'Ladies and gentlemen, in 1810 you would with equal insistence have demanded an overture of Weigl.'

Ferruccio explains to his readers that as in 1810 the Viennese preferred the old-fashioned Joseph Weigl, whom they knew, to the revolutionary Beethoven, so they now preferred Beethoven to the rugged novelty of Brahms. Ferruccio at this time was no whole-hearted adorer of Brahms, and in his last years he seemed to take little interest in his music.[1] As a young man he frequently played the Variations on themes of Handel and Paganini. Of the Symphonies he was critical, and had no hesitation in saying that Brahms was an indifferent pianist when he played a concerto of his own in public; for the Variations on a theme of Haydn he had an enthusiastic admiration. But to Brahms as a man he was evidently much attracted, and it may well have been that Brahms, who knew Italy well, felt an equal attraction to Ferruccio. Ferruccio thoroughly understood and appreciated his lovable qualities. His apparent modesty and his refusal to listen to praise of his works were merely a thin disguise for a very good opinion of himself, in which, as Ferruccio observes, he was perfectly justified. Praise from those incompetent to judge was of no value to him; and it was equally a waste of time, said Brahms, to give indications as to how he wished his works performed. If people could not understand them from the printed notes they were incompetent to play them.

[1] He played the Paganini Variations almost up to the end of his life, but he spoke of them with very detached criticism.

Brahms never encouraged intimacy, but Ferruccio, even when Brahms made it clear that he was not wanted, felt instinctively at home with him in a way that he never did, for example, with Richter. He called one day to bring some compositions of his own which he had dedicated to Brahms. Brahms was at the pianoforte playing Scarlatti; he told Ferruccio he would try his music over for himself. Ferruccio made his bow and went away, leaving his compositions on the pianoforte, but he had hardly reached the staircase when he heard Brahms call out, 'Now let us put away Scarlatti and have Busoni instead!' It was pleasanter for a young composer to be sent away like that than to be introduced to Bülow in a crowded artists' room and be received with a spluttering explosion after the manner of Alfred Jingle: 'Young composer—perform his works?— no, no—quite impossible!'

Rubinstein was more genial; he had the manners of a man of the world—'a cigarette always ready for a male visitor, a kiss for a lady'. He suggested an alteration in one of Ferruccio's works; Ferruccio was not very ready to accept the correction, but politely answered that no doubt Rubinstein was right. 'It is not that I am right,' Rubinstein retorted, 'but that is exactly how it must be (*ma è precisamente così*).' One morning Ferruccio came into Rubinstein's room at the hotel and found a young Italian lady playing a nocturne of Chopin to him. Rubinstein seized her hands and protested in the caressing tone which he always employed with ladies, 'No, my dear, that's wrong, that's wrong; you have entirely misunderstood the style.' He sat down and played the nocturne for her. The instrument seemed transfigured; Ferruccio and the girl were in ecstasies of delight. Perfectly impassive, Rubinstein played on, turning his head every now and then to make some remark to the pupil—'There— you see—here—more feeling, more passion, more *morbidezza*!' Just at the end he struck a wrong note, smiled and exclaimed, '*Too* much feeling!' Ferruccio felt that that one nocturne had given him a whole course of lessons.

59

Hanslick's coolness towards himself had not prevented
him from reading Hanslick's famous book on *Beauty in
Music*, and it is clear from a long article which he wrote in
L'Indipendente that the book gave him the foundation of
his own aesthetic principles. There is no need to sum-
marize the essay here, but it may be observed that it shows
a remarkably firm grasp of philosophical principles; its
arguments are well marshalled and expressed with clarity,
vigour, and wit.

No sooner were father and son settled at Frohnleiten
than they sent for various things required from Trieste.
Ferdinando wanted his clarinet, some music, and the
Method for Clarinet which he had written himself, which
shows that he had not played for some time. Ferruccio
asks his mother to send Bach's *Matthew-Passion*, Mozart's
Symphonies, and two or three volumes of Proske's *Musica
Divina* containing masses and motets of Palestrina. On
his first visit to Leipzig he had seen in the dark little
office of Kistner the publisher an old man with a white
beard and long white hair falling over his shoulders.
Kistner was replying to his talk by signs—the old man
was completely deaf. It was Robert Franz. Ferruccio
was thrilled at meeting 'the great Bach scholar and the
successor of Schubert'. Kistner wrote Ferruccio's name
on a piece of paper and handed it to Franz. The old man
at once rose, laid his hands on Ferruccio's shoulders, and
said, 'Ah, you are Italian?' Then, lifting his hands to
heaven, he went on in the voice of an inspired preacher,
'Palestrina! Lotti! Scarlatti! Oh, those were men indeed! what minds, what minds!'

Kistner made him understand that Ferruccio was a
composer.

'Take these men as your models,' said Franz; 'they are
the treasure of your nation.'

Ferruccio seized his hand and kissed it; it was the only
way in which he could express the sudden sense of affection and devotion which the ancient prophet had awakened
in him. Ferruccio throughout his life had a touching

veneration for those whom he believed to be really great men; but he was sometimes disappointed when the great men did not keep up their characters as such in a personal encounter. The baptismal name of Michelangelo seems to have led him to expect the grand manner of Moses as a matter of course. Franz evidently possessed it by nature. As regards the old Italian church composers, Ferruccio needed no fresh encouragement to study them. He was already familiar with sixteenth-century music before he went to Dr. Mayer, and Dr. Mayer found him avidly receptive in the matter of historical studies. He had heard a Mass of Palestrina sung in the Palace Chapel at Vienna, and was thrilled by the sound of the boys' voices as well as by the sight of the ceremony in that gem of medieval architecture. 'Palestrina's music', he wrote, 'will continue to exist when there are no more priests and no more incense.' At Vienna he spent several days copying Monteverdi's *Ritorno d'Ulisse* in the Court Library for Mayer; he proposed to edit it himself for publication, but his father wisely forbade him to waste time on so unprofitable an enterprise.

They had invited the Cimosos to come and see them in the summer, but as this was not practicable, they asked Anna instead. She seems to have required some pressing; money was short and she was never fond of long journeys. But they insisted. She was to pledge her jewellery to Beppe Cimoso to pay her fare, and was not to forget to bring papa's meerschaum pipe, some of his favourite tobacco, the *Decameron*, the *Divina Commedia*, and the German Dictionary. She came; but Ferruccio did not altogether enjoy her visit. Mother and son were gradually drifting farther and farther apart. Ferruccio had fallen in love. There had been a long and painful entanglement at Graz with an elderly married lady who wrote him fantastic letters about superior humanity, but these things were beyond Ferruccio's comprehension. He had answered the lady somewhat uncivilly, and the faithful Kapff had to do his best to prevent a quarrel. She eventually consoled herself with another young man of genius and not long afterwards was removed to a lunatic asylum. The love-affair at Frohnleiten was of short duration and came to an unpleasant end. Kapff was told to say never a word about it in his letters to Ferruccio; on the least hint both Ferdinando and Anna would be sure to find out everything.

Anna went back to Trieste at the end of August, and Ferruccio began to realize that the financial situation was becoming troublesome. The only remedy was for Anna to sell her pianoforte. Ferruccio observed that she might well do so, as it was in such a state that it was no pleasure to play on it, and Ferdinando thought she might accept 200 florins (about £15) for it. Ferruccio said she would be lucky to get that much. The grandfather came to the rescue, and appears this time to have become a little more generous. Ferruccio gave four concerts at Trieste in October and November; the old man came to two of them, *tutto gongolante e ringalluzzato* ('pleased as Punch and proud as a turkey-cock'), to Ferruccio's great delight.

The winter was severe. Ferruccio began work on *Sigune*, but the opera progressed slowly. He sent for his easel and brushes and turned to painting for a change. Money matters went from bad to worse. The good ladies at Vienna were not very punctual in paying his allowance, but Ferruccio was not going to write every month to the Baroness to beg for her 'filthy florins'. So life went on, day after day—

> Espère, enfant, demain, et puis demain encore,
> Et puis toujours demain, . . .[1]

The quotation, he felt sure, would appeal to his mother.

April 1886 brought his twentieth birthday. His mother sent him Chateaubriand's *Génie du Christianisme*, telling him to read a page every day. He replied, thanking her

---

[1] Victor Hugo, *Espoir en Dieu* (*Chants du Crépuscule*, 1835). Ferruccio had set the poem to music as a song, probably at Anna's suggestion (date not ascertainable, but certainly before 1880).

for the '*Génie du Crétinisme*'; a page a day, he calculated, would take him two years exactly, so he promised to read it from beginning to end, but a chapter at a time, as he felt inclined. 'I suppose it is a book which besides exalting things and views which are not to my taste is full of old-fashioned philosophical doctrines which cannot possibly be applied to the social conditions of the present day.' Anna feared that he was forgetting his Italian. He admits that German is beginning to get the upper hand, owing to his large German correspondence; he is contemplating a book in German on the musical conditions of Italy. Anna gently replied that it would be good practice for his Italian style if he wrote to her a little oftener. She found him 'changed' indeed.

Ferdinando took up his clarinet again and practised assiduously. There was little else for him to do at Frohnleiten. He gave a concert of his own at Leoben in May, but in spite of a brilliant success came back to Frohnleiten in a very bad temper, which was not improved by a letter received from Anna. Even Ferdinando had at last come to the conclusion that her position at Trieste was most unsatisfactory, but he seems to have had no suggestions how to improve it. Ferruccio saw quite clearly what ought to be done; his parents ought to live together and try to put their affairs on a sound basis, leaving him meanwhile to fend for himself and not be a burden on them. The situation was indeed difficult. The summer would reduce the number of Anna's pupils; there was serious anxiety at Trieste on account of cholera. At the same time father and son were not in a position to take her away from Trieste for good. Something must be done before the autumn. Meanwhile 'Baronesse and Wertheimstein *tacent*'. Another matter which was troubling Ferruccio was his liability to military service; but after a good deal of correspondence with Empoli and an interview with the Italian Ambassador at Vienna he was definitely exonerated, either on grounds of health or as being an only son responsible for the support of his parents.

They drifted on through the summer months with
nothing to break the dreariness of life except a charity
concert organized by the poet Peter Rosegger in June, at
which Ferdinando played Cavallini's Fantasia on *Don
Pasquale* and Ferruccio Liszt's on *Don Giovanni*. Ferruccio's patience began to give way. It was more and more
difficult to live in peace with Ferdinando. Day by day his
querulousness increased, day by day debts mounted up.
He brushed aside any suggestion of his son's as to seeking
his fortune elsewhere, telling him not to be rash, to make
sure of his future, to wait for the opportune moment—
anything, in fact, rather than take decisive action. Ferruccio would have taken counsel with his mother and with
Kapff, but was obliged to tell both of them not to say a
word of these things in their letters, because the old man
loved nothing better than ferreting out any papers which
his son had particular reason to conceal from him.

If only he could get away from Frohnleiten! He used
to walk down to the railway almost every day, just for the
pleasure of seeing a train speeding north from Trieste to
Vienna—from Vienna to the real land of music. Another
pleasure to be expected sometimes at the station was a
meeting with the Statthalter, Herr P., who at the sight of
an engine drawing up, would invariably assume an expression of terror, press his hand to his brow with the fingers all
touching at their tips, shake his head ominously and exclaim, 'Bless my soul! this invention! what do you say to
it? Magnificent! Appalling!' In 1886 the steam-engine
was still something of a mystery in Styria.

November came, and nothing more had been done about
a change. All that Ferruccio could suggest was that Anna
should go to live with her nieces, Ersilia and Carolina. It
would at least be an economy. But Ferruccio had his own
plans, which he was not going to reveal until he had made
sure of them. He made some money by playing at Graz,
both publicly and privately, and hoped that the sum would
be sufficient to pay his father's debts and his own fare to
Leipzig. Ferdinando would not hear of his going away.

Ferruccio thought the problem out for himself. To stay on at Frohnleiten simply meant accumulating a heavier load of debt with no possible opportunity of paying it off. He would be a prisoner in idleness there, with no chance of making his way; he would be forgotten, whereas all Dr. Mayer's other pupils were coming to the front in other countries. He felt a bitter sense of shame at having to be dependent partly on the indulgence of creditors and partly on the somewhat spasmodic generosity of Frau von Wertheimstein and Baroness Todesco.

Suddenly he made up his mind. He went to Vienna on November 17, saying nothing to his father about his future intentions. He had enough money to live for a few days and hoped to make enough to take him to Leipzig. As soon as he reached Vienna he wrote a letter to Melanie Mayer:

'I write to you in the joy of freedom at last secured, and in the glorious consciousness of the tasks which await me—a consciousness which is glorious when one feels in oneself the power to overcome them—sustained by the uplifting sense of the responsibility laid upon me.

'I can hear your mother cry out, "Isn't that the regular young artist of twenty, who has just found his wings?" Yes, I know it is; but this momentary and perhaps over-romantic enthusiasm shall not for an instant hamper my serious effort. I mean to accomplish something. This morning I said good-bye to my father; it was harder for me than I was able to show, just as on Tuesday evening at your house I did not show all that I was feeling. But you and your mother will have understood.'

The next day he wrote fully to Anna. He was tortured by the thought of leaving his father in a position that was unsatisfactory and indeed critical; but what else could he do? 'Stay with him there and watch the snow falling together? No, certainly not! Have no anxiety about me, and trust my character.'

At Vienna he lost no time in seeing all those who might be of help to him. Richter, as usual, was not to be found; he was burying his mother-in-law. He called on Eugen

d'Albert, whom in Berlin he had rather disliked; this time
he changed his mind, after seeing d'Albert read his *Studio
Fuga* straight off at sight. Busoni thought little of
d'Albert's compositions, but was pleased with his manners
and his absence of pose. By a stroke of luck Signora
Giovannina Lucca, head of the music-publishing house in
Milan, was at Vienna; massive and heavily moustached,
inseparable from her snuff-box, she chattered away in
affectionate Milanese to her *caro mio Büsonetto*, and paid
him 100 florins on the spot for some pianoforte pieces
which he had not yet composed. She was the friend and
protector of all the 'modern' young Italian composers.
Ferruccio called on the Baroness and also on Frau von
Wertheimstein. They agreed to his plans and provided
him with money, a good proportion of which he sent off
at once to his father.

Anna's anxieties never abated. He comforted her as
best he could. 'I take your warnings to heart,' he wrote,
'but at the same time I am a fellow of sufficiently upright
character not to take the wrong road. As regards religion,
you know what I think; as regards women, I value my
talents too highly to sacrifice them to a futile and short-
lived pleasure. So set your heart at rest.' To his father he
had written nearly every day. He left for Leipzig on the
last day of November. Within two days of his arrival he
sends his father a complete balance-sheet of his affairs.
The Baroness had given him 200 fl.; hotel bill at Vienna
30 fl., tips 8 fl., journey to Leipzig 40 fl., sent to his father
50 fl.—in hand 72 fl. Ferdinando had a rigorous standard
in the matter of accounts, provided that they were not his
own.

Ferruccio found rooms with a captain's widow on the
third floor of Centralstrasse 14, a pleasant situation, with
board and lodging for 75 marks a month. The house was
opposite the Thomaskirche—'an ever-present injunction
to industry'. Having to pay the month's rent in advance,
he was left with 10 marks in his pocket. Four days later
he was penniless. By good luck that same evening he met

Schwalm, partner in the firm of Kahnt, who offered him 150 marks if he would write a little easy fantasia on Cornelius's *Barber of Bagdad*. Ferruccio was to have 50 marks on account and the rest on production of the fantasia. The next morning he called at Schwalm's office for the first instalment, pocketed his 50 marks, and produced the fantasia. He had composed it that night, between nine and three in the morning, without a pianoforte and without knowing the opera before. There was not a single correction in the manuscript. Schwalm paid him the remaining 100, and the next day he sent 80 marks to his father. Some of the rest went to buy a copy of Vasari—his own Christmas present to himself.

For the first few months at Leipzig life was crowded with new experiences. The sense of complete independence and freedom, the escape from Frohnleiten and the perpetual worry of parental interference, the joy of being able to earn money by his own efforts, together with the satisfaction of being really in a position to send help, however modest, to his father and mother—all these things contributed to make Ferruccio feel that he had entered on a new world in which he would be able to accomplish without hindrance the tasks to which he felt himself called. Publishers, whom he had formerly pursued with little success, were suddenly cordial; Kahnt offered him a favourable contract; he was for a time on good terms with Dr. Abraham of the firm of Peters, and friendly relations began with Breitkopf and Härtel which were to last up to the end of his life. Leipzig was full of interesting people. Through Dr. Abraham he met Grieg, who was making his home at Leipzig for the time, and it was Grieg who introduced him to Frederick Delius with the words, 'This is a most remarkable pianist—and perhaps something more.' Another young musician then living in Leipzig was Gustav Mahler. Ferruccio was not on terms of great intimacy with any of them; but in the case of Delius and Mahler the friendship was renewed with deeper cordiality in later life. The only people with whom he

67

was really intimate were Henri Petri, the violinist, and his wife—not to mention their small son Egon, then about five years old, to whom Ferruccio was no less devoted than Luigi Cimoso had been to him; and even in the case of the Petri family Ferruccio hardly realized the extent of his affection for them until his sojourn in Leipzig came to an end.

Life must have been too busy for intimate friendships. It was hard enough to earn a living for himself; as long as his father stayed on at Frohnleiten he had to make a living for two. He was obliged to undertake any drudgery that was available—fantasias on operas, the pianoforte score of Goldmark's opera *Merlin*, and articles for musical papers. It was fortunate that he could write German well enough for this last purpose. He did not do much teaching. Only in later life he discovered that teaching can be a pleasure, and then he discovered that it can be no great pleasure unless it is done for nothing. One of his gratuitous pupils at Leipzig, the son of a music-seller in a provincial Austrian town, was a youth of typically Austrian feckless-ness. He was always on difficult terms with his father. That in itself was reason enough for Ferruccio to make friends with him and do everything he could to help him. The boy had spent his Christmas in bed because he had no money to get anything to eat or to light a fire. Fer-ruccio induced Dr. Abraham to help him, and as he found that he was deriving no benefit from his lessons in counter-point with Jadassohn, set to work to teach him counter-point and musical form himself. Later, when he revisited Austria, he called on the boy's parents and did his best to bring about a reconciliation.

Another student friend was the son of a wealthy noble family, who was also learning counterpoint with Jadassohn, and finding his teaching equally unsatisfactory. Again Ferruccio had to come to the rescue; he gave him piano-forte lessons too, but without much pleasure. The young nobleman's musical abilities were hardly up to Ferruccio's standard, but at any rate he was a pleasant and companionable youth who thoroughly enjoyed the pleasures of life and was only too ready that Ferruccio should share them with him. One of Ferruccio's publishers too was a *bon-vivant di prima forza*, and there were now and then some lively suppers in a private room at the Hôtel de Prusse, where Ferruccio and the young nobleman were his guests, not to speak of guests of the other sex too.

But Ferruccio, in spite of these friendships, felt himself lonely. The Austrian lad adored him, 'almost like Luigi Cimoso', as Ferruccio said, but he wanted something more than adoration. Luigi Cimoso had been a man from whom he could learn something; to his contemporaries at Leipzig he felt himself always in the relation of a teacher. He wanted some one who could understand him and be interested in him, feel proud of his successes and stimulate him to further efforts. Luigi Cimoso and his tragic fate still haunted his dreams.

'Here I have not been able to make a single friend', he wrote to Melanie Mayer, 'who is on my own level. There are two who learn from me, and so I get nothing from them except the pleasure of watching their progress under my teaching. That is the worst of precocious talent—one cannot associate with people of one's own age, and older people do not wish to associate with one—hence complete isolation! If I had not the gift of being able to adapt myself for the moment to other people—which does no harm now and then, for after all man is here to be with other men—I might well spend the whole of my life in utter solitude.'

He solved the problem by buying himself a dog— 'Lesko', a black Newfoundland bitch to whom he grew daily more devoted. There was no money to spend on a summer holiday that year. Ferdinando's complaints grew more and more peevish, but Ferruccio was unable to satisfy them. One day in August Ferdinand Pfohl, afterwards a musical critic in Hamburg, recognized Lesko in the street with a man whom he at first took for a blacksmith, and wondered if she had been stolen. A closer inspection showed him that the blacksmith was none other than Lesko's own master, who was enjoying a substitute for a holiday by dressing as a labourer and disappearing altogether from his usual social circle. On another occasion Kathi Petri, Henri's wife, was horrified to discover him not merely in this unconventional attire but actually addressing a party of real workmen on the doctrines of Karl Marx. Worse still, he was having an uproarious success as a socialist orator. These were the first symptoms of a habit which afterwards became very characteristic of him. In all probability it was his reading of Dickens, possibly too of Tolstoy and Dostoievsky, to whose works he was introduced at Leipzig by a Russian student acquaintance, that awakened in Ferruccio a curious passion for observing the humble life of great cities, though he discontinued speech-making after he left Leipzig. It must not be supposed that in maturer years he continued the practice of disguising himself as a blacksmith, nor that he had at any time the least inclination to what is called 'bad company'. But he never had at any time Beethoven's passion for the open country; he could appreciate landscape as a painter might, but not as a peasant. The one thing that interested him most throughout life was humanity.

Ferdinando's affairs were a perpetual source of anxiety. Thanks to the generosity of Blüthner, Ferruccio had been able to send him 640 marks in April, but such large sums could not be raised every month. Ferruccio tried to obtain him a post in an orchestra at Rotterdam, but without success. He must at all costs be got away from Frohnleiten, where his situation became every day more hopeless. Ferruccio advised him to try to come to terms with his creditors as best he could, so as to be free to leave the place. 'Consider how one deteriorates both morally and artistically by living in such a place in such conditions.' Ferruccio had begun to take a strong line with his father. His father entirely refused to understand. He had lived most of his life by borrowing and seemed to think that Ferruccio might borrow from any one he could in order to support him. What had an artist to do with finance?

He desired his son to send him the trumpet parts of a
concerto by Spohr which he was practising.

In October Ferruccio played twice at Hamburg. His
programmes included Tausig's transcription of Bach's
D minor Toccata and Fugue for organ, Liszt's transcription of the waltz from Gounod's *Faust*, the Fantasia on
Lucrezia Borgia, a nocturne and polonaise of Chopin,
some works of his own (with an improvisation), and
Tausig's transcription of the *Walkürenritt*. He had reached
a phase when he was very much—too much indeed—the
virtuoso. German criticism naturally fell foul of his freedom of style, especially in his use of the pedal. His almost
orchestral effects on the pianoforte were something new,
and Hamburg was hardly ready for them. Hamburg also
thought it very strange to play *Lucrezia Borgia* to a cultivated German audience. As for Tausig's *Walkürenritt*, it
had already caused a scandal at Trieste, where Ferruccio
was told that such music was only fit for a steam-engine.
Indeed the attitude of the critics to Ferruccio at this date
was much the same as that of the old gentleman at Frohnleiten to the locomotive—'Magnificent! Appalling!!'

The news of Ferruccio's successes at Hamburg only
roused Ferdinando to worse displays of bad temper. If
the concerts had been so successful, why did not his son
send him some money? But the expenses had been heavy,
and there had been no profits. The Baroness and Frau
von Wertheimstein were apparently intending to discon-
tinue Ferruccio's allowance. At last Ferruccio in despair
went to Dr. Abraham, explained the situation without
reserve, telling him the whole story of his father's life, and
asked for his advice and help. Dr. Abraham viewed the
situation as any reasonable man would. He was only too
glad to help Ferruccio, in whose ability and character he
had complete confidence, but he saw no reason why he
should make himself responsible for maintaining Ferruccio's father in a life of idleness. It is extremely probable that
the two ladies in Vienna would have agreed entirely with
Dr. Abraham, who saw at once that it would be useless

71

to pay Ferdinando's debts and send him back to Italy, as he would simply go from bad to worse. He refused to do anything to help unless Ferdinando obtained a regular post in an orchestra. Ferruccio could only beseech his father to write to the theatre at Bologna. Even if he were only a month or two in an orchestra, even if the contract were only a pretence, the situation might be saved. The conversation with Dr. Abraham took place in November 1887; it was nearly a year before Ferruccio was able to shift his father from Frohnleiten.

For Christmas Ferruccio went to Trieste, playing in January 1888 both there and at Graz. The programme of his recital at Graz on January 12 may be given here in full:

1.	Organ Fantasia and Fugue in G minor	Bach-Liszt
2.	Sonata in C minor, Op. 111	Beethoven
3.	Variations and Fugue on Chopin's Prelude in C minor	Busoni
4.	*a.* Toccata	Schumann
	b. Rondo in A minor	Mozart
	c. Gigue	Mozart
	d. Perpetuum mobile	Weber
	e. 'Man lebt nur einmal'	Strauss-Tausig
5.	Improvisation on a given theme	Busoni
6.	Tarantella di Bravura (*La Muette de Portici*)	Auber-Liszt

It is obviously the programme of a virtuoso, but it has a character of its own. It is a typical Busoni programme, although it belongs to his first period as a mature artist. Bach, Beethoven, Mozart, Weber, Chopin, Liszt—these are the names which are to recur most frequently in the recital programmes of the succeeding years. Schumann's Toccata did not remain long in his repertory, and it was almost the only work of Schumann which he cared to play.[1]

[1] At one time he played the *Études symphoniques,* and the *Abegg* Variations appeared for several years in his programmes. *Carneval* he detested. Although in later life he had no esteem for Schumann at all, he wrote with great enthusiasm of the Symphonies of Schumann which he heard at Vienna.

72

Melanie Mayer was there to hear him, and naturally had much talk with him too. She wrote down her impressions of the meeting, and they sketch a vivid portrait of Ferruccio as he was at twenty-one.

'He was about to start a new chapter in his development. His individuality had given unusually early signs of maturity and enlightenment; it seemed as if he now desired to shake off these precocious fruits and to put forth new buds. He admitted frankly that he had hitherto allowed reason to have too predominant an influence on his work. His whole personality now seemed veiled in a quality of gentleness, his former over-severity and hardness softened; it reminded me of the mysterious light of the hour when the stars begin to pale and the sun has not yet risen.'

Melanie, like Anna, found Ferruccio 'changed'; but unlike her she viewed him with a sister's understanding. It was their last meeting for many years to come.

CHAPTER V

MARRIAGE

THERE was plenty of occupation for Ferruccio on his return to Leipzig in January 1888. He played there and also at Halle and Dresden, where he saw the picture gallery and the opera, and spent a pleasant evening at one of the private music-meetings of the Tonkünstler-Verein, a society of professional musicians which both for the excellence of its performances and the friendliness of its hospitality is famous throughout Germany. Composition progressed steadily. For a long time he had been working at his opera *Sigune*; it was now nearing completion, at any rate in the rough, and Ferruccio was particularly proud of the *duetto d'amore*, which he thought the best thing he had ever written. It is curious to read of his enthusiasm for this number in view of the utter condemnation of all operatic love-duets which he pronounced in later life. A new Quartet had been finished; it was played on January 28 by Petri and his colleagues. It had a great success with the public, but was severely handled by the critics. The Suite for orchestra was to have been played on February 23, but as the King of Saxony unexpectedly announced his intention of attending the concert the programme was changed. Ferruccio wrote himself to the King telling him of his disappointment after all the years of struggle which he had endured, and hoped that King Albert would put his detractors to rout by commanding the Suite to be performed. King Albert 'washed his hands of the whole matter', and all that Ferruccio could do was to send his father a comic caricature of His Saxon Majesty as the King of Spades with himself kneeling in prayer before him.

He was also able to send his father a considerable sum of money, thanks to the generosity of Theodore Steinway, head of the American pianoforte firm. Steinway had been

greatly impressed with Ferruccio's powers and was pro-
posing a contract for a tour in America, which would
have established him at once in the front rank of pianists.
For some reason the tour was postponed and no definite
contract made. Theodore Steinway died suddenly in the
following year. Busoni always considered that his death
had been the greatest misfortune of his own life.

In April, through the recommendation of Professor
Hugo Riemann, Ferruccio suddenly received the offer of
a post as teacher of the pianoforte at the Conservatoire of
Helsingfors, the term to begin on September 15. He had
no idea where Helsingfors was, but accepted at once.
The post promised an assured income for the year, at any
rate. He immediately suggested to his mother that she
should come and live with him there. At last he was in
a position to fulfil his long-cherished desire of making a
home for Anna. Anna was completely taken by surprise
and replied with a letter so incoherent that Ferruccio could
hardly make out what she wanted. Naturally quite incapable of seeing the situation from her son's point of
view, she proposed that Ferdinando should go to Helsingfors instead of herself. She could only think of Ferruccio
as a child, who needed a parent to take care of him; she
apparently could not grasp the idea of his taking care of
her. It would solve the problem of Ferdinando, and
meanwhile she could go on earning a little money for him
at Trieste. Ferruccio explained things to her with his
endless patience and kindness. He took it for granted that
she agreed to join him and forthwith made clear and
practical plans for her journey. In August he went to the
Bayreuth Festival as the guest of Steinway. Towards the
end of the month he was giving his mother the last
directions about packing up his possessions and joining
him at Leipzig where she was to stay with the Petris.
Suddenly, at the very last moment, she decided that she
would not go. In the first week of September Ferruccio
and Lesko, the adored Newfoundland, set off for Helsingfors by themselves.

75

They went by a night train to Lübeck, Lesko giving some trouble on the way; after a day at Lübeck they embarked on a small and uncomfortable steamer for Helsingfors. The voyage took three whole nights and days, the first two of which were stormy and rough. It was Ferruccio's first experience of the sea, and he found himself then, as on all subsequent voyages and Channel crossings, a very bad sailor. When they reached Helsingfors late on the fourth evening, he was completely hoarse from seasickness and remained practically voiceless for over a week. He had already met one of his future colleagues on board the boat, the second pianoforte teacher, but when he found that this gentleman not only read but positively enjoyed the short stories of *Die Gartenlaube*[1] he cut conversation short. He had better luck with a young university lecturer returning from three years' study in Italy. At the harbour Ferruccio was met by a portly and cheerful gentleman with a face like Silenus, a little pointed beard and a mane of pale fair hair, who carried him off to supper; it was Martin Wegelius, the Director of the Conservatoire. Wegelius, then a man of just over forty, was an interesting and attractive personality. He was a sound and well-read musician, who had travelled widely and had made friends with musicians in all countries; even in later life he made a point of visiting foreign schools of music in order to see what he could learn from their methods and organization. He was genial and kindly, with a strong sense of humour and a cordial friendliness towards young musicians; to meet his new subordinate at the boat and take him to supper was a very characteristic act of hospitality.

Ferruccio was fascinated by his first view of Helsingfors with its picturesque buildings and its rocks, bays, and islands, but he could hardly help feeling painfully lonely in a place where he was a stranger to everybody in language, habits, and general ways of life and thought. He was horrified at the Conservatoire and its artistic

---

[1] *Die Gartenlaube* has been for many years the favourite literature of German women of the lower middle classes in provincial towns.

standards. Wegelius talked hesitatingly of Bach—'yes—Bach's Inventions are what we may regard as a foundation—plenty of Bach, plenty of Bach! Mozart and Beethoven too, Liszt . . .'—he must have known that he was thinking more of his own ideals than of what could actually be carried out. Ferruccio soon found that Clementi and Cramer were about all that his pupils could attempt. He had an average of four hours' teaching a day, with an occasional ensemble class. The majority of his pupils were girls; the few men among them were little superior to them in intelligence. He wrote to Petri that he felt like a clown in a circus with a troop of performing geese. Helsingfors possessed no opera; the Conservatoire could not even produce a professional quartet. There was a violin master, a Hungarian Jew who played in the Viennese manner, taking no interval without a pronounced slide, and a violoncello master who three years before had been a commercial traveller; the inner parts had to be taken by pupils. Outside the Conservatoire there was an orchestra led by a brother of Hans Sitt and conducted by Robert Kajanus, a young Finnish musician of some talent. Orchestra and Conservatoire looked somewhat askance at each other. Ferruccio thought the orchestra the more energetic institution of the two and determined to cultivate its friendship; there was a chance of his playing concertos at concerts and even a possibility of his Suite being performed.

Ferruccio was soon in demand as a private teacher, and by the middle of October he had a dozen private pupils, but he detested teaching in private houses, for he felt that he was being treated like a servant by the wealthy parents who employed him. Besides, he felt that every hour given to teaching was robbed from composition; but, as he significantly wrote to his father, he was firmly determined never to run into debt, in order that he might be free to leave Finland as soon as his year's contract came to an end. Early in October he gave a Beethoven recital—Sonata Op. 2 (probably the F minor), the *Appassionata*,

77

and Op. 111, the *Eroica* Variations and Fugue, and the *Écossaises*; Helsingfors had heard nothing like it since the visits of Rubinstein and Bülow. The Beethoven recital was followed by a series devoted to a complete survey of pianoforte music, beginning with Bach, Mozart, Scarlatti, and Handel, thence proceeding onwards to Brahms, Rubinstein, Liszt, Grieg, Sgambati, and his own works. Composition proceeded steadily; he was still working at *Sigune*, and found time too to write some Bagatelles for violin (for little Egon Petri) and a Suite on Finnish folk-tunes for pianoforte duet.

In spite of his success he felt terribly lonely. Lesko was his only friend and to her he became more and more devoted. His young Austrian admirer was in difficulties again, as usual, and he did his best to comfort and encourage him, but he felt that his own case was the worse of the two, for the other at any rate was living in a place where music was seriously cultivated. Ferruccio missed his friends and missed his parents too; in addition to the mere fact of loneliness he suffered perhaps even more acutely from the fear that in the backward environment of Helsingfors his own talents would deteriorate. It is evident from his letters that what troubled him most was not the temporary hindrance to his ambition, the consciousness that he had no opportunity of appearing before a cultivated public and winning fame as a pianist, but the fact of his being regarded in Helsingfors as a marvel, while he knew all along that, even if he were acknowledged to be in the front rank, he was in reality only on the very threshold of what he inwardly felt himself called to become. He did not feel the need of teachers; what he intended to achieve he knew he could only achieve by his own efforts. But he needed, and knew that he needed, the stimulating influence of an environment with the highest possible standards; and it may be that he had not yet quite outlived the phase in which, as he confessed later to Petri, competition with his fellow students was a keener spur to him than the pursuit of the ideal itself. The applause of

Helsingfors made him more than ever doubtful of his own value; it was a certain sign of his own mediocrity, he felt, if he pleased an audience of mediocre minds.

The northern winter set in, and naturally intensified his depression; amid snow, granite, and the eternal monotony of the pine-trees he remembered sorrowfully that he was born in the warm shadow of the cypresses.

'Your refusal to come with me', he wrote to his mother, 'made me very sad. Here I am all alone and long to be near you. I wish you could be with me, to follow my occupations at first hand, my progress, both in my art and in my career. You would enjoy the good food and admire the magnificent landscape before me. This solitude, although disturbed by continuous duties, is terrible; in the evening when work is finished, I am obliged to do nothing for an hour or two and then I feel a most painful sense of emptiness. I hope I shall have you with me next year . . .

'When my work was published by Peters (the Bagatelles for Violin) I thought again of Luigi Cimoso and how overjoyed he would have been about it. That friendship and admiration of his were a great spur to me. His letters are an irreparable loss.'

After giving an account of his hours of work he goes on to

'what is most important of all—the will and the effort not to neglect composition, the everything of my life, the ultimate object of my existence, without which all that I have achieved so far would be relatively worthless . . .

'Musical conditions here do not satisfy my requirements; I want a country where it is a case of surpassing the highest that has yet been reached, not one where much work has yet to be done to reach the average level of other countries. As you know, it would be a great satisfaction to reform and educate taste, to establish orchestral concerts in a backward country; but this is a duty and a satisfaction which I feel only towards Italy, and later on I certainly mean to dedicate a great part of my life to laying the foundations, along with others, of a new epoch in the musical life of my own country. There! I have let out one of my secret plans . . .'

The term came at last to an end, and Ferruccio hurried off to Leipzig. He must have arrived in a state of very overwrought nerves, for on New Year's Eve an episode happened which nearly brought about a complete rupture with Henri Petri. There had been a party at Petri's house in honour of his old teacher Joachim. Petri, who was always anxious to do his best for Ferruccio, pressed him to play his Chopin-Variations to the great man. Ferruccio had taken an antipathy to Joachim and flatly refused to play at all; there was a somewhat painful scene which was made all the more painful by Petri's good manners and Joachim's perhaps rather condescending kindness. Ferruccio went home and sat up for what remained of the night writing an acrimonious letter to Petri. After he had written it he re-read it, thought better of it and refrained from sending it off. The quarrel was averted, and he joined Petri's Quartet in a concert at Halle a week later; but it required all Petri's kindness of heart to heal the breach. As Ferruccio admitted in his letter, the affair of the party for Joachim was merely the last drop in the cup. The letter might well give a reader the impression of nothing more than an outburst of wounded vanity. Petri was a man who had a wife and children to support; he was one of the finest violinists of his day—Reinecke told Ferruccio that he considered him the obvious successor to Joachim—but he was also a Dutchman who valued the comforts of life and was extremely glad to have reached comparatively early in his career an eminence which enabled him to maintain his household in a good social position. No man was more ready to be kind to rising talent, but rising talent, when it had risen to a certain height, was apt to find Petri too conventional and too desirous of standing well with persons of influence. Ferruccio did not take criticism with humility, and what roused him to even more fury than the criticism of his own work was Petri's respect for Reinecke and Joachim as composers and his condescending disparagement of Ferruccio's own contemporaries Sinding and Richard Strauss. The letter was the expression of a noble and generous temperament; but Ferruccio was wise not to post it.

Ferruccio had complained of loneliness at Leipzig, but

for all that Leipzig had brought him contacts which were
to develop into lasting friendships. It is probable that in
those days he little realized how vivid was the impression
which his own personality made on other people. The
unposted letter to Petri championed Richard Strauss and
Sinding. Ferruccio had recognized at once the outstanding
abilities of Strauss, though Strauss was never one of his
intimate friends, and to the end of his life his admiration
for Strauss never wavered, however acutely he might
criticize his work in detail. For Christian Sinding, Ferruccio had a personal devotion of touching intensity. They
had become acquainted at Leipzig in 1888. To most
people Sinding at first sight appeared insignificant and
unattractive. He was a painfully shy and nervous young
man with a large domed forehead and a little pointed
beard. When he first met Ferruccio he had no idea that
he was a pianist. One day Sinding brought him the manuscript of a pianoforte quintet which he had just written;
Ferruccio sat down and played it through at sight. Sinding
was completely taken by surprise and thereupon insisted
that Ferruccio should play the pianoforte part at its
first public performance. It was played at Leipzig on
January 19, 1889, the string players being Brodsky, Becker,
Nováček, and Klengel. The audience received it with
enthusiasm, but the critics were hostile; one of them, who
occupied a conspicuous seat on the platform, ostentatiously
ate sandwiches throughout the work.

Sinding's later musical career led him into paths very
remote from Ferruccio's, but friendship remained un-
impaired. Many years afterwards Sinding, Delius, and
Busoni met in Paris; they were then all three married and
accompanied by their wives. Busoni, who was in a cheerful mood, burst out suddenly with one of his characteristic
observations:

'Here we are, three composers and their wives; and
every one of the ladies is thinking that *her* husband is the
greatest of all!'

Delius was a little uncomfortable; it was 'the sort of

81

thing one didn't say,' he felt. But for all that explosion of
laughter with which Busoni, as usual, followed up his
remark, it was probably true enough; certainly few composers have ever had such devoted wives as those three
friends. And two more of the players at that Leipzig
concert entered into Ferruccio's later life; Nováček was
to become one of his constant intimates until his early
death, and Brodsky remained a faithful friend too,
although he and Ferruccio had but few opportunities of
meeting.

Yet Helsingfors, in spite of its backwardness, had
somehow contributed to Ferruccio's development. He
undoubtedly learned much from association with Wegelius, who both appreciated his talents to the full and had
too a strong personal affection for him. None the less he
had suffered acutely from loneliness—a loneliness far
drearier than that of Leipzig. Solitude had perhaps
taught him to know himself more thoroughly. When he
gave a recital at Hamburg in January 1889, playing
among other things the first of his own transcriptions from
Bach's organ works, it was acknowledged that he had
acquired a greater variety of style and an altogether
deeper insight into music. One critic spoke of his wonderful reproduction of full soft organ tone on the pianoforte.
It was Kathi Petri who first suggested to him that he
should transcribe Bach's organ music. She and Ferruccio
went into the Thomaskirche one day and heard the
organist play Bach's Prelude and Fugue in D major. 'You
ought to arrange that for pianoforte,' she said to him. He
had never yet attempted anything of the kind, but a week
later he played it to her. He had not even written it down.
This was not merely the beginning of the transcriptions,
but what was of far deeper import, it was the beginning
of that style of pianoforte touch and technique which was
entirely the creation of Ferruccio Busoni. 'That angelic
old Theodore Steinway,' as he called him, came over from
Brunswick to hear him, and talked of arranging an appearance in London for him in the summer. He felt him-

self that this Hamburg concert was the beginning of a new stage in his career, and that he had better things to do than to 'go sour', as he put it, at Helsingfors.

Ferruccio returned to Helsingfors in no very cheerful frame of mind. Hamburg had given him hopes for the future, but his sense of loneliness was aggravated by what had happened at Leipzig. He had escaped a complete rupture with Petri, but none the less the cordiality of his relations with him was for the moment impaired. There had been too another and a severe shock inflicted on his nerves. Friendship with a married woman had deepened on both sides into passion, and a husband's neglect had encouraged plans for an elopement. Fortunately the lady was a woman of intellect and reasoned the matter out with herself; Ferruccio, who in his relations with women was always to some extent inhibited by his reasoning powers, probably did the same. At any rate the elopement never took place, and Ferruccio soon came to realize the error from which he had been saved.

By the middle of March he was thoroughly depressed. He was tired of Helsingfors and the pettiness of its life, tired of his unintelligent and indifferent pupils. He had had a quarrel with Dr. Abraham over the publication of the Finnish duets; Schwalm had sold his business, which endangered the publication of *Signune*; Theodore Steinway was dying and the chance of playing in London had vanished.

One Monday evening in March a pupil of his, a lively young man called Edi Fazer, persuaded him to come and see some *tableaux vivants* which were being given in aid of a charity. Somewhat reluctantly he went. After the performance there was a supper and a dance, at which Edi introduced him to Gerda Sjöstrand, the daughter of a Swedish sculptor who had settled in Helsingfors. They met again the next day; on the Wednesday he came to her father's house, and within a few days more they were engaged to be married. Gerda told her father at once. Carl Aeneas Sjöstrand had studied sculpture in Italy and spoke Italian fluently.[1] He received Ferruccio with cordiality and gave his unhesitating approval to the match. Ferruccio, perhaps remembering his own family history, had feared that he might be uneasy about allowing his daughter to marry a young musician of uncertain prospects. The sculptor had no uneasiness whatever; his art had taught him to be a quick and shrewd reader of character, and he accepted Ferruccio as a son-in-law with complete and unquestioning confidence.

On Ferruccio's side matters were very different. It was some months before he dared announce his engagement to Ferdinando and Anna. Ferdinando might possibly approve of Gerda; his son's marriage would mean another mouth for Ferruccio to feed and the possibility of more, but at the same time Ferdinando was a man of experience where women were concerned, and viewed matrimony with the blunt common sense of an Italian. 'Now that you are a man,' he had often said to his son, 'you must live a regular life; so either buy yourself a woman or marry one.' It would be much more difficult to break the news to Anna; she could not think of Ferruccio except as her child, her only child, the only thing for which she lived, and she could never bear the thought of another woman coming between them.

As regards marriage Ferruccio, like his father, was an Italian. He had no desire for a romantic Egeria to inspire him; inspiration was his own affair. Nor did he desire the sort of woman who would always be considering her social position and the position which her husband ought to take in the world. What he wanted above all things from woman was *Empfindung*—intuitive feeling. He wanted a helpmeet who would follow him through all the risks and troubles of an artist's life, a woman who should be his and his alone, a woman who should be the mother of his children. Difficult as his position with Anna had become, he none the less appreciated what a mother's love

[1] He had been chiefly a pupil of Bissen at Copenhagen; Bissen was a pupil of Thorwaldsen.

and devotion meant, and it was his ardent desire to be himself the father of children who should grow up in happier surroundings under the same affectionate influences. His Italian temperament showed itself at times in almost grotesque outbursts of jealousy. Gerda, who was already beginning to earn her own living as a pianoforte teacher, had been brought up with all the freedom of the northern nations and with the additional freedom and knowledge that came from close and constant association with her artist father. Her mother had died in 1884. Ferruccio had on his first arrival in Finland been horrified at the general freedom of manners, and his Italian mind could not altogether understand that outward liberty might be compatible with complete inward self-possession. He discovered that Gerda had spent some time in Germany; she had frequented theatrical society in Berlin, and at Bayreuth she had lodged with one of the 'flower-maidens'. Ferruccio put the worst construction on these escapades; he was convinced that the 'flower-maidens' were notoriously as dangerous in their private lives as they were supposed to appear when on the stage. On one occasion his jealousy drove him to such a pitch of excitement that without realizing what he was doing he destroyed a whole boxful of Sjöstrand's cigars, taking them up one by one and crushing them in his fingers until no more were left.

He stayed on at Helsingfors to the end of May. The only musical events to be noted were two Chopin recitals, at which he played very characteristic programmes—the *Études* and *Préludes* complete at the first, at the second five Polonaises, two Ballades, the *Berceuse*, and the *Tarantella*, four Nocturnes, and the B flat minor Sonata. At the beginning of June he went to Weimar, where he lodged with Liszt's cook at Schröterstrasse 23a. Wegelius had converted him to a serious interest in Liszt as a composer, and although he had not yet begun to make himself the champion of Liszt, he no doubt felt attracted towards the town which Liszt's influence had made into an artistic

85

centre where musicians, poets, and painters met on friendly terms and worked in peace and quiet. At the last moment of leave-taking he had almost persuaded Gerda to come with him. She refused, not so much from want of courage as from the intuitive knowledge that it would be best for him to be alone with his work for a time. He was not altogether alone, as Edi Fazer had come too to be assistant to Stavenhagen the pianoforte teacher; but Edi spent most of his evenings exploring the diversions of Weimar with a young Englishman. He had not even the companionship of Lesko; she had been left to look after Gerda. Ferruccio had no inclination to amuse himself and preferred to sit at home and write letters. Correspondence with Gerda presented difficulties; Ferruccio had learned little Swedish and she knew still less Italian, so that the language of their courtship was German. He had mastered German thoroughly and wrote it with the prolixity of an Italian and the added prolixity of any one who knows a foreign language well enough to write it with ease but not with concision. Gerda had been at school in Paris, and spoke French fluently, but her German had been merely 'picked up' in Berlin. She was obliged to write her love-letters with a dictionary, and long as they were, Ferruccio found them disappointingly short. But they were full of sound sense, and when he pestered her with questions about Bayreuth and Berlin she replied with serenity and dignity. Ferruccio had reason enough to be nervous; he had asked his mother to come to Weimar, and the day of her arrival was drawing near. His father had at last left Frohnleiten in the autumn of 1888 and after a visit to Tuscany had settled down again at Trieste with his wife, but Trieste was never very congenial to him, and he would have been glad of any excuse to make a move. Anna was ill in June and unable to travel. Ferdinando proposed to take her to Vienna, suggesting that Ferruccio should come to Vienna to meet them; it would be a good opportunity for discussing plans. Ferruccio saw that this was merely an excuse for a trip to Vienna at his son's expense. As to plans, Ferruccio had made his own and was not going to change them. Anna was to join him at Weimar, where he intended to stay to the end of the year, except for occasional concert journeys to Hamburg, Frankfurt, and other places. In January he was going back to Helsingfors and intended that his mother should go with him. He suspected that what Ferdinando wanted was for father and son to make their home in Vienna; against this plan he set his face firmly.

'Austria I mean to avoid for some time. I detest Austria for all the privations and discouragements which it brought me; I have only the most bitter remembrances of that country and I will not go back to it until I am called thither—that is, until I have become so famous that they will be forced to invite me to Vienna.

'Those were terrible times, when I could move nowhere except between Trieste and Vienna, always in disaster. I bless my decision to escape to Leipzig; from that moment I was born again, I became a man, I know what I want and I know what I am doing. I only wish I could tell you to follow me too, but you see how impossible it is. Yet I would like to do so, if only to pull you out of that black-and-yellow filth once for all. And once more at Vienna, are you going to stick fast there again? I cannot recommend it. Dearest Father, I pray and beseech you for the love of God to try not to start another chapter like that of Frohnleiten!'

By the middle of July Anna was well enough to travel, and on the 16th Ferruccio went to Leipzig to meet her. To his surprise he found that Ferdinando had come with her. He showed them round Leipzig and brought them to Weimar in the evening. They were much aged and altered, he found, more narrow-minded and timid, more superstitious and absorbed in religion; he suddenly felt the vivid contrast of Gerda's sunny joyousness and youth. Anna noticed the photograph of her on the writing-table the moment she came in.

'Who is that?' she asked.

'That is a girl whom I like very much.'

'And who is this in the locket?'

'The same girl.'

Anna seemed not to have heard his answers. They

went out to supper. When they came back Anna looked at the portrait again.

'How do you like the girl, Mamma?'

'I have not looked at her yet, the frame is so pretty.'

'But the portrait?'

'*Oui, elle n'est pas mal, mais elle ne serait pas mon idéal.*'[1]

'She is *my* ideal,' said Ferruccio, 'and that is enough.'

'But the frame is pretty,' Anna repeated, 'and now good-night.'

She could not bring herself to say more; Ferruccio knew that he was his own master.

The next morning she went up to the portrait again.

'That is a very intelligent young woman,' observed Ferruccio.

'Yes, one sees that.'

Ferdinando came in and looked at the photograph too. He always had an eye for a woman.

'Now, who's that? That's a fine girl!'

And to Ferruccio's complete surprise his mother chimed in, 'Yes, isn't she a beauty?'

At luncheon at the *table d'hôte* conversation turned on women smoking.

'Does that girl in the photograph smoke?' asked Ferdinando cheerfully.

'Yes,' replied Ferruccio, 'when I ask her to smoke—otherwise not.'

'Aha!' remarked Ferdinando, 'then there's something between you!'

'Yes, we are engaged to be married.'

They drank Gerda's health and the parents gave their blessing. They were not unprepared; they had talked it over together, and evidently Ferdinando had persuaded Anna to accept the situation.

She accepted it in the way that she accepted all situations, with the resignation of a devout Christian.

[1] Yes, she's not bad, but she would not be my ideal.'

Ferdinando did not stop long at Weimar, but went to
Empoli to stay with his brothers. They gave him no very
cordial reception, but that did not prevent him from remaining at Empoli for the next six months. Anna did her
best to reconcile herself to the idea of Ferruccio's marriage,
but conversation on the subject (and it may well be
imagined that it was the daily subject of conversation)
often became painful. At the beginning of August
Ferruccio could bear it no longer and went off to Helsingfors for a few days, returning via Berlin—'that odious,
dreary, lazy, ostentatious, *parvenu* and expressionless
town of Jews', as he called it. He was offered a very
lucrative post at the Cincinnati Conservatoire, but declined it. He felt that he could not bear to stay more than
one year there, and that in view of travelling expenses,
payments to his parents, and the interruption to his artistic
career it would not be worth his while.

His original intention had been to stay at Weimar to the
end of the year. Early in September he suddenly decided
to go back to Helsingfors and to take his mother with him.
The step was taken without consulting Ferdinando. The
fact was that Ferdinando was becoming restive at Empoli.
Ferruccio may well have feared that his father would
inflict his company on him again unless he put the Baltic
between them. Another reason was that Anna's profoundly Catholic piety did not prevent—indeed it may
have encouraged—her tendency to develop a curiously
suspicious attitude towards Gerda, and she had been
somewhat unscrupulous in trying to suggest to Ferruccio
that she might not be the right sort of wife for him. He
replied to this by leaving one of Gerda's letters on his
writing-table, knowing that his mother was certain to pry
into it. Caught in the act, she said nothing, but grew daily
more and more mistrustful. He may well have felt that
Weimar under such conditions was no longer bearable.
In any case a return to Helsingfors had become necessary
in order to provide money for his parents. Ferruccio and
his mother arrived at Helsingfors in the second week of

89

September, travelling via St. Petersburg, as Anna refused
to face the sea—indeed she was not in a fit state of health
to take the risk. Gerda met them at the station; when the
old lady descended from her long journey, gaunt and
haggard, with a large wart on each side of her aquiline
nose and a disordered mass of wavy white hair standing
out all round her head—even at that age it was put into
curl-papers every night—she thought she had encountered
one of the witches out of *Macbeth*. Anna greeted Gerda in
French, calling her *ma bonne*—it was a long time before
she could bring herself to anything more affectionate than
that. French was always her language of communication
with Gerda, and even after her marriage Gerda always
wrote to her in French, at any rate until she had acquired
complete command of Italian.

Anna did not take kindly to life at Helsingfors. The
Sjöstrands did everything in their power to make her
happy, but it was useless. The strange climate, strange
language, and strange food, above all the loss of most of
her religious observances,[1] all contributed to make her
more and more depressed and irritable in her relations
with Ferruccio and Gerda. Gerda was quite sensible
enough to see at once that Anna's hostility was not really
directed against her own personality; she was hostile towards any prospective daughter-in-law. When Ferruccio
went away to play at St. Petersburg and Leipzig matters
only became worse. For him the concert-tour must have
been a welcome relief. At St. Petersburg there was much
talk of his settling there as a teacher; he was also corre-
sponding with Henri Petri (now established as leader of the
royal band at Dresden) about a post at Breslau. In Leipzig
the reception of his *Concertstück* for pianoforte and orchestra was unfriendly, but both at Leipzig and St. Petersburg
he had a brilliant success as a pianist. He had an extraordinary power of self-control when on the concert-plat-
form; once at the pianoforte he could lay aside all the

[1] There was a Catholic church at Helsingfors in those days, but apparently it did not fully satisfy her devotional requirements.

nervous agitation caused by his domestic affairs and concentrate his entire mind on his playing.

It was a fortunate gift, for at this moment he had cause enough for agitation. Ferdinando was clamouring for money and writing long letters to his wife which embittered her relations with Ferruccio still more. He had somehow become obsessed with the idea that his son was living a life of riotous immorality and was doing his best to convince Anna of this belief. It became gradually evident to Ferruccio that his father really had no great desire to live with his wife; he never admitted this, but he was always ready with some pretext or other for refusing to consider his son's plans for bringing them together. It was urgent, he maintained to Anna, that Ferruccio should have his mother to look after him, for then 'certain things' would not happen. Ferruccio retorted that it would be very much better for her to be looking after Ferdinando. Anna refused to allow her son to say a word against his father.

Throughout the whole spring and summer of 1890 these anxieties continued without respite. In the early summer Ferdinando managed to leave Empoli and go back to Trieste; but Trieste was evidently a place where he was too well known to be comfortable. He tried Gorizia, gave a concert, lost money and sank deeper into debt. Ferruccio advised him to try Milan; in a big town he might find occupation both as a clarinet-player and as a journalist. Ferruccio was by this time firmly determined to be rid of his mother. Had she been a widow he would have borne the burden, but as she had a husband living, it was only reasonable that the parents should live together and leave their son to marry and lead his own life. He was perfectly prepared to support his parents, but he pointed out to them plainly that what he had to spend in maintaining Anna in Helsingfors would serve amply for the two if they would only join forces. Finally the matter was settled for them by Ferruccio's appointment to a post at the Moscow Conservatoire. He took up his duties there in the second

week of September; the month had already begun before
he could bring his parents to a decision. Probably Anna
refused to face a fresh transplantation to a country still
remoter from all her normal associations than Finland.
Ferruccio paid his father's debts at Gorizia and sent his
mother off to join him there. There was no necessity,
they agreed, for Ferdinando to meet Anna at Vienna, as
Ferdinando seems to have suggested; he was not to go
farther than Nabresina.[1]

Anna's jealousy was driving Gerda to despair. One day
she told her straight out that she ought never to have
allowed herself to become engaged to Ferruccio when she
knew that his parents were dependent on him; his first
duty was to his parents and he had no right to found a
family of his own. She was holding her prayer-book in her
hands as she said this, and was so overwrought that she
tore it to shreds. It was no wonder that by the end of
the summer poor Gerda's courage completely broke down
and she suggested to Ferruccio that it would be better to
break off the engagement. It was a noble act of self-
sacrifice on her part. Her only thought was for the happiness of Ferruccio; she thought the problem out and came
to the conclusion that his life would really be happier if it
were spent with his mother. Naturally Ferruccio would
not hear of such a thing for a moment. As soon as he
reached Moscow he wrote to her and told her to join him
at once. Ferruccio's original idea had been that they
should be married with Catholic rites, to please his
parents, but the church authorities made difficulties owing
to Gerda's being a Protestant. Neither of the young
people cared very much whether they were officially
married or not. On the morning of September 27, 1890,
Carl Aeneas and his two daughters, accompanied by the
beloved Lesko, arrived in Moscow. Ferruccio met them
at the railway station and told them that as the German
Protestant pastor, who had agreed to marry them, was

[1] Nabresina is a junction twenty-five miles from Gorizia, where the
line to Gorizia diverges from the line from Vienna to Trieste.

going away for his holiday that day, the ceremony must take place at once. Gerda had brought a new dress for the occasion, but there was no time to change. The pastor refused to wait; the wedding party drove straight from the train to his house, and Gerda was married in her old red knitted jersey.

H

CHAPTER VI

THE VIRTUOSO

Busoni began life at Moscow, as he began every new life, with high hopes. In the summer he had won the Rubinstein prize (its first adjudication) for composition with his *Concertstück*; in the opinion of the majority of the judges present, he ought undoubtedly to have won the prize for pianoforte-playing as well. After the examination several of them did in fact congratulate him on winning both prizes; but Rubinstein himself interposed. Not all of the appointed judges had been able to attend in person, and the absentees had all handed over their votes to Rubinstein, so that he was in an impregnable position. It was the first award of the prize, he said, and the award was being held in St. Petersburg; one of the prizes at least must be given to a Russian. Busoni having obtained the prize for composition, the other was bestowed on Dubassov. Busoni was quite ready to admit Dubassov's merits as a pianist. Five years later the prizes were awarded for the second time; the scene was Berlin, and Busoni himself a member of the jury. Safonov, then Director of the Moscow Conservatoire, made a long speech relating the whole history of the first award. He ended with the words, 'Here stands the man who ought to have received both prizes,' and pointed to Busoni.

In any case the composition prize was in itself sufficient to bring Busoni's name into prominence when he entered the musical life of Russia, and he never bore the slightest ill-will towards his more successful rival at the pianoforte. But residence in Moscow was a very different matter from flying visits to St. Petersburg.

The first sight of Moscow brought a certain sense of disillusionment. Helsingfors had been bewildering enough to a young Italian—'I expect one never feels happy at first in any strange town where one knows that one has got to settle for some length of time,' he wrote to Gerda—but Moscow was far worse, with its immediate impression of appalling beggary, ostentatious luxury, and a general state of filth which seemed to achieve positive virtuosity in filthiness. Furnished rooms were so dirty everywhere that he was finally obliged to take a couple of unfurnished rooms and furnish them himself. As Gerda's arrival drew near he began to see Moscow in a more favourable light. The Conservatoire, at any rate, was admirably organized and provided with the best possible teachers. Siloti received him with unaffected cordiality and he took it for granted that his colleagues would do the same. He could assure his father that his position even on his first arrival was a considerable one and that he hoped in time to make it even more important. It was not long before his view of the situation changed. By November he had discovered that he had no friends in Moscow and that his colleagues were all jealous of him; in addition to that there was also the growing sense of nationalism among the Russian musicians which intensified their hostility towards a foreigner. He had a large number of pupils and was obliged to teach for thirty-five hours a week, but he soon found that his increased income was balanced by increased expenses, although Gerda was a cleverer and more careful housekeeper than her mother-in-law, so that the difficulty of providing for his parents became greater than ever. His first concert appearance, in a concerto of Beethoven, brought him immense applause, but no profits. He soon began to long for Hamburg and Leipzig; in Moscow he felt himself hopelessly cut off from European culture and could only look forward to his concert tour in the Christmas vacation.

He returned to Moscow only to become more and more dissatisfied with its social and musical conditions. One of the Steinways in New York urged him to go to America. He began to learn English and decided to accept Steinway's invitation to take up a teaching post at Boston. The stipend offered was three times the amount which he was receiving at Moscow, and there was a further attraction at Boston in the fact that his old friend Nikisch was established there as conductor. During the whole of this period Ferdinando Busoni had never ceased grumbling and complaining from Trieste. Nevertheless he sent affectionate messages to his daughter-in-law, whose beautiful character, as Ferruccio assured him, made her a helpmeet beyond all price. What Anna thought about it all may be well judged from the following letter, which was written in February 1891 to a Fräulein Sarah Hess at Hamburg. Anna never met her in person, but as she was a friend of Ferruccio's she often sent the old lady press-cuttings of his concerts, and Anna seized the opportunity of relieving her feelings to another woman, especially as she could have no designs on Ferruccio. The letter, polite and formal as it is, gives a curiously vivid picture of the writer.

Trieste, 12 February 1891

Come un baleno rapido
    La sorte mia cangiò.[1]

Dear Madam,

It gave me the greatest pleasure to see your handwriting once more, and I tender you infinite thanks both for your kind remembrance of me and for your courtesy in sending me the newspapers which speak so favourably of the successes of my beloved son. I am entirely in agreement with you that Ferruccio is wrong in not dedicating himself more to composition and in thus laying aside his Opera, with which he might acquire fame and money more easily than by becoming a teacher. To be sure, when one forms a family everything becomes more difficult and one is obliged to think about securing one's position. And for that reason I consider that Ferruccio should not have dreamed of taking a wife until his reputation had become more widely spread in all the branches of his Art, all the more as he is still too young to bind himself and to take up all the burdens of a family. You will understand without further explanations from me that this decision of his destroyed my most cherished dream of living close to this son of mine who is doubly

---

[1] 'As in a sudden lightning-flash
      My fortune all was chang'd.'
These lines are probably quoted from some Italian opera.

dear to me, for I love him not only with a mother's affection but with the heart of an artist as well.

This being said (between ourselves) Ferruccio is still the best of sons, but living so far off I can no longer enjoy his companionship which is so dear to me, nor enrapture myself at the touch of his fingers, nor rejoice in the creations of his fervid fantasy! I beg, dear Madam, that you will not repeat a word of what I have said, when you write to Ferruccio. I allowed myself to pour out my poor heart to you, for although we have never met, I felt sure that our opinions would harmonize. I shall therefore always be thankful whenever you remember me and write to me.

Believe me, dear Madam, with esteem and gratitude,

Your most affectionate and obliged

ANNA WEISS BUSONI.

Be so kind as to write to me in Latin characters, as it will then be easier for me to decipher your German.

Busoni and his wife sailed for Boston at the end of August 1891. It was a step of doubtful wisdom; a concert career in Germany might have done more to establish his position. But with the thought of his parents always uppermost in his mind, he did not dare take the risk of finding himself without any financial security. Hermann Wolff, the Berlin concert agent, encouraged him to go to America and he followed his advice. A few weeks of Boston disillusioned him. Conditions were far worse than in Helsingfors. At Helsingfors resources were primitive, but Wegelius realized Busoni's value and gave him a free hand. At Boston there was a great show of business efficiency but little artistic enthusiasm. The New England Conservatory was none too firmly established and the teachers were all in chronic fear of an imminent collapse. Pupils were accepted whether they had talent or not, as long as they paid their fees. Lessons were given at the rate of four in one hour, and the first pupil had to stop in the middle of a bar when the second arrived. Busoni endured it for a year and then resigned. His colleagues were astonished, but admired his courage. 'You can risk it,' they said to him; 'you are strong enough to stand on your own feet.'

97

On May 24, 1892, at Boston, a son was born to him and given the name of Benvenuto. In the summer they moved to New York, where the free life of a travelling virtuoso was more agreeable than the restrictions of Boston. In some of his letters Busoni attributes the narrowness of the American outlook and the dreariness of the American Sunday to Protestantism; but as a matter of fact it was an aspect of Protestantism which troubled him only in America and England. He had plenty of concert engagements at first, but after the first year that source of income seems to have become more precarious. He felt himself terribly cut off from Europe and deprived of the intellectual and artistic atmosphere which he needed to stimulate him. He could regard this sojourn in America only as a period of transition. 'In America', he wrote, 'the *average* is better than elsewhere, but along with that there is much more *average* than elsewhere, and as far as I can see it will soon be all average!' It was increasingly difficult for him to do his duty by his parents; finally, in the spring of 1894 he decided to go back to Europe. He had no prospect of a teaching post, and his experiences at Moscow and Boston made him firmly resolved, in this phase of his life, not to tie himself down to one anywhere. The career which he anticipated was primarily that of the travelling virtuoso, and with that career in view he determined to make his home in Berlin, simply from the fact that Berlin was the geographical centre of his future field of action, a field bounded for the present by Helsingsfors on the north, Moscow on the east, Trieste on the south, and Brussels on the west.

Yet America was not without happy experiences for him. There was the inspiring contact of Nikisch, and the friendship of Eugene Gruenberg and Charles Martin Loeffler, as well as other musicians, among whom the most devotedly attached to him was Rudolf Nováček the violinist and composer. The Nováčeks were a family of musicians from Temesvar in Hungary, a father and four sons; the father regarded Busoni with especial gratitude for all his kindness to the family and called him 'the friend of all Nováčeks'. Rudolf's brother Ottokar, with his flashing eyes, heavy moustache, and thick untidy black hair, was the typical Hungarian violinist of his period, riotously exuberant in manner, both in conversation and in correspondence. He was not in America with the Busonis, but was a constant visitor in Berlin. He was always in love with some woman or other and generally in financial difficulties; he looked up to Busoni as an altogether superior being and as a friend who could be counted upon in any emergency. For Gerda he had—like every one of Busoni's friends who came in contact with her—a respect and affection that amounted almost to a religious devotion. Busoni did his best to assist him, and even played a concerto of his later on at Copenhagen; but even Busoni's playing could not make it a success, and his early death[1] prevented his fulfilling such promise as he showed. To Ferruccio and Gerda, in those early days of their marriage, the brothers Nováček, Ottokar and Rudolf, were friends whose extravagant loyalty and affection were a support and encouragement which they acutely needed and never forgot.

Another joy which America brought them was the birth of their first child. Busoni had always a profoundly Latin feeling for family life, and fatherhood was an indescribable happiness to him. The companionship of his sons in later life, whether as children or as young men, was always a delight to him, and the painful memories of his own childhood induced in him a peculiarly tender sympathy for all the difficulties of adolescence. One of his happiest recollections of America in these days was their last Christmas in New York in 1893, when Nováček came to supper and Benni astonished his father by making his appearance dressed as Puck—the American Puck, not Shakespeare's—in nothing but a sky-blue dress coat and top hat with a pink scarf, carrying in each hand a diminutive bottle of champagne.

[1] Ottokar Nováček died in New York in February 1900.

For the next few years Busoni was known to the musical world only as an executant. 'I have great successes as a pianist,' he wrote to a friend in 1896; 'the composer I conceal for the present.' It was not that he had lost faith in himself as a composer, but he had become critical of his early works and realized inwardly that he must go through a new period of study and self-development before he could produce original work that would satisfy his own judgement. The judgement of the critics on his compositions was in most cases hostile; his music had at least the merit of arousing ill-will, and in his later phases as a composer this hostility was steadily maintained and indeed intensified in certain quarters. As a pianist he often secured the enthusiasm of his audiences at this period of his life, but the next morning brought severe censure in the newspapers, and it must be admitted that the judgement of the critics was in general not altogether unreasonable. The Busoni of thirty was an executant of astonishing virtuosity, but he had not yet attained that maturity of mind which makes virtuosity the servant of intellectual interpretation.

It was a phase through which many young artists have to pass; in Busoni's case it was rendered more acute by the nature of his early education. His father was a virtuoso by temperament; as an artist he had never been anything else. His mother was a musician of far deeper sensibility and of wider technical accomplishment; but she too from the nature of her environment and from the musical period in which her artistic character was formed—a period and environment of which Thalberg is the most representative name—had become a virtuoso by force of circumstances. It was at any rate to Ferdinando's credit that he divined the extraordinary artistic abilities latent in his son at quite an early age, and that although he was often mistaken in his educational methods he never for a moment wavered in his conviction that Ferruccio was destined to achieve the summits of artistic fame. He impressed the conviction of this calling upon Ferruccio with ruthless tenacity, and

Ferruccio as a grown man felt sincerely grateful to him for having done so, even though his ambition, which was by nature unusually keen, was systematically developed by a perpetual show of dissatisfaction on his father's part.[1] He valued this treatment, cruel as it seemed, because he felt that it was only with the arrival of manhood and the sense of personal independence that he began to experience the true artist's selfless devotion to his art for its own sake. He told Petri in 1890 that until a few years before he had hated the pianoforte and neglected it, preferring literature to the practice of music (*früher habe ich lieber gelesen als musicirt*).

Brought up to this almost fanatical ambition, associating always with grown-up people and finding himself entirely without friends of his own age until he was twenty, it is not surprising that Turgeniev's *Fathers and Children* should have sunk deeply into his soul. Bazarov, the hero of that novel, was the first Nihilist, and the book, on its appearance in 1862, had been the subject of fierce controversy; it is not surprising that even in 1885 it should have still startled readers in Germany and Austria, and that the young Busoni should at once have identified himself spiritually with the young Bazarov, all the more since the portraits of Bazarov's father and mother bore a striking resemblance to his own parents. He confessed afterwards that at nineteen he had deliberately cultivated a Bazarov pose which he had found very effective for the purpose of startling ladies of the 'intellectual' type. As he naturally could not accept Bazarov's denunciation of art in all forms, he adapted it to the extent of maintaining, and maintaining with inward conviction, 'that art was a technical facility in reproducing life in colours, words or forms', and that the feelings aroused by art were to be accounted for on purely physical and physiological grounds. In that spirit he had begun to compose a string quartet, but had had to lay it aside after writing two pages, not to take it up again

---

[1] Frederick Delius said that what struck him most about Busoni in their Leipzig days was his passionately intense ambition.

until after two years, during which period his views on
the relation of art to emotion had considerably changed.

Busoni's personal character is another factor which
must be taken into consideration at this point. 'I never had
a childhood,' he was heard to say in later days, and one
might well imagine that the experiences of his early years
would have embittered him for life against his father and
against the world in general. Yet he was not merely
patient in bearing with the querulousness of his parents
but positively and whole-heartedly devoted to them; it
was natural that he should in childhood have dreaded the
violence and brutality of his father, yet even in comparatively early years he regarded him as a friend and a wise
counsellor in many respects, simply because his father
was the one man who never lost faith in his genius, however severe he might be in criticizing his actual accomplishment. None the less, certain traces of embitterment
remained, and remained almost throughout his life. His
mother's Christian resignation was a quality which he
could never share, though in later years he might come
to understand it with the vision of an artist through some
of the more ecstatically devotional works of Liszt. At the
time of his marriage he could only face his career with
a spirit of grim determination to fulfil his destiny in some
way or other, and to make up for the miseries of his own
youth in the resolve to let pass no opportunity of giving
such help as he could to musicians younger and less fitted
for the struggle than himself.

Of those three giants of the pianoforte belonging to
the previous generation, Liszt, Rubinstein, and Bülow,
Rubinstein was the only one with whom he had come
much into contact. Liszt he had heard only when he was
a boy of eleven and Liszt an old man long past his prime.
With Bülow his acquaintance was but slight. Rubinstein
had been the first great musician whom he had met in
early life; he had frequently heard him play at concerts
and had had several opportunities of developing his personal knowledge of him. It was thus natural that his own

style should have been strongly influenced by Rubinstein's; it was to Rubinstein, more than to any one else,
that he owed his 'monumental' conception of his art. But
a monumental style is not to be achieved on the threshold
of a career, and the pursuit of a virtuosity which to many
hearers seemed exaggerated, if not indeed positively repel-
lent, was a necessary preparation for the higher development of intellectual interpretation. It must also be
remembered that Busoni's early life had been spent in a
strictly professional atmosphere; he had had no tempta-
tions, unless from within his own temperament, to adopt
the cultured amateur's outlook and to rate instinctive
feeling higher than technical skill. The only musician
of culture whom he had known was Brahms, but in spite
of the attraction which Brahms had for him he never
became a member of his intimate circle. Towards the
other leaders of the Brahms group, such as Joachim and
Clara Schumann, he felt antipathy rather than sympathy;
they were too closely associated with the world of small
courts, orders, titles, and decorations—a world for which
Busoni, especially as a young man, had a natural and
hearty contempt.

Yet behind all this parade of virtuosity Busoni had
during the last few years laid the foundations of his two
great works of musical scholarship, the annotated editions
of Bach and of Liszt. In 1890 he had published his
edition of Bach's *Inventions*, and these were followed in
1894 by the first volume of the *Forty-eight Preludes and
Fugues*. His mother, it may be mentioned, was highly
indignant at his having published these works with letter-
press in German and English, instead of in Italian. He
replied to her rebukes by saying first that the publishers
had commissioned the work in German, and secondly that
in spite of the most energetic efforts on their part it had
been utterly impossible to induce any Italian publisher to
bring out an Italian edition. As regards Liszt, it was
Wegelius who first suggested to Busoni the idea of studying him seriously. He received a further impulse in

America, where a lady who had been his pupil at Boston presented him with some rare original editions. This gift led him to write to his mother and ask her to make a catalogue of such early editions as she herself had acquired in her girlhood. Busoni eventually formed a very important collection of original publications of Liszt's pianoforte works; it need hardly be explained that they are of peculiar interest owing to Liszt's habit of frequently revising and re-writing. Bach and Liszt make frequent appearances in the programmes of Busoni's next few years, but it was some time before he began to regard these two composers as the main features of his repertory.

Helsingfors, Moscow, and America, in spite of their disappointments, had all contributed something to Busoni's inner development. Leipzig and Weimar, following on Vienna and Graz, had made him almost more German than Italian. Tchaikovsky, meeting him and hearing his Quartet at Leipzig in January 1888, had thought him completely Germanized. When he arrived in Boston he began to discover that his real personality was anything but German. He wrote to Wegelius from America saying that he had become much less German and much more cosmopolitan. All the rest of his life he consciously set out to be cosmopolitan; he never for a moment denied or even resisted his Italian personality, and it would have been superfluous to assert it. In Helsingfors, Moscow, and Boston he had begun to realize his vocation as a teacher, but he also realized only too painfully what the routine work of a regular Conservatoire teacher was forced to be. Had he obtained a reasonably good post in a German school of music he might well have found conditions more tolerable and might even have run the risk of settling down as a part in the vast machinery of German musical life. It was fortunate for him that he escaped to places far enough removed from that machinery to make him see its limitations as well as its magnificent organization. He came back to Germany to make use of it, but never to let himself be absorbed into it.

The summer of 1894 was spent quietly in Berlin, where he had taken a ground-floor flat at Kantstrasse 135. Charlottenburg in those days was a remote suburb, and the present western quarters of Berlin had hardly begun to exist. His mother was annoyed at his not coming to Trieste, and his father still more annoyed at not receiving more regular supplies of money, but it was a difficult time for Ferruccio, as the concert-season was a long way off and his only source of revenue was editorial work. He was working hard (*come un cane*) at the second volume of the *Forty-eight* in September, and at the same time practising the pianoforte for five hours a day in view of his opening concerts. Anna sent him news of the deaths of two old friends, Signora Lucca and Frau von Wertheimstein; the latter especially he remembered with a profound sense of affection and gratitude.

October 22 brought a concert at Hamburg, a place where he was always sure of a cordial success. With Mahler as conductor, he played Weber's *Concertstück* and his own arrangement—made in America—of Liszt's *Rhapsodie Espagnole* for pianoforte and orchestra with the addition of a contrapuntal introduction on the theme (used by Liszt too) of the *Folies d'Espagne*. On November 3 he played at Berlin in the Singakademie; the programme included the same two works and also Liszt's Concerto in A major and his own transcription of Bach's *Chaconne*, with *La Campanella* as an encore. Later in the month he played for the Liszt-Verein at Leipzig and two more concerts were given in Berlin, at the last of which he played Beethoven's Sonata Op. 106. In December he played at Liége and St. Petersburg. It was a strenuous life; the programmes in themselves were fatiguing enough, and the inevitable railway journeys involved a further exhaustion of his energies. The last Berlin concert was on December 1, the concert at Liége on the 8th; as soon as he returned from Liége he had to devote three days to practising a concerto of Rubinstein which he had not played for six years; then two nights and a day in the train to St. Petersburg, sleeping two nights there for the rehearsal and a concert in memory of Rubinstein, with two more nights and a day in the train to come back to Berlin. He played again at Berlin in January 1895, outraging the critics by his interpretation (modelled on Rubinstein's) of Chopin's Sonata in B flat minor; he was at Helsingfors in February, a few days later at Brussels, and in March at Christiania, after a very bad journey which made him forty-eight hours late. Thence he went back to Berlin, where he was laid up for a week with influenza and gastric fever; after that there was a chamber concert followed immediately by a night journey to Leipzig, a rehearsal at ten the next morning and a concert in the evening.

The following verses, which were probably written about this date, give an amusing picture of a travelling pianist's discomforts. It was fortunate for Busoni that he had a sense of humour which never deserted him.

Virtuosenlaufbahn

Vorerst das Kursbuch. Sich zurechtzufinden!
Doch schliesslich lernt man's—Seite 103.
Kein Anschluss. Lässt es sich denn nicht verbinden?
Und auch kein Wagon-lit? Nun einerlei!

Verschlafen, fröstelnd, komm ich elf Uhr an.
Da steht ein Mann: 'Die Probe wartet schon!'
—'Ich hab' noch nicht gefrühstückt.' Sagt der Mann:
'Mir leid, doch öffentlich ist die Repetition.'

Nun hin denn! Das Hôtel wird übersprungen,
Der Stadtrath, der empfängt mich sauer-süss:
'Sie sind ein bischen spät! Schon längst gesungen
Hat ihre Nummern die betreffende Miss.'

Ich stürze an's Clavier. Die Reisekleider
Sind nicht gewechselt. Und die Hände kalt.—
Nun ist's vorbei. Der Kritiker war leider
Schon da. Zum Spät-ausgeh'n ist er zu alt.

Was hilft es, dass es Abends glänzend geht?
Die Recension bespricht das Probespiel.
Nur keine Zugabe, sonst wird's zu spät,
Und bis zum Bahnhof ist's ein weites Ziel.

Noch 'nass' erreich' ich richtig mein Coupé—
'Abfahren!' und der Zug ist schon im Gehn.
Und wieder musst' ich fort ohne Souper,
Und morgen früh die Probe ist um Zehn.

Career of a Virtuoso

Where is my Bradshaw? How do I get there?
Ah! Page a hundred: here's the only train.
Change—can I risk it? Three minutes to spare.
No sleeping-car? Well, useless to complain.

Next morning, at eleven, half awake
And shivering, I arrive. A man comes up.
'Make haste! Rehearsal's waiting! You must take
A cab at once!' No time for bite or sup.

No time to change or wash. 'You're rather late,'
Says the presiding magnate. 'You must know
The rehearsal's public. We have had to wait;
The songs were all sung half an hour ago.'

Straight to the platform—play as best I can—
Hungry and dirty, fingers frozen quite—
That's done! Why, there's the critic! 'Poor old man,
You can't expect him to go out at night.'

The concert's a success—but what of that?
The critic writes on how *he* heard me play.
Encore? No time. I seize my coat and hat,
For to the station it's a goodish way.

Into the train just as the whistle blows—
On to the next place, supperless again,
Clammy with sweating, still in evening clothes—
To-morrow the rehearsal is at ten.

The record of Busoni's outward life for the next few years is little more than a list of his repertory, a diary of concert engagements, and a collection of press criticisms.

His first important appearance was at the Berlin concert of
November 3, 1894. Criticism was not altogether friendly;
his marvellous technique and his variety of tone-colour
were fully acknowledged, and it was admitted that virtuosity with him was a merely secondary matter, but his
transcriptions were disparaged and his additions to Weber's
Concertstück were censured. When he played Beethoven's
Sonata Op. 106 at Berlin a month later he was cordially
praised by Otto Lessmann in the *Allgemeine Musikzeitung*.
Lessmann was always one of his staunchest supporters.
He had heard Liszt play the *Adagio* 'in hours of especial
consecration'; Bülow's performance he found too coldly
analytical, Rubinstein's too careless of detail. He regarded Busoni's interpretation as the greatest which he
had ever heard; it was more than pianoforte-playing, it
was orchestration.

His playing of Chopin was always difficult to accept.
The smaller works of Chopin he never cared to play at all,
except for the *Préludes*, which remained in his repertory
up to the end; he said that they were the most 'prophetic'
things which Chopin ever wrote, those which looked
furthest into the future. The *Mazurkas*, which many
admirers of Chopin have regarded as his most characteristic compositions, did not appeal to him; he preferred
the *Études* and *Ballades*. His conception of Chopin was
always terrifyingly grandiose; passages which most pianists
play dreamily and tenderly he would bring out with a
solidity and dignity which seemed ruthlessly severe. In his
younger days he adopted Rubinstein's well-known method
of interpreting the *Marche funèbre*, representing the arrival
and departure of a procession. It brought the melody of
the Trio into unusual prominence, and his Italian appreciation of a melody obviously inspired by Bellini led his
critics to accuse him of exaggerated sentimentality. The
last movement—one which has always bewildered every
listener—he evidently took as the traditional picture of
'spirits hovering over the grave'; even Lessmann found it
'ghostly and confused'—we can see that Busoni even at

that date had begun to visualize the possibilities of his
much later style in which he often sought to pass beyond
clear intellectual interpretation to a mysterious kind of
'impressionism' demanding that music should be appre-
hended as a direct vision in which detail of every kind was
entirely transcended.

His recitals, even then, were only suitable for a public
of regular *habitués*; he seemed to assume that his audience
knew the classics as thoroughly as he did himself and had
no need for them to be explained in the conventional
manner. He naturally alienated the sentimental adorers
of Chopin, and was charged with eccentricity in his reading of Beethoven. The fact was that whatever he played
he threw some entirely new light upon it. His devotion
to Liszt was a further cause of scandal, not only in Germany but in other countries. Brussels saluted Liszt with
a 'Hélas!' The *Journal de Liége* in 1894 apostrophized
Busoni with regretful admiration:

'Ferruccio Busoni! enigmatic artist, ironic lightning-flash hurled
at all pianists and pianofortes, swift meteor that vanishes as soon as
it appears; why do you depart after having graved on the tablets
of our memory no more than the undecipherable hieroglyph of your
virtuosity, without having forged for us from the hard and sparkling
metal of your talent the lock and key that would have opened for
us the secrets of a masterpiece?'

His audience needed time to accustom themselves to
the dazzling light of this new comet. But understanding
deepened as years went on, and in 1902 *Le Guide musical*
(Brussels) could describe him both outwardly and inwardly
with more sympathetic appreciation:

'When Busoni sits down to the pianoforte and waits for a
moment in meditation before he places his evoking hands with
deliberation on the shuddering keyboard, I feel myself penetrated
by a sense of security. . . . To those whose feeling for the spirit of the
music is vague he makes the musical language of feeling precise; to
those who stammer he speaks clearly; for those who think they
know, deluded by arbitrary traditions, he corrects and sets right;
and to those who have already responded in understanding, he shows

I

new features of beauty which his genius and sagacity have divined and uncovered.'

The author of this last criticism was Marcel Rémy. A letter which Busoni wrote to him defending himself against the charge of 'modernizing' the classics, gives an interesting sidelight on his principles of interpretation:

'You start from false premises in thinking that it is my *intention* to "modernize" the works. On the contrary, by cleaning them of the dust of tradition, I try to restore their youth, to present them as they sounded to people at the moment when they first sprang from the head and pen of the composer.

'The *Pathétique* was an almost revolutionary sonata in its own day, and ought to sound revolutionary. One could never put enough passion into the *Appassionata*, which was the culmination of passionate expression of its epoch. When I play Beethoven, I try to approach the liberty, the nervous energy and the humanity (*liberté, nervosité et humanité*) which are the signature of his compositions, in contrast to those of his predecessors. Recalling the character of the man Beethoven and what is related of his own playing, I built up for myself an ideal which has been wrongly called "modern" and which is really no more than "live".

'I do the same with Liszt; and oddly enough people approve in this case, though they condemn me in the other.'

Rémy had evidently criticized Busoni's 'alterations' in the *Prélude, Choral et Fugue* of César Franck.[1] Busoni replies quite plainly that Franck did not always know how to obtain the effects which he wanted from the pianoforte. Busoni had already noticed uncertainties of this kind in Liszt and still more in Chopin. A phrase which is to be soft or loud must be laid out for that purpose, orchestrated, as it were. Franck at the organ could pull out different stops to make the same music sound loud or soft; at the pianoforte one must lay the music out differently under the hands, use thin harmonies or full and extended ones. This is the basis of all Busoni's interpretations and transcriptions, as well as of his own compositions, a theory which he ultimately formulated in his *Neue*

[1] Busoni played this work for the first time in January 1902 at Berlin.

Aesthetik der Tonkunst (1907). He refused to see anything
sacred and unalterable in the written notes of a piece of
music, or in the sounds produced by any one particular
instrument. What interested him was the music itself, the
music as it existed in the composer's imagination, before
it had been written down on paper, even before it had
been approximated into tones and semitones, a music as
yet unheard by human ear. He sought to seize the unwritten conceptions of Bach or Mozart and to make them
audible to his own generation; it was only natural that in
doing so—especially at this period of his life—he should
employ as his medium the instrument to which he was
best accustomed.

One can see that even as late as 1902, the date of the
letter to Marcel Rémy, Busoni was still young enough to
enjoy the sensation of being a revolutionary; his attitude
to the *Pathétique* and the *Appassionata* is still that of the
reader of Turgeniev and the amateur socialist orator at
Leipzig. His exuberant vitality was a scandal to conventional critics, as it sometimes was in private life to
conventional neighbours; but even though he himself
would have admitted later that his playing at this time
sometimes erred in the direction of extravagance, it was
still controlled by a severe intellectualism. Intellectualism
in music is indeed far less willingly condoned by most
critics than emotional extravagance. It was Busoni's intellectualism that made them find his playing hard and
unfeeling, because he refused to allow himself the slightest
concession to current conventions of sentimentality. His
alleged 'modernizations' of the classics, like his transcriptions, may still be distasteful to those who approach old
music in the spirit of antiquarian scholarship, but at the
same time it would be unjust to suppose that they were
directed only by a haphazard emotionalism. They were
designed with aesthetic purpose and worked out with
careful skill. Busoni, even at the moment when virtuosity
seemed to come uppermost in his ambitions, never ceased
to be a scholar.

At Moscow in 1895 Safonov had said to him, 'Your playing is a revelation; I said good-bye to you as a young man, and you come back a great artist.' Gevaert said to him at Brussels, 'Tone, virtuosity, poetry—you have everything!'

A series of four concerts given at Berlin in 1898 to illustrate the history and development of the pianoforte concerto shows the extent of his repertory at this time:

I. Bach in D minor, Mozart in A major, Beethoven in G major, Hummel in B minor.
II. Beethoven in E flat major, Weber's *Concertstück*, Schubert's *Wanderer-Fantasie*, Chopin in E minor.
III. Mendelssohn in G minor, Schumann in A minor, Henselt in F minor.
IV. Rubinstein in E flat major, Brahms in D minor, Liszt in A major.

To these may be added Liszt in E flat major, Rubinstein in D minor, Grieg in A minor, Beethoven's *Choral Fantasia*, Nováček's *Concerto Eroico*, Saint-Saëns in F major and G minor, as well as his own *Concertstück*. Not all of these were kept up in later years; Liszt and Beethoven remained, and in course of time he made a more intensive study of Mozart's concertos. For Saint-Saëns he always had more admiration than met with approval in Berlin; as late as 1910 he proposed to play one of his concertos at Cambridge.

'I have the feeling that from now onwards my career is going to develop splendidly,' he wrote to his mother; 'three years of pause and work have been a great help to my *début*, and my calculations seem to be coming out right.' To Busoni life was a perpetual series of new beginnings. To the old man at Trieste it was an unending series of reproaches. His letters have not been preserved; but one can obtain some idea of their style from his son's answers.

Berlin.
27 March 1895

Dear Father,

I had to reflect a little on your letter and now I answer it. To say that I have concealed my affairs from you is an accusation which

I must definitely repudiate. I have only talked to you about my triumphs. I hoped I should give you pleasure in telling you the brightest parts of my career and keeping the less agreeable things to myself alone; but I made a mistake. In any case I have told you what my engagements were, and if I have not named the precise total of my fees, you must know that as a rule symphony concert engagements are generally paid at the rate of 400 marks, francs or roubles according to the country. For long journeys an allowance for travelling expenses is made.[1] This winter—the first, you may say, since I began my career in Europe afresh—was devoted chiefly to the object of making a name for myself, and I am happy that this should have completely succeeded, leaving the material fruits of this success to future years. . . . Do you imagine, my dear Father, that travelling, playing, working like a horse morning and evening, writing for the press, to say nothing of letter-writing, and on the top of that *being always in order with one's affairs*—that that is a mere nothing?'

A statement of account follows:

Concerts at Berlin	2,500 marks
Newspapers (presumably press-cuttings and advertisements)	300
Breitkopf and Härtel	500
Furniture	400
House (rent)	800
Tailor	180
Payment of an old debt	400
House expenses, 50 a week . . .	2,600
(without counting extras and travelling)	
Sent to you	1,820
Total	9,500

On the back of the envelope Ferdinando did a small sum in pencil. Four hundred apiece for seven concerts— he had the press-cuttings, so he knew how many there had been—at Legi [*sc.* Liége], B[russels], Li [*sc.* Leipzig], P[etersburg], M[oscow], M[oscow], and Cr[istiania], made

[1] In another letter Ferruccio says that he received 800 francs for playing at Brussels. He sent 400 to his father; of the rest 200 were spent on the journey, and 80 would have to be paid to his agent

2,800, from which he subtracts 200 sent to himself. And the boy had the impertinence to ask for a clear statement of his father's debts!

A concert at Prague in May with the Bohemian Quartet brought him 400 marks; he sent 300 to Anna. Then came two concerts at Helsingfors and a recital at the Conservatoire, where he played for the first time Liszt's *Bénédiction de Dieu dans la Solitude*, 'a most beautiful piece of music with great depth of feeling and a stupendous sonority for the pianoforte'. In June he moved from Kantstrasse to Tauentzienstrasse 10, near the Zoological Gardens. His mother pressed him to come to Trieste, but he wrote to say he thought it better to send her the money which the journey would have cost him. Letters from Trieste became more and more painful to him. If one came at breakfast-time he would lay it aside until he had enjoyed his meal; if they came by the evening post he would put off opening them till the next morning. Sometimes they lay unopened for two or three days.

Ferruccio had no desire to spend the summer at Trieste. In Berlin he had a home of his own. Gerda was unchangeable—nothing could ever disturb her serenity. And Benni was two and half, with a most delightful sense of humour and a passion for pictures which made his father feel quite certain that he would become a painter when he grew up. Grandfather Sjöstrand was asking to see him too. It would be very unadvisable to arouse jealousy between grandfathers. Benni's father decided to keep him for himself.

CHAPTER VII

NEW PATHS

IN the year 1893 there occurred one of the most astonishing events in the whole history of music—the production of Verdi's *Falstaff*. Busoni heard the opera at Berlin
on April 22 of the following year.

'I heard *Falstaff* the day before yesterday,' he wrote to his
mother: 'it is a little masterpiece of its kind. It is really un-
believable how a man of eighty can still do things which he has
never done before in his life, and not only that: several things which
no one else had done before him. *Falstaff*—to put it shortly—is a
most original, lively and amusing work, and without doubt the best
Italian comic opera since the *Barbiere*. And that's saying a good
deal.'

Busoni's attitude towards Italian music of his own time
had hitherto been decidedly sceptical. In 1886 he had
contributed a series of several articles to the *Grazer Tage-
blatt* on the conditions of music in Italy, reviewing all
aspects of Italian musical life with the ruthlessness of a
young artist only too well instructed by personal experience. Italy, he pointed out, had never fully accepted the
romantic movement. In Germany there had been a steady
development in opera from Weber to Wagner; in Italy
there was a wide gap between the age of Rossini, Bellini,
and Donizetti, and that of his own contemporaries, who
were trying to write in the modern idiom without having
mastered either its technique or its intention. Catalani
and Puccini, at that time (1886) the hope of the younger
generation in Italy, would come to nothing, he prophesied.
History has indeed verified his prophecy; Catalani died
young and Puccini adopted a business career.

It is noteworthy that Busoni in his younger days had
no very high opinion of Verdi. No Italian opera had impressed him so powerfully as *Carmen* did in 1884. Writing on *Carmen* that year in *L'Indipendente* (Trieste), he

observes that after Donizetti all Italian music was immersed in darkness. To this he added the following footnote on Verdi:

'In saying this I do not presume to ignore altogether the great merits of Verdi and the many high qualities of his music, but it seems to me that he has done too little to raise the standard of a degraded period, and very little at all when one compares his productions with those of the other contemporary schools.'

Neither *Aida*, the *Requiem*, nor the String Quartet, was in Busoni's opinion sufficient to place Verdi among the great composers of his day. Boito he respected profoundly as a man; as a composer he could only regard him as an amateur. From *Otello*, which the Graz essay just mentions as being on the verge of production, he anticipated a step towards the higher plane. But Busoni's musical education had been so completely German that it was a long time before he could come round to a view which at the present day is maintained more vigorously in Germany than even in Italy itself. One might easily be led to imagine that Busoni suffered a sudden conversion on hearing *Falstaff*. He began to draft a long letter to Verdi, in which he said definitely that *Falstaff* had been a turning-point in his artistic life; but in spite of the fact that no gradual process of change can be traced continuously in his letters and other writings, there can be little doubt that the spiritual experience of *Falstaff* was one for which his mind had been prepared, however subconscious the preparation might have been.

Busoni's compositions up to the time of his marriage had been numerous, too numerous indeed. In later years he said of the Violin Sonata in E minor, Op. 36a, composed in 1899, that it was his first really good work. In earlier life he had regarded composition from a perhaps too professional standpoint. In adolescence it is natural enough for a young musician to be fascinated by the mere idea of being able to compose music at all. Busoni acquired at an early age an extraordinary facility in composition, and his studies with Dr. Mayer gave him a complete mastery of traditional technique. He was acquiring simultaneously an astonishing mastery of technique in pianoforte-playing, so that it is not surprising that in many of his early works technical skill, both in composition and in designing pianoforte effects, is the most prominent feature. He was Latin enough to avoid by nature the sentimentality of the second-rate Germans, and at the same time too German to fall into sentimentality of an Italian type. Tchaikovsky, meeting him at Leipzig in 1888, was at once attracted to him as a young Italian; when he listened to his Second Quartet in the Old Gewandhaus, sitting with Delius and the Griegs, he passed his hand wearily over his face and longed for it to come to an end. It was far too German, he thought; yet it was Italian for all that. The Muse who looked over the young composer's shoulder was assuredly Florentine, but instead of being Tchaikovsky's Pimpinella, it was Cherubini himself.

The most important works of Busoni's young manhood are the Variations on a Prelude of Chopin, Op. 22 (1884), the Second Quartet (1888), the *Concertstück* for pianoforte and orchestra which won him the Rubinstein Prize in 1890, and the *Symphonisches Tongedicht* composed in America in 1893. All these are more or less influenced by German models, mainly by works of Brahms. It is especially in the handling of the pianoforte that Brahms is recalled with some suggestion of Schumann's *Toccata* and *Études Symphoniques*; the orchestral style approaches more to that of Liszt and Wagner.[1] It was in America that he began to understand Liszt, and Liszt was his natural link with Italy because Liszt was Italian and romantic at the very moment when the Italians themselves were ignoring romanticism. If Busoni wanted to write music of his own

---

[1] The *Symphonisches Tongedicht* bears pessimistic mottoes from Lenau and Leopardi; but Busoni afterwards repudiated them, saying that they were added on the ill-considered advice of friends, and that he wished the work to be heard simply as music alone.

day that was definitely Italian he could only do so by
following in the steps of Liszt; there were no real Italians
to help him find his native language, for the only Italian
composers whom he could at all respect were at that time
doing their best to write German music.

Suddenly the new light on his path appeared with
Verdi's *Falstaff*. To approach the composer was a difficult
matter; the sentences were written and re-written as if
Busoni found himself a stranger to his native language.
The letter was never finished and never dispatched. None
the less its tortuous and to a non-Italian reader often ful-
some phrases show that the moment had come when the
writer realized the necessity of sloughing off the chrysalis-
membrane of his German education. He had already
begun to see the dangerous side of German musical life,
though it was not until some years later that he expressed
himself clearly about it. A letter to Henri Petri about the
education of his son Egon, written in 1901, sums up the
experience through which he was now passing. He even
regretted Egon's matriculating at a German university;
it showed too much respect for all that was traditional and
'respectable'; he deplored the provincialism and the
musically *bourgeois* atmosphere in which the boy had been
brought up. He hoped that maturer life would show him
the difference between the *bourgeois* and the artist, between
the German and the cosmopolitan. Writing to Egon himself in 1905 he asks whether the Germans are musical
at all.

'The German is sober, sentimental and awkward—all that goes
against art. A Menzel and a Ludwig Richter—that is what he likes.[1]
The German is the greatest sufferer from *Heimweh*: he loves to
make poems about it. Art is at home everywhere. The German
is *bourgeois*, art is aristocratic.

'And then *Tiefsinn* (profundity)! Profound is the highest epi-

[1] This momentary outburst was not altogether consistent with Busoni's
habitual attitude to Menzel and Richter. He often expressed the pro-
foundest admiration for Menzel and he actually collected books illustrated
by Richter.

thet of praise for a composer. Something that sounds low in pitch, carefully crawling or angrily growling: that is "profound". That is what the Germans hear in Beethoven and timidly admire in him. A man who has walked, jumped, or dived into the abyss has no more reverence for depths; that is only for people who stand on the edge and dare not go down. The free bird Music runs the risk of being shut up in a cage if it comes near the Germans. The Germans are becoming custodians of museums. Germany is the country in which the *Lex Heinze*[1] was passed and is brought into force.'

In December 1895 Busoni went to play in Italy. It was strangely exciting to him to revisit Verona, Milan, and Parma. 'It gives me a *childish* pleasure to talk Italian, to be a stranger and yet not a stranger.' Milan disappointed him; he felt that he was received with mistrust, and it required his utmost effort of strength and will to secure recognition. Orchestras and conductors, he wrote, were hopeless. 'It would be a giant's work to bring Italy up to the musical level at which Germany stood years ago.' Parma pleased him better; the audience were not so stiff as at Milan. But what pleased him most was the completely Italian character of the town; there were abbés and asses there—objects which he seems always to have regarded as essential features of the Italian landscape. One is reminded of another Italian musician and idealist, Guido Podrecca, to whom the ass and the abbé were the symbolical fauna of his country. 'We must go to Italy as tourists,' he wrote to his wife; 'enjoy the old things, the food and the wine—all the rest is worth nothing.'

Ferdinando was complaining again. Ferruccio decided to spend a night at Trieste and have it out with him by word of mouth. To judge from the letter which he wrote afterwards the visit must have passed off agreeably; but Ferruccio was always considerate for his mother's feelings. On his way north he stopped at Vienna and went to hear

[1] The notorious *Lex Heinze* was a law against obscene publications, the application of which by the police against famous masterpieces of painting and sculpture brought it into odium and ridicule.

d'Albert play. Bösendorfer encountered him in the hall and at once arranged for him to play in February 1896 at a Philharmonic concert. It was a triumphal return and a successful 'revenge' after the disappointments of ten years before. Hanslick was stiff and ceremonious, sitting 'like an Egyptian divinity' and going to sleep once or twice, but hailed him as the only pianist who could approach Rubinstein. And Brahms was there too—it may well have been the last concert that he ever attended.

Early in 1897 Ferruccio took Gerda and Benni to Trieste. It was Gerda's first experience of Italy and of Italian family life. The little flat at Trieste was a severe shock to a woman brought up to northern standards of cleanliness and sanitation. It was also something of a shock to see how completely abashed her husband was in the presence of his father. Ferdinando was more quarrelsome than ever. A nephew of his from Empoli had been to visit him; he was newly married, and neither he nor his wife—they were both under twenty—had ever travelled farther than Florence in their lives. Uncle Nando took them out to a café, flew into a rage with the waiter over the bill, called him a German pig and threw his wineglass at him, cutting his head open. All three had to go to the police-station—a pleasant experience for a young bride on her honeymoon.

At home Ferdinando was more free to have his own way. He had no regards for any one else's feelings, least of all for his wife's.

'Anna! Anna!' he would shout; Anna would hurry in from the kitchen.

'What is it?'

'Anna! give me my handkerchief.'

The handkerchief lay before him on the table; Anna had to pick it up and hand it to him.

Ferruccio did his best to be friendly with the old man—he had a genuine affection for 'King Lear', yet it was impossible to talk to him without raising a storm. Anna would invite a few friends and Ferruccio would be asked to play. If there was one thing Ferruccio detested, it was

playing in a drawing-room; but he could not refuse his
mother's request. While he played, his father would sit
there in a red cap with a long pipe in his mouth, thumping
the table and calling out proudly, 'I taught him, I taught
him!' He had given up his dogs, much to Ferruccio's
regret, and had adopted parrots instead; there were seven
of them, and Benni at any rate found them fascinating.
But after the family went back to Berlin Benni made the
acquaintance of a parrot who could talk, and from that
moment his admiration for those of the '*grosse Vater*' began
to wane.

In the summer of 1896 the Busonis had had a holiday at
Göhren on the island of Rügen; the following year Ferruccio sent Gerda and Benni away to the country and
spent the summer alone in Berlin to work quietly by
himself. For several years this became his regular practice, and it was during these more or less solitary summers
in Berlin that most of his works were composed. The
main work of 1897 was the *Comedy* Overture. It was
written on a sudden inspiration; late one night in July he
sat down and wrote steadily till the morning. The first
draft needed revision, but the whole Overture was on
paper after that one night's work. Busoni seems to have
been taken by surprise himself at both the method and the
style of composition; it was a throw-back to the manner
almost of Mozart. The *Comedy* Overture was in fact the
first result of the change which *Falstaff* had wrought in
Busoni. The German romantic manner was dropped;
Mozart was going to lead him on to *Turandot*, *Arlecchino*
and his dreams of an Italian comic opera.

It was in the autumn of 1897 that he paid his first visit
to London. London enthralled him at once; here was a
real great city, here were characters from Dickens to be
seen in every street. He felt that Berlin and New York
were merely 'average' and characterless by comparison
with London. But London was a difficult place in which
to make a start. He described himself as 'a Sisyphus of
débuts'; Liszt and Rubinstein were not making fresh starts

at thirty-one. But Sauer and Paderewski had had to begin
in the same way, playing to empty halls and cold-blooded
critics. As time went on he grew more accustomed to
London; he made friends with the Willy Hess Quartet,
with Enrique Fernandez Arbós, and with Arthur Friedheim. Friedheim must have forgiven Busoni's satirical
description of him at Vienna, if indeed he had ever read it.
He gave him useful suggestions about certain works of
Liszt which he had often heard Liszt play, and pleased
Busoni by telling him that he had 'arrived' in spite of not
being one of Liszt's own pupils. He met an Italian friend
of Liszt's named Ducci, and played him his own waltz
Frohsinn (Cheerfulness), on which another Italian present
observed that he must belong to the school of Bologna
because his music was so serious. Arbós was very much
discontented with London; society was passing through a
period of decadence, over-refined, superficial, and seeking
'sensations'. A bad place for an artist, he said; one had
only to look at the style in which Alma Tadema lived and
compare it with Rembrandt's way of life. But in any case
South Kensington was no place for Busoni; English 'good
taste' was dominated by the influence of Joachim and
Clara Schumann—Liszt and his followers were anathema.
Nevertheless Busoni made his mark in London, and his
London success helped him to engagements in Paris and
Budapest.

The following spring brought a renewal of the friendship with the faithful Kapff, who had almost disappeared
from Busoni's life after Busoni left Frohnleiten. Kapff
had married before then and had gone to live in Vienna,
a city which Busoni visited as seldom as possible. When
he met Busoni again in 1898 he was in very difficult
circumstances; it required all Busoni's delicacy to induce
him to accept the help which Busoni regarded as the
grateful repayment of a long-standing debt of kindness.
He did not often see Kapff again, but just at this time he
acquired a new friend who showed him the same sort of
quiet and faithful devotion—Emilio Anzoletti, a young

man from Bologna who had come to Berlin to study engineering. Anzoletti was another link with Italy—a link never broken to the end of Busoni's life.

London was revisited in June 1898, and again in December. The more Busoni saw of London the more he felt at home there. English people can hardly realize how Dickens has made London live in the imagination of every foreigner who reads him. To them the London of Dickens is unreal, or at least a London long forgotten. The foreigner who has read him, when he visits London for the first time, creates an imaginary London in which the familiar characters come to life again; and as Dickens with his vast humanity has made them all—even the bad ones—lovable, the foreigner not only sees every Englishman as a character out of Dickens, but feels that he must approach him as a friend. And there were other friends there too for Busoni, unexpected friends from other parts of the world. Delius was there, and Richter.

Richter took him to the Gambrinus and unburdened his heart about Mahler.

'I say, I was sorry not to be in Vienna when you played' (Richter's Viennese brogue is impossible to reproduce in English), 'but I heard that Mahler gave you a lesson at the rehearsal. That puts the lid on it. He can't stand any soloists because he has got no routine and can't conduct at sight; but a conductor ought to be able to do that just as much as a pianist—come!'

After more in the same strain Busoni politely said that he congratulated the Viennese on Richter's decision to stay there.

'I'm not so sure of that. I shall think the matter over *very* carefully. I don't think I could stand it.'

'But the newspapers all state it as a fact.'

'Well, paper is a long-suffering material.'

Other friends were Teresina Tua, whom his father had once expected him to marry, Teresa Carreño, Camilla Landi, Johannes Wolff the violinist, Hollmann the violoncellist, and Dr. Muck, who was a frequent guest of

Busoni's hospitable friends the Matesdorfs. A Melba
concert in which he took part brought him the acquaintance of Ysaye, whose extraordinary magnetism reminded
him at once of Rubinstein. Ysaye had Rubinstein's laugh,
and Rubinstein's mixture of animalism, vulgarity, and
kingliness. He could not make up his mind whether he
liked him or not. Later on he was to be thrown much
with Ysaye, and in spite of occasional friction made a firm
friend of him. He made friends too with Sargent, who
had an idea of painting his portrait. There were other
concerts at Nottingham, Glasgow, and Manchester. At
Manchester he met the Brodskys and William Dayas, an
American pupil of Liszt, whom he had known in Leipzig
and recommended to Wegelius as his own successor at
Helsingfors. After he had played the Fantasia on *Norma*,
Dayas, with eyes starting out of his head, exclaimed, 'What
a pity the old man never heard you! he would have blessed
you and died happy.' Dayas and Brodsky played his first
Violin Sonata (in C, Op. 29—one of the works which won
the Rubinstein Prize); afterwards there was a dinner given
by Dayas with the Brodskys at which Dayas drank nearly
two bottles of port out of a tumbler. Brodsky was in a bad
humour, Mme Brodsky unable to eat anything at all; but
she had a queer Russian kindness of heart which (like her
queer Russian accent) always delighted Busoni, and was
quite ready to enjoy the party on account of '*derr sym-
patischen Atmosferre*!'[1]

There was another visit to London the following June,
with a variety of comic episodes. 'Pädäruski' (as Busoni
represents the English pronunciation of his name) played a
Concertstück written for him by Cowen—'twice-cooked meat
with *sauce piquante*'; he himself had to play Tchaikovsky's
Concerto—'once and never again!'(these words in English).
'I felt as if I had a new pair of boots on; they looked very
smart, but I was glad to get them off!'

---

[1] Tchaikovsky wrote of Mme Brodsky as 'a really good Russian woman'.
(Modeste Tchaikovsky, *Life and Letters of P. Tchaikovsky*, translated by
Rosa Newmarch.)

And he was interviewed—'May I ask you, as I understand that you have been playing in public, what is your
profession?'

'But I am a musician, as you know!'

'Oh yes, exactly; but, I mean, what instrument do you
specially play?'

Between these visits to London he played in Switzerland.
Basle reminded him of some Italian provincial town;
Zurich was 'ungrateful and full of gossip'. He detested
small towns. When he played in Holland he established
himself with a pianoforte at a hotel in The Hague, and
came back to sleep there after concerts in the other places
rather than spend a moment longer than was necessary in
the provincial atmosphere. Slow trains and hotels lit by
candles had no attractions for him. In one small town
he was invited to the home of a pupil; it reminded him
painfully of Sudermann's *Heimat* (*Magda*), and still more
painfully of the house of his own parents. It was a relief to
stay at Brussels and to meet Fauré and Saint-Saëns there at
Ysaye's.

'London is always beautiful—what a pity that I must
leave it to-morrow night!'

The summer of 1900 brought a new experience. On the
invitation of the Grand Duke Carl Alexander of Saxe-
Weimar he spent July, August, and September in Weimar
to teach a class of advanced pupils and carry on the
tradition of Liszt.

In the Memoirs of Prince von Bülow, Duke Carl
Alexander is described as having been the original of the
typical 'Serenissimus' so often caricatured on the German
stage. It was he who had made Weimar the artistic centre
which it became in the days of Liszt's residence there; his
amusing oddities (which Busoni, needless to say, appreciated to the full) did not prevent him from having a
singularly generous and high-minded conception of his
duties and obligations as a prince. Busoni had long ago
made up his mind that he would never accept another
teaching post at a Conservatoire, and he was equally

K

unwilling to give private lessons, but the *Meisterklasse* suggested by the Grand Duke was work which was thoroughly congenial to him. About fifteen students joined him at Weimar, all pianists who had reached a high standard of technique. The Tempelherrenhaus, a picturesque building in the park, was placed at his disposal as a studio. Built early in the nineteenth century to look like a ruined medieval chapel, it had been designed originally for a mausoleum and had later been converted into a sort of summer tea-house. The interior formed a large rectangular room with a flat painted ceiling; along the walls were holland-covered sofas alternating with enormous marble statues of the Muses. The long south wall consisted entirely of large windows opening down to the ground.

Twice a week Busoni and his pupils met there; those who had prepared a work played it, while the others sat round and listened. After that there would be general discussion, overflowing on to the lawn outside. Visitors were admitted, and sometimes there were more than was convenient. Busoni seldom discussed matters of pure technique; technique was taken for granted, and he preferred to talk about the music itself. But when he sat down to show his pupils how a work ought to be played they soon realized what they still had to learn in technical matters, and their independent discussion of these things taught them to learn from one another as well as from the master. For his teaching was by no means confined to the hours in the Tempelherrenhaus; his pupils were with him for most of the day and a good part of the night as well. Busoni wanted to know them all intimately and to study the personality of each. His own house was always open to them, and Gerda, in spite of having to look after the baby Raffaello, who had been born a few months earlier, was more than a hospitable hostess; she was a kindly sister to every one of them. And there were lively evenings at the Hotel Erbprinz, so lively indeed that respectable Weimar was often rather scandalized at this Bohemian invasion of the town.

The Busoni pupils thoroughly enjoyed scandalizing Weimar. Their costumes and *coiffures* were eccentric and startling; they hailed each other with shrill musical cries, danced along the streets like a *corps de ballet* and fell into each other's arms with extravagant embraces, offering the most shocking examples of deportment to all the well-bred young ladies who walked out two and two in the sacred city of Goethe. The town took its revenge as best it could. When Busoni gave a concert with a contralto one evening, the lady received an unflattering notice in the local paper, and the next day the office was invaded by 'a young gentleman of about thirty with a sallow face, a modern moustache and beard, wearing an elegant light-grey suit and speaking with a foreign accent'.

Without any preliminary courtesies he brusquely fired off the question, 'Who wrote your concert criticism of yesterday?'

The editor replied by another—'Will you tell me your name?'

'No,' shouted the visitor and made for the door, turning back in the doorway to roar out, 'You're a dirty dog!'

The editor told the full story of the interview in his next issue and hinted broadly that the light-grey gentleman was Busoni himself. At any rate, he maintained, Busoni ought to make some statement on the matter. Busoni did nothing of the kind; it was evident that the paper would have gladly done him an injury but did not dare attack him directly owing to the fact that he was protected by the Grand Duke. As a matter of fact the excitable champion was not Busoni, but the husband of the singer. He was a quixotic individual who amused the Busoni circle by flourishing a sword-stick when he went out. He could not sleep at his lodgings on account of a cock which crew, so he attacked the bird with this weapon; but the cock still went on crowing.

The old Grand Duke took a personal interest in the class; he would sometimes put in an appearance himself, especially on the occasions when Busoni gave an evening recital in the candle-lighted studio for the pupils and other friends. He at any rate was not scandalized; he had always been a loyal supporter of the arts and it was he who made the historic observation to Busoni about Liszt— 'Liszt *was* what a Prince *ought to be*!' He did his best to induce Busoni to come and live permanently at Weimar, but Busoni refused. As Gerda wrote to her mother-in-law, 'Ferruccio does not like little towns'. But he accepted the Grand Duke's invitation to come back the following summer, and the classes were continued in July and August of 1901.

Among the Weimar pupils of 1901 was Maud Allan. Busoni soon discovered that her real talent was for the dance; it was he who first suggested to her that she should become a dancer. One day in Berlin they cleared a space in his music-room; Gerda dressed her up in a costume improvised on the spur of the moment and she made her first experiments in interpretative dancing to Ferruccio's accompaniment at the pianoforte. For her it was the prelude to a distinguished stage career, for Gerda and Ferruccio the beginning of a life-long friendship.

Busoni held two more *Meisterklassen* in later years—at Vienna in 1908 and at Basle in 1910—but both in his own memory and in that of his pupils the Weimar classes stood out as a unique experience. Not all of the Weimar pupils were to rise to fame—some indeed were eventually to abandon all hope of it. But distinguished or undistinguished, fortunate or unfortunate, they were all to enjoy his friendship and the never-fading radiance of his inspiring personality. At thirty-five he was in the full flush of health and strength, exuberant in affection as he was in humour, ready to absorb with delight all that was wonderful in art, literature, and life, and absorbing it only to share his joy in it with those around him. He had read widely in various languages, he had often astonished the learned by his extraordinary knowledge of painting and architecture, his travels and his experiences of life had brought him into contact with human beings of endless variety; his forceful intellect, always the dominating factor of his personality, had trained him ever more and more to understand, and passionately to desire to understand, not only music and the other arts, but men and women of all social grades and conditions. Those of the Latin races are often egotistic in conduct, not from natural want of kindness, but from a certain sense of duty and obligation to their own immediate families; Busoni, despite his Italian blood and upbringing, despite all his Italian devotion to his own parents, had acquired—was it through marriage?—an habitually keen and penetrating interest in other people. It was not because he liked them instinctively—so it seemed—that he took trouble to be kind to them; they interested him, and it interested him to get to know them, to understand them, and through understanding to find his way to their affections.

From year to year after his return to Europe Busoni's horizon was widening rapidly. His concert appearances became more and more numerous and his travels took him farther and farther afield. He began to be conscious of weariness, but Ferdinando was always pestering him for money, and during the months from October to the end of the London season in July there could be no respite. England was at any rate the country in which he could earn the most money, but earning money in England meant touring the provinces. In London he could count on an intelligent audience; besides, in London there were friends like Ysaye. He played trios with Ysaye and Becker, but found Becker *troppo alla tedesca* to make a suitable partner. And Ysaye occasionally preferred bed to a morning rehearsal, which infuriated Busoni; but no quarrel could last long with Ysaye. The provincial round became more and more depressing; he began to feel a horror of the virtuoso's life. There came even a moment when he ceased to take trouble about his own playing on these dreary tours with a concert party, and the consciousness of such a state of mind filled him with a deeper horror. There was only one place outside London where he suddenly felt inspired to play his best—Cambridge, 'with its distinguished academic public and its enthusiastic undergraduates sitting on the orchestra'. Supper in college rooms after the concert was a new and apparently pleasant experience for him.

Busoni had often deplored the narrow-mindedness of German musical life, and for some years to come he was still to be the object of perpetual attack on the part of German critics. But Berlin, for all its musical convention-ality, was at any rate a place in which experiments could be tried. In other countries Busoni might earn fame and even money, but only by asserting himself as a virtuoso at the pianoforte. In Berlin he had by this time attained a certain position of notoriety, if not of whole-hearted respect. His personal followers might be few, but they were at any rate passionately loyal to him, and their num-bers were gradually increasing; they could be at least recognized as a party, if only as a dangerous one. What-ever he undertook in Berlin was certain to attract attention, however hostile. The very solidity of the German musical organization gave him an opposition worthy of challenging. He formed the plan of a series of orchestral concerts to be devoted entirely to new works or to older works which were seldom performed. The plan was spread over a number of years, twelve concerts being given between 1902 and 1909.

Busoni had no ambition to pose as a star conductor. He had discovered at Helsingfors that he had a certain ability for conducting, and orchestral players in various countries were always delighted to play under him, though his utter lack of all affectation of gesture generally led critics to doubt his competence. His primary object in organizing these concerts was to assist young and unknown composers, and he regarded it as most important that they should conduct their own works; it was only when they refused to do so, or were unable to come to Berlin, that he made himself their interpreter. It was a period in which new works found little encouragement in Germany, especially if they were not of German origin. The conventional German attitude of those days was not without its justification. No historian could possibly deny that the main stream of European music from 1800 to 1900 had been predominantly and consistently German. It was only natural that the average German, especially after the political development of the German Empire, should believe as a matter of course that music was a purely German art and that other countries could only be considered musical in so far as they imported music and musicians from Germany. To call this doctrine chauvinism or even patriotism would be quite unjust; it was more in the nature of a religious creed far too firmly established to engender fanatics. Even outside Germany it had its adherents; there were musicians in England and Italy who certainly practised it, if they did not preach it. No wonder that foreign music had little chance of acceptance in Germany; if it was tolerable, it was 'German', and native Germans could produce as good themselves; if it was not 'German', it was not music. The most dangerous revolutionary of the moment, Richard Strauss, was at any rate in the direct German tradition; the men whose new methods of musical expression were to change the whole face of music within the next generation were not Germans at all. The broadest-minded of German conductors might well hesitate to introduce novelties, and to give entire concerts of novelties was utterly inconceivable.

Busoni gave his first concert of new works on November 8, 1902.[1] It was not surprising that the Berlin critics greeted it with a chorus of abuse. The *Prelude and Angel's Farewell* from Elgar's *Dream of Gerontius*, which was the first item, was described as 'the most barren piece of senseless music-fabrication that has been heard for a long time'. At the next concert Delius's *Paris* offered an obvious opportunity for comparing it to the next-morning feelings induced by a 'night out'. The *Berliner Neueste Nachrichten*,

[1] The complete programmes of these concerts are printed as an Appendix.

with that high sense of moral responsibility so characteristic of German musical criticism, added that 'after the
complete fiasco of the second concert, the announcement
that these orchestral concerts would be continued in the
autumn of 1903 sounded little short of blasphemous'.
The *Germania* paid Busoni the ironic compliment of
saying that he must indeed be an accomplished conductor
to be able to conduct such stupidities. Busoni, it need
hardly be remarked, was entirely unabashed by these rebukes. He did not wait for the autumn, but gave a third
concert in January. To quote further criticisms would be
superfluous. But there was a public for the concerts, and
a public which gradually became more and more apprecia-
tive. When Vincent d'Indy conducted his *Symphonie sur
un chant montagnard* in November 1906 it was received
with so much enthusiasm that Busoni asked the composer
to repeat it at the next concert along with his second
symphony (in B flat). At the last of the concerts (January
1909) Béla Bartók conducted the Scherzo from his Suite;
it was described as 'another of those outrages on good
taste which he has gradually made his speciality', and the
critic added that it was an insult that such music should be
played in a concert-hall which bore the sacred name of
Beethoven. The reader of to-day may recall the story of
Bülow at Vienna related in an earlier chapter.

Busoni seldom included compositions of his own in
these programmes; the *Comedy* Overture and the Violin
Concerto may well have been put in only to lighten their
severity, for both of them are cheerful and attractive in
character without any pretence of being revolutionary
in style. It was not unnatural that he was accused
of neglecting German composers to the advantage of
foreigners; he replied that German composers in general
had more chance of performance elsewhere and therefore
had less need of encouragement from him. He pointed
out further that as a matter of fact several German works
had found a place in the programmes. It was no part of
his object to perform music by such well-known people as

Strauss, Mahler, or Schillings. The reader of to-day will observe that practically all the non-German names in Busoni's programmes have become universally famous, whereas of the German composers only one, if any, is known outside Germany—Hans Pfitzner. Pfitzner in those days had an almost smaller following as a composer than Busoni himself; his genius had been recognized only by such men as Mahler and (in later years) Oskar Fried.

The ten years between 1890 and 1900 had wrought a remarkable change and development in Busoni's personality, a change difficult to sum up in a few words. The causes of the change were manifold and various; they can be traced separately, but it must be borne in mind that their effect was due to their simultaneous interaction. The first and probably the most continuously intimate influence on his character came as the result of a marriage which to the very end of his life was uncloudedly happy. In all probability it was only the sense of moral security derived from Gerda's companionship that gave him the courage to abandon for ever—after Helsingfors, Moscow, and Boston—any idea of settling down to the routine of a permanent teaching post in a school of music. The experience of those three places, followed by the still wider experience resulting from his travels as a virtuoso to such centres as Brussels, Paris, and London, gave him a deeper confidence in himself and an ever intenser consciousness of the international ideal of the artist. Tours in Italy revived his devotion to the land of his birth and parentage, a devotion already stimulated to some extent by the study of Liszt's impressions of Italian life and landscape. Verdi's *Falstaff* opened his eyes to the possibility of a new type of Italian music that should be prophetic of the future as well as rooted in the noblest traditions of the past. Then came the call to Weimar, and in that 'holy city' he realized that he was no longer an ambitious youth striving frantically for the recognition of his own individual talent, but a mature artist with an inward vocation to leadership. To spend his whole days in educating

and inspiring those joyous and ardent young people who
surrounded him in the Tempelherrenhaus was a very
different matter from the drudgery of scales and exercises
timed by the clock of the New England Conservatory.
Busoni knew in Weimar that although there would never
be an end of acquiring knowledge it would be of little use
to him unless he could give it out again generously to the
younger generation. At Berlin his concerts of modern
works brought him yet more closely into contact with the
younger generation and with the international world of
pioneers in music. Before his marriage he had practised
his art for himself alone and had in consequence suffered
all the agonies of spiritual solitude. With the new century
he had become, and knew that he had become, a leader.

CHAPTER VIII

'ALL'ITALIANA'

'FERRUCCIO BUSONI', wrote Dr. Adolf Weissmann in the *Roland von Berlin* on November 17, 1904, 'provided his friends on Thursday with a surprise. He appeared without his beard and with a great pianoforte concerto, or rather with a long one.' Dr. Weissmann, usually so up to date, was in this case a good way behind the times; Busoni had shaved off his beard more than a year before.[1] As to the concerto, Dr. Weissmann summed it up as a *Höllenspektakel*—which may be translated 'Pandemonium let loose'. The work was greeted with abuse from almost the entire Press. At the performance it was received with hostility; the majority of the audience pointedly called for the conductor, Dr. Muck. Busoni's party, consisting mostly of women, did their best for the beloved master, and a Hungarian pianist, Joseph Weiss, stood up and shouted for Busoni 'like a general storming a barricade'. The concert ended in a scene of wild tumult. The *Tägliche Rundschau*'s description may be taken as typical:

'During five movements we were submerged in a flood of cacophony; a *pezzo giocoso* painted the joys of barbarians lusting in war, and a *tarantella* the orgies of absinthe-drinkers and harlots; finally the *cantico* showed us to our horror that a composer can take seriously the facetious humour of a male-voice choral society. It was frightful!'

Busoni had deliberately challenged his German critics by giving his concerto an Italian title with sub-titles in Italian for the different movements. This was enough to

[1] Busoni shaved off his beard in the summer of 1903, to the horror of his friends. He was obliged to grow it again in the autumn because the manager of his American tour regarded it as indispensable to his success in the United States. Its final removal took place in the summer of 1904.

set patriotic critics against him, even before they were
roused to fury by the aggressively Italian character of the
music itself.

The Concerto was the fruit of some two and a half
years' thought. The first suggestion of it in Busoni's
letters occurs in one written from London in February
1902. Tired out with a provincial tour in the company
of Ysaye, John Harrison the tenor, and Percy Pitt as
accompanist, he had cancelled his concert at Aberdeen—
'only three or four times more, *then 'tis over*.'[1]

'As soon as I feel myself free, ideas come, and that is the real and
only joy of life. I have been considering setting Oehlenschläger's
Aladdin, not as an opera but as a *Gesamtwerk* of drama, music,
dance and magic—if possible compressed into one evening. It is my
old idea of a stage work with music *where necessary*—otherwise
music must not hamper the living word. As a spectacular piece and
as a profoundly symbolical work it might become something like
the *Zauberflöte*, but with a better meaning, better words, and with
a subject that no one can despise.

'Besides that I have planned six works for the summer, the
chief one being the Pianoforte Concerto.'

It was only in the summer that Busoni could work
seriously at composition; during the spring he was continuously on concert tours. From London he went to
Turin, Florence, and Trieste. At Turin he was to have
played Liszt's Concerto in E flat, but although he rehearsed the orchestra in it himself, two conductors attempted to conduct it in vain; each in succession came to
grief in the middle and the work had to be abandoned.
'Viva l'Italia!' was his only comment on the episode. At
Florence he met his cousin Orfeo Busoni from Empoli,
to whom he was always very much attached; he visited his
parents at Trieste with less cheerful feelings. May saw
him back in London again, tired out with concert-playing,
but much encouraged by performances of his Violin
Sonata in Paris by Ysaye and Pugno.

Towards the end of May he settled down in Berlin

[1] These last three words in English.

again (he was now living at Augsburgerstrasse 55) with
the intention of working steadily there at composition until
October. Gerda went away for her usual round of summer
visits and he was left alone with Lello, who was now two
years old. Anzoletti was in Berlin, and there were various
survivors of the Weimar classes who came in to see him.
It was from the Weimar classes, and later on from those
at Vienna and Basle, that Busoni's habitual circle was
recruited. His usual habit was to work by himself all the
morning; after luncheon visitors would drop in until about
five, when he would either retire to his work again or go
for a solitary walk. If he worked in the afternoon he
would often go for his walk in the evening. One might
meet him in the most unexpected quarters of Berlin. He
loved the life of a big city, and in Berlin, as in London,
he was fascinated by the sight of odd characters who
might have stepped out of a novel of Dickens. He used
often to say that his best inspirations came to him during
these solitary rambles. After supper he would generally
go to one of the little Italian restaurants which then existed
in Berlin, mostly in the Potsdamerstrasse and its neighbourhood. Bartolini's, where he was always a welcome
guest, has been vividly described by Sudermann in his
novel *Das Hohe Lied*. Bartolini himself was a broadly-
built Florentine, speaking the most exquisite Italian; his
wife came from Trieste and was a first-rate cook. The rest
of the company were young painters of the 'Secession'—
Konrad von Kardorff, Oppler, Linde-Walther, Finetti,
most of whom have now reached professorial status; there
were a few journalists and poets such as Wilhelm Herzog,
afterwards an apostle of pacificism, and various members
of Busoni's own circle. Occasionally an Italian painter
would come in. Those were memorable evenings, for the
painter played the guitar and would persuade Bartolini to
sing old-fashioned Italian opera songs with an attractive
light tenor voice and a natural gift for elegance of lyrical
style.

The eternal circle of admirers, most of them women, was

a source of perpetual amusement and occasional irritation
to Busoni's older musical friends. It was only natural that
the group should consist mainly of former pupils who had
either not yet attained success or had for some unfortunate
reason been compelled to abandon all hope of it. A well-
known German pianist called them 'the caryatides of the
house of Busoni'. They clustered round him because his
friendship was perhaps the only thing left to give them
any sort of inspiration for the battle of life, and Busoni,
with all his impatience of 'Hamlet types', had too profound
a sense of pity to rid himself of any person who had ever
awakened his sympathy. It certainly was exasperating for
a man like Delius to find, after being invited to call and
discuss the interpretation of one of his works, that he had
to sit for three hours unable to get a word in edgeways
and then be dismissed at five o'clock when Busoni went
for his solitary walk; and other occasional callers found
only too often that any serious talk with their host was
impossible owing to the perpetual interruptions and ejacu-
lations of the adoring angels. But as Delius said, 'how
good Gerda was to them!' There was one sure way of
catching Busoni's attention, and that was to say something
to him in Italian; but naturally that method only infuriated
the rest all the more. The fact of the matter was that
Busoni, after working all the morning, wanted intellectual
relaxation. His composition was too important to him
for him to waste brain-power on other people's intellectual
interests. He would sit at the table smoking one cigar
after another, letting off occasional flashes of an outrageous
wit, bantering the young ladies, sparring for a moment
with any chance visitor who provoked him to it, and ending all discussion with a volcanic eruption of laughter
which burst like a thunderclap and then rolled away in
distant rumblings. He was always fond of the society of
women, and many women liked to pretend that he was in
love with them. As a matter of fact there never was any
woman but one in whom he took a serious interest, and
that was Gerda. Intellectual comradeship on equal terms

was not a thing which he expected from women; would-
be intellectual women definitely repelled him. He had
had enough of that type in Vienna. What he wanted
from women was *Empfindung*, intuitive sympathy, dog-
like adoration. 'Lello wakes me every morning—it is very
charming and pretty, and reminds me of Lesko,' he wrote
to Gerda in July of this year 1902. But the Newfoundland bitch's bulk and appetite, as well as her all too
frequent production of puppies, made it impossible for
Busoni to keep her in a small second-floor flat in Berlin,
and for Lesko's devotion human substitutes had to be
found. A Russian pupil asked him 'what he was to say
to Wolff (the concert-agent)?' 'What, do you want to
play? have you technique enough?' 'Yes, I think I can
play all right, but I must get a dress suit made, and I have
no money.' Busoni loved him; he was 'so straightforward,
so serious and intelligent—like a dear dog'.

Every two or three days Busoni sent Gerda news of the
Concerto and its progress. To judge from the letters and
the comic little drawings which often illustrated them one
might imagine that the Concerto was a huge piece of
descriptive music, especially the *Tarantella*, which was to
include a picture of popular festivities in Rome and Naples,
with the Italian *bersaglieri's* song,

> E sì, e sì, e sì, che la porteremo,
> la piuma del cappello,
> avanti al colonello
> giuriam la fedeltà!

a serenade, a night of love, and an eruption of Vesuvius
into the bargain. Ideas, especially Italian ideas, came so
thick and fast to him that the *Tarantella* was soon over-
burdened with material. But lucidity of form was always
a far more important thing to Busoni than vividness of
picturesque description. An operation was performed on
the *Tarantella* at a later date; its details are not described,
but a careful study of the Concerto leads one to suppose
that the *Tarantella* was divided into the two Italian quick

movements which precede and follow the *Pezzo serioso* in the middle of the complete work.

The Concerto was still in this embryonic state when the autumn arrived and the concert season began; no more work could be done on it until after another exhausting tour in England during the spring of 1903. He returned to the Concerto in July; he had an engagement to play in London towards the end of the month, but cancelled it in order to prevent his composition being interrupted. It meant a loss of some £70 to him, and he feared that Gerda would reproach him for it, but he hoped to make up the loss by a concert at Harrogate in August. Gerda telegraphed her approval; she never reproached him, although he was often conscious of having given her good cause to do so.

The result of this sacrifice was that the first movement was completely sketched in the next three days. He worked continuously, 'with the regularity of a Zola'. Besides composing he was practising the pianoforte with equal regularity. A week later he had finished the second movement. The slow movement, in which he incorporated fragments of the opera *Sigune*, as well as a theme (in D flat) from an unpublished *Étude* for pianoforte composed some twenty years earlier, proceeded satisfactorily, but the *Tarantella* was still 'a hard nut to crack'. It was about the end of July that he shaved off his beard; he did not inform his wife, but she heard of it from friends, to whom his change of appearance caused no little shock. About the end of the first week of August the slow movement was finished in sketch form; the *Tarantella* had been hewn into shape, and the final *Cantico* cannot have taken long to write. Two preliminary sketches of the complete work exist; the first is dated simply 1903, the second, in which the solo part is complete and the orchestral accompaniment sketched, is marked *Secondo abbozzo, in esteso*,[1] and dated August 18, 1903. The work of instrumentation was begun at once and proceeded through the month of September—

[1] Second sketch, at full length.

a month made memorable by Busoni's first meeting with
Arnold Schönberg, who had been sent to him by Heinrich
Schenker.

In the autumn work was interrupted by the usual concert tours. The English tour was more tiring and depressing than ever; this year he had not the pleasure of Ysaye's
company. In December he had a notable success in Paris, in
spite of having to play on an atrocious pianoforte, as indeed
was generally the case whenever he played in France.
The first three months of 1904 were spent in America,
playing at New York, Boston, Chicago, and Detroit.
America had not changed in the least since he was
there ten years before, he thought; he poured out his
antipathy in scathing terms to Anzoletti and Gerda. He
detested the impertinence and ignorance of American
women; he detested their husbands still more for their
complete indifference to all artistic interests and their
utter contempt for all other languages, all other countries,
and all other professions than that of an American business
man. 'Really, my poor despised fellow-citizens of Empoli
are men of genius in comparison!' The voyage home gave
him time to rest and meditate. 'It is a source of eternal
unrest to me that what has yet to be done occupies me
more intensely than that which I have done, even though
the latter were the more difficult task.' He read *Dr. Jekyll
and Mr. Hyde*; it is interesting to note that he at once
compares the hero to Hoffmann's Cardillac. He was also
reading with keen and friendly interest Strauss's newly-
published *Sinfonia Domestica*; 'the score looks like the
streets of New York!' There was a good Steinway pianoforte on board; he would have liked to play, and the
passengers were naturally pressing him to do so, but he
refused—he could not get over his 'prudish dislike of
half-publicity'. For Busoni there were only two possible
environments for pianoforte-playing, the concert-hall and
the private practice-room—it was only amateurs who
played 'for amusement', whether for other people's or for
their own.

L

Another summer brought him back again to the Concerto, and on August 3, 1904, he finished the fair copy of the complete full score.

Brahms was once severely criticized for daring to compose a pianoforte concerto in four movements instead of the conventional three; Busoni was even more indignantly handled for writing one in five. The first movement of Busoni's Concerto—*Prologo e Introito*—is marked *allegro, dolce e solenne*. The three adjectives exactly describe its character; it moves swiftly but unhurriedly, beginning and ending in a mood of quiet serenity, rising in the middle to a sumptuous and solemn climax. The second movement—*Pezzo giocoso*—begins in C major, but ends in D; it has the character of an intermezzo and needs the following movements for its completion. Its themes are vividly Italian in character; the first is robust and almost brutal, the second languorous and mysterious, vanishing at the end into a ghostly and fantastic scurry of notes curiously characteristic of Busoni's later manner. The third movement is called *Pezzo serioso* and is in D flat major. It has four subsections, headed respectively *Introductio, prima pars, altera pars,* and *ultima pars*. In construction it is extremely complicated, and the form of the whole concerto is difficult to analyse in words on account of the way in which themes are transferred from one movement to another. The work has to be considered as a continuous whole, and Busoni always desired it to be played straight through without interruption. The slow movement is followed by what in his letters he calls the *Tarantella*—here headed simply *All'italiana*. This is the real finale of the Concerto, treated with all the breadth of development suitable to a last movement. Its themes are reminiscent of Italian popular songs and military marches; one can well imagine how horrified the German critics must have been to hear such atrocities 'in a hall sacred to the name of Beethoven'. It may well have provoked a scene of tumult, for it is a scene of tumult in itself, whirling madly from one frenzy to another, becoming ever faster and more

furious, until after a wild stretto and an elaborate cadenza
for the solo instrument it pulls up abruptly in the key
of C, only to let the orchestra enter with a B held softly
in octaves, leading gradually to E major, in which key
the chorus of male voices (invisible) enters singing mysterious words from Oehlenschläger's *Aladdin* to the middle
theme of the first introduction. A coda follows, recalling
various themes from previous movements, and the Concerto ends with some rather conventional effects of brilliance in the original key of C major.

Like Brahms, Busoni was at once accused of having
written, not a concerto, but a symphony with pianoforte
obbligato. The accusation was not unjust; in fact, as
Busoni's own wife quite rightly pointed out to him, it
was a symphony in form and proportions, and the pianoforte part was so exacting that very few pianists were
ever likely to undertake it.

It is undoubtedly true that most pianoforte concertos
of the last hundred years, as Busoni himself wrote, can
be criticized as being either 'symphonies with pianoforte'
or mere exhibitions of virtuosity. If we consider for a
moment the methods of Mozart the phenomenon can be
explained. With Mozart a concerto was a more important musical event than a symphony. In his days the composer of a symphony remained in the background; the
conductor who in our days is the most conspicuous figure
on the platform did not exist in the eighteenth century.
The honours of publicity would have been divided between
the *maestro* who accompanied at the harpsichord or pianoforte and the leader of the first violins.[1] But when a
concerto was performed the composer would be in a far
more conspicuous position. Mozart, playing a new concerto to his admirers, would appear before them not

---

[1] When Haydn appeared in London at Salomon's concerts he accompanied his symphonies on the pianoforte, and some of his improvised
arpeggios were handed on traditionally and later written down from
memory by an English musician who had heard him play them. (Information from the late Rev. J. R. Lunn.)

merely as a virtuoso but as a composer as well. Hence in Mozart's concertos we see that the solo player stands out from the orchestra not so much because he has the most difficult music to play, as because his part has a far greater musical interest. Indeed Mozart invariably makes a point of reserving one or two of his most delightful themes for the pianist alone. They are not announced by the orchestra in the introduction; they are suddenly produced by the soloist-composer as if he had thought of them on the spur of the moment. It is by such devices as these that Mozart almost creates the illusion of composing his concerto in front of the public—an illusion by no means unreasonable in days when public improvisation was expected from a composer as a matter of course.

With Beethoven the centre of interest is shifted from the soloist to the orchestra. The symphony becomes a more important and serious form of music. Moreover, whereas Mozart's chief interest lies in his themes themselves, Beethoven takes themes of little intrinsic interest and devotes the greater part of his creative energy to their development. Simultaneously there comes an enormous development of pure virtuosity in the world of pianoforte-playing. It is easy to see that in these conditions a composer who was a virtuoso and little else would produce concertos in which virtuosity was the sole characteristic, while the composer who took his art seriously would tend, as Beethoven himself did, and as Liszt and Brahms also tended, to confide his innermost thoughts to the orchestra, and to leave little but decorative passages to the pianoforte. Even in the case of Liszt, who has only too often been charged with the exaggeration of virtuosity, we feel (especially in the Concerto in A major) that the pianist is not creating ideas before us, but is listening to them; what the soloist has to play is a transcription, a romantic memory, of themes which have been suggested to him by the orchestra. It is the same romantic attitude as that which produced Field's and Chopin's Nocturnes, Liszt's transcriptions and operatic fantasias.

Despite the incredible difficulty of the solo part, Busoni's Concerto at no point offers a display of virtuosity. Even its cadenzas are subsidiary episodes. At the same time the pianoforte hardly ever presents a single theme in its most immediate and commanding shape. It is nearly always the orchestra which seems to be possessed of the composer's prophetic inspiration. Busoni sits at the pianoforte, listens, comments, decorates, and dreams. The technical treatment of the pianoforte is, as one would naturally expect, derived mainly from that of Liszt. Busoni's study of Liszt had soon enabled him to see, as he points out in one of his essays, that all Liszt's pianoforte writing is based on a limited number of habitual figures. We can recognize these as the foundation of Busoni's passage-work, but Busoni has conceived the whole concerto on so grandiose a scale that devices used by Liszt for occasional episodes are developed here for long stretches at a time, and what in themselves might be striking effects of virtuosity are treated by Busoni as mere backgrounds to subjects given out by the orchestra. The solo part thus makes the most exhausting demands on the skill and endurance of the player while giving him curiously little opportunity for conspicuous display. The wealth of invention shown in the purely decorative passages of accompaniment is extraordinary. Here as elsewhere in his writing for the pianoforte Busoni shows an inexhaustible resource of colour effect. This only increases the difficulty of the Concerto, for the player is often required to play passages of acute technical difficulty with the subdued quality of tone appropriate to a simple accompaniment of broken chords.

Those who heard Busoni play will remember vividly how under his hands the most complicated passages of Beethoven or Liszt seemed transformed into washes of pure colour, although one could not fail to be aware that every single note was accurately played and nothing smudged or blurred. This preoccupation with colour effects on the pianoforte began to make itself evident after Busoni had begun to devote himself to the serious study of Liszt, but it remained to dominate his mind up to the end of his life. Even after he had played in public for the last time he was considering the problem afresh. At certain times in his life there were moments when his playing seemed to some hearers inexpressive and over-intellectual, because he was bent on playing long passages in one carefully graded and absolutely equal tint of tone, as if he wished to produce the effect of an organ. He knew that the more radiant beauties of pianoforte colour were only attainable on a basis of faultlessly accurate technique; there was no possible short cut to them. Liszt's St. Francis walks a storm of roaring and rumbling waves; but the effect of roar and rumble can never be adequately produced unless every note is struck with precisely the right graduation of touch.

It was a mistake to suppose, as many critics and listeners did, that Busoni played Liszt merely for the sake of vulgar ostentation. As a matter of fact the greater works of Liszt, which minor pianists turn into mere displays of virtuosity because their technique is inadequate for anything beyond that, often sounded strangely easy and simple when they were played by Busoni. The glittering scales and arpeggios became what Liszt intended them to be—a dimly suggested background, while the themes in massive chords or singing melodies stood out clear because Busoni had acquired so perfect a control of touch that his tone seemed to become more and more beautiful as it grew louder, even when its actual loudness seemed to surpass the force attained by any other player.

It is such qualities as these which are demanded of the soloist in Busoni's Concerto, and he is required further to have the will to put himself deliberately into the background when necessary,[1] however difficult his technical

[1] When Vincent d'Indy conducted his *Symphonie sur un chant montagnard* for Busoni at Berlin in 1906, Rudolf Ganz, who was to play the pianoforte part, was unable to appear at a rehearsal through illness. Busoni took his place, reading the part at sight; Ganz played it at the concert. It was very noticeable that whereas Ganz treated the part like the

task may be, and to have the musical intelligence to see
the concerto as a whole, to grasp the significance of themes
which recur in unexpected places and to mould the shape
of long heroic phrases designed in the manner of Liszt
but extended over far broader periods.

At this distance of time it can be seen that the musical
style of Busoni's material was derived in the main from
late Beethoven, Brahms, and Liszt, with the addition of
an insistent Italian element easily recognized but less
easily traced to its historical sources. The same com-
ponents are clearly visible in the well-known Violin Sonata
in E minor. Most great composers betray the fact that
they have been influenced by their predecessors not so
much in general style as in a haunting reminiscence of
some particular work or movement. What Busoni derives
from Beethoven and Brahms is a characteristic atmosphere
of serenity. In the slow movement there is an episode
which at once sets the hearer in the mood of certain
movements of the posthumous Quartets and more especially in that of the *Benedictus* from the Mass in D.[1] Other
moments recall the variations from the Sonatas in E minor
(Op. 90) and C minor (Op. 111) or those in the Trio in
B flat (Op. 97). From these there is a natural link to the
Paganini Variations of Brahms. Such movements must
have appealed to Busoni both as a pianist and as a musical
thinker; the result appears in the Concerto in frequent
passages of complicated decoration marked with such
directions as *senza agitazione, morbidissimo, velato, senza
inquietudine alcuna*.[2] From Liszt come the heroic manner
and also the diabolic manner which became more and
more pronounced in Busoni's music as he became more
and more saturated with the imagination of E. T. A.

solo of a concerto, Busoni played it as the composer intended—with an
exact understanding of the pianoforte considered as a component part of the
whole orchestra.

[1] The *Benedictus* was actually transcribed by Busoni for violin and
pianoforte.

[2] 'Without agitation—very velvety—veiled—without the least sense
of unrest.'

Hoffmann. Here too we can note his characteristic Italian directions—*sontuoso, tuonando, fantastico, spettrale, scherzando senza allegrezza*.[1] Yet in spite of all the orgiastic frenzy let loose in the two 'Italian' movements the prevailing impression left by the Concerto as a whole is one of grandeur and serenity.

Writing a few years later about Brahms, Busoni confessed himself repelled by his 'Germanism' and by his *Bequemlichkeit*—his tendency to take the line of least resistance and to avoid facing any new problem. The opening phrase of the Concerto is a musical illustration of this criticism; its serenity and beauty at once remind us of Brahms, but as it moves on its way it deliberately explores modulations which Brahms would never have attempted. The Berlin critics were quite right in finding Busoni's music too Italian for them; it never has the least trace of genuine Germanism. Even the final chorus, if rightly interpreted, is free from the *Liedertafel* taint at which they scoffed. One may indeed wonder why an essentially Italian work should end with verses in praise of Allah. The plain fact was that Busoni at the moment happened to be interested in Oehlenschläger's poem *Aladdin* and had set the final chorus to music. When he planned the Concerto he saw that this chorus, which has something of the mystical character of the concluding stanzas of Goethe's *Faust*, was exactly the music to give the general sense of serenity that he required for his own finale. It was from the original *Aladdin* chorus that he took the theme which occurs in the first movement; when he came to write out the last movement he felt that he missed the words, and therefore directed that a chorus of men's voices should sing them. The actual meaning of the words hardly matters. The chorus is directed to be invisible; it sings in plain chords, like a body of soft trombones added to the orchestra. The effect which Busoni desired was stated by him once in a letter to a friend who had mistakenly suggested to him that it might

[1] 'Sumptuously—thundering—fantastically—like ghosts—jesting without merriment.'

be better to re-write the chorus for mixed voices; he replied that he had no desire to convert his Concerto into an oratorio; he insisted that the chorus should be invisible, and said that its function was 'to add a new register to the sonorities which precede it'.[1]

Leo Kestenberg, then a young pupil of Busoni, wrote an enthusiastic account of the Concerto in the *Neues Montagsblatt*. Beginning with a remark of Goethe to the effect that Bach's music expressed for him the innermost feelings of God as He created the world, he compares Busoni's Concerto to the successive stages of the Creation: the *Introito* suggesting the Spirit of God moving upon the face of the waters, the *Pezzo giocoso* the joy of light and air, the *Pezzo serioso* showing us the creation of Adam and Eve, the next movement the Garden of Eden with the tree of life and the tree of knowledge, while the *Cantico* 'sets to music the last and highest revelation, that of the eternal verity—"and they were both naked, the man and the woman, and were not ashamed" '. We may be tempted to smile at so fantastic an interpretation, but the author was not exceeding the bounds of reasonable criticism if he meant to convey the idea that the Concerto evoked in his mind a memory of the frescoes of Michelangelo.

[1] 'Il Coro nel Concerto dovrebbe del resto rimanere *invisibile*, ed aggiungere un nuovo registro alle sonorità che lo precedono.' One might say that it was to provide a new depth of general tone such as an organist provides when he suddenly adds the 16 ft. stops on the manuals after previously holding them in reserve.

CHAPTER IX

THE CITY OF DISAPPOINTMENT

AFTER the performance of the Concerto Busoni paid a short visit to England, playing in Manchester on November 24. Fog and frost made him see Manchester as 'an ingeniously contrived department of Dante's Hell, where travelling virtuosi, who threw away the best part of their lives for the sake of fame and money, gnash their teeth in blindness'.

In December he returned to Berlin for a series of recitals devoted entirely to the works of Liszt. These recitals, coming at the same time as some of his orchestral concerts of modern music, were a fresh challenge to his critics. At the first concert he played the *Études d'exécution transcendante* and the *Paganini-Études*; the second programme consisted of original compositions by Liszt, the third entirely of Liszt's transcriptions. It can well be imagined how horrified the Berlin critics were at programmes of this type; but they seem to have enjoyed them against their will. Otto Lessmann, of the *Allgemeine Musikzeitung*, understood them better, for he had often heard Liszt play himself, and recorded how Liszt had explained to him the origin of the operatic fantasias. In the eighteen-forties it was the regular habit for pianists to improvise publicly on given themes; after Liszt had played several such *impromptus* on themes from the popular operas of the day these began to take a definite shape, became fixed, and eventually appeared in print. Lessmann very rightly says of them that they must be played as if they were improvisations on the spur of the moment.

'The melody is the chief thing; a pianist who makes it evident that he is playing them for the sake of the virtuoso passages which decorate the themes can never make the right effect with them, the effect which Liszt himself used to make. Busoni understood their style and that was the reason why his performance aroused an enthusiasm such as is seldom seen in the concert-rooms of Berlin.'

Busoni understood the operatic transcriptions because he was an Italian. If he had not heard the great Italian singers of Liszt's youth, he had at least heard his father play similar operatic transcriptions on the clarinet with all the combined sensibility and virtuosity of the romantic era. It was not for his virtuosity at the pianoforte that Busoni worshipped Liszt. He was not converted to Liszt until he began to see Liszt as something more than a virtuoso, as the only link that there had ever been between the Italy of Bellini and the Italy of his own time. The recital of operatic fantasias had its appropriately romantic end— from the galleries near the platform the adoring young ladies drenched their hero with a shower of violets.[1]

In May 1905 Busoni went with his wife to Madrid for the tercentenary celebrations in honour of Cervantes.[2] *Don Quixote* was one of the first books which he had read as a child, and throughout his life he had an intense devotion to it. They spent just over a fortnight in Madrid, so that they were there for three Sundays. Each Sunday Gerda said that they ought to go and see a bull-fight, as it was the proper thing to do in Spain. Each of the first two Sundays Ferruccio refused, making some excuse or other—it was a wet day, or some other engagement had to be carried out. Finally on the last Sunday she got her way and they went. After about ten minutes Gerda began to feel faint and wished to go away; Ferruccio had no pity on her but said to her severely, '*You* wanted to see a bull-fight—now you must stop.' Seven bulls were to be killed; after the first had been dispatched he got up and said he could stand it no longer—it made him sick. They went out, and at the exit found the usual crowd of boys waiting to secure the tickets of those who came away early. Busoni tore the tickets into tiny fragments, threw

[1] It was a form of homage often practised in Russia and on this occasion was organized by a Russian pupil.
[2] *Don Quixote* was first published in 1605.

them in the boys' faces and exclaimed with disgust, 'And
for people like that I have to play the pianoforte!'

Busoni played both at Madrid and at Lisbon and
Oporto; the concerts in Portugal had been arranged
through the good offices of his close friend José Vianna
da Motta. In Portugal he joined forces with Kreisler;
Gerda went with Frau Kreisler to Paris. A curious episode
took place during the tour in Portugal. One day when
Kreisler and he were travelling together and had just
finished luncheon in the restaurant car, Busoni looked
at the wine-list and proceeded to order a half-bottle of an
extremely expensive Burgundy. The waiter told him that
they had whole bottles only; Busoni told him to bring
one. He drank a few sips and then gave the rest to the
waiter. Kreisler was horrified at Busoni's extravagance,
for the bottle was priced at about 50 francs, and he was
well aware that Busoni and his family were none too well
off. He remonstrated with Busoni in plain terms.

'What!' replied Busoni, 'you, who are a great artist,
have the soul of a *commis*? I have an idea; I must get
myself into the mood to find it. I have to make a transition
from one subject to another; I cannot find it and I must
get myself out of myself in order to find it.'[1]

He was no doubt meditating on some portion of the
Turandot-Suite, the first sketches for which date from
1904. The episode, trivial as it may appear, aptly illus-
trates Busoni's mentality. To him there could be nothing
of greater importance than the perfect solution of his inward musical problem. As to the wine, he had not the
least intention of getting drunk or even mildly drunk; he
approached the wine as an artist and a connoisseur—a few
sips were enough to take him away from his everyday
surroundings and set his inspiration free.

A new link with Italy was forged in the summer by the
composition of the *Turandot-Suite*. This was conceived
originally as a concert work suggested by Gozzi's play.
Gozzi's *Turandot* had been freely adapted for the German

[1] Information kindly supplied by Herr F. Kreisler.

stage by Schiller, and Weber had written incidental music
for it—music which has always had a certain historical
interest on account of the Chinese melodies (derived from
Athanasius Kircher) which Weber employed in it. Busoni's
view of the German *Turandot* was that Schiller and Weber
between them had merely ruined a great work of Italian
literature. In 1905, however, he seems to have had no
definite idea of getting the play put on the stage again.
It was only in October 1911 that Busoni's music was re-
arranged for stage purposes to accompany a new adapta-
tion of the play made by Karl Vollmoeller and produced
by Max Reinhardt at the Deutsches Theater in Berlin.

Early in March 1906 Busoni played at Trieste. He
did not stay at his parents' house but went to an hotel.
He was not in good health at the time, and the prospect
of visiting the old people made him none the happier.
He spent three hours trying to make up his mind to call
on them; although he found them better than he expected,
it was a painful visit as far as he himself was concerned.

'There is nothing worse', he wrote to Gerda, 'than looking back,
or than places, people and things that lead one to do so. I seldom
look back, and wish I never could; but here I cannot help it. And
so I feel uncomfortable, as if I had been shunted off the main line,
in the night, on to a side station where no trains run. It is an interruption of my real self, which in the world outside is famous, active
and forward-looking, whilst here a child that has grown up is
forced back twenty-five years to the unchanged environment of his
childhood.

'Escape into life again! that is the cry within me, and I think of
the idyllic end of the *Adagio* and the *Tarantella* which follows it in
the Concerto.

'But after the end of the *Tarantella* ? The air here is almost like
that of Rome: it hypnotizes one and draws one with gentle arms
towards the South and the placid joy of life in Italy. Will that be the
end?

'Let us not think about that yet.'

Yet if Busoni would not think about the end, he was
always thinking about the future. He played the Concerto

at Bologna in May, the *Turandot-Suite* being also included
in the programme. Anzoletti had been of great service
to him there, writing notes for the programme and giving
help in many ways. After the concert Busoni wrote to
him from Berlin, sketching out the plan of a permanent
Italian symphony orchestra to be centred at Bologna and
to supply concerts for Trieste, Milan, and Florence as
well. He admits that it could only be a dream for the
present, but the letter shows how Italian music was always
in his thoughts, and Italian music with Bologna as a centre.

A new work was taking shape in his mind; this was the
opera *Die Brautwahl*, which was ultimately performed at
Hamburg in the spring of 1912. From the summer of
1906 onwards Busoni's letters are full of the opera and its
progress, but the detailed history of its composition must
be postponed to a later chapter. By June the work was
well advanced and he was occupied with it during his
visit to London, where he played in a Patti concert at the
Albert Hall. It was very much an 'all-star' programme—
Patti, aged 63, as he notes, Santley, aged 72, a girl
violinist aged 11, and Ben Davies '100 kilo schwer'. With
memories of Spain fresh in his mind he remarked that the
Albert Hall was more suitable for bull-fighting than for
pianoforte-playing. Busoni was always interested to hear
other pianists, and even when he was not much interested
he often went to their concerts out of courtesy. This time
in London he heard Mark Hambourg and Pachmann;
he wrote to his wife an amusing description of the latter
playing the *Invitation à la Valse*. After he had played it,
Pachmann turned to the audience and said, 'Mr. Godowsky—has made an arrangement of this piece—*very*
difficult! He can't play it himself—he, he—I—he, he
—don't play it yet—before—the public—must be careful—careful—he, he, he!' then laughed, shrugged his
shoulders and disappeared.

In the summer, while Gerda and the children went to
stay with Caroline Gomperz-Bettelheim at Habrovan in
Austria, Ferruccio went for a little tour by himself to

think out his ideas for the opera. Starting by Munich, he went on to Innsbruck, Bozen, and Trent. At Innsbruck he hated the tourists with their green suits, chamois-beards, and bare knees; Trent he thought would please him better. He had curious recollections of playing there as a boy of thirteen in the stone hall of the Palazzo Salvotti; it had been so cold that he could hardly play, and he remembered the audience sitting in their overcoats with the collars turned up. And he remembered having been kissed by a red-haired chambermaid in the hotel, and how his mother had been very much annoyed about it. But when he reached Trent it rained for three days. Trent is a dull town even now, and it was duller still in the days of the Austrians. Busoni was infuriated with its 'spirit of resignation'—Empoli was quite American by comparison! The search for romance was disappointing; he consoled himself with the letters of Giusti, always one of his favourite writers, as he was of Ferdinando too.

'Enjoy life: melancholy is a fashionable foolishness.'[1]

The autumn was spent in Berlin, where some new pupils had been added to the circle—Gino Tagliapietra and O'Neil Phillips. Busoni was now forty, and with the advent of middle life he was coming to see more and more that his chief interests lay in composing and in teaching. 'Both as man and as artist I prefer to look forwards rather than backwards, and I suppose that is why I prefer to have younger people around me'—so he had written in 1904. 'And may it be so up to the end, for when that ceases, it brings depression.' It was in many ways a happy period of life for him, for the number of his disciples was increasing, and all who frequented his house in the Augsburgerstrasse derived inspiration from his talk according to their capacities for receiving

[1] Busoni, writing to his wife, quotes the sentence in German: 'Geniesse das Leben! Die Melancholie ist ein eleganter Blödsinn.' The original Italian is: 'Goditi la vita: la malinconia è una corbellagine elegante.' (G. Giusti to Pietro Papini, 30 July 1841; *Epistolario*, ed. F. Martini, Florence, 1904, vol. i, p. 356.)

it. His circle was not confined to pupils and professional musicians. On one occasion the usual group of disciples was startled by the appearance of a nervous maidservant announcing 'Herr Hauptmann von E—', followed by the entrance of a Prussian officer in uniform accompanied by his very stately wife. Most of the party were by no means accustomed to such visitors, but Gerda, it need hardly be said, was on all occasions a perfect hostess, and the situation was saved by Lello, then aged six, who inquired in a loud voice if that was the 'Hauptmann von Cöpenick', which reduced the whole company, including the captain and his wife, to helpless laughter.[1]

The concerts of modern music were still going on, and were still received by the critics with a good deal of hostility. The two symphonies of Vincent d'Indy and Alkan's Cadenza for the C minor Concerto of Beethoven had caused much indignation; a few days later Busoni came into Bartolini's restaurant with a letter expressing his own indignation, which he proposed to send to the Press. The disciples were naturally full of admiration, but an English friend, who had had experience of musical journalism, told him that he would be ill advised to send it, as critics love nothing better than baiting an angry musician. This plain speaking was blasphemy to the faithful, but Busoni did not send the letter.

Playing in public, except at his Berlin recitals, for which he could choose programmes with the deliberate intention of challenging criticism, was gradually becoming more and more distasteful to him. But he could not afford to sacrifice the earnings of a provincial tour in England, and went off early in December to play at Manchester, Edinburgh, Aberdeen, Glasgow, and Bradford. He missed

[1] The 'Captain of Cöpenick' was a poor shoemaker from Cöpenick, in the 'East End' of Berlin, who had recently made the whole of Germany laugh by putting on a captain's uniform and entering the local Town Hall, in which the officials were completely deceived and meekly allowed him to arrest the Mayor and take possession of a large sum of money from the municipal cash-box.

156

Ysaye sadly; his partner this time was Sarasate. Sarasate was sixty-two, and had, according to Busoni, neither brains nor temperament. He irritated Busoni by his 'Olympian egoism' and by a peculiarly Latin quality which reminded Busoni painfully of his own father—'*urteilslose Ablehnung*' —the utter refusal to discuss or even consider ideas which were outside his own mentality. Busoni happened at that time to be keenly interested in César Franck. All that Sarasate had to say of him was, 'He was a bad accompanist.' But Sarasate had known many interesting people and seen a great deal of the world; that gave him at least 'a certain historic varnish'. And Busoni was certainly fascinated by a story of Rubinstein. Sarasate and Rubinstein were playing cards together one evening in a Leipzig hotel. About 10 o'clock people came in from a Gewandhaus concert at which a new symphony had been performed. Rubinstein had refused to go and hear it.

'Well, how was the symphony?' he asked.

'Oh, very *musikalisch*,' was the answer.

'That settles it,' thundered Rubinstein, striking the table with his fist; 'when the Germans call a work *musikalisch*, you may be sure it is tiresome.'

It was towards the end of 1906 that Busoni was informally approached with a view to his conducting a *Meisterklasse* for the pianoforte at the Vienna Conservatoire. In itself the idea of the class was attractive to him after his experience of Weimar, but Vienna was a place in which he had known too many disappointments. He hesitated for a long time before accepting. His first step was to consult his old friend, Ludwig von Bösendorfer, who had shown him unfailing kindness ever since his first appearance in Vienna at the age of nine. He explained to Bösendorfer that since he left the Boston Conservatory in 1892 he had enjoyed complete freedom and felt himself incapable of submitting to academic discipline. To transfer himself from Berlin to Vienna would mean a complete change of environment and habit, as well as the sacrifice of much of his own work. He must insist on being entirely

157

M

independent of the Director's authority and free to choose his own pupils and teach them as he pleased. He further demanded a reasonable amount of leave to go away on concert tours, especially as he had some expectation of being engaged for a tour in America.

Busoni's terms may well have seemed impossible to persons living under the ordinary routine of a school of music, but from his own point of view the acceptance of the post, even on his own conditions, was a considerable sacrifice. Thanks no doubt to Bösendorfer's influence and the tact and genuine friendliness of Dr. Botstiber, the secretary of the Conservatoire, Busoni's conditions were accepted, and he agreed in February 1907 to undertake the class for one year at any rate.

The year 1907 was one of unusually varied activities. In March he played at Marseilles—a place 'with the ignorance of Naples and the catchwords of Paris'; the long journey wasted a whole week. Then there were records to be made for the 'Welte-Mignon' at Freiburg, followed by concerts at Munich and Florence. The summer was spent mostly in Berlin, working at *Die Brautwahl* and practising the pianoforte. Early in August he had to play at Norderney. The weather was stormy and bitterly cold; it made him think of the opening of the *Flying Dutchman*, and by a curious coincidence, just as he entered the concert-room for a rehearsal, he heard the orchestra begin the overture. After the rehearsal Count Oeynhausen, the 'royal bath-commissary', came up to him and said that the two sisters of the Emperor were present and would be glad if he would play a little more. That was the sort of thing which infuriated Busoni; needless to say, he refused. 'It is a curious feeling, being obliged to play in public after three months' pause,' he wrote to his wife; 'I feel the *shamefulness* of it more than ever.'

Another task before him was the preparation of the complete works of Liszt. A committee, which met at Weimar, had been formed for this purpose, and Busoni, who was to edit the pianoforte works in some twenty volumes or more, astonished his collaborators by his extraordinary knowledge on minute points of bibliography and textual criticism. The work demanded scholarship of a high order, for Liszt frequently revised his compositions, and it was a matter of some difficulty to collate the various versions. Busoni had begun collecting first editions of Liszt since the year 1892, and probably few public libraries possessed such a wealth of material as he did.

In September he went to Vienna to examine pupils for his *Meisterklasse*. It was a depressing business; they were mostly girls, and as indifferent in talent as they were in looks. From Vienna he went to London, having to play at the Cardiff Festival and at other places in England. At Manchester he visited Egon Petri and his wife. Their house was always 'an oasis in the desert' for him, but in spite of all their kindness he never could adapt himself to what he called the *Cottage-Stimmung*—the domesticity of a small suburban house. Even travelling was a relief from that. It was not luxury that he demanded, but the sense of contact with the swarming life and activity of a big town. In October he was back at Vienna and starting his class.

'You can safely look about for a nice flat in Berlin for next autumn,' he wrote to Gerda; 'I will bet my head against a hair of yours that not much result will come out of the K. and K. [Imperial and Royal] city. My father knew a mysterious man in Italy (I forget his name) who had invented a secret process by which corpses could be preserved for centuries (so he maintained) exactly as they were in life, with the colour of the skin and lips and with perfect flexibility of all muscles and joints. I rather think the K. and K. city is a corpse of this sort.'

The class was on a level with that at Moscow; there was only one man with whom he could discuss pictures, books, or anything of human interest. Fingering, pedal, rhythm, *piano* and *forte*—that was all he could teach them; for the psychology and aesthetics of music they had no understanding. 'I have noticed that very sensitive young

159

men are not much good at the pianoforte. People with aesthetic sensibility bring refinement into the profession, but they cannot reduce the instrument to obedience.'

A characteristic sentence from one of Kalbeck's criticisms annoyed him and set him thinking. 'Liszt's *Triumph of Tasso* was a defeat for the composer but a victory for our orchestra.'

'I begin to realize', wrote Busoni, 'that the ruin of the Viennese, as regards their attitude to art, comes from newspaper criticism (*Feuilletons*). This systematic daily reading (for half a century) of *causeries* on art, witty and superficial, *short*, and all turning on an obvious catchword, has destroyed for the Viennese their own power of seeing and hearing, comparing and thinking with any seriousness. These little Viennese have something Parisian in their thirst for enjoyment and their "superiority", and in their chase after sensations they are often badly taken in, like the Parisians.'

It was a long time before his Viennese pupils began to have any idea of the standards that he set before them, but the class gradually improved. The men at any rate showed intelligence, and by way of inspiring them with something of the spirit of Weimar, he would invite them to supper and try to gain closer intellectual contact with them. By the end of November things were going better. Friedmann, one of the men, had given him an English mezzotint; that pleased him enormously, not merely because he loved prints but because it indicated an aesthetic sense in his pupil. It is evident from the letters that Busoni was giving them all much longer and more careful lessons than he was paid to do; for a fortnight he taught the class for four hours every day.

One evening he went to hear *Madame Butterfly* at the Opera. After twenty minutes he left the theatre, went for a walk and had supper, returning for the last act. All he could say of it was 'Es ist *unanständig*'. It is difficult to give the sense of this word in English: it is best translated *indecent*, and is used in all the senses in which English people use that word, implying anything, moral, social, or artistic, of which one ought to be ashamed.[1]

In January 1908 he gave a recital himself in Vienna. It was like a début, he said, for nobody in Vienna had any idea of his playing. He felt as if he were back in the Vienna of 1884, and he did in fact frequent only the society of friends whom he had known in those days. The pupils were becoming more and more devoted to him, and among the men were some who were eventually to attain distinction—Louis Closson, a young protégé of Ysaye, Leo Sirota, and Louis Theodor Gruenberg.

Trouble began in February. On the 10th Dr. Botstiber received a letter from Busoni's secretary in Berlin saying that he had been obliged to cancel his second recital owing to illness. Although still unwell, he was to start that day for Switzerland to play at concerts; further engagements had to be fulfilled in Paris and London. He admitted that this postponement of his classes in Vienna was irregular, but pleaded previous contracts. He hoped to return to Vienna by April 21 and would then be willing to devote the whole of May, June, and July to the *Meisterklasse*.

The Directorate of the Conservatoire replied on the 14th that they had already had cause to complain of Busoni for irregularity in his hours of teaching and that they now considered their contract with him to be terminated on the ground of non-fulfilment on his part. They did not wait for a further reply from him, but allowed statements to appear in the Viennese Press to the effect that he had been dismissed for neglecting his duties. It was further stated that Godowsky had been appointed to take the class over. From Vienna the news spread at once to Berlin, where the *Börsen-Courier* applied to Busoni himself for information and published on February 25 a letter from him, in which he maintained that there was no breach of contract. It had been understood from the beginning that this first *Meisterklasse* was merely a trial year, and that he was to

[1] In 1920 Busoni expressed cordial admiration for the masterly theatrical skill of *Il Tabarro*.

have freedom to go away on concert tours. He had under-
taken to give 280 hours' teaching and was prepared to
make up the full number in the later months.

He had as a matter of fact been teaching every day for
a fortnight and then taking a fortnight away. Before his
last departure at the end of January the Directorate had
expressed their satisfaction to him and the hope that he
would continue the class the following year. Illness had
prevented him from giving the next fortnight's teaching,
and after that he had to start for Switzerland. Meanwhile
the Director sent for the pupils to ask who could play a
concerto at a concert on March 20 to represent the class.
It was not the Director's business to interfere with the
class in this manner; Busoni alone had the right to decide
who might play at a concert. Indeed the first instinct of
the class was to remain loyal to Busoni and refuse to
answer the Director's question; but the chance of a public
appearance was too much for one of the young ladies. She
timidly offered a concerto of Beethoven; another young
lady promptly countered with a concerto of Liszt, and
after that there was nothing to be done but for all the
pupils to say what they could play. Busoni was informed
of all this by one of the men, and was naturally much
annoyed at the Director's action.

He wrote in the same sense to Dr. Botstiber, who all
along had been ready to take Busoni's point of view and
replied in a tactful and conciliatory spirit. Meanwhile the
pupils, who after all were the most important people concerned, although it naturally never occurred to the
Directorate of the Conservatoire to consult them, took
matters into their own hands. Several of them wrote to
Busoni, expressing their distress, which was in some cases
serious, since most of them had come from other countries
to join the class at considerable financial sacrifice. An
American girl, Georgine Nelson, summoned a meeting of
the class at her lodgings, and it was unanimously agreed
that if Busoni were not reinstated by the Directorate, the
whole class would follow him to Berlin. Georgine Nelson

was not a girl to be frightened of the Director and went to see him herself, and present what was called a 'petition' from the class. It was more like an ultimatum.

Her letters[1] to Busoni in London gave an amusing account of the affair.

'We are fighting nobly. "Busoni expects every man to do his duty!" I went to Director Bopp and the Secretary, Dr. Botstiber, and "demanded their intentions". They were quite meek, when I told them that we should all leave unless they arranged the affair, and said they hoped very much that it could be done, if you would *entgegenkommen*[2] by returning before April. You *must* come back to us as we should *die* of grief, otherwise! On Wednesday I am going to play the Chopin F moll Concerto for Director Bopp. You should see him accompany! He *is* so big and fat, and looks like an inflated balloon when he sits at the piano, from the back view! He 's quite nice, though: he has behaved quite decently about this stupid affair.'

Miss Nelson's letter is dated March 2; she appears to have interviewed the Director on February 27. On March 3 Busoni wrote in strong terms from London to the Directorate, protesting against their unjust action and undertaking to come to Vienna on March 14 for a week, and after that to devote himself exclusively to the school from April 21 onwards. The Directorate replied by telegram that they could not alter their decision. The telegram was published in the papers. The pupils then sent a statement to the *Neue Freie Presse* (March 11) announcing their intention of following Busoni to Berlin. Busoni replied at once with a letter to the same paper saying that he would meet his pupils at the Hotel Bristol in Vienna on March 15, and that he intended to continue the class from April 21 to July 15, independently of the Conservatoire, but in Vienna, in order to prevent the students from having to incur any additional expense.

A postscript to the letter threw a little more light on the whole affair. It had been alleged that Busoni had treated the Director with discourtesy at a Board Meeting. Busoni

[1] In English.   [2] 'Meet them half-way.'

told the plain story of the matter. He had been summoned to the Board of Professors to discuss the question of whether listeners should be admitted to the *Meisterklasse*, as they were at Weimar. The Directorate was against their admission, Busoni for it. He addressed the meeting and gained his point; the admission of listeners was agreed to by a majority. The meeting then proceeded to discuss matters which did not concern Busoni, but the chairman politely asked him to stay, and out of politeness he did so. But the discourse of the President (Hofrat Adolf Koch von Langentreu) was somewhat long, and as it continued 'with the even monotony of a distant Gregorian plain-song', Busoni's attention wandered. He noticed a portrait of Beethoven on the wall, life-size, and hitherto unknown to him; without thinking, he rose from his seat and went to inspect the portrait more closely. The President took this amiss, and made some pointed remark to Busoni; he apologized and took his departure.

It must have been a very human scene. From Busoni's own letters it is clear enough that he did not take much trouble to be friendly with the Conservatoire people; it was natural too that they should feel a certain resentment against him as a teacher from outside who refused to submit to their authority, although they themselves had appointed him. The episode of the Board Meeting was simply the last straw.

Busoni returned to Vienna in April, as he had promised, and took up his quarters in the Palais Todesco-Oppenheimer, placed at his disposal by his old friend Baroness Jella Oppenheimer, daughter of the Baroness Todesco who had befriended him in boyhood. There were twenty-five pupils and about a dozen listeners; lessons were given regularly twice a week. This, at any rate, was what he told Bösendorfer when the class came to an end; from his letters it is clear that he often taught for four hours a day. Teaching the class was in fact the one thing that made life in Vienna endurable; he hated the place.

'O this city! If I did not know that Beethoven had done great work here, I should think that nothing could ever be done here.

But perhaps the composing-element in the air of Vienna has been used up or diluted, to judge by the descending scale of BEETHOVEN, BRAHMS, hugo wolf.

'Vienna is medieval and provincial at the same time. Events are manufactured here, as they were at Weimar. When boredom has gone on too long, a procession is arranged, or a monument unveiled.' (He gave his wife a comic description of the unveiling of the Brahms monument in the rain.)

An Italian opera company came to Vienna, and he went to see *Rigoletto*. He had not seen it since he was about nine years old.

'I remember an evening in the Via Geppa at Trieste, when my mother told me the story of it—"arranged for the young". For some days I have been pursued by an idea, stronger than any previous ones; that after the *Brautwahl* (as the natural result of this whole five years' development) I must write an Italian opera! I feel that only thus can my style unfold itself in full flower. The *libretto* is the difficult question. I thought of Boito, and of Italian amusing *novelle*, but it is safer to take a ready-made stage figure, like Falstaff. Goldoni will not do—Gozzi hardly; but perhaps I ought to think that out more carefully.

'Yesterday I met the Gerickes. When I talked of my comic opera Frau Paula said that sort of thing was unsuitable for a serious man like me. She and Melanie are clever heads.'

One day the faithful Kapff reappeared. It was an unfortunate moment; Busoni had just finished a lesson and was tired and inclined to be ill-tempered. Poor Kapff was in his usual state of pessimism and stayed for two hours.

'I can't help it, but I cannot do with people who have finished with life. This rummaging in the past is an abomination to me. Either one has accomplished something which one can never accomplish again, or one can do it better now than one did it then. Both memories are irritating. I felt neither friendship nor sympathy for Kapff; I should like to have made him a present of a revolver. It was the first time that I found myself so hard-hearted. Is that a bad sign?'

It was certainly not a sign of a change of character in Busoni; it was only a moment of nervous irritation. But it was caused by an incident typically Viennese, and it was Vienna that had made poor Kapff, an East Prussian *Junker* by birth, the pitiful figure that he had become.

There were happier moments. One evening in June Baroness Oppenheimer invited all the pupils to the house. Like her mother and her aunts, she was a *grande dame* of the old school, with a dignity and reserve which Busoni occasionally found a little frightening, but she had inherited all the large-hearted generosity of the Gomperz family. In the midst of that Vienna which Busoni hated so bitterly she was the one surviving link with that other Vienna which had enchanted him as a child. And Melanie (now Frau Dr. Prelinger) was there that evening too— Melanie, who had been a friendly sister to him in his adolescence and still gave him a sister's comradeship and affection. He played to them for two hours and knew that he was at his best. It was a typical Busoni programme— Bach's *Chaconne* and two *Choralvorspiele* arranged by himself, *All'Italia* and *Turandots Frauengemach* from his own new *Elegies*, and the twelve *Études d'exécution transcendante* of Liszt.

In the middle of July the class came to an end and Busoni returned to Berlin.

CHAPTER X

'DIE BRAUTWAHL'

THE composition of the Pianoforte Concerto and the Violin Sonata in E minor had marked a change in Busoni's development, but these works were only the prelude to a much more striking development in his whole personality, a development marked by the composition of many works in a new style and also by a considerable literary output. Although his audiences and even some of his critics had by this time begun to realize that he was not only a virtuoso of unique technical accomplishment but also an interpreter such as had not been heard since the days of Liszt and Rubinstein, he himself was rapidly becoming more and more disgusted with the career of a public performer. 'The artist exists only for artists,' he wrote from America in 1904; 'the public, the critics, the schools, and the teachers are nothing but stupid and harmful parasites.'

With that perpetual tendency to self-analysis which pursued him throughout his life (though it must be remembered that the examples of it quoted here were intended only for the eye of his wife or of some intimate friend like Henri Petri) he wrote in July 1905: 'I have a feeling of so many interweaving hopes and memories that I hardly know whether I am an old man or a mere youth. Perhaps now for the first time I realize my actual age.' He goes on to quote the lines of Rückert—'Mit vierzig Jahren ist der Berg erstiegen'—which the music of Brahms has made so well known to all musicians. He was not actually forty at the moment of writing, but he had passed his thirty-ninth birthday. And he might well feel that he was in some ways an old man, when he remembered his childhood and youth, his premature development and the burden laid upon him by his parents at an age when most children have little idea of what the burdens of life may be.

A letter of August 1907 gives some idea of the changes that were taking place:

'This summer I have noted one of the greatest steps in the progress of my development. With regard to my musical tastes, I began, as you know, by getting beyond Schumann and Mendelssohn; I used to misunderstand Liszt, then worshipped him, and then more calmly admired him. I was hostile to Wagner; later I was amazed at him, and then, as a Latin, turned away from him. I allowed Berlioz to take me by surprise (*überrumpeln*). One of the most difficult things was learning to distinguish between good Beethoven and bad. Latterly I discovered the most recent French composers by myself, and when they became too quickly popular, dropped them again. Finally I have come to a closer inward understanding of the old Italian opera-composers. These are metamorphoses which cover twenty years. And all through those twenty years there stood unchanged, like a lighthouse in a stormy sea, the score of *Figaro*. But as I looked at it again a week ago, I found signs of human weakness in it for the first time, and I rejoiced at the discovery that I do not stand so far beneath it as I did—although on the other hand this discovery means not only a positive loss, but also points to the transitoriness of all human achievement. And how much more transitory must my own be!'

During this period of development four great composers of the past had a predominating influence on Busoni—Liszt, Verdi, Bach, and Mozart. Liszt had interested him as a pianist, but had stirred him far more deeply as an Italian. The intensive study of Liszt's music bore fruit in three directions: in the publication of Liszt's works under his editorship, in the mission to which he felt called to spread the knowledge of them both as pianist and conductor, and, more inwardly, in the recognition of Liszt as a pioneer in composition, as the ancestor of almost all the newer developments in music. The public of to-day perhaps hardly realizes how unfamiliar Liszt's music was to concert-goers of thirty or forty years ago. The Hungarian Rhapsodies and the *Liebestraum* were almost the only works of his which were commonly played, and they were played so often by indifferent players that serious musicians very naturally came to regard Liszt with aversion or contempt. It was chiefly Busoni's marvellous interpretations of the Sonata, of the *Legends*, the *Années de Pèlerinage*, as well as of many works of the later period, which led pianists of the present day, and critics too, to take a wider view of Liszt. The later works of Liszt, such as the *Trauer-Gondel*, *Valse Oubliée*, *Mephisto-Walzer*, and *Weih-nachtsbaum*, are still very little known, even to well-read musicians. Busoni played them, but not very often; some of his pupils studied them with him, and they must have sunk deeply into his mind, for they certainly suggested the direction which he took in his own later compositions, especially in the short pianoforte works.

The Verdi whom Busoni admired was the Verdi of *Falstaff*. *Falstaff* is the only opera with which *Die Braut-wahl* has a direct affinity. Here again Busoni recognized at once the prophetic character of *Falstaff* and saw the direction in which it could lead him to a still newer style. The *prophetic* character, as he himself called it, was a quality for which he was always on the look-out in music of older days; it was especially this quality that kept him faithful to Chopin's *Préludes* after he had discarded most of Chopin's other works.

The influence of Mozart and Bach is less obvious at first sight. The *Comedy* Overture hints at Mozart in the manner of a *jeu d'esprit*, but it was not until about twelve or fourteen years later that Mozart seemed to come uppermost in his compositions or in his concert-activities. Yet he was constantly studying Mozart and it is to 1906 that the *Mozart-Aphorismen* belong—a string of short observations, some of which show a very penetrating insight.

It was Mozart that had led him to the serenity of the Pianoforte Concerto: that is clear from the reference to *Die Zauberflöte* in connexion with Oehlenschläger's *Alad-din*. And the next step taken in the spirit of Mozart was towards comedy opera—a transition natural enough when one remembers that the German word *Heiterkeit* can mean both *serenity* and *merriment*. Later on it was to lead him beyond the romance of *Die Brautwahl* to the Comedy of Masks and so towards Italy.

Still deeper below the surface was the influence of Bach. The transcriptions of his organ music and of the *Chaconne* were preliminary steps towards the more elaborate studies which are in the nature of commentaries on Bach written not in words but in music. Contrapuntal studies had always fascinated Busoni, and he had already grasped the contrapuntal aspect of certain works of Mozart. When studying a classical work he was always on the look-out for ideas which pointed towards the future, and would then often proceed to sketch out the music to which those ideas seemed to lead on. This may be noted, for instance, in his treatment of the ground bass in Bach's *Capriccio sopra la lontananza del fratello dilettissimo* and in the cadenzas which he wrote for the pianoforte concertos of Mozart. The climax of his Bach study came in 1911 with the *Fantasia Contrappuntistica*.

Editorial work on Bach and Liszt had further turned Busoni's thoughts in a literary direction. To this period belongs the *Entwurf einer Neuen Aesthetik der Tonkunst* (1905), as well as a number of small essays and dramatic sketches. From 1906 onwards his letters become much more copious both in number and in interest. The chief literary influence on his mind was that of E. T. A. Hoffmann; it was to Hoffmann that he turned for the subject of his new opera *Die Brautwahl*, and so profoundly did he steep himself in Hoffmann's works that his vivid imagination led him almost to believe that the spirit of Hoffmann had taken a sort of demoniac possession of him.

To those outside Germany Hoffmann's name is known chiefly through Offenbach's popular opera *Les Contes d'Hoffmann*, which can hardly be said to give an adequate representation of him. Ernst Theodor Amadeus Hoffmann (1776–1822) was one of the most original figures of the early German romantic movement. He is famous as a writer of fantastic stories; he was also a composer of music, with a certain vein of originality, though amateurish in execution. During his erratic and eccentric life he was by turns opera-conductor, scene-painter, and caricaturist, as well as lawyer, musical critic, and novelist; his own existence was hardly less fantastic than those of the personalities which he created. Brought up on German romantic literature from boyhood, Busoni could not fail to be attracted by him, and he was by no means the first composer who had sought a subject for an opera in Hoffmann's stories. The fascination of Hoffmann's tales, which seem old-fashioned only by reason of their leisurely style of narration, lies in the fact that, unlike many of his contemporary practitioners in mystery, he had the singular gift of combining his sense of the morbid and macabre with a delightful sense of everyday humour, and achieved the most grotesque results by mixing up fantastic supernatural adventures with absurdly commonplace characters in the most unromantic surroundings. English literature of a later epoch often shows similar methods, from Dickens's *Christmas Carol* down to more recent examples. To a musical reader Hoffmann possesses the additional attraction of being a musician himself, and composers have naturally felt drawn towards him as a source for a libretto because so many of his stories have a musical background. That musical background too had a special attraction of its own for Busoni. Hoffmann was a devoted admirer of Mozart—it was for that reason that he dropped his original name of Wilhelm and called himself Amadeus; and apart from Mozart, the music which we are invited to listen to in many of the stories is the Italian music of the seventeenth and eighteenth centuries. Hoffmann in fact was, like Liszt, a link between German romanticism and classical Italy.

The effect of Hoffmann on Busoni's psychology was very curious. His letters show more and more that he acquired a habit of looking at everything from a Hoffmannesque point of view. Busoni was certainly not a man of morbid temperament, but he took a great delight in literature of the fantastic type. His devotion to *Don Quixote* has already been mentioned. Edgar Allan Poe was another of his favourite authors, and in 1907 he was reading De Quincey's *Murder as a Fine Art*. The mere fact of his being an artist meant that he was a man of excitable imagination and highly-strung nerves; the eventful nature of his life, with its constant change of scene, made further demands on his nervous energy, and it is not surprising that he suffered constantly from dreams and nightmares, especially when he had to sleep a night in the train. After giving his wife an account of one of these nocturnal visions in a letter from Trent in July 1906, he exclaims, 'Oh E. T. A. Hoffmann! can it be that thou still livest in the spirit? and takest possession of me by night? I almost believe so.'

Needless to say, one must not take this apostrophe literally; it meant no more than that Busoni tended to dream about the books which he was reading. But those books, and, in addition, his constant preoccupation with the opera, caused him to note on his travels any picture or episode that might be stored up in memory for operatic treatment. Fantastic experiences left their mark indelibly on his brain; episodes which to other people might have seemed trivial often struck him, both at the moment and in later recollection, as things which could only have occurred in a story of Hoffmann. One day, during the time of his residence in Zurich, he jotted down a number of notes of episodes, people, and things which he wished to remember in view of writing his autobiography. Some of them refer to things which even his nearest relatives and friends are now quite unable to identify and explain; others have been traced with considerable difficulty. Among them is a note of 'Ysaye's *Todtentanz*'. What was Ysaye's 'dance of death'? It was just one of these characteristically 'Hoffmannesque' episodes.

In February 1902 Busoni was playing at Birmingham with Ysaye. As usual, he had spent most of the day by himself; as soon as he arrived at a new place, he would send his luggage on a cab to the hotel and would explore the town alone in search of old books, returning just in time to dress for the concert. When leaving, he would always put off packing until the very last moment. After this concert at Birmingham the party had to proceed elsewhere by a night train. They were given supper by Max Mossel, who was living permanently in the Queen's Hotel; after supper Busoni went to his own room to pack, while Ysaye and the others looked at Max Mossel's collection of old instruments. Among these Ysaye found a little *pochette*—a kit or pocket violin such as was once used by dancing-masters; he tuned it up and began to play the *Chaconne* on it, producing the most unearthly squeaks, to the great amusement of the party.

'Let's go and serenade Busoni!' he said, and went into the passage where Busoni's room was, playing caprices by Paganini and any other virtuoso music that came into his head, the effect of which on this ridiculous instrument was indescribable. Busoni had lain down for a moment to rest; when he first became aware of these strange sounds he thought he was dreaming. They continued; was it a hallucination, he wondered—or the beginning of some terrible nervous disease like Schumann's? He became quite frightened. He looked into the passage; all was dark. The conspirators had retired round the corner. Suddenly the diabolical serenade began again. It was like the ghost of Paganini, Ysaye purposely exaggerating all the worst mannerisms of the typical virtuoso. Summoning up his courage, Busoni determined to pursue the sounds and track them down. The hotel was in darkness; he stumbled from one corridor to another until suddenly he found himself confronted by Ysaye. To Ysaye the whole episode was just a huge joke; he was amazed to find Busoni white with terror. It was a long time before his nerves recovered from the shock, and for years afterwards he could never forget the sight of Ysaye's vast bulk and the grotesque contrast of the tiny little violin. It was a scene from an unwritten tale of Hoffmann.[1]

[1] For the details of this story I am indebted to Mr. Percy Pitt, who was present on the occasion.

N

Reading Busoni's letters one is often reminded of those of Mozart. Mozart, as all musicians know, had a wonderful power of quick and graphic portraiture; it seems as if he saw everybody whom he met as a character out of an opera. Busoni had had a far better education than Mozart, both literary and artistic, and his letters are very much more self-conscious. When he appears to look at life as an opera, however, he does not so often sketch single figures as groups and scenes; he seems to see situations and backgrounds rather than personalities. Another thing which one learns from the letters is that his mind was always looking ahead of the work on which he was actually engaged. Thus during the years in which *Die Brautwahl* was taking shape he had already conceived the idea of an Italian comic opera, which eventually materialized as *Arlecchino*, although the libretto of that opera was written in German, not Italian. Beyond *Arlecchino* he had the vision of the great Italian opera which was often discussed but never actually composed; and beyond that again he was beginning gradually to conceive the germ of *Doctor Faust*. There was a natural sequence of thought in these ideas; the story of *Die Brautwahl* ends in Italy, and like his own hero Busoni, as he grew older, felt more and more drawn towards the land of his birth. When he came to consider plans for a greater work that should be entirely Italian in conception and centre in some majestic figure of Italian history, it was Leonardo da Vinci whom he chose for his hero. And then, as he came to study Leonardo more closely, he began to see Leonardo as 'the Italian Faust'. For reasons which will appear later the opera on Leonardo was abandoned and the story of Faust became the theme of his last creative effort. But Faust had been in his mind for many years previously, even though at that time he may perhaps not have realized himself that Faust was to be the figure in which all the experience of his own life was to be finally summed up.

The first mention of *Die Brautwahl* in the letters occurs at the beginning of June 1906; he had then finished the second act of the libretto, which he was compiling himself. The letter from Trieste in March of that year, quoted in the previous chapter,[1] may very likely have reference to the opera in its suggestion of an end in Italy 'after the *Tarantella*'. Busoni continued working at it on his travels and in London in June—'it goes on by itself and takes me with it'. The visit to Trent in July was apparently in search of architectural suggestions for the church scene; the complete libretto is dated June 1906. By the middle of March 1907 the music of the first act and some other scenes had been sketched; a good deal of work on it was done in July in Berlin, but progress was hampered by the necessity of pianoforte practice and the work on the collected edition of Liszt. There were further interruptions in 1908 owing to the class at Vienna, although he was still working at the opera there in the summer, so that it was not until March 1909 that the orchestration of the first act was finished. By the middle of July the complete score came back from the binder, coinciding with the arrival of a cupboard in the 'Biedermeier' style which he had just acquired. Busoni was a great collector of old furniture, and the 'Biedermeier' cupboard gave him especial pleasure at the moment because of its associations with Albertine, the heroine of his opera.

Albertine—it is time that the story of the opera was told—was the charming daughter of Commissionsrat Voswinkel, a wealthy business man in the Berlin of 1815–20. One afternoon, as they were drinking their coffee in the Tiergarten—the park which lies between Berlin and Charlottenburg as Hyde Park lies between London and Kensington—they made the acquaintance of a young painter called Edmund Lehsen,[2] who naturally fell in love with Albertine at first sight. Edmund enjoyed the protection of a mysterious personage known as Leonhardt, who had apparently lived for several centuries and was

---

[1] p. 153.

[2] Hoffmann drew Edmund Lehsen from the painter Hensel, whose sister married Mendelssohn. *Lehsen* is an anagram of *Hensel*.

possessed of magical powers. That same evening Leonhardt, wandering about the streets of old Berlin, comes across another lover of Albertine, one Thusman, a middle-aged State official, fussy, pedantic, and self-important. He stops him in front of the old Town Hall, much to Thusman's annoyance, as he is in a hurry to get home. It is the night of the equinox, says Leonhardt, and at eleven o'clock on this night there appears a vision of the girl who is to be the year's happiest bride in Berlin. The clock strikes eleven, and to Thusman's amazement the figure of Albertine is seen at a window in the Town Hall tower. Leonhardt at once hurries the unwilling Thusman off to a tavern, where they meet Manasse, an old Jew, who like Leonhardt appears to have survived from remote ages and is also a master of uncanny arts. In the tavern the two wizards wrangle over some ancient quarrel and display their magical powers one against the other until Thusman flies in terror.

Edmund has made so favourable an impression on old Voswinkel that he commissions him to paint a portrait of Albertine. This naturally leads to a love-scene, which is interrupted by the unexpected entrance of Thusman, followed by Voswinkel and Leonhardt. Thusman's indignation is drastically stifled by Leonhardt, who takes one of Edmund's paint-brushes and covers his face with bright green paint. The paint is bewitched and refuses to come off; Thusman in despair attempts to commit suicide by throwing himself into the 'Frogs' Pond' in the Tiergarten, but Leonhardt rescues him and removes the paint as easily as he put it on. Meanwhile another suitor for Albertine has presented himself in the shape of Manasse's nephew, Baron Bensch, a dandified young Jew from Vienna. Leonhardt persuades Voswinkel that the only way for him to decide between the three is to leave the choice to chance. He stages a scene in the manner of the casket scene in the *Merchant of Venice*. Needless to say the casket containing Albertine's portrait is chosen by Edmund. Leonhardt, however, will not allow him to marry

Albertine at once; he must go to Rome and pursue his studies in painting for a time. Before the lucky choice is made he shows Albertine a vision of an Italian church, in which Edmund is painting a copy of some old fresco whilst an invisible chorus sings an ode in Latin to the glory of art.

Hoffmann leaves Edmund in Rome, and hints that once there he very soon forgot all about Albertine.

Many composers seem to have identified themselves in some way with the heroes of their operas, and there is something of the young Busoni in Edmund Lehsen. The fact that Busoni wanted Leonhardt to look like Liszt at the age of fifty[1] points clearly to this. The importance which he attached to the vision of Italy further corroborates it. The vision was one of the first scenes that he sketched, and we have already seen that he paid a visit to Trent in order to refresh his memory of Italian architecture for it.

Trent disappointed him, as Italy only too often did. A letter from Verona (September 9, 1908) shows how intensely and how simultaneously he felt the disappointment, the fascination, and the inspiring force of Italy:

'One could weep tears over the state of this country. The sun shines perpendicularly, blinds and oppresses without cheering one. The people are idle and care-free; inquisitive and unfriendly, they take stock of the passing stranger and criticize him. On the steps of beautiful palaces the lower classes sleep like animals. The shops are shut for most of the day, made fast with shutters and padlocks. The women have neither education nor taste, they look neither to right nor left and betray only ignorance and want of *naïveté*. This town is even more terrifying than Spain, where there is at least a certain *bravura* of deportment.

> O Italia, Italia mia,
> O foste tu men bella,
> o almen più forte! [2]

[1] Letter to Robert Freund, April 22, 1912.
[2] Inaccurately quoted from the famous sonnet of Vincenzo da Filicaia (1642–1707):   [*Continued next page*]

'My room and bed are a zoological garden—I heard every hour strike till five, and this morning counted twenty-six mosquito-bites on my forehead. The heat is still broiling. . . .

'The towns are corpses, but the country lives. Siena is the classic example. And I begin to wonder whether the towns have gone backwards or whether they have stuck fast in the Renaissance: the latter, I almost believe.

'When you look at them closely, these old buildings are no better than ours of to-day. With a few exceptions, the majority are quite plain (*recht simpel*). O heresy! But the modern buildings in Italy are bad. I believe—this is a good idea—that just as in music it is not the "theme" but the co-operation of all threads in the mind of the composer that gives the music its value, so the "charm" of Italy consists in an infinite number of simultaneous conditions.

'And the charm is there. You come out of a theatre at night, as I did this evening, and after the false light of the stage you see the sky outside in its motionless beauty, the houses lit up with a reddish glow from the street-lamps; silhouettes hurry round corners and are lost in unimaginable angles, the moon sits in triumph above fantastic shapes of roofs, the loud singing of the theatre makes you all the more conscious of the silence—all this is really nothing, but here it counts far more than anywhere else.

'Dear Gerda, this evening a great idea has begun to dawn on me. I should like to give this Italy a national opera, as Wagner gave one to Germany, for the Italians have none as yet. I feel that I can do it and that it will be the work of my life. Verdi had no definite aim (*hatte kein Ziel*) and what came after him is harlotry (*Hurerei*). Mozart might have been the classic of Italy, but they hardly know anything of him. I mean to think much about this.'

It is as a stage scene that he describes Verona, and as a

[*Note* 2, *page* 177, *continued*]
        Italia, Italia, o tu, cui feo la sorte
        Dono infelice di bellezza . . .
        Deh, fossi tu men bella, o almen più forte,

.   .   .   .   .   .

(Imitated by Byron in *Childe Harold's Pilgrimage*, Canto iv. 42 :
        Italia! oh Italia! thou who hast
        The fatal gift of beauty . . .
        Oh God! that thou wert in thy nakedness
        Less lovely or more powerful . . .)

scene from Hoffmann. Here is another Hoffmann picture
—this time from Bordeaux (February 16, 1909):

'An old musician whom I had met at Erard's asked me to come
for half an hour to his house. He lives in a little round *place* that
must be over a century old and has only tiny one-storied houses,
clean and quiet, with never a soul nor a carriage to be seen there.
Inside it was very pretty and comfortable. With his wife I found
a young lady of striking beauty and distinguished expression, dressed
in deep mourning. She was a pupil, who was engaged to the old
musician's nephew, a painter in Paris. The old man besought me—
with a mixture of pleading and pride—to hear her sing. She sang
four or five songs of Fauré with a warm deep voice, with great
feeling and taste, and with a very expressive play of features—all
within the bounds of *noblesse*; it was a picture of Donna Anna in
Don Giovanni.

'This little intermezzo leaves a tender and almost fantastic
memory; fantastic, because it seemed to be quite outside our own
time and rather to take one back to the days when the little *place*
was built.'

A lady at Vienna had expressed her astonishment at
Busoni's writing a comic opera. A few months later he
wrote her a letter—one of those letters which he never
posted:

'Your remark that I was too serious a man for a comic opera
set me thinking. It sounded like censure, but as I know you had no
such intention at the moment, I must attribute it to a difference
between our ideas of what seriousness is. I find more seriousness in
humour than in tragic *Spanpanaderln*.[1] To me *Die Meistersinger*
is more serious than *Cavalleria*; *Figaro* more serious than *Le Prophète*; Leporello is the creation of a more serious mind than Fidès;
Don Quixote profounder than the *Kampf um Rom*.[2] Want of humour
is as dangerous a sign in a poet as exaggeration of the pathetic, as
Victor Hugo shows.

'Beethoven is master only of psychological tragedy; the tragedy of
a situation is quite dull with him—the tragedy of a situation which

[1] The word might be translated 'rumbustious bombast'.

[2] *Ein Kampf um Rom*, by Felix Dahn (1876), was a novel much read
in Busoni's younger days; it described the life of ancient Rome with a
great parade of archaeological learning. It was translated into English
as *A Struggle for Rome* (1878).

requires a conflict between at least two persons, whereas psychological tragedy unfolds itself within a single person. Beethoven would have been the man for a higher type of comic opera.

'In a word: The tree of seriousness has humour for its flower. One sees that in Shakespeare and Ibsen.

'So it is a very serious matter indeed if I write a comic opera.'

The opera was interrupted in its progress by many strange events and experiences, and it was also the source of various by-products. The *Aesthetik der Tonkunst* (to begin with the most important of these latter) is not a treatise on aesthetics but a loosely strung collection of observations on all sorts of musical principles. No idea is pursued to any length, but the little book is full of stimulating and provocative thoughts. The difficult technical problem of reducing Hoffmann's tale to an opera libretto stimulated him to further dramatic efforts. One was *Der Mächtige Zauberer*, a libretto after a short story by Gobineau (1905); another (1909) was an original libretto for a musical comedy, *Frau Potiphar*, described by its author as *sehr unanständig*. There were also suggestions for a ballet to trace the life of a man, beginning with his childhood in a scene showing a fair and a puppet-theatre; at the end this scene was to recur, with a later generation of children enjoying themselves while the funeral procession of the man passed across the stage. A still more strange idea was a 'philosophical drama', the scheme of which is obviously derived from Goethe's *Faust*, especially from the Second Part. A man sells his soul to the Devil in exchange for three lives, as an artist, a lover, and a prince of industry; the Devil loses his bargain because in each life the man has given the greatest benefits to mankind. As an artist he plans a perfect town; as a Don Juan he makes all women happy and leaves behind him the happiest memories and the most beautiful progeny; as a millionaire he organizes the perfect town with machinery to do all the unpleasant work, secures peace by buying up the disputed territories and provides handsomely for all his offspring begotten in the previous act. 'He is the new and last Messiah.

Epilogue: the apotheosis of art, love, and human welfare brought about by labour and capital.' This curious project deserves mention because it shows how the idea of Faust was germinating in Busoni's brain. It also shows an interesting conception of Don Juan: not (as generally presented) the man who sacrifices all women to his own lust, but the man who provides all women with the most glorious experience of their lives.

More important than these efforts are the various musical compositions, which are also closely connected with the opera. The set of *Elegies* for pianoforte was finished in December 1907. They are transcripts of fragments from the Pianoforte Concerto, the *Turandot-Suite* and *Die Brautwahl*, preceded by a movement headed 'Nach der Wendung. Recueillement'. It is intended to express the pause for meditation which followed on the change of musical outlook which Busoni had experienced in these recent years. He was beginning to evolve a new musical style, in which the musical anatomist can still trace memories of Berlioz, Liszt, and Brahms; but these memories have by now been absorbed into Busoni's own personality, and take on a new significance from the new type of harmony with which they are associated. The Pianoforte Concerto, the *Comedy* Overture, and the Sonata and Concerto for violin, for all their originality, belonged still to the music of the last century; the *Elegies* have left that music behind and look forward to the future. They are studies in expression rather than in form; it was always Busoni's view that new experiments could be tried best in short 'mood-pictures', and with the exception of the operas, the *Fantasia Contrappuntistica*, and the *Indian Fantasy*, all Busoni's later works are in comparatively short forms, whether written for pianoforte or for orchestra. And the *Recueillement* sets the direction of them all; we shall see the work of Busoni growing steadily more and more meditative, more other-worldly and remote in spirit until the end.

The opera was completed in 1909—it had taken six

years' work—but it was some time before it was put on
the stage. Busoni very much hoped that it might be produced at some Italian theatre. In March 1909 he was in
Milan and consulted Boito about it. Boito was friendly
and seemed to think there would be no difficulty in
finding an Italian publisher and an Italian theatre, but
Busoni saw that it was no use suggesting that he should
make the Italian translation, though he had insisted on the
importance of having the opera well translated. Boito was
no longer young, and was preoccupied with his own affairs,
especially with *Nerone*, of which he had published the
libretto in 1901. Augusto Anzoletti translated *Die Brautwahl*, but to no purpose; in November 1909 Ricordi declined the opera. Busoni talked to Richter about it in
London, but Richter's reply was devastating. 'So was
führt man nicht auf!' (One doesn't perform that sort of
thing). But by the spring of 1910 negotiations were
pending with Hamburg. Busoni was at that time in
America, and could not settle matters in a hurry. 'Hamburg can go on with d'Albert and Puccini for the time
being.' He had no patience with people who treated the
passing moment as if it was as important as eternity; he
was content to wait. The score was not entirely completed
yet, as he wrote in April from Chicago; he expected the
production to take place about November. But by November the score was still far from being finished; in the early
part of 1911 Busoni was in America again and still
wrestling with the third act. 'Two acts of the opera are
finished and printed,' he wrote to Anzoletti from New
York in March. 'I shall want another four months' work
to finish the score. New ideas have arrived and this
blessed score is taking on the character of a ruminant.
Toscanini is interested in it, so it is possible that New
York may see and hear it before Italy.' He left America in
April with the intention of going to Hamburg, but in May
the opera was still unfinished. 'This summer I can think
of nothing but the opera, which threatens to grow old
under the pen.' In July he was expecting to finish it in the

middle of August; in September he went to Italy with his son Benni, and wrote from Varese, 'Die Brautwahl is suffering from constipation, like its composer. . . . *Espère, enfant, demain.*'

The opera was finished at last on October 8, 1911, and in the spring of 1912 it was brought out at Hamburg (April 13). It had a *succès d'estime*, but did not survive for more than three performances. The interpretation was hardly up to Busoni's standards. The orchestra was mediocre, some of the singers unequal to their parts, and the scenery too realistic—Busoni wanted it to be more in the style of a picture-book or a puppet-show. And the mechanism of the Hamburg theatre was inadequate for his effects of magic.

It was hardly an opera for Hamburg, with its stiff and conventional audiences. And it must be admitted that the opera as a whole suffered from the way in which it had been composed. To begin with, Busoni had forgotten that his audience could hardly have so intimate a recollection of the story in every minutest detail as he had himself. His libretto contains hardly a word beyond those which Hoffman actually records as spoken by his characters; the result is that to a reader unfamiliar with the original the libretto is most bewildering. Busoni would have said that that was perfectly reasonable: an opera libretto ought not to be complete without the music. The music suffers from its very wealth of ideas and still more from the elaboration with which they are developed. The first decade of the twentieth century was an age of large orchestras, and Busoni could hardly help falling in with the fashion, however he might jest about Mahler with his 'alto, tenor, and bass hippopotamuses, chromatic serpents, pedal-birds-of-paradise and all the passengers of Noah's ark'. The opera is by no means undramatic, so long as characters are on the stage; it is not that the music holds up the action. Nor can it be said that the parts are ill written for the voices; on the contrary, there is always a strong sense of Italian vocal line, just as in *Falstaff*. But

183

none the less the elaborate orchestration is distracting, and
there are long stretches of instrumental music which do
not at once explain their relationship to the drama. A
typical example is the introduction to the scene in which
Thusman proposes to throw himself into the 'Frogs'
Pond'. Hoffmann in his story describes the Tiergarten at
night, and mentions how Thusman heard the postilion
blowing his horn as he drove along the straight high-road
from Berlin to Charlottenburg which runs through the
middle of the park. This is merely a picturesque adjunct;
the postilion's horn plays no part in the story. Before
the curtain rises on this scene Busoni builds up a long
introduction on the theme of the postilion's horn, intended partly as an ironic parody of German romantic
feeling. Considered merely as a piece of music it is one
of the most beautiful and haunting episodes in the opera.
Dramatically, it leads a listener to suppose that the horn
motive is going to become the point on which the whole
of the next scene will turn; the curtain rises, and the
postilion has vanished for ever—he has never been seen,
and he is not heard again.

Another moment at which the music fails to explain
itself is in the church scene at the end. One hears a
chorus in the distance; if one vaguely catches a Latin
word, one might suppose it to be a church service going on.
The voices have mainly long-held chords; the treatment
of the chorus is similar to that at the end of the Pianoforte
Concerto and the general musical intention is much the
same. As in the Concerto, the chorus 'adds a new register'.
It is beautiful music, but it leaves the spectator utterly
mystified. Yet when one knows both story and opera one
can imagine Busoni seeing himself as Edmund—remembering how in his youth he was almost desiring to
give up music for painting—and feel with him the emotion
of those inward spiritual voices calling him away from the
everyday turmoil of Berlin to the pursuit of that ideal for
which Italy was the symbol.

Busoni was always very much pleased with his characterization of Thusman, and Thusman certainly stands out as a very original comic figure—something of a modern Monostatos, just as Albertine has a reminiscence of Pamina. The opening scene is admirably effective, with a small band on the stage playing the march from Rossini's *Moisè in Egitto*, and a good contrast is provided by the scene in front of the Town Hall, with Thusman's agitation and the romantic vision of Albertine, the music of which exhibits Busoni's new style in singular beauty. The 'hocus-pocus' duel between Leonhardt and Manasse is a brilliant piece of orchestral virtuosity, but perhaps the scenes which haunt the memory the most vividly are those of Albertine at the spinet and Thusman at the 'Frogs' pond'.

The opera was revived at Mannheim in 1913 under Bodanzky and again at Berlin in 1928, but without lasting success. It is too complex, both in its music and in its psychology, to become a really popular work, but it at any rate deserves to be remembered, like *Euryanthe* and *Les Troyens*, among those operas which all musicians admire, and which are still periodically revived and revived again despite all the discouragement which they receive from the hasty-minded and unthinking.

CHAPTER XI

THE SKELETON WITH THE TORCH

VERONA had suggested to Busoni the idea of a national opera that he should write for Italy. It could not be considered seriously until *Die Brautwahl* was finished and presented to the public, but Busoni's active brain was always full of new projects, and it is evident from his letters and note-books that he had a remarkable power of planning out his intentions as a composer. At different periods of his life we can see the emergence of some central idea in his mind, around which work of apparently varied character is grouped, even if, as in the case of the national Italian opera, the central idea never came to fruition. The public, as he once wrote, often likes to associate genius with solitude; but 'I am not a genius', he added, and his ideas came best to him in the life to which he was accustomed—a perpetual wandering from place to place, or a few months of residence in a great city.

Merejkovsky's book on Leonardo da Vinci, which he was reading in the autumn of 1908, suggested a hero for the Italian opera.

'The historical background of the Sforzas is splendid, and one could make Leonardo a central figure of the action, like Hans Sachs in *Die Meistersinger*, and a much more attractive one. The episodes in which he designs the festivities for the Court of the Sforzas and invents various wonderful devices remind one quite of the part which Faust plays at the Court of the Duke of Mantua [*sic*] in the puppet-play, which Goethe also used in the second part of *Faust*. The *milieu*, mainly Milan, seems to me favourable and promising. I shall work at it later on; but *Die Brautwahl* must come first.'

Leonardo and Faust: for a long time their names are intertwined in Busoni's imagination, and for some years to come Leonardo was to seem the substance and Faust the shadow.

During the autumn of 1908 Busoni was playing in England. A provincial tour was always a martyrdom to him. 'The journeys are depressing,' he wrote from Newcastle in November; 'the life here is horrible, grey and joyless. Everything within me is asleep, and I dream restlessly, of unattainable things, great works, beautiful countries—and rest!' A few days later he gave a recital in London. 'It was one of my most successful achievements; for a few hours I was really happy. I feel that a change is not far off.' Another thing which made him happy was that he had been able to introduce young Szigeti to Ysaye and his own pupil George Boyle to Henry Wood, with the result that Szigeti received lessons and Boyle an engagement. Many people in London thought Busoni too much wrapped up in himself because he refused social invitations, but he was always prepared to take endless trouble to help younger musicians in their pursuit of a career. And he had played Liszt's *Legends* for the first time to English provincial audiences. Most people imagined that Busoni played Liszt because Liszt's music was showy. That was not the case; Busoni believed in Liszt as a great composer, and played his works, especially the unfamiliar works, wherever he went, in a spirit of missionary fervour.

January 1909 saw him in Vienna, where he heard bad news of his parents, both of whom were seriously ill; his father's case was considered hopeless. He went over to Trieste for a few days. Ferdinando and Anna lay in the same room, with a screen between their beds, nursed by the nieces Ersilia and Carolina, with the help of a sister of mercy and an 'indescribably ugly' maidservant.

'Papa is like a naughty child of three; if he is left alone for two minutes he screams like a baby. He is horribly pale, with head bowed down and hardly any expression in his eye. The cousins take endless trouble and are beyond price in their care and patience. Mama has got over the danger and Papa drags on. It is sad and undignified to have to say that the most dreadful thing was the list of debts.'

To stay on was impossible. Busoni had to play at Bordeaux and Lyon in February, and after that in Milan and other Italian towns. Bordeaux and Lyon he found attractive; Milan was an unpleasant contrast with its provinciality, its small-mindedness, and its malicious gossip. His only pleasure was in Gerda's daily letters, and in his plans for 'Leonardo'. For the moment he saw his hero as perhaps he saw himself—his every plan for a great work coming to nothing, his friends turning away from him one after another, while Leonardo himself, lonelier and lonelier, attains his highest wisdom and dies with prophecy on his lips.

From Venice on a wet day—'this unspeakably depressing town, which might have been imagined by Edgar Allan Poe'—he sends an amusing comment on Italian social life. One of his young friends had become engaged to be married, and Busoni was invited to meet the prospective father-in-law. ' "You see," he said, "the young man came so often to our house that people began to talk, and so a decision had to be made." That is how marriages are made in Italy.' The general impression of Italy was disappointing. The Anzolettis were the only people with whom he really felt in sympathy. His Italian audiences were incapable of understanding what he had to offer them; he had been too long absent from Italy and they felt his musical outlook to be that of a foreigner. In Rome he sketched a preface to the Italian edition of his *Aesthetik*. He took up the famous dictum of Verdi in 1871—*Torniamo all' antico, e sarà un progresso*.[1]

'That is a pacificist's war-cry. To what "ancient" are we to turn back? Palestrina? Cimarosa? Donizetti? We might put Monteverdi and Caccini on the stage again: an experiment of that sort would certainly be of value. We should not return to the ancient, but we might draw from the ancient sources an art that was new and at the same time Italian. The motto we need is the one we shall always need: "Let us go forward and let us remain Italian." '

Every one of Busoni's greater works is preceded and

[1] 'Let us turn back to the ancient and it will be a step forward.'

surrounded by smaller ones which are studies towards it and comments upon it. In Rome it occurred to him that he might prepare the way for the great Italian opera with a comic opera in one act; his first idea for a subject was some full-blooded old Italian tale of women and monks—the phrase suggests that he had been reading Casti. Perhaps too it was due to the 'shortage of women' in Italy, to which he makes allusion in the same letter. Busoni always loved the society of women, but Italian women were too cloistered and domestic for his taste—they had no intellectual freedom and never talked with any men except their brothers and uncles. Italy, he felt, was in the condition of his own father—dying slowly of old age.

A letter about his elder son's literary education sums up his view on life and letters. Benni was now seventeen, and already keen to educate his father in the appreciation of modern German poetry.

'He ought to read what will spur him on, not what will discourage him. Shakespeare, and whatever is artistically good, provided it be not pessimistic or erotic. *Don Quixote*, Goethe's poetry, Kleist, Gottfried Keller, the *Arabian Nights* (erotic, I admit, but the eroticism is quite secondary to the imaginative element), Cellini's Autobiography, Dickens, Edgar Poe, Ibsen, the German romantic school; but not Lenau, Schopenhauer, *Werther*, or Leopardi—"the suicide-club"[1] of literature.'

He paid another hasty visit to Trieste in March, and found Ferdinando out of bed. Anna was very weak. She gave him her blessing, in her solemn formal Italian way, saying to him, 'I bless you, for all the joy and help that you have brought to your mother; God will reward you for it and all shall be well with you.' The remembrance of visits to Sgambati and Boito brought a sudden sense of the beauty of old age: 'in old age there is the truth, for only the kernel of the whole man remains, and he has not strength to hide it'. On May 12 Ferdinando died. Anna survived him only a few months. She lived to hear Gino Tagliapietra play her the Fantasia after Bach for

[1] These three words in English.

o

pianoforte which Ferruccio wrote in memory of his father, and died on October 3. On October 4, the day on which he heard of her death, Busoni wrote in his diary what might have been her epitaph—'Our Lady of Sighs'.[1]

In August he went to Italy again for a short holiday. Florence, like Milan, irritated him by its provinciality; but early one morning he walked out towards Fiesole to see a villa which he thought of buying. The call to Italy was insistent and irresistible; for some years the thought of the Tuscan villa haunted him. October brought the Festival of Newcastle, at which he conducted his Concerto, the solo part of which was played by Egon Petri.

A new stimulus came to him in January 1910 at Chicago, where he met Bernhard Ziehn and his pupil Wilhelm Middelschulte, two German musicians who had settled there and devoted themselves mainly to the teaching of counterpoint. It was Ziehn who gave him the first idea of how to solve the problem of Bach's unfinished fugue in the *Kunst der Fuge*. Busoni had been very thoroughly trained in counterpoint by Dr. Mayer at Graz; at Chicago he took up the study afresh with all the experience of a mature musician, and the result was the *Fantasia Contrappuntistica*, written in the midst of a concert tour which took him to Cincinnati, Louisville, New Orleans, Atlanta, Dayton (Ohio), and Toledo. From every place he sent Gerda news of the great fugue and its progress, as well as occasional short essays and sketches, most of which are printed in *Von der Einheit der Musik*. He was fascinated by the idea of the south and the Gulf of Mexico, but somewhat disappointed by the reality. None the less, as an Italian, he felt at home there, and was amused at the inability of his tuner—a German-American from New York—to understand the southern mentality. He tried to explain to him that in Europe inventions had been

---

[1] These words in English. Mr. Lawrence Haward has kindly pointed out that they refer to 'Mater Suspiriorum, Our Lady of Sighs', the second sister in De Quincey's *Levana and our Ladies of Sorrow*, appended to the *Suspiria de Profundis* (Masson's Collected Edition, vol. xiii, 1897).

made to meet wants, whereas in America the inventions came first and the wants were found for them; in Europe railways were built to join towns, while in America the railways were built first and the towns afterwards.

There were visits to 'dear old Boston', a place for which Busoni always cherished a sentimental affection, though he had no great love for it when he had to stay there. Everything was just as it was in 1892—the same people with the same remarks and the same ideas, although a new concert public had grown up to the age of Benni. But Boston—'almost a second Vienna!' is a town of inherited traditions, and the elderly waitresses in spectacles made him feel as if he were in a hospital.

Natalie Curtis, one of his old New York pupils, introduced him to the music of the Indians, and he at once seized on the possibilities which it suggested to him. In spite of the exhausting succession of thirty-five recitals, with their attendant journeys as well as their astonishing programmes,[1] he could work simultaneously at the *Fantasia Contrappuntistica*, *Die Brautwahl*, and endless minor projects. At Cambridge (Mass.) he made the acquaintance of Arnold Dolmetsch, and at once determined to make use of the spinet in his opera. He spent his forty-fourth birthday at Colorado Springs, where he found himself without a single acquaintance, and wrote long letters to Gerda and Anzoletti, inspired by the sight of the mountain range which at once recalled the pictures of Segantini, so like the Alps of the Engadine that he felt as if Italy and Anzoletti must be just the other side. 'No year of my life was ever so full as this last one, the richest in work, in experiences and in achievements. And I feel that I am still going upwards. The Good, dear Gerda, is with us.'

He returned to Europe in May, and in August held a *Meisterklasse* at Basle. To the autumn belong the series of pianoforte pieces called *An die Jugend*, the first *Sonatina*

---

[1] A specimen programme: Beethoven, Sonata Op. 53; Brahms, Paganini Variations; Chopin, Sonata in B minor; Liszt, *Erlkönig, Au bord d'une Source*, and sixth Rhapsody.

and the *Berceuse Élegiaque* written in memory of his mother. They continue the change of style which was first manifested in the *Elegies*. *An die Jugend* is not music such as is generally called 'for the young', but it is addressed to those who are young enough to look at music in a new way. Busoni was often sceptical of new experiments in music, and the judgements which he expressed in private were devastatingly severe; but he was still more severe on those who were content to follow the beaten track, however respectfully the outer world might regard them. 'Composing only deserves the name when it busies itself ever with new problems,' he had written (in English) to Louis Gruenberg. A composer who knows that he has nothing new to say has no business to write music at all.

Another tour in America was made in the early part of 1911. It was even more exhausting than that of 1910, and Busoni came more and more to believe that he was being forced to bring profits to his agent rather than to himself. At Boston he heard his *Turandot-Suite* played and also (apparently for the first time) the *Don Quixote* of Richard Strauss. His criticism on it is worth quoting:

'It is a work of great qualities: vulgar in the lyrical parts, uncommonly stimulating in the grotesque, a mixture of peasant *naïveté* and exaggerated cultivation. The form is badly held together, the texture of sound masterly. As a whole it is at any rate one of the most interesting works of our time and one of the richest in invention, perhaps the best work of Strauss. I listened with the greatest attention and at times with the greatest pleasure. No illustration of Don Quixote has ever quite satisfied me, not even this of Strauss; but it is one of the better and cleverer and less literal. I admit frankly that *Turandot* was thrown into the shade by it; luckily I have grown out of *Turandot* myself and can recognize the fact.

'Strauss reminds me of Tiepolo, and I foresee a reaction of a Cornelius-school to follow, but perhaps without the stiffness and awkwardness of the "Nazarenes". Possibly the appearance of Palestrina after the earlier Netherlanders would supply a better parallel for the change which we may expect to see.'

Boston, as usual, roused the devil in him. It was one of the few places in the world about which he himself could be sentimental; he could never forget those first years in America, with their friendships and the new sense of artistic independence which they brought him; above all he could never forget Gerda's devotion in those early days of struggle. But the moment that the Bostonians themselves began to be sentimental about 'the dear old place' (he writes the words in English), he was reminded of Vienna. 'I could spit on everything here, if spitting wasn't so heavily fined.'

'If the European artists were to boycott America, America would be like a great hall in which the electric light had suddenly gone out; they would have to find their way with matches and burn their fingers.'

At New York he met Mahler, who conducted the *Berceuse Élégiaque*. It had some success, but Busoni knew its value. 'The public doesn't like the piece,' he said, 'but it likes me.' Mahler was not quite at home in it; the rattling rhythms of *Turandot* suited his style of conducting better. Toscanini heard it and was delighted with it; Busoni was delighted with Toscanini—'the most intelligent musician I have ever met, except perhaps Richard Strauss'. Another old acquaintance in New York was Dr. von Hase, the head of Breitkopf's, who 'carried a facetious Leipzig atmosphere about with him'.

The tour in the West was a protracted agony. He was constantly ill, and the perpetual travelling made sleep almost impossible; but in spite of pain and fever contracts had to be fulfilled. In March, at Kansas City, he heard of the sudden death of his English pupil O'Neil Phillips in Montreal. He had always regarded Phillips with great affection and wrote often of the pleasure it had been to meet him and talk with him in America. 'Poor Phillips! what a broken life, and how much he must have suffered!' Few tragedies affected Busoni so profoundly. Work was his only consolation. He was gradually developing the

193

idea of utilizing Miss Curtis's Indian themes, but felt that he must begin with small experiments. It would be ridiculous, he said, to follow Dvořák's example and write a symphony on Indian tunes to the Leipzig pattern. He conceived a series of scenes on some quite primitive scheme—'Mother Son Bride War Peace'—and *ohne Raffinement* (without too much ingenuity or over-elaboration). 'It is already the height of ingenuity to overhear such things rightly and then reproduce them.' His book for the moment was *The New Machiavelli* (H. G. Wells), and he quotes from it: 'I feel one [we] might do so many things, and everything that calls one, calls one away from something else.' Kansas City had yet another inspiration to give him; it was there that he heard of a villa for sale near Settignano. It was called Monte Sole—the very name was a dream of Tuscany and the sun.

By the middle of March he was at Los Angeles, becoming daily more and more irritated over the conduct of his agent; he was in that state of nervous exhaustion when even a kindly action is apt to cause annoyance.

'Artists have just as much to do with the public as religion with the church. I regard religion as something inward and personal, like talent; the church is an "institution", ostensibly for the average mass, really for the benefit of the priests.

'Telegram from my agent: "Congratulations on success in Los Angeles signifies much for the future." My God! If this greasy devil could only keep quiet; but he must be telegraphing. Am I a person who seeks a future in California? But perhaps he means California's future—I wish it all prosperity.'

He quotes Wells again: 'Most of the good men we know are not really doing the very best work of their gifts; nearly all are a little adapted, most are shockingly adapted to some second-best use.' The agent suggested an extension of the tour to Honolulu. 'It is a very interesting trip.' Busoni's wrath boiled over. 'It is all a nightmare; I am dispatched like a parcel, ill and without news.'

At San Francisco he fell into the hands of the local German group of musicians.

'They hold the traditions high on the Pacific Ocean, these con-scientious folk! To think what a mischief that rat-hole of a Leipzig can spread! Oh these Germans! Oh these Bismarck-columns and fairy woods, with beer and male-voice part-songs thrown in! I think that expresses the whole of it.'

There was an Italian group at San Francisco too, who also struck the patriotic note and made a great nationalist noise. In one of his letters he describes the scenery; he ends with the cynical observation that people probably admire nature so enthusiastically because they know that it has not been made by some other, and more gifted, man.

At last the tour came to an end. Just before his birthday (April 1) he wrote to Gerda: 'It is with a grave joy that I think of my home-coming. I feel that my most important period is beginning, and that it is the definitive one.'

After a visit to London in March 1912 came the pro-duction of *Die Brautwahl* at Hamburg in April. Towards the end of April Busoni took Benni with him to Italy, leaving him to stay for a while with Emilio Anzoletti at Bergamo. Busoni's impressions of Italy were no more favourable than before, except for one which stood out vividly in his memory for years to come. At Bologna he saw a performance of an old mask comedy, *L'Inutile Precauzione* (1692), acted by Arnaldo Rossi's 'Compagnia delle Maschere', which was reviving the repertory of the Italian actors in Paris in the seventeenth century. An actor named Picello[1] took the part of Harlequin, and when he appeared in the disguise of a captain Busoni was at once reminded of Callot's etchings. He described him in a letter as 'un Arlecchino di stile tale, che teneva del monu-mentale' (a Harlequin of such style as to seem almost monumental); he drew a sketch of him in pen and ink. The seed of yet another opera was sown in his brain.

Leonardo had been laid aside for the time being in favour of Faust. In the prologue which he eventually wrote for *Doctor Faust* Busoni alludes to his having once thought of composing an opera on Don Juan, and having

[1] Information kindly supplied by Dr. Francesco Vatielli.

195

immediately discarded it because he knew that it would
be impossible to compete with Mozart. His veneration
for Goethe made him equally modest as regards taking
Goethe's drama as the basis for an opera. An English
friend, acting on a suggestion thrown out in conversation,
sent him the plays of Marlowe. 'They will encourage me',
Busoni wrote in reply (May 20), 'to take up the problem
of Faust and perhaps to finish what will probably be my
principal work. Meanwhile my thoughts are turning towards another opera, on which I mean to set to work this
summer.' He had returned the day before from Italy,
after having 'at last', as he notes himself, obtained success
as a pianist in Rome.

What was the opera to which he referred? In January
he had come across a new idea, derived from Villiers de
l'Isle-Adam, a libretto with the title of *The Secret* (*Das
Geheimnis*), and he at once decided that for the present it
was to remain a secret. In the course of the summer yet
another aspect of Faust was brought to his notice. He was
invited to write incidental music for Frank Wedekind's
Franziska—twelve short numbers for an orchestra of
twenty. At first the suggestion attracted him, and he began
to plan the music out. These pieces for small orchestra
would be an interesting and not too laborious task; the
production would offer all the advantages of a distinguished
'first night' and might be of help to his further theatrical
career. On the other hand, he feared—knowing the ways of
the theatre—that he might have all his trouble for nothing.
In any case he might find himself entangled in the Wedekind circle, for which he had no great desire, and he would
be taking the Faust idea away from himself, for Wedekind's
Franziska is, as he writes himself, a parody of Goethe's
Faust. He decided to refuse the offer. It was more urgent
to revise *Die Brautwahl* for performances at Mannheim,
and to make a concert Suite out of some of the numbers.

The negotiations with Wedekind seem to have taken
him to a theatrical café in the Nollendorfplatz. One day
the head waiter told him that the bandmaster of the café

intended to play one of his works there. He could not
remember the title, but knew that on the cover there was
a picture of a woman at a cradle. 'Dear Gerda, if that
happens when I am there I shall meet with Meyrinck's
"mauve death"; I shall turn into mauve gelatine and be
served up as wine jelly to the first Jewess who comes in.'

Negotiations with Karl Vollmoeller, who was acting
for Wedekind, do not seem to have proceeded very easily.
Even Gerda hinted that Ferruccio had been somewhat
capricious. He defended himself to her on the plea that
if he undertook any work on a large scale he would have
to lay aside 'the secret' on which his whole mind was set.
The 'secret' was not the opera on the Faust legend itself,
but that on *The Secret*, first mentioned in January. Suddenly he veered round again to Leonardo. In August 1912
he paid a visit to Paris, where he met Gabriele d'Annunzio.
The immediate object of his visit to Paris was an idea—
never mentioned previously—of buying a small property
in the neighbourhood of Vincennes. He was amused at
a comment of Widor, who betrayed unconsciously the
mentality of *la France fonctionnaire*: 'When you acquire
a property you will be counted as one of our own people.'
The cost of the house was prohibitive, and the idea came
to nothing.

One evening he dined at the Hôtel Meurice with Vollmoeller and d'Annunzio. The party was all very elegant,
rather to Busoni's embarrassment, and there was a lovely
lady there with a sumptuous Spanish title which 'sounded
like a whole play of Calderon'. Both Vollmoeller and
d'Annunzio paid him compliments on his literary learning. 'I know you are a classical scholar,' said the poet;
Busoni was evidently gratified, but at the same time
sceptical. He found his host 'charming, a quick and lively
thinker, a fascinating *raconteur*—a little "scented" and
affected, yet sometimes shy and confused'. D'Annunzio
talked of a new work which he was writing for Ida Rubinstein and half suggested that Busoni should compose
music for it. Busoni thought the idea attractive, but

Vollmoeller warned him that it would be waste of labour: 'D'Annunzio thinks a great deal of success—hence his unlimited respect for Wagner and even for Puccini!' None the less, Busoni left Paris with the feeling that he had carried his plan a step farther. Cynical as he might appear to be in his talk, he could never bring himself to believe that other great artists might have less disinterested ideals of art than himself.

November brought a new and strange experience, a tour in Russia, where Busoni—not having played there for some years—was received like a prince. At Moscow he noted with delight that all the best architecture was Italian. The Kremlin was built by Italians, the church in it modelled on St. Mark's at Venice; the theatre and the 'Halls of the Nobility' were the work of Italian architects too. There was a quiet interval spent at Riga, where he was charmed by the resemblance to Helsingfors and the quaint architecture of the old town, which reminded him of the Town Hall scene in *Die Brautwahl*. But he soon found himself uncomfortable; he was perpetually tied to a small group of people who seemed to have come out of a play by Strindberg—outwardly well-behaved but inwardly ravaged by frustrated ambitions and desires. Yet Riga as a whole was a pleasant interlude.

'I often love such little towns with quiet church squares, crooked lanes and old buildings—but I come to a queer conclusion: all these things please me more as memories. Memory is a great artist in her neglect of petty details. She gives us an artistic picture of experience—the sketch of genius; one should learn composition from her. I remember how surprised Benni was when I said to him at Basle—"that will be a beautiful memory". I see now what I then hit upon unconsciously.'

In January 1913 *Turandot* (as a play with music) was given at the St. James's Theatre in London. Busoni saw two acts and fled, consoling himself with *Le Rouet d'Omphale* at Queen's Hall. His delight in the music of Saint-Saëns never failed. Mahler's seventh symphony, which he also heard in London, was 'a small satisfaction and a

great disappointment'. *Turandot* opened Busoni's eyes to
the musicianship of the average English theatre-manager.
'An orchestra of about twenty, that played out of tune;
some bits played four or five times over, other parts cut;
the whole thing in the style of a music-hall. And as there
was then too little music for the producer, pieces by Saint-
Saëns and Rimsky-Korsakov shoved in! Imagine!'[1] Oskar
Fried conducted; Vollmoeller was also in London. To
hear those two talk about money-making, said Busoni, was
like a scene from Molière. 'What do you think about
Turandot', he wrote to Gerda, 'as an opera, in Italian of
course, to the words of Gozzi?' He signs himself, 'Your
Ferruccio, who finds himself at a moment of indecision.'

He was in bad health and exhausted with work; he
found rest and comfort at Maud Allan's house in Regent's
Park, where he remained inaccessible to all but intimate
friends. His agent was told to keep his address a secret,
and this caused some difficulty with the Philharmonic
Society, which had proposed to perform a work of his.
Busoni offered them the *Fantasia Contrappuntistica*, which
had been orchestrated for him by Stock of Chicago. The
Fantasia was composed, as Busoni stated openly in print,
simply as a piece of music—without any consideration
for the instrument on which it was to be played. Busoni
himself published it as a pianoforte solo, in which form it
is hardly playable, and as a duet for two pianofortes.
Middelschulte arranged it for the organ and Stock for
orchestra. The Philharmonic directors were quite ignorant
of all this, and Busoni never thought it necessary to en-
lighten them.

At the rehearsal he found that Stock's orchestration
was not always satisfactory, and began suggesting alterations. The directors present were naturally somewhat
surprised to note, first, that Busoni had had his work
orchestrated for him by some one else, and secondly, that
he seemed never to have seen the score himself until
the rehearsal. On the other hand, one can quite well

[1] This last word in English.

understand Busoni's own point of view. In composing the Fantasia he had concentrated his attention on counterpoint and construction; for this particular work orchestral colour was of little importance. That was no doubt the reason why he had allowed Stock to orchestrate it. The Philharmonic concert offered a convenient occasion for 'trying it out'; he knew how quick and intelligent the London players were at seizing anything new, for Henry Wood had once allowed him half an hour at a rehearsal to try out the score of the *Berceuse Élégiaque*. The concealment of his London address made it impossible for the directors to see the score beforehand so as to judge of its length and difficulty, and the time that it might require for rehearsal. As it was the Fantasia had to be withdrawn at the last moment, for it was impossible to get the proposed alterations copied into the parts in time. Busoni wrote an injured but very courteous letter to Sir Alexander Mackenzie, who naturally did everything he could to smooth matters over. The directors asked Busoni to substitute some other work of his own which was printed and could be rehearsed in time, but Busoni preferred to retire from the conflict altogether.[1] The secretary, William Wallace, was very much puzzled by the fact that Busoni's letter to Mackenzie bore the postmark 'Holloway'. If he had known Busoni better he would have guessed that he posted it on one of his solitary rambles in unfamiliar (and to most people unattractive) quarters; and that before posting it he had taken some time to think over the question of whether it would be advisable to post it at all. It was a habit of Busoni to write letters in order to relieve his own feelings; it was fortunate that he also had the habit of not always putting them into a letter-box.

Walking one day in the Strand a poster caught his eye; it advertised a film, the subject of which was 'Dante's Hell'. At once there flashed across Busoni's brain the idea of an opera on Dante. Dante, whose poetry was the possession of all Italians of all classes, far more familiar

[1] Information kindly supplied by Mr. William Wallace.

indeed than the *Nibelungenlied* to Germans, would provide the ideal material for the great Italian national opera. It should open with Dante dreaming on the famous stone in the Piazza della Signoria: a picture of medieval Florentine life, with Beatrice passing across the stage. Then should follow about six scenes taken from the *Divina Commedia*: Ugolino, Paolo and Francesca, and other episodes with more opportunity for a massed stage. He would not stop at Hell, like the film on the poster, but at the same time he felt unequal to the presentation of Paradise. The opera should end at the meeting with Beatrice and their ascent to Heaven. 'And of course, *in Italiano*. There, that is at any rate an anchorage for a longish time.'

By February he had veered round to Leonardo again, influenced by the good advice of his wife. 'Moi, je raisonne trop.' He had passed the last three months and more in a state of indecision, unable to work, and in consequence more than ever liable to nervous irritation; yet he was determined, as always, to regard these periods of interruption as periods of subconscious ripening. To become clear about himself—that is a phrase which recurs over and over again in his letters: to know, quite definitely, what he wanted to do and how he was to do it—that was the perpetual ideal of his life.

March took him back to England. To encourage Maud Allan, who was rather depressed at the moment, he sketched a ballet for her—a sort of dance of death, ending with a scene before an altar with angels and Death himself. The music was apparently to be patched up from various sources—'but I have no stuff for the temple scene: that is what composers call oratorio (*it's English, you know*).'[1]

He had written to d'Annunzio to suggest another meeting, but owing to his concert tour in Italy during April and May it could not take place until June. D'Annunzio welcomed him one morning in a Japanese kimono—a good

[1] These four words in English.

deal aged, and looking like Mephistopheles receiving the Student in Goethe's *Faust*. Leonardo happened to be the man of the moment. The famous 'Gioconda' had been mysteriously stolen from the Louvre. The poet revealed the secret at which the police and the newspapers of all the whole world were guessing in vain.

'I am just writing a book now,' he told Busoni, '*L'homme qui a volé la Gioconda*: for the Gioconda is in my possession, and I shall send her back to the Louvre as soon as the book is published. The man who stole the Gioconda is descended from a family of mystical painters going back for six hundred years. He brought the picture to me at Arcachon.'

Busoni notes that the police had already traced the thief to a Paris–Bordeaux train.

'So many centuries of adoration and love', the poet continued, 'had accumulated in this figure, that at last the passion of many thousands of men had communicated its own vitality to the picture. To be sure, it was still necessary that one man should be slain, that the immediate heart's blood should become hers. The mystic action was performed, and I lived for four days with the Gioconda. My power did not suffice to hold her for longer, and she vanished. On the canvas there remains only the landscape, and in the landscape there remains only her smile. The gesture of her smile has been impressed upon it, but the figure has disappeared. In this state the Louvre will receive the picture back again.'

They talked of Leonardo as a subject for an opera. The poet was at first little in favour of it. He felt shy of putting his own words into Leonardo's mouth, as he might hesitate to give words to Christ or Napoleon. Leonardo was no figure for the stage, on account of his lack of passion and feeling—he was 'a skeleton bearing a burning torch instead of a head'. Busoni's phrase 'an Italian Faust' suggested more possibilities—not the historical Leonardo but a symbolical one: the mystical element dominating a series of pictures without dramatic connexion. D'Annunzio seemed to be completely won over, and they talked of working together at Arcachon.

At the hotel Busoni met Marinetti and Boccioni, who

were making energetic propaganda for 'futurism'. Futurism was in those days quite new; and Busoni saw futurist sculpture for the first time and discussed its principles with Boccioni. 'Compared to *this* sort of art and the incarnation of Monna Lisa as Gabriele's mistress, *Pierrot Lunaire* is mere tepid lemonade!' One evening he went to the Châtelet to see Ida Rubinstein in *La Pisanella*, with music by 'Ildebrando da Parma' (i.e. Ildebrando Pizzetti). After two acts he came away. He was bored by Pizzetti's music, bored by the stage with its Russian scenery, with the play's elaborate symbolism of colours and scents, irritated with the 'neighing' sound of conventional French declamation, and infuriated by the audience consisting mostly of Russian women, one of whom suddenly addressed him as 'Monsieur Chaliapine'.

He found Paris exhausting and bewildering; it was full of people who wanted to see him for some private interest of their own, and full of experiences that interested him but left him cold. 'How old-fashioned and over-ripe this Paris is! it unites all interests and is openly indifferent to everything. I expect it is really the right place for d'Annunzio, as it was for Oscar Wilde and Meyerbeer.' He had more conversations with d'Annunzio, but could never feel quite certain of him. He noticed in his room a row of books on Cyprus, old and new. Each book had one or two strips of paper sticking out of it; he divined at once how the poet had a quick eye for the passages which he could utilize for his own work (*La Pisanella*). 'He does not really know things; he uses learning when he wants it. After all, he is an artist, not a researcher.'

He began to see through d'Annunzio, and the poet soon saw that he was seen through. He remarked that he had only two more years to live—'in just the same tone in which he said he had lived four days with the Gioconda'. A Russian lady present took him quite seriously; Busoni laughed aloud. D'Annunzio, as always when he was seen through, smiled disarmingly and said

'Yes, but it really is so.' He was anxious to hear some of Busoni's compositions, and this immediately made Busoni suspicious. Was he to be put through an examination? D'Annunzio spoke of Tito Ricordi, who was to arrive in a day or two. The whole question of their collaboration would depend on Ricordi's approval, it seemed. Busoni began to feel as if he had been offered a glass of poisoned wine. If only d'Annunzio would begin to write the libretto, he felt, he was convinced that everything would develop as he desired; but he was worried and confused both by d'Annunzio's mystifications and by his sense of the practical. Yet after all, as d'Annunzio had said himself—'why should we toil and trouble for three or four years and then find that nothing could be done with the work when it was finished?' Busoni had half a mind to go away from Paris at once and leave the whole business as it was. His last letter from Paris, written on June 27, ends by saying that he would think it over and make his decision in the evening. A few days later he was back in Berlin. The skeleton with the torch lit his way no more.

CHAPTER XII

'BONONIA DOCET'

ITALY was hardly ready to accept the great Italian opera of Busoni's dreams, but during the last few years his name had become more familiar to Italian musicians, and he had perhaps more friends and admirers in his own country than he himself imagined. The directorship of the Liceo Rossini at Bologna fell vacant in 1912 on the retirement of Enrico Bossi, and after some months of waiting it was offered to Busoni.

Anzoletti had been considering the possibility of his accepting the post as early as August 1912; in April and May 1913 Busoni went to Italy to give a series of concerts at Milan, Bologna, and other towns. The success of these concerts was remarkable, and no doubt much of it was due to the helpful influence of Anzoletti. Busoni began to feel more confident of his reception in Italy. He came to a preliminary agreement with the authorities at Bologna in April, and it was formally confirmed by the town council in July. He was to begin work at Bologna in October.

At Parma in May there was an amusing incident which put him in a good humour. The concert-hall was an old one, dating from the days of Marie Louise and exquisitely decorated in the Empire style. Just before it began an old lady called to see Busoni; she had white hair and a black bonnet adorned with strings that hung down below her waist. She had been a great friend of his mother and remembered him as a little boy. Busoni became rather bewildered and worried as she poured out her endless reminiscences, but listened to her with his invariable courtesy until the concert began. She took a seat in the middle of the front row. Busoni, seated at the pianoforte, waited, as he always did, for silence; but the longer he waited, the more restless the audience seemed to become. Finally the old lady stood up, leant forward towards him and said very sweetly, 'Sono le sedie!' (it 's the chairs!)

205

P

The chairs were of the same period as the room, and a century of concerts had made it impossible to sit on them without a great deal of creaking and cracking. The old lady had that delicate but penetratingly clear utterance characteristic of Italian gentlewomen of her generation, and her words were at once audible all over the room; the audience burst into a roar of laughter, in which Busoni himself could not help joining. Trivial as the episode may seem, it was in the combination of its details essentially Italian; it could have happened nowhere but in Italy.

The non-Italian reader may find it strange that Busoni should have been prepared to sacrifice his activities in Berlin and northern Europe in order to become director of a provincial school of music in Italy. It could hardly have been the stipend that attracted him. Devotion to Italy was his one and only motive. Throughout his wandering life he had persistently dreamed of an ideal and perhaps imaginary Italy. He began to dream of an ideal and equally imaginary Bologna. Bologna had indeed as distinguished a musical tradition as any Italian city. In the seventeenth century the passion for music in Bologna had been so extravagant that popes and cardinals fulminated against it in vain. The most famous of all Italian musical academies is the Accademia Filarmonica of Bologna, founded in 1666; Mozart was admitted to membership of it at the age of fourteen and Busoni himself when he was one year older. Mozart was prepared for his examination by Padre Giovanni Battista Martini of Bologna, the most learned contrapuntist and musical historian of his time. From his monastery at Bologna Martini corresponded with musicians of eminence all over Europe, and his large library and collection of musical portraits are now the treasured possession of the Liceo Rossini.

The Liceo Rossini, now officially called Liceo G. B. Martini, was founded in 1804 as a sort of municipal university of music. Its principal activity in those days was the training of singers, for since the seventeenth century Bologna had been the chief centre of operatic study, especially for women, as we can see from Marcello's satire *Il Teatro alla Moda*, in which the prima donna (as well as her stage mother) talks the Bolognese dialect as a matter of course. In 1804 the only other schools of music in Italy were the historic Conservatorii of Naples and the Ospedali of Venice (for women only), dating from the sixteenth century. Outside Italy there was the Paris Conservatoire, founded in 1795—the oldest non-Italian school of music. The foundation of the Liceo at Bologna was therefore an event of considerable importance in the history of musical education.[1]

The first Director of the Liceo was Martini's favourite pupil and confessor Padre Stanislao Mattei (1750–1825), who had to renounce holy orders to accept the post. Rossini and Donizetti were among his pupils. Rossini was 'Councillor' of the Liceo from 1839 to 1861; his residence in Bologna conferred great musical distinction on the town, and this distinction was well maintained throughout the nineteenth century. It was Bologna that was chosen by Verdi as the appropriate site for the sole performances of that joint *Requiem* which he invited the Italian composers to write in collaboration with himself in memory of Rossini. The Teatro Comunale of Bologna, built by Bibbiena in 1763 and burnt down in 1931, was the first Italian opera-house to open its doors to the music of Wagner; *Lohengrin* was performed there in 1871. In 1875 Bologna accorded a decisive success to Boito's *Mefistofele*, which had been damned by Milan in 1868. The Liceo reached its highest level under the directorship of Giuseppe Martucci (1886–1909), who held much the same position in Italian music as his friend Stanford did in that of England.

As a centre of operatic industry Bologna, once pre-eminent, had long yielded its position to Naples and

[1] It may be useful to give the dates of foundation of the chief remaining Schools of music: Milan 1807, Prague 1811, Brussels 1813, Florence 1814, Vienna 1821, London (Royal Academy) 1823, Liége 1827, Genoa 1829, Madrid 1830, Budapest 1834, and Leipzig 1843.

Milan. Bologna, in music as in literature and science, stood for learning. For centuries the life of the town had been dominated by its ancient and famous university, and the university had set an intellectual standard to which music, like the other arts, was made to conform. At the beginning of the present century Bologna was a highly prosperous provincial town, and one of its chief charms was that it was thoroughly Italian. Tourists passed it by in an age that despised the pictures of Guido Reni and the Caracci; its architecture was considered quaint rather than imposing. It was thus delightfully free from either the commercialism of Milan or the cosmopolitanism of Florence and Rome. The university still impressed its character on the town, and the presence of Carducci as professor of Italian literature gave it a unique distinction. It is not surprising that Busoni should have imagined Bologna, of all Italian cities, to afford him that opportunity which he had so long sought for regenerating the musical life of his own country.

Yet it was difficult to tear himself away from Berlin. He had moved into a new flat in the Victoria Luise Platz, where he had space for his ever-increasing library and his collection of old furniture and pictures, as well as a large music-room with two grand pianofortes. There was a studio above, to which he could retire when he wished to be completely alone and devote himself to composition. The house presented a strange jumble of incongruous objects, and one saw how his taste had altered as years passed on; but the rooms were comfortable and well adapted for entertaining, and the very incongruity of the decorations suggested wide artistic sympathies, and a mind always open to appreciate new forms of art. Busoni became more and more attached to this flat, and especially to his library; he was an ardent collector of old books, although he was never able to afford the purchase of rarities. The happiest period of the year for him was always the summer spent in Berlin, where he could work out his unending series of projected compositions.

Bologna attracted him, but he accepted the post with a certain amount of his habitual scepticism. He had no intention of giving up the flat in Berlin. He meant to spend his summers there as before. Needless to say he insisted on a certain freedom to travel and give concerts. For so many years he had dreamed of a villa in Italy; now that the moment came when he might take a house there and establish himself permanently, he hesitated.

In a letter to Egon Petri he had summed up his impressions of Italy after his concert tour in the spring of 1912.

'Has this Italy at last come to its last end, or is there to be a new beginning? There is a very high intelligence and culture among the *élite*, but the proportion of *imbecilli*, of indifference and ignorance is terrifying. Then there is the Americanism of the business and sporting world, from which the optimists expect new strength. A confused ideal of "smart business man"[1] and "lawn-tennis parties"[1] obliterates what was characteristically Italian; and what has become of painting and sculpture, the most legitimate offspring of the country?

'And a new disease has appeared: the regular visits of second-rate German conductors with "classical" orchestral concerts. The Italians are becoming "educated" and consequently boring, like women who attempt intellectual conversation. The great man, Toscanini, spends his winters in the north and his summers in the south—of America. If he did his damned duty and stayed at home, people would put every difficulty in his way; that is unfortunately in the blood of all Italians, owing to their little narrow towns—it is the inheritance of a past that is all too rich in tales of treachery.'

The summer months were spent as usual in Berlin, where he devoted himself chiefly to the composition of the *Indian Fantasy* for pianoforte and orchestra. Its progress was slow and difficult. Another change was gradually taking place in his musical outlook. Ever since his meeting with Ziehn and Middelschulte at Chicago he had become more and more concentrated on counterpoint as a medium of expression. But although the *Fantasia Contrappuntistica* was conceived as music independent of

---

[1] These words in English.

instruments it was far from being merely an exercise in ingenuity. It was intended above all things to be the expression of emotion no less intense than that which prompted the composition of the *Berceuse Élégiaque* in memory of his mother, although Busoni never seems to have worked on the deliberately pictorial principles of Liszt. And during the years in which he was composing and revising the Fantasia he was also planning his edition of the second book of the *Wohltemperiertes Clavier*. The first book had emphasized the pianistic element in Bach's work; the second was to be a study of his technique as a composer. It was to stand towards the first as the second part of Goethe's *Faust* to the first, and it was a work which he could entrust to no one else, not even to Egon Petri, because it might involve a complete reversal of values; the good principle of the first book might have to be presented as the evil principle in the second, just as the moral values are reversed in the two acts of *The Magic Flute*.

We see here something of the way in which Busoni's mind worked. He was perpetually seeking—and quite consciously and deliberately seeking—to penetrate the ultimate mystery of all music. He knew from quite an early age that this mystery was never to be solved by what might be called Dionysiac inspiration, but only by the steady progress of trained intuition based on clear thinking and accurate scholarship. But he knew also that there was something beyond even scholarship. A word which frequently occurs in his writings about music is *sich auflösen*—to melt or dissolve. He would have agreed with the poet that the ultimate function of music is to

> Dissolve me into ecstasies
> And bring all Heaven before mine eyes;

but the process of solution into a transparent and saturated liquid could not take place unless the substance had previously existed in all the clarity and precision of perfect crystallization.

The *Berceuse*, the *Gesang vom Reigen der Geister*, and the

Nocturne Symphonique had already illustrated this *Auflösung* from a more harmonic than contrapuntal point of view. The *Indian Rhapsody* carries the principle still farther. Busoni's strange harmonies arise out of the interplay of melodic parts. His orchestration is tenuous and translucent; he had begun to discover the weaknesses of Wagner's scores and had a horror of mere filling up for the sake of sonority. He tended more and more to treat the orchestra as an assemblage of solo players, and some of these works are written for small and unusual combinations of instruments. In one of his letters to Egon Petri he speaks of the aversion which he feels towards scoring *tutti* passages; these loud outbursts were dynamically necessary at times, but he felt that they were always interruptions to the natural flow of his thought in composing for orchestra.

The more he became immersed in composition the more he hated playing the pianoforte in public. It was not that he hated the instrument; he was keenly interested in the development of his technique as a means to the expression of new ideas, but he felt that there was something shameful in appearing before a public which obviously did not understand his outlook. Success pleased him, all the more as it was by no means assured; yet what interested him more was to observe his own performance critically as he played. He had written to Petri from London in October 1912:

'This week was very exhausting; if I could only rid myself of this feeling of shame at playing in public! I think my playing has become different again. I observed myself carefully the first evening and collected (my own) criticism. Something is still wanting. My Violin Sonata begins to please people—Kreisler, for example.[1] For me it is dying (*mir stirbt sie ab*). It has a few good moments of feeling and is honest work. Life becomes shorter and shorter—the goal ever farther off; what an inhuman task! *Enfin*, if one can only see that——'

The appointment to Bologna offered the chance of beginning a new life. A new beginning—*Neuer Anfang*—

---

[1] Kreisler played Busoni's Violin Sonata in E minor with him in London in October 1912.

was an ideal that constantly haunted him. He was conscious of passing through a period of uncertainty and hesitation. To accept Bologna meant at least that a definite decision would be made. It would be a new experience to be director of a historic school of music, and he had indeed sometimes regretted that he had never before considered a position of the kind. He thought the whole matter out carefully in relation to his own artistic development. The moment had come when he needed Italy as a background to his own public position, and as a source of inspiration for the great Italian opera which he was still determined to compose.

The town council of Bologna was ready to make a very liberal-minded agreement. Busoni's appointment was to be for life, but at the same time he was free to resign after the first year if he were not satisfied. The stipend offered was higher than the previous director's, though from a German point of view hardly more than nominal. On the other hand, Busoni was to be relieved of all administrative and business duties, and he was not required to give regular teaching. Bologna desired his presence as a leader of musical life, and was apparently ready to carry out his projects; it seemed as if he would be able to make Bologna once more a great European musical centre.

Busoni left Berlin in September, intending to make a leisurely journey to Bologna. Almost every other day he wrote to Gerda. His first stop was at Heidelberg; he paid a visit to Bodanzky at Mannheim, and the next day proceeded southwards. Southwards: the very word, he wrote, made one a poet! Bodanzky suggested that he should compose new music to *Peer Gynt*; Busoni noted with keen interest the progress of a younger mind. Bodanzky had in earlier years been whole-heartedly devoted to Wagner; now he was all enthusiasm for *Les Huguenots*. Busoni began to envy the new generation who had not had to bear the burden of Wagner throughout most of their lives. He stopped again at Basle, to meet Benni, who brought a ray of sunlight into that dismal and depressing city; Basle, he thought, was one of those places that one should preserve as a memory and never visit a second time. He went on by Geneva to Milan, where he was alone; the only friend that he saw was Boito driving past in a cab. He began to feel nervous about Bologna—'if there were only one person there who really knew me and with whom I could speak my mind in real confidence!' He went on to Bergamo, to stay with the two Anzolettis in their mysterious old house in the upper town. Emilio managed a factory; Augusto was an orthopaedic surgeon. There was no pianoforte in the house, and what was more strange to Busoni's mind, there were no women; how could one go on living in this picturesque but remote little place, seeing nobody, with every day exactly like every other day? Bergamo reminded him of a toy theatre which he had possessed as a child; it had a magnificent scene representing a town, but it had always made him feel a little melancholy—it was a very fine town, but there were no people in it. His nervousness about Bologna increased; it was like stage fright before an important concert.

'I have come to the monstrous conclusion', he wrote to Gerda, 'that the Italians of to-day have no feeling for art. They read, hear and see badly; they build in an ugly style and furnish their houses without taste. They are ignorant in all these things, or under bad influences; they draw a thick line between what is historic and what is of the present. At bottom (history shows it) they are merchants and politicians; like the Americans they are aggressive and claim the *right of opinion*,[1] which is simply disrespectful bad manners.'

It was a grey Sunday; they had come back to the house at eight in the evening and Busoni had slept badly; Italy was a depressing country.

By the end of September he was at Bologna, living for the time being at the Hôtel d'Italie (Baglioni). The brothers Anzoletti had come to spend a few days with him. Through empty and sun-baked streets they walked to the old monastery which houses the Liceo. At the door the

[1] In English.

porter met them; he had known Busoni thirty years before and remembered him at once.

'L'ho conosciuto giovanetto, ora è divenuto tanto grande!'

His wife, fat and cheerful, with white hair and a pronounced moustache, opened her arms to welcome him.

'Ben venuto, signor Direttore, Lei che è amato da tutti!'[1]

Within the Liceo, as in the silent square outside, everything spoke of the past. In the great hall and in the lofty corridor there hung the portraits of Padre Martini's musical friends—John Christian Bach painted by Gainsborough, Dr. Burney by Reynolds, and many others, all rather neglected, dusty and blackened with age. In the library were Padre Martini's books and music—one can hardly go in there without expecting to find him teaching Mozart how to write a fugue. And in another room, next door to the director's study, stood Rossini's Napoleonic bed, and by the bedside, under a glass shade, Rossini's wig.

There was administrative work to be done before the pupils came back, local authorities to be interviewed, concert programmes to be drawn up. In addition to the directorship of the Liceo, it was hoped that Busoni would organize the concerts of the Società del Quartetto, collaborate in producing a new musical periodical, and also become a member of the committee which was responsible for the Opera. When he came to make definite plans, he found that there was always some obstacle to their being carried out. It was like being presented with an island, he said, with no boat by which to reach it. He began his reforms with the simplest and most urgent necessities. Within a week of his arrival he wrote to the town council demanding the instant reconstruction of the Liceo's sanitary arrangements, which probably dated from the days of Padre Martini. In this department at any rate his efforts were crowned with success; the rebuilding of the

[1] 'I knew you as a little boy, and now you have become such a great man!' 'Welcome, Mr. Director, you who are beloved of everybody!'

sanitary arrangements was actually begun as early as April of the following year.

Busoni began to feel depressed with Bologna. It was a pleasure to receive a visit from Baroness Jella Oppenheimer and take her to see the seven strange and beautiful little chapels of Santo Stefano, or to drive out with the Anzolettis up to San Vittore in the Apennines and look out over the whole of the Lombard plain. But Bologna was 'a town without water, without trees and without women'. He found a new and secret way to the Liceo, in order to avoid meeting tiresome acquaintances—a crooked street known to the populace as the Via dell' Inferno, one of those curious streets which exist in almost every French or Italian town, though the traveller seldom hits upon them unless he has lost his way—a street inhabited exclusively by prostitutes, who sat at their doors (as Busoni said) like goats in a stable. Bologna is famous in Italy for the beauty of its women. There are trees in Bologna too, but even if Busoni had taken the main streets he would hardly have noticed them, for they are hidden behind the armoured gates of old palaces, and only rarely does one catch a glimpse of a garden, or sometimes, when there was not room for a real garden, of a garden painted in illusive fresco on the back wall of a courtyard.

A visit from Isadora Duncan was embarrassing. She had lost her two children six months before, one of them a boy of three whom she believed would have become the great genius of the future, dancer and composer in one. She told Busoni how she had seen three black birds hovering perpetually about her for a month before the catastrophe; she was now nothing more than a spirit herself, she said, and wanted to consult him about an idea of dancing symbolic dances to choruses of Palestrina. Busoni was reminded partly of his old pupil Maud Allan and still more of d'Annunzio and the *Gioconda*.

He was too compassionate a man to show any signs of impatience with poor Isadora's fantastic outpourings, but on other occasions he dealt with troublesome people less ceremoniously. There was a Polish singer at Bologna who pestered him relentlessly; one day when she had attached herself to him at luncheon in the Hotel Baglioni Dr. Anzoletti suddenly came in. Busoni seized his opportunity and sprang up to shake hands with him.

'Oh my dear doctor! Here's a fine bottle of wine for you! Here's a fine cigar for you! Here's a fine figure of a woman for you! Amuse yourself well! Good-bye!' With this exclamation he left the surgeon to look after the lady and disappeared.

Bologna recalled, more and more, the memory of Trieste, and Busoni hated memories of his youth. There was some notion of his occupying a set of rooms in the Liceo itself, but he had no great mind to do so, after his experiences with the sanitation, still less as there was no electric light in the building, and he would have to find his way at night with a candle across the great hall and the draughty corridors. A glass of wine too many, he thought, and he would have to make the acquaintance of the old gentlemen on the walls, to the music of Padre Martini's harpsichord. There was a dwarf among the 'old masters';[1] Busoni felt sure that one night he would come into his room wearing Rossini's wig and insisting on his playing the piece of music which he carried in his hand.

He looked at a house in the arcades beyond the Porta Maggiore; through a door in the wall he came into a garden with a view right up to the Apennines. He began to plan his future life—spring and autumn at Bologna, concert tours in the winter, Christmas perhaps in Berlin, and certainly the flat in Berlin for July and August. The flat in Berlin must on no account be abandoned: the summer devoted to composition would be the only thing that could prevent him falling into a premature old age. The house outside the Porta Maggiore was to let; it belonged to a Marchese Marsigli. But the rent demanded

---

[1] It is a portrait of Adrianus Coclicus, known as Le Petit, a pupil of Josquin des Prés, who was expelled from Rome on account of his immoral conduct.

was too high, and Busoni decided to wait. He was beginning to feel tired of Bologna. Towards the end of October there was a strenuous week of examinations at the Liceo; he was pleased with the singers and still more so with the string players, but the pianoforte pupils did not satisfy his standards. As an examiner he was severe, being accustomed to criticize himself severely. After one of the pupils had played for her diploma, Busoni turned hesitatingly to his fellow-examiners. 'Can we possibly let her pass?' His colleagues were amazed; they were all for giving her full marks. 'Full marks?' asked Busoni, incredulous; 'why, if I were a candidate myself I should not give myself more than fifty per cent!' Needless to say, diplomas granted by Busoni soon came to be regarded as honours of rare value.

He became more and more conscious of the provincialism of Bologna; everybody seemed to be old, like their historic institutions. The one consolation was a stock of Montepulciano wine which he had discovered.[1] Montepulciano, as he explained to Egon Petri, was not (as one might suppose) a mountain which gave birth to fleas; mountains of that kind were less common than those which produced mice. It was significant, he observed, that the phrase *parturiunt montes* was created in Italy. He wrote to Gerda at Berlin, telling her to pack her trunks and join him at St. Petersburg.

He arrived at St. Petersburg with influenza, and would gladly have put off his concert, but yielded to the pressing request of the conductor, Kussevitzky. He was to play his own Concerto—'the skyscraper',[2] as he called it in a letter to Petri; he was obliged to miss the first rehearsal, but left his bed to rehearse and play at the concert on the same day. It was a great triumph, and the audience persistently demanded an encore. Busoni, despite his exhaustion, sat down again to the pianoforte, intending to play a fugue of Bach. Suddenly the silence was pierced

[1] 'Montepulciano d'ogni vino è il rè' (Francesco Redi, *Bacco in Toscana*): translated into English (*Bacchus in Tuscany*) by Leigh Hunt, 'Montepulciano's the king of all wines.'   [2] In English.

by the shrill scream of a female voice from the topmost gallery of the theatre: '*Cam-pa-nyé-laa!*' Busoni left the stage at once, and it was a long time before he could be persuaded to go back; eventually quiet was restored and he played the Bach fugue.

Gerda returned to Berlin and Busoni went on to Warsaw alone; a postponed concert at Lemberg kept him away from Berlin until Christmas. Christmas in Berlin with his family was a thing which Busoni hated to miss, and this year his holiday was a short one; he was back again at Bologna early in January 1914.

Bologna was under snow and colder than Berlin. He looked at the Marsigli villa again and liked it less. After two or three busy days of administrative work he left for Strassburg, Paris, Nantes, and Bordeaux. He spent March in Berlin, where he gave two recitals, and in April went back to his duties at Bologna. The spring made him feel more hopeful. His plans for a permanent orchestra were taking shape; another plan of his, to convert the abandoned church of Santa Lucia into a concert-hall, met with approval, and the sanitary arrangements of the Liceo were positively under active reconstruction. For the present concerts had to be given in the opera-house, where the stage was ingeniously converted into a site for the orchestra by means of scenery which continued the architectural design of Bibbiena's superb auditorium.

Gerda followed in a few days, and as they could not obtain possession of the Villa Marsigli until the autumn, they took rooms in another house. It was a large villa outside the town, and to reach their own part of it they had to pass through several unoccupied apartments, furnished as bedrooms, but with truly Italian parsimony. As long as his wife was there to look after him, Busoni was happy enough, but after she left Bologna at the beginning of June, he could bear it no longer. The evenings were unendurable, and every night when he came home he felt a horror of walking through the long series of great empty rooms, dark and draughty—'like hospital wards', he described them. One day he suddenly made up his mind and went to live at the Hotel Baglioni. Hotel life gave him a new sense of comfort: not merely the comfort of a well-managed hotel, but the sense of being on his travels again. It was a chilly summer. A general strike broke out; even the old porter at the Liceo struck, though he could not tell Busoni what was the reason of it all. There were no newspapers and no trams; Bologna was just duller than ever. Busoni suddenly realized with delight that by moving to the Baglioni he had 'disappeared'. Dr. Augusto Anzoletti came to Bologna, but he too managed somehow to 'disappear'; no one knew where he slept. Bologna seemed to have become mysterious, like Berlin or London. One could 'disappear' even in Bologna; there was even said to be a criminal quarter in the town.

June came to an end, and with it Busoni's patience. The bad weather continued and he had a slight attack of illness, though Dr. Anzoletti told him that he might safely leave his cure to nature and his own constitution. Bologna had become intolerable. Life there was a perpetual series of misunderstandings with everybody—'it is as if one had married the housemaid'.

Busoni found himself in an embarrassing state of indecision, and few things tormented him more than being forced into a situation where he could not see a clear course before him. Bologna must be given up; that was clear enough. There was an offer from America, but Busoni knew only too well what a tour in America meant. His private inclination drew him to Berlin, or at any rate to his own house in Berlin. But he felt that he could not reconcile it with his artistic conscience to go back to Berlin unless he could accomplish there what he had failed to accomplish in his own country. He consulted Isidor Philipp, the famous pianoforte teacher, with whom he had become very friendly during his recent visits to Paris. Philipp was only too anxious to bring him to Paris, but Philipp knew Paris well enough to understand that Busoni's career in Paris must be that of a pianist, and

Busoni was quite clear in his own mind that he had finished with the life of a virtuoso. He knew himself inwardly to be a composer and perhaps something more; it is not too much to say that he knew himself to be a philosopher and a prophet. It was not mere personal vanity or ambition that dominated his thoughts; any weakness of that kind he had shaken off years ago. What made it impossible for the world to understand him was that he felt himself to be a man with a mission. The ordinary artistic world can understand easily enough a man whose motives are purely commercial; it can even extend a certain tolerance to mere vanity; but a man who regards his art as if it were a religion which he has been called by Heaven both to preach and to practise, regardless of worldly conventions and understandings, finds himself in an impossible position. He is like a stranger speaking a language which no one understands and offering riches in a currency which the local money market does not acknowledge.

By the end of June 1914 Busoni was back in Berlin, and spent July preparing the collected edition of Bach's clavier works, about which he was in perpetual correspondence with his collaborator Egon Petri. The outbreak of war at the beginning of August did not at first make much impression on him; in all countries it was believed that the war would be a very short one, and the successful advance of the German army during the first few months led many people to believe that artistic life would not suffer much from political troubles. It was only natural that Busoni, who had never interested himself in politics, should at first have been merely roused to contempt and indignation at the patriotic outbursts of German musicians and critics. Patriotism brought out in Germany, no less than in other countries, the worst side of narrow-minded middle-class stupidity. Busoni, in any case, was an Italian. Germany had never regarded him as anything else, and he had never had any illusions about the essentially Germanic qualities in music.

He signed the contract for his American tour and wrote to Bologna to ask for a year's leave of absence. He had not given up all hopes of returning to Bologna, and he was gratified to hear that there was some hope of his plans for a concert-hall there being carried out. Besides, Italy was neutral as regards the war, and in the autumn of 1914 that neutrality seemed likely to be maintained, in spite of d'Annunzio's fervid appeals for brotherhood between Italy and France. Busoni foresaw, by the middle of September, that the war meant the cultural ruin of Europe. Italy was his one hope; Italy would have to become the chief rebuilder of intellectual and artistic life after the war was over—whenever that might be.

He stayed on in Berlin over Christmas, concentrating as far as possible on his work, and playing occasionally in public; a Bach recital for the benefit of war charities was received by the musical patriots with discourteous ingratitude. It was the first time that any pianist had ever devoted a whole recital to Bach in Berlin.

And a new work had at last begun to take definite shape. Three days after Christmas he completed the poem of *Doctor Faust*; it had been written down almost with a sense of inspiration, without hesitation or interruption. He was due to start for America on January 5; three days before he was still hesitating whether to sail or not. The hesitation was but momentary; after compulsory stoppages at Zurich, Genoa, and Naples, he sailed with his wife and sons on the Dutch boat *Rotterdam*, reaching New York on January 20. He summed up his feelings in a letter to Egon Petri: 'When shall we ever meet again? This state of uncertainty (*Planlosigkeit*), after ten years of deliberate constructive work, at the climax of my vital strength, is the hardest of all blows to bear!'

America gave Busoni a cordial welcome; at his first concert in New York his audience included six famous pianists—Harold Bauer, Carl Friedberg, Percy Grainger, Mark Hambourg, Josef Hofmann, and Raphael Joseffy. But he was in no mood for social gatherings, and it

221

required all the charm and tact of 'Mrs. Bach-Busoni', as she was often called, to smooth over the difficulties caused by her husband's irritability. 'Even with a war Europe is better!'

In March he started on a concert tour in the western States. Wherever he went he noted the characteristic signs of American culture—the New York journalist who said to him in all seriousness that the three greatest organizations which the world had ever seen were the Catholic Church, the German army, and the American Oil Trust Company; and the programme of a concert in San Francisco at which Marcella Sembrich sang 'Down the sweet river' and Kreisler played Dvořák's *Humoresque* on a muted violin. A cheerful letter from Petri provoked the melancholy comment that he himself had always made the mistake of regarding the pleasures of life as things of transitory value, not worth enjoying to the full, and that now such pleasures seemed to him to be like the picture-books in a dentist's waiting-room.

A strange and tragic happening befell him in one of the far western cities. At the end of his recital there came into the artists' room a repulsive-looking man of about fifty, with a woman,whose crudely painted face and bright yellow dyed hair, coupled with her sodden features and painful expression, showed only too plainly that she had touched the lowest depths of moral and physical degradation. Years ago she had been one of Busoni's most ardent pupils. She had been given a ticket for the concert on condition that she came to it sober. Busoni's only feeling was one of compassion and horror, not so much at her downfall as at the social conditions which had made it possible. To help her was his first instinct, but as he was obliged to leave at once he could only console himself with the knowledge that a lady in the town had offered to take charge of her.[1] For three nights in the train he was haunted by the memory of that ghastly encounter.

In April he came back to New York. His prospects were

[1] She died not long afterwards.

none too favourable. His agent had tried to arrange a tour in California, but without success; New York was full of celebrated pianists—there were some twenty of them, and the result was that nobody would go to hear them play. Saint-Saëns was there too; it was always a pleasure to Busoni to meet him. He little thought what a scandal it would create in Berlin when he was seen talking to Saint-Saëns in a box at the Opera during a performance of *Carmen*!

By May he had decided that he must leave America; he could bear it no longer, and he knew that when he left it he would never again return. And there was another reason for leaving. Italy had entered the war, and he felt that he ought to go back to Italy. What he expected to do in Italy during the war he probably did not know himself; it was obvious that at the age of nearly fifty, and in a very precarious state of health, he had no intention of offering himself as a soldier. At any rate he felt the call to 'defend the fortifications of art, as far as it may be granted to me to do so'.[1] The months spent in America had not been altogether wasted. He had finished the *Wohltemperiertes Clavier* and his edition of the *Goldberg Variations*; of his original compositions the *Indian Fantasy* was complete, and the *Rondo Arlecchinesco* very nearly so. Besides these he had written the libretto of the opera *Arlecchino*, and had succeeded in obtaining the construction of his long-planned harmonium in thirds of tones—an instrument which he hoped would lead towards a new system of musical composition.

He had decided to leave America, but for several months he still hesitated. Owing to a series of misunderstandings with his agent and with the pianoforte manufacturers, he found himself without any chance of concert engagements for the coming autumn. One of his most loyal friends in New York, Mrs. Lanier, the foundress of the 'Society of Friends of Music', tried to persuade him to complete the score of *Arlecchino* at once, in the hopes of getting it

[1] Letter to I. Philipp, May 20, 1915.

produced at the Metropolitan Opera House in the winter
under the direction of Bodanzky. Busoni knew quite well
that *Arlecchino* would be no opera for the Metropolitan.
The longer he remained in America the more disgusted he
became with American life, musical and otherwise. He
was determined to go back to Europe. To go back to his
home in Berlin was impossible; he hoped for a welcome in
Italy.

Early in September he sailed for Europe with Gerda and
Lello, leaving Benni in America, as he had rights of
American citizenship, having been born at Boston. They
landed at Genoa and proceeded to Milan, where Busoni
had to wait some time, partly on account of illness, partly
on account of difficulty in obtaining a passport to enter
Switzerland. The only welcome that he had received in
Italy was the offer of a subordinate post as teacher of the
pianoforte at Rome. By the last week of September he was
at Lausanne with his friend the pianist Émile Blanchet,
who had been one of his pupils at Weimar.

It might be asked why Busoni did not return to the
Liceo Rossini at Bologna. The situation at Bologna had
become hopeless. Busoni had started work there under
a municipal administration which promised him every
possible support. This administration, however, did not
remain long in office; it was followed, after the strikes of
June 1914, by the advent of a royal commissioner whose
powers were very limited. At a later stage a socialist
administration came into power. This new town council
considered that Busoni was neglecting his duties in being
too frequently absent from Bologna. Busoni replied with
a letter saying that if the town council would carry out the
reforms that he demanded at the Liceo he would come
back. The town council made no promise of carrying out
Busoni's wishes, but merely granted him leave of absence
for a definite period, adding that if he did not return before
its expiry he would be considered to have resigned his
directorship. To this letter Busoni made no answer. The
result was that by the time Busoni came back from

America the Bologna authorities had acted upon their threat and had appointed another director.

'The Italians could do everything that is done in other countries,' Busoni used to say to his friends in Bologna, 'if only they had the will.' The one and only result of all his efforts in Bologna, the sole memorial of his directorate— *aere perennius* in white glazed tiles—was that reconstruction which he had demanded in his first week of office, a reconstruction which in all probability he little thought he would ever have to initiate and thought still less that any Italian town council would ever see carried out.

CHAPTER XIII

THE CITY OF REFUGE

SWITZERLAND was a country which hitherto had had little interest for Busoni. From a musical point of view it was of no particular importance; musicians who took their tone from Berlin or Vienna regarded Switzerland as a region even more provincial than the 'provinces' of Germany and Austria. To the German mind the non-German parts of Switzerland counted for nothing at all; and in so far as German Switzerland ever produced anything of intellectual or artistic interest the German mind naturally claimed it as being 'German'. Busoni's impression of Basle, quoted in a previous chapter, was characteristic of him; it was a place to have seen once, a place to remember but not to revisit. For beauty of landscape Busoni appeared to have curiously little feeling. He would sometimes admit to what one might call a tourist's enjoyment of natural beauty, but he confessed quite frankly that he hated the realities of country life. His attitude was a perfectly logical and reasonable one. 'Nature', he maintained, was everywhere, and to the imaginative mind one single tree in a street might signify more than a forest. If 'nature' was to mean virgin land where no sign whatever of mankind was to be seen, then one could have no relation to it, unless one approached it professionally, as a botanist, a geologist, an agriculturist, or something of that kind. Any other approach was 'amateurish', and that word, in Busoni's vocabulary, always expressed contempt. He would have agreed heartily with Pope's famous dictum—'The proper study of mankind is Man.'

He had acquaintances in Switzerland, but perhaps had hitherto hardly realized their true value. Busoni sometimes gave the impression of being inclined to judge people more by what they could accomplish than by what they were as human beings. His own mind was always tensely concentrated upon some definite end; if for a moment he felt in doubt as to his ultimate aim he was miserable. He had a horror of the 'Hamlet' type, as he called it, but at the same time it was often just those very 'Hamlets' who became indispensable to him, when once he came to know them intimately, on account of the affection which they gave him. Kapff was a typical case. Busoni's keen critical and analytical faculty led him to write of them occasionally with an insight that might seem merciless, but such criticisms were generally intended for Gerda's eyes alone. They were an intellectual exercise, one might say, perhaps even a form of vicarious self-examination, for Busoni was often inwardly unsure of himself and feared nothing more anxiously than this very sense of inward insecurity. It was for this reason that such friends were necessary to him. Professional contacts, on the other hand, did not so often afford the opportunity for analysis of this kind, and in the strictly professional moments of life Busoni was too completely concentrated on purely artistic matters to admit the distraction of personal feeling. It came as something of a surprise to Busoni in Switzerland that men whom he had hardly known except in a professional association, whatever their artistic abilities might be, should reveal themselves—and just at the moment when he needed it the most—as loyal and warm-hearted personal friends.

By the end of October 1915 he had settled in to a small flat in Zurich at Scheuchzerstrasse 36, on the hill to the north of the lake. He had been driven out of America by an overwhelming sense of disgust—*dégoût* is the word he used, and the French word used in a German sentence might perhaps be better translated 'intellectual and moral nausea'. When he arrived in Europe and found that Italy was impossible for him to live in, he suddenly became conscious that he was utterly homeless, and that he had really never had a home in his life, except in so far as the flat in Berlin was a home. The war had made all the

227

belligerent countries impossible for him, not on any political or legal grounds, but simply because in all those countries the war had produced—as most of us can now clearly see—a mental condition that bordered on insanity. Busoni spoke of Europe and America as a 'monster madhouse'; towards all these countries he felt as embarrassed and disgusted as a sober man in a company of more or less intoxicated people. Switzerland attracted him because it was neutral; it was not the only neutral country, but it was the only one whose neutrality was certain to be proof against all pressure, the only neutral country which did not more or less definitely side with one or other of the belligerent parties, and the one country in the world which prided itself on being constitutionally international.

The war had made Zurich an international metropolis. That was one of its great attractions for Busoni. It was the one place in the world where he had the chance of meeting people of every nationality. At the same time the enormous influx from every country of people who found their own countries unbearable had given Zurich a doubly international aspect: it was the meeting-place of international idealism, and also of the international underworld. It would be grossly unjust to suggest that Busoni frequented what is called 'bad company', but he undoubtedly took a perpetual delight in those aspects of city life which had first fascinated him when as a boy he read the novels of Dickens.

After the homelessness and friendlessness of America the warmth and cordiality of the welcome that he received at Zurich was astonishing to him. It is a significant symptom of Busoni's psychological condition at this moment that he was ready to appreciate it and to be honestly and profoundly grateful for the friendship that was offered him. Inwardly Busoni was always grateful by natural temperament, but a certain inhibition had often made it difficult for him to admit his gratitude, even to himself; it was only towards his wife that he was always conscious of it and always happy in expressing it.

To no one among his Swiss friends had he more cause

for gratitude than to Dr. Volkmar Andreae, the conductor of the Zurich municipal orchestra. It was to Andreae, more than to any one else, that he owed that penetrating sense of repose and refreshment which he derived from his residence at Zurich—an intellectual and moral influence on his character which prepared him for the serener years of his later life and gave him the power to create those works in which at last he realized the true fullness of his own personality. As the son of an Italian mother, Andreae was temperamentally attracted towards Busoni's Italian character. As a musician he was very different from any of the prominent conductors whom Busoni had come across in Germany. He was entirely free from the inordinate vanity of the modern virtuoso conductor; he was firmly rooted in Zurich and devoted all his energies to the development of Zurich's musical life. He had all the qualities which the romantic artist is inclined to despise—efficiency, punctuality, organizing ability; and he applied these qualities—not without a touch of military precision acquired in his function as a colonel of Swiss artillery—towards furthering the cause of music and to the artistic support of other musicians. He had for a long time cherished a whole-hearted admiration for Busoni as a musician and an affectionate and loyal appreciation of him as a man; he rejoiced in the opportunity which now presented itself of showing his devotion in a practical form and also of securing the inspiring force of Busoni's immense personality for the musical life of Switzerland.

An opportunity presented itself almost at once. Andreae was called up for military service early in 1916 and therefore proposed that Busoni should conduct the second half of the winter's subscription concerts. The programmes were already to some extent settled, but for the most part they were of a type that Busoni could conduct with satisfaction. The remaining few months of 1915 Busoni devoted to the edition of Bach's clavier works, in collaboration with Petri, who was living in Berlin, and to the composition of his opera *Arlecchino*.

In January 1916 he played Beethoven's Concerto in
E flat, the *Indian Fantasy* and Liszt's *Totentanz* at a concert conducted by Andreae. In February he began his
duties as a conductor with a whole programme of Liszt—
Les Préludes, the Concerto in A, played by Petri, and the
Faust Symphony. The March concert, at which he had
to conduct Tchaikovsky's Violin Concerto and *Wotans
Abschied*, provoked a characteristic outburst in a letter to
Petri about 'gods and heroes on stilts, the nightmare of
my fifty years' life—heroes, as Heine says, who have the
courage of a hundred lions and the brains of two donkeys!'
He contrasts them with the *Teatro dei Piccoli* which he had
seen just before at Rome, in a performance of a comic
opera written by Rossini at twenty. The next Zurich
concert brought the Italian Symphony of Mendelssohn,
one of the few works of the romantic era that Busoni
always admired, and his own *Rondo Arlecchinesco*; at the
last, in April, he had to conduct the *Eroica* Symphony,
about which he was by this time beginning to grow somewhat sceptical.

'The Latin attitude to art,' he wrote to Petri, 'with its cool
serenity and its insistence on outward form, is what refreshes me.
It was only through Beethoven that music acquired that growling
and frowning expression which was natural enough to him, but
which perhaps ought to have remained his lonely path alone. Why
are you in such a bad temper, one would often like to ask, especially
in the second period.'

Busoni had again been taken by surprise at the success
of his concerts in Rome.

'I had a wonderful reception,' he wrote to Petri, 'and was shown
both respect and affection. A delightful circle of intelligent younger
musicians surrounded me at once. The people there (i.e. at Rome)
are naturally very clever. So was the orchestra, which at once understood everything new and unfamiliar, tackled it at once and carried
it out rightly. I feel very grateful. And I am grateful to you for
coming and for playing: it is not forgotten in spite of all that has
happened since.'

Besides the concerts in Zurich and Rome there were four pianoforte recitals at Zurich, devoted respectively to Bach, Beethoven, Chopin, and Liszt. He played also in other Swiss towns. Swiss people might seem dull to Busoni at times—he quotes a dictum of Carl Spitteler to the effect that if the Swiss had made their own mountains they would have been very much flatter—but in spite of their narrowness they had a certain culture, and he could feel some likelihood of finding his artistic ideals appreciated.

In June 1916 he was the guest of a new friend, Marchese Silvio Casanova, at San Remigio near Pallanza. Marchese Casanova was a man of considerable culture, with a singular devotion to German literature which induced him to write poetry in German himself. He was also keenly interested in music, and one of the reasons which led Busoni to cultivate his acquaintance was the fact that he possessed unpublished manuscripts of Liszt. Another guest at San Remigio was Boccioni, the painter, in whom Busoni had been interested for several years. During the three weeks that they were together Boccioni painted a striking portrait of Busoni. In July he was called up for military training (he had already served seven months as a volunteer in a cyclist battalion directly after Italy entered the war) and in August was killed by a fall from his horse. Busoni was deeply distressed at his death, and bitterly indignant at the way in which the death of a gifted young artist was treated by patriotic journalism. The *Corriere della Sera*, as did many newspapers of other countries in similar cases, spoke of the young painter as if his military service was a matter of infinitely greater value than his future career as an artist. Busoni wrote a notice of Boccioni in the *Neue Zürcher Zeitung*. Along with the *Corriere*'s obituary he quoted a letter written by Boccioni to himself early in August:

'I can only thank you for giving me the courage to endure this appalling life. . . . The first days were unbearable. . . . After this existence I shall have an utter contempt for everything but art. There is nothing more terrible than art. Everything that I am now

231

facing is child's play compared to a rightly made stroke of the brush, to a harmonious line of verse or a properly placed chord.'

Busoni was enraged at the 'conspiracy of silence' by which such unforgivable wrongs as the sacrifice of young artistic hopes were glossed over with patriotic commonplaces. He ended by quoting the motto inscribed by Goya on *Los Desastres de la Guerra*—'La verdad es muerta!'[1]

Busoni had cause enough to exclaim that truth was dead, for he had himself been the victim of perpetual persecution in the newspapers. He was an international 'celebrity', and though no one cared much about his merits as a composer, it was a matter of journalistic interest to know what side he took in the war. He had already been annoyed by the impertinence of American and German comments on his meeting with Saint-Saëns in New York. No sooner had he settled down to life in Switzerland than it was rumoured that he had naturalized himself as a Swiss subject. A few months later Maurice Kufferath, the former director of the Théâtre de la Monnaie at Brussels, stated in the *Journal de Genève* that Busoni had given a concert at Brussels by desire of the German military authorities. It was absolutely untrue; Busoni had never even been invited to play at Brussels. He was too proud to answer these charges, and felt it to be insulting that he should be expected to 'prove an *alibi*'. His friend José Vianna da Motta, who was living at Geneva, and in constant correspondence with him about the edition of Liszt's pianoforte works on which they were collaborating, drew his attention to the statement, and himself wrote to contradict it. The *Journal de Genève* published a very half-hearted rectification—'bien que M. Busoni eût refusé son concours etc.'. But the damage was done; the misstatement was copied into Italian papers and procured further annoyance for Busoni in Italy. It was amusingly characteristic of Busoni that he attributed Kufferath's indiscretion to the fact that Kufferath was an enthusiastic devotee of Wagner! Busoni had unearthed a letter of

[1] 'Truth is dead.'

Wagner to Bülow in which he admitted having obtained many of his new harmonic devices from Liszt, 'but must one tell the public that at once?'[1] It suggested the morality of a fraudulent bank, Busoni said; it also accounted for Wagnerite standards of truth.

As regards his alleged change of nationality, Busoni expressed his views clearly enough in a letter to Émile Blanchet at Lausanne.

'*Tutto il mondo è paese*,[2] one finds defects everywhere, and everywhere one can discover—if one will—qualities. All the nations, taken *en masse*, are antipathetic (yes, all!), and each nation produces *personnalités d'élite*. For this one and most important reason it would seem to me a pity to *change* my nationality, since it has never been proved that any one, all told, is better than any other. It is for this reason that I have *not* become a Swiss, and you can make this *démenti* in Paris, if people attach so much importance to it. It is quite enough to have been born with one nationality ticketed on one's body!'

It was only a week before Boccioni's death that Busoni completed the music of *Arlecchino*. It was accepted for production at the Zurich opera-house, and as it was not long enough to occupy a whole evening, Busoni suddenly determined to convert his incidental music to *Turandot* into a short opera with spoken dialogue. *Turandot*, the full score of which amounted to three hundred pages, was finished early in March; the work had taken him a hundred days, and he was not a little pleased at his achievement in rapid workmanship. The two operas together

---

[1] Wagner to von Bülow from Paris, 7 October 1859: 'There are many matters which we are quite frank about among ourselves (for instance, that since my acquaintance with Liszt's compositions my treatment of harmony has become very different from what it was formerly), but it is indiscreet, to say the least, of friend Pohl to babble this secret to the whole world.' (Letters of Richard Wagner, ed. W. Altmann, tr. M. M. Bozman. J. M. Dent & Sons, London, 1927.)

[2] 'All the world's a village'—a well-known quotation from Goldoni's play *La Vedova Scaltra* (Act i, scene 1), in which an Italian nobleman, dining in Venice with an Englishman, a Frenchman, and a Spaniard, follows up these words by saying that a gentleman is at home in all countries.

were to be considered as examples of a new 'comedy of masks' (*la nuova commedia dell'arte*). *Arlecchino* was less of a new comedy of masks than a ferocious satire on the theatre, the conventional opera, the war, and human nature in general. It has had more performances than any other opera of Busoni's, but it has never become popular, for it leaves an audience bewildered and somewhat uncomfortable.

The first performance of *Turandot* and *Arlecchino* took place at Zurich on May 11, 1917. The part of Arlecchino, which is for an actor, not for a singer, was taken by Alexander Moissi; it would have been impossible to find a more ideal interpreter of the character.

Arlecchino—Busoni described it as *ein theatralisches Capriccio*, a theatrical caprice—is in the nature of a play for puppets. Harlequin, speaking but never heard to sing (except for a few bars of *larallera* which are heard off stage and sung actually by another voice), stands apart from the other characters as Kasperl does in the traditional German puppet-plays, talking sometimes as a personage in the drama, and sometimes turning to the audience as the author's mouthpiece. He appears in four aspects—as rogue, as soldier, as husband, and as conqueror. The scene is laid in Bergamo, the traditional home of Harlequin. Ser Matteo, an elderly tailor, sits at his work in front of his house, reading Dante; he is a man of lofty ideals and ridiculous appearance. Above his head, on the balcony, Harlequin is making love to Matteo's wife. In order to frighten Matteo out of the way, Harlequin tells him that the town is being invaded by 'the barbarians—the nation of music and philosophy'.

Harlequin reappears as a recruiting-sergeant, to a distorted reminiscence of the march in *La Figlia del Reggimento*, and calls up Matteo for military duty, after having thrown out some cynical observations on militarism and patriotism. Next appear two more traditional characters, the Doctor and the Abbé, who seek refuge from the imaginary invaders in the tavern.

Harlequin has a wife of his own, whom he naturally neglects. Columbine yields to the fascinations of Leandro, a typical operatic tenor, who parodies both the romantic German singer and the classical Italian one of the days of Scarlatti and Leo. Harlequin discovers them, lays out Leandro with his wooden sword and runs away to resume flirtation with the wife of Ser Matteo. It is growing dark. The Doctor and the Abbé come out of the tavern, both rather unsteady on their legs, but all the more uplifted by humanitarian principles. The Doctor stumbles over the corpse and the Abbé calls for help. One by one lights appear in the windows of the surrounding houses and heads are protruded, but as soon as the Abbé makes his pathetic appeal for compassion, every window is slammed to. Providence will not desert us, says the pious priest, and lo! round the corner comes a donkey drawing a cart. '*Asinus providentialis!*' sings the Abbé, as they lift Leandro on to the cart, which takes him off the stage. Dawn breaks, and Matteo returns from the war to find his wife flown. He sits down philosophically to his tailoring again and once more takes up the *Divina Commedia*, while to the strain of a lively minuet the other characters, including the donkey, take a formal and ceremonious leave of the audience, and Harlequin speaks an epilogue.

There is no need to tell the well-known story of *Turandot*, which keeps closely to the original play of Gozzi, though much compressed. The most original creations of Busoni are the Queen Mother, a fantastically adorned negress who crosses the stage with her women bewailing her son, one of the princes who has just been executed for failing to guess Turandot's riddles, and the chief eunuch Truffaldino, another modern Monostatos like Thusman, but more amiable in character.

Few of Busoni's compositions gave him so much satisfaction as *Arlecchino*; both from a literary and musical point of view he regarded it as his most individual and personal work. One reason for its lack of popularity up to the present is' that it demands an unusual alertness of mind

235

on the part of the spectator. The libretto is extremely terse in style, and was considerably reduced in the process of setting it to music, for Busoni was always determined to make the musical form the deciding factor in his works for the stage. With the older composers this principle led to the expansion of the libretto by frequent repetition of words; with Busoni it led to compression. The whole action of the play undoubtedly moves much too quickly for the average German audience; at the same time *Arlecchino* is an opera conceived for production under the technical conditions of a modern German theatre, and it would be singularly difficult to translate into any other language, especially as a good deal of Italian is employed, and the mixture of languages adds to the humour of the situations.

Yet behind the momentary joy in the creation of his opera there was a grim background of depression. April 1, 1916, had been Busoni's fiftieth birthday, and he reflected that in spite of all the work achieved at Zurich his future was still uncertain. He was never much concerned for his financial future; what troubled him was the thought that the greater part of his life lay behind him, and that he must lose no opportunity of making the best use of what remained. As long as the war kept him an exile and a prisoner in Switzerland, it was impossible to make plans. There were always recitals to be given, but he had reached an age when he loathed practising the pianoforte. Da Motta had suggested his taking a pianoforte class; he replied that he could no longer bear to sit and watch students going through all the labour that he himself had gone through years ago.

He began to feel intensely lonely. Deprived of his library in Berlin, he began to collect books again in Switzerland, but after a year or two he had exhausted all the second-hand booksellers, for they received no fresh supplies from other countries. Switzerland was full of interesting people who had taken refuge there, but as the war went on they became less and less accessible to human society. At the beginning of 1917 Da Motta left Geneva to become head of the Conservatoire at Lisbon. Busoni congratulated him on having the chance, at fifty, of starting a new life and of taking a position of importance in his own country. 'I feel homesick for great cities,' he wrote to Philipp; 'life is exhausted in work. I have no talent for "organization" and small hope of gathering the fruits of my efforts. Still I remain serene.'

By the middle of 1917 he began to feel that he had exhausted the resources of Switzerland. He did his best to keep in touch with the younger musicians, but there were very few of them to talk to and educate. In the first month of his arrival in Switzerland he had made friends with Philipp Jarnach, the son of a Spanish painter, born and educated in France. Jarnach was an excellent pianist and a clever composer. He soon became Busoni's *famulus*, as he called him, and was employed by Busoni to make the pianoforte arrangements of *Arlecchino* and *Turandot*. He delighted Busoni by his Latin clarity of mind, as well as by what Busoni called a German outlook on music in general; that meant merely that Jarnach took music seriously, not that he was burdened with the *bourgeois* romantic outlook. During the first two years in Zurich Busoni had made his house—cramped and uncomfortable as it was—something of a social centre, as he used to do in Berlin; and there were many cheerful and animated evenings spent in the restaurant of the railway station. Busoni was always fascinated by the station; he would even sit there alone in the evenings, watching the arrivals of trains from other countries with their strange company of passengers. The station at Zurich may well have reminded him of those early days at Frohnleiten, when he used to watch the trains that came up from Trieste to travel on to Vienna and Berlin. And the street which leads to the chief station of Zurich, the Bahnhofstrasse, was the regular evening promenade of the town. A Swiss writer describes Busoni as walking along the Bahnhofstrasse *quaerens quod devoret*, looking at every woman with

237

R

the eye of a connoisseur. But Busoni, though always attracted by women of all kinds (except intellectual women), looked at everybody. An English pupil of his, who tended him like a daughter when he visited London in later years, found it uncomfortably embarrassing to walk with him; half absorbed in his own thoughts, half fascinated by the human types around him, he would stop and stare at any one with a disconcerting air of both curiosity and absent-mindedness.

In 1916 Busoni had acquired a young St. Bernard dog, to whom he gave the name of 'Giotto'. As the invariable companion of Busoni's solitary walks Giotto soon became a well-known figure in Zurich, and his master, who was utterly unable to keep him in order, contributed, no doubt with secret pleasure, to Giotto's becoming something of a 'character'. He was a most amiable dog, but he insisted on going his own way. One hot day in summer he thought he would like to take a bath in the fountain opposite the railway station. The basin was small and Giotto large, so that a good deal of water was splashed about, but Giotto thoroughly enjoyed himself. A policeman came up to Busoni and informed him that dogs were not allowed to bathe in the fountain; Busoni merely said to the police-man in his politest tones, 'Won't you go and tell him so yourself?' On another occasion, when Busoni was sitting in the station restaurant, a Swiss officer in uniform came in. He divested himself of his sword and leant it up against the wall; Giotto, being in restless mood, knocked it down. The officer looked a little annoyed, so Busoni bowed to him and remarked very sweetly, 'Please excuse him; he is an anti-militarist.' It was impossible to resent or even resist the monstrous friendliness of Giotto.

But in the autumn of 1917 Busoni gave up drinking wine with his friends at the station restaurant and took to spending his evenings at home with Giotto and his books. There was always work to be done, and he had already started on the music of *Doctor Faust*; but he did not work happily in solitude, 'although solitude is often associated with men of genius—I am not one'. Among the minor works of this autumn were some of the exercises and studies eventually collected under the name of *Die Klavierübung*. They are intended mainly for virtuoso pianists, but even the amateur can attempt some of them, and they are all extraordinarily interesting and stimulating. They are interesting too as helping to elucidate some of Busoni's other compositions, for the studies show how certain of his harmonic devices grew out of purely pianistic principles based on definite positions of the hands on the keyboard. Every one of the studies has genuine musical originality, and even the exercises to be repeated in all keys are a good deal more musical than such forms of torture are generally made to be. The last work of 1917 was the exquisite little *Sonatina in diem Nativitatis Christi*.

Another year began, and Busoni's depression deepened. Benni was called up for military service as an American citizen; Busoni wrote anxious letters to Mrs. Lanier in the hopes that he might in some way be released. Through Baroness Jella Oppenheimer, with whom he was in fairly frequent correspondence, he heard that the faithful Kapff was in great distress. Baroness Oppenheimer was anxious to help him, but Kapff's scrupulous sense of honour in all financial matters made it impossible for him to be dependent on her, and only Busoni could persuade him to accept a gift from 'an anonymous benefactor'. Busoni gave a few pianoforte recitals in Berne and elsewhere, but the main work of the year was the score of *Doctor Faust*. Loneliness grew more oppressive; he felt himself more and more cut off from the rest of humanity, even from such intimate friends as Petri and Anzoletti. Letter-writing was no great pleasure if every letter was read by a censor when it crossed a frontier. More than once Busoni had to do what he could to soothe an irritation which some hasty outspoken words of his had caused, for everybody in all countries was suffering from a mental fever which inevitably led to misunderstanding.

In November the armistice brought the whole world

relief from the interminable agony of the war. Busoni
saw at once (as is clear from a letter which he wrote to
Marchese Casanova) that the military defeat of Germany
was the signal for Germany's spiritual resurrection, that
the Revolution would set free the voices of those elect
souls who had hitherto been condemned to silence, and
that Germany would find a nobler way in which to show
her greatness than in the pageantry of flying flags and
glittering helmets.

The final conclusion of peace made it possible to travel
again, and after a series of five concerts at Zurich in the
spring of 1919 designed to illustrate the history of the
pianoforte concerto, Busoni set out for Paris and London.
He had at first no idea of playing in Paris; London was
his main objective, and his chief purpose in visiting Paris
was to seek the advice of his old friend Philipp.

'Zurich is exhausted,' he wrote to Philipp, 'and now that peace
is concluded, the town is returning to its normal condition; I see
that it is time for me to make an end of its limitations.

'Do you think that Paris would welcome me, and have you any
suggestions to make? You are really the only man in whom I have
complete confidence, so bear with me.

'For four years I have lived in a state of inward hostility towards
this remote world, from which I have shut myself off. While judging
it to have become uncivilized, I have perhaps become uncivilized
myself. On the other hand I think that my art has become more
subtle, and that it expresses all that remains of "good" within me.'

Busoni reached Paris in the middle of September.
Paris to him seemed strangely Americanized, and for a
victorious city it was strangely melancholy.

'One sees a great many American soldiers with insolent and
expressionless faces, and even officers of my age with cheap cocottes
who have got themselves up smart for the occasion. They walk
along with them without talking or laughing, simply because they
think it is the proper thing to do in Paris. They call themselves
"Knights of Columbus". People do not like them.' [1]

Busoni was thankful that he had avoided the belligerent

[1] Letter (in French) to his wife.

countries during the war. He called on Philipp, but in
spite of being touched by Philipp's devoted affection and
admiration for him, there was still a faint sense of misunderstanding between the two men. Busoni could not
understand the 'conception féroce' which Philipp, like
most Frenchmen, had of Zurich. Philipp could not understand why Busoni resolutely refused to go back to Bologna.
Busoni wanted him to say that he must make his home in
Paris; Philipp talked of concerts at Paris in the spring,
but would go no farther. Busoni described him to Gerda
as beginning to look like 'un Clemenceau bienveillant'.
If he was lonely in Zurich, he was still more lonely in
Paris. 'I think of Giotto,' he wrote to Gerda; 'I feel
touched whenever I see a dog.'

A few days later he was in London. His first impression
was a happy one, for there was a letter waiting for him
from Gerda, to say that Benni had arrived in Zurich.

'Kiss Benni for me,' he wrote to her, 'tell him I want him to feel
happy and to like the little town that has given us so much that was
good—until things take a turn for the better. He ought to consider
now what path he means to follow, get over America and that
drifting life, develop his splendid abilities.

'I expected a redemption from London, and I certainly have had
beautiful first impressions. The town has not changed, but I have.
I notice that I expect nothing *from outside*, whereas formerly I
expected everything. This does not make me unhappy, but it makes
me more tranquil and more solitary. Nothing that has been ever
returns, says Anatole France; that gives the past its charm. England, which before the war was the most democratic of all countries,
is now—though unchanged—the most aristocratic, compared with
the others. What a sense of dignity there is here! How attentive
and individually considerate people are, in spite of all the rush and
hurry!'

The old friends were unchanged too, from Henry Wood
to the little second-hand bookseller in Shaftesbury Avenue.
Before the end of September the great railway strike broke
out—it was 'the very Bach of strikes, so polyphonic and
contrapuntal!' Busoni left his hotel, where butter, milk,

and sugar were scarce, and took refuge with Maud Allan at her house in Regent's Park. 'She has such a motherly way of realizing a situation.'

'What I like best about London is the Embankment, the river with its bridges, Westminster, St. Paul's, the Tower, the wharves and the ships, the wonderful rich façade of Buckingham Palace. One can see some of it from the back windows of the hotel,[1] always beautiful whether in sunshine or in fog. I look at the people less than I used to do; their expression is very unpleasant to me. The architecture of London I should describe as "cautious" (*vorsichtig*). It is as if some one played a piece of music accurately, tastefully and not without understanding, but too slow and too softly. I remember what I said before, that the English can be men of taste, but not artists. Even in their architecture they want "not to attract notice", and woe, when they do try to attract notice! I remembered too, how the architecture stands out as a quiet and firm background to the movement of history; *that* I call strength and victory.'

One of his most striking impressions was that of Marylebone Road at sunset with the endless perspective of yellow street-lamps—'a *féerie* that no theatre could ever reproduce'.

Busoni's first recital at the Wigmore (formerly Bechstein) Hall was an unexpected success, and he was deeply touched by his reception. 'You will find me very much changed,' he wrote to one of his English friends. But his public had changed too; England, despite his despair over first impressions, had become more musically intelligent since his last visit, and was ready to appreciate him in a way that it had never done before. Whenever he played in London he chose the Wigmore Hall for his recitals; it held only a small public, but that public was certain to include the fine flower of London musical life. After one of his London recitals Pachmann ran up to him, kissed his coat-tails and called out—'Busoni grösster Bachspieler —ich grösster Chopinspieler!' There were concerts in the provinces too, but those, as always, filled Busoni with nothing but disgust.

[1] The Savoy Hotel.

'You ask me if I am happy,' he wrote to Philipp. 'I confess I am not. To begin this strolling player's life[1] again is humiliating at my age, and at the moral and artistic phase that I have reached, it is unendurable. And I see no end to it.'

London provided Busoni with another of those curious experiences which affected him with a Hoffmanesque sense of mystery. One afternoon as he was coming back from a solitary walk he found himself enveloped in a thick fog. He managed to reach Regent's Park, but once inside it, the fog was so thick that he lost his bearings completely. A man came up to him through the gloom and Busoni asked if he could direct him to West Wing; the stranger took him by the arm and without the least hesitation led him straight to the house. In the light of a street-lamp Busoni realized with a sudden shock that his guide was blind. The episode would have seemed less disturbingly mysterious if Busoni had been aware that the roads in Regent's Park were all provided with a handrail to guide the blinded soldiers living at St. Dunstan's Lodge, next door to the house where he was staying.

In December Busoni passed through Paris again on his way back to Switzerland. He went with Maud Allan to see M. Carré, the director of the Opéra Comique, about certain projects of hers. At the end of the interview, M. Carré, as one might expect, took a polite leave of Miss Allan—'Je suis charmé et flatté, Mademoiselle, de vous serrer la main.' To Busoni he merely said, 'Bonsoir, Monsieur.' He apparently took Busoni for a hired interpreter. Most people would have taken this episode as a joke, and laughed over a typical Frenchman's ignorance of all that concerned music apart from his own professional interests. Busoni was deeply aggrieved, and expected Philipp to take some step towards an explanation.

The ordinary reader may well be led to think that Busoni was a man of inordinate vanity. This certainly was not the case. There can be no doubt that he was genuinely surprised at the respect with which he was

[1] 'Cette existence de saltimbanque.'

243

treated in London after an absence of nearly seven years. The period of seclusion at Zurich had caused him to concentrate profoundly upon himself and upon his own interior development. He had almost forgotten, one might say, that he was a pianist; to himself he was a composer, as indeed he had been all his life. Solitude had formed in him a habit of living in the future, rather than in the present. Each work that he completed was but a step towards the next. No sooner had he conceived the first germ of *Doctor Faust* than his mind looked forward to it as a finished achievement. For years he had seen himself in imagination as the prophetic leader of Italian music. It was no desire to be enthroned as a national newspaper hero like Puccini or Caruso; it was a sense of duty rather than a desire, an intense inward conviction that a mission lay before him which he only could fulfil. It was a mission to the whole art of music, not merely to Italy alone; Italy, he felt, was only to be the chosen instrument through which that mission was first to be launched. Italy rejected him. At this moment of his life he did not know which way to turn. But the consciousness of the mission remained as steadfast as ever. M. Carré's polite indifference offended him not as an insult to himself but as an indifference to the whole future of music.

Christmas was spent at Zurich. Here Busoni was content to be a father and no more; Benni had come back from America 'like Caspar Hauser from his prison', and needed all the affection that father, mother, and brother could give him. Busoni had always recognized his artistic gifts as a painter, and he had been resolved from the first that Benni should have a happier chance of developing them than he himself had had under the parental discipline of Ferdinando. 'He is a gifted boy of sound character,' he gently described him to Philipp, 'but at this moment he needs tender handling.'

Concerts for Paris had to be planned, and as soon as his own Concerto was suggested, Busoni immediately proposed that he himself should conduct it—in order that he might thus secure an opportunity for Petri to make an appearance in Paris. 'Petri is a Dutch subject—how wretched to be obliged to add that!' There was a short visit to Italy early in 1920. 'My impressions of Italy were discouraging. Italy will soon be nothing but a historical curiosity.' Philipp tried to soothe his irritation, but hardly understood Busoni's inward thoughts. 'I expressed myself badly,' Busoni replied; 'it is *not success* which I miss, it is the possibility of *working* in peace, whereas I have to waste my strength and the years that are slipping by for a thing which has always been of secondary importance to me. *Voilà.*'

He went to Paris in March, accompanied by Gerda. She had not left Switzerland since they first established themselves at Zurich. The years of trouble had told upon her too; her health had suffered severely. But there were few things she enjoyed more than travelling with Ferruccio on his concert tours, looking after him—he needed it badly—and sharing in the pleasure of his successes. Her presence radiated affection and kindness; if Ferruccio was unsociable and difficult of approach, she was always gentle and serene. Since the first years of her marriage she had been beloved of all her husband's friends and pupils; she accepted their love and rejoiced in it, for she regarded it as but given to her in trust, not so much for herself as only for Ferruccio.

There were six concerts at Paris, three recitals and three concerts with orchestra. In Paris, as in London, Busoni was overwhelmed at the cordiality of his welcome. The superb playing of the French orchestras aroused his enthusiastic admiration, and at the same time he was delighted at the success won by his Swiss friend Edmondo Allegra of Zurich, who played the solo in his Concertino for clarinet. The visit brought him into contact with some of the most distinguished French musicians, and of these none attracted him more than Maurice Emmanuel, whose immense learning, sensitive musicianship, and keen philosophical intelligence made him a man

245

thoroughly after Busoni's own heart. And in addition
to all the artistic and intellectual side of Paris there was
the magnificent and affectionate hospitality of an old friend
whom he had not seen for forty years—Leonhard Tauber,
once the young innkeeper at Klagenfurt who had listened
to him as a boy, now the proprietor of a number of the
most sumptuous hotels in Paris, still passionately devoted
to music and the generous friend and host of all musicians.

Another visit to London followed in June, when he
conducted the *Brautwahl* Suite and Liszt's *Faust* Symphony, as well as playing the solo part of his own *Indian
Fantasy*. This concert provoked an amusing and characteristic letter from Bernard Shaw, who advised Busoni to
produce his compositions under another name, since the
public could never be induced to believe that one man
could be so supremely great in two departments of music
at once. Busoni was considerably puzzled by the letter,
never having met the writer personally, and it took some
little explaining to make him understand that it was the
expression of a whole-hearted admiration, in spite of the
jesting language in which it was couched. Maud Allan
arranged a meeting between the two; it was not quite
so successful as she had hoped. Busoni's experience of
Germany had led him to expect the world's great men,
or those who considered themselves such, to behave in
a more monumental manner. Mr. Shaw seemed to adapt
himself only too charmingly to the elegant *badinerie* of
a lady's drawing-room.

From London Busoni wrote to Andreae at Zurich:

'The London Symphony Orchestra, which I had at my disposal, is
quite excellent, technically accomplished and equally quick at understanding. And it has kept the dignity and good manners too that
I appreciated so much before the war. . . . In this clear and sunny
season London is enchanting, though I take a peculiar delight in the
mystic drama (*Mysterium*) of the fog.

'I note that my years in Zurich have not been without an effect
for me in other countries; my position in the world of music has
distinctly risen, without any help from me, just as a work ripens

within oneself, without one's being consciously occupied with it. I am all the more grateful to your country for the quiet activity which it made possible for me. But now that chapter too is finished; sadly and seriously, I must say good-bye. . . . Parting will not be easy, but my sense of form tells me that the length of this movement must not be exceeded.'

On the same day he wrote to Petri in much the same words. For a year he had been unable to make up his mind where the next chapter of his life was to be spent. The decision came from outside. The German Revolution had affected music as well as politics. Busoni's pupil Leo Kestenberg had been appointed to an important post in the Prussian Ministry of Education. The result was that Busoni was offered the direction of a class for advanced musical composition under the State (formerly Royal) Academy of Arts and Sciences. The State Opera was planning the production of *Turandot* and *Arlecchino*. Busoni decided to go back to Berlin. The future became clear to him at once. He would have a position of honour in Berlin under the new régime and an opportunity for carrying on his mission as a trainer of young composers. For six months in the year he would be free to travel. He visualized his new life as divided between Paris, London, Berlin, and Rome. America should see him no more.

Yet still he hesitated; the contract with Berlin should be for one experimental year only. There had been other contracts for an experimental year—with Vienna and Bologna.

It was with a sense of homelessness that Busoni had come to Switzerland. There were many cities that he loved—Helsingfors, London, Paris, Bergamo—but none had ever been a home to him. Not even Berlin had ever given him that sense of home which means that one belongs to the place rather than that the place belongs to oneself. In Switzerland a new feeling seems to have taken possession of him, however little he may himself have been conscious of it. Affectionate by nature, it was impossible for him to receive so much affection as

247

surrounded him in Switzerland without responding to it in a degree that subtly influenced his whole personality. To those who were cut off from him during the years of war he appeared changed in many ways. The change in his outward appearance was indeed distressing, and hardly less distressing the sense of melancholy remoteness that he so often conveyed. Those characteristic explosions of laughter had begun to seem almost artificial, spasmodic, and deliberate attempts to recover something of his old self, or to disguise—perhaps to himself as well as to his friends—the transformation that had taken place within him. One might think him grown less exhilarating, even less cordial; but he had acquired a new gentleness and tenderness, a new power of tranquil inspiration for those who had the sympathy to receive it. He had entered into Swiss musical life in a way that was new to him; he had made friends with the Swiss composers, had learned to take a helpful interest in their works and in their aspirations, almost as if he belonged to Switzerland himself; he had in fact come to feel himself spiritually at home in Switzerland—far more intimately than the foreign musicians who bought themselves properties in picturesque landscapes, even when they found it convenient to acquire legal Swiss nationality.

When the University of Zurich conferred an honorary Doctorate of Philosophy upon him in July 1919, Busoni expressed his thanks in an open letter to Andreae both for this honour, which he sincerely felt to be the most distinguished that he had ever received, and for all that Zurich and Switzerland had done for him. He had felt that he himself was receiving help and benefit from the high level of intellectual and artistic culture that characterized the Swiss; the consciousness that he was understood and that others were willing to bring him understanding had produced an ideal harmony of collaboration.

A pale autumn settled down upon Zurich; it had lost all that made it tolerable during the 'good' time of the war! Busoni tried to devote himself to composition, but it was impossible in a house full of packing-cases and straw. The one person who seemed to enjoy the situation was Giotto, who pushed his way between the packing-cases like Gulliver in the streets of Lilliput, looking for a heap of straw on which he could settle himself to sleep.

'He looks up at me and his eye says, "I've no business here, but you won't turn me out, will you?" Poor Giotto—I can hardly bear that look of his; he seems to know.

'My heart is bursting. I leave my sons behind. I am going—at 54—into the unknown.' [1]

[1] Letter to I. Philipp, September 7, 1920.

CHAPTER XIV

THE CITY OF LIGHT

USONI had good reason to be nervous about returning to Berlin. He had departed in January 1915 from a Berlin that was imperial and confident of victory, a Berlin fermenting with hatred for everything foreign and especially for everything that expressed the Latin spirit. As the war went on, he had been the subject of malignant criticism in the German press. By 1914 Berlin had just begun to acknowledge him as the greatest of living pianists, and there was even a certain appreciation for him as a composer. The war-spirit inevitably drove Germany back to the music of the romantics. War conditions, in Germany as in other countries, produced a general lowering of intellectual and artistic standards. National unity involved everywhere the acceptance of an 'average' type in all thought and feeling. Busoni might hand over the gross receipts of his farewell concert in Berlin to a fund for destitute musicians, but that did not prevent him from being attacked for deliberately avoiding German music in his American programmes—the reason being that he had played his own *Indian Fantasy* and the F major Concerto of Saint-Saëns! At the same moment the American papers alleged that he had refused to conduct concerts at Rome because he said he could not make up a worthy programme without the inclusion of music that was German. A few literary friends who remained in Berlin had written occasional articles in his honour, perhaps as *ballons d'essai*; it was pointed out that unlike most prominent artists he had kept the strictest silence as regards his political sympathies, and had retired to the obscurity of Switzerland rather than accept lucrative engagements in Paris or London. It was even said that he was longing to return to Berlin. It is highly probable that he was always longing to go back to his flat and his library; but it is significant that in not one of the letters which he wrote between January 1915 and June 1920 did he ever say a word which could suggest the possibility of his considering Berlin as a place in which to live.

The Berlin of 1920 was a changed city. In one way it might indeed have made a keener appeal to Busoni—at any rate in his 'Dickens' mood—for the first thing that a stranger noticed on revisiting Berlin after the war was its general griminess. There was only one building in Berlin which had had a fresh coat of paint since 1914—the British Embassy. The Friedrichstrasse, once the busiest street in the town, was a chaos of sand and wooden planks; some day there was to be an underground railway beneath it, but in 1920 Berlin was too depressed either to proceed with the railway or to remake the pavement. War had produced poverty and poverty crime. In 1914, as to-day, honesty could be taken for granted in any German town, at least as regards everyday trifles; in 1920 it was assumed that everything would be stolen if the opportunity was not carefully prevented. Berlin had adopted for the time being the standards of old-fashioned Italy. On the railways and in the restaurants one was perpetually conscious of the shortage of certain materials—textiles, leather, metal. In Berlin's best hotels the knives and forks were in a disgraceful state; and in the cafés of Amsterdam one was given a little glass rod to stir one's coffee because the Germans who came to Holland stole all the spoons.

It was early in September when Busoni came back to Berlin. Gerda had stayed behind at Zurich to finish packing up. The flat in the Victoria Luise Platz was in perfectly sound condition; one of the 'caryatides' had watched over it throughout the war, and had taken care that on his return Busoni should find everything exactly as he had left it. Busoni missed Giotto terribly, but it was impossible to keep a dog of that type in a third-floor flat in Berlin. The flat and the library were unchanged; but Busoni noticed at once the change that had come over the town. He noticed too that the people had changed—they had become more *humain*, as he described them to Philipp, more kind and friendly. Friendliness even took surprising forms; Busoni had hardly been a week in Berlin before he ran into jovial Hans Herrmann, 'Berlin's King of Song', well-known for his extremely popular ditties, who at once hailed him with: 'Hullo, Busoni, what luck to meet you—want you to sign your name on a fan for a lady!' There were certainly some features of Berlin which were the same as ever.

Berlin at once stimulated Busoni to composition. As soon as he had finished the *Toccata* for pianoforte, begun at Zurich, he amused himself by writing a set of waltzes for orchestra (*Tanzwalzer*) suggested by the accidental hearing of a Strauss waltz at the door of a café. They do not, however, remind the hearer so much of Strauss as of Bizet; they were actually studies for the ballet music in *Doctor Faust*. But work was only an anodyne for anxiety. There was an inward crisis to be overcome. 'These weeks have been the most difficult of all my life,' he wrote to Gerda. He tried to remain incognito, but old friends insisted on seeking him out. To explain the crisis is difficult; Busoni himself said little of it. But even amidst his familiar books he still felt that he had 'gone out into the unknown'; the future was still undecided, and he was haunted almost to agony by the sense that the greater part of his life lay behind him and that the remaining years must be put to their fullest and most intense purpose. His friends became anxious. One took it upon herself to telephone to Gerda at Zurich and beg her to come to Berlin at once. Busoni was extremely annoyed when he discovered this; it was perfectly senseless, he said, and most unjustifiable. 'You must do exactly what you yourself think necessary,' he wrote to Gerda. It was characteristic of his unfailing consideration for his wife, and his unfailing confidence in her judgement.

She arrived in a few days.

'Yes, it is bearable,' he wrote to Philipp. 'I am something between Don Quixote and the wandering Jew. I have had a short postcard from Lello.[1] He is in Paris, enthusiastic. To be twenty and be in Paris is certainly pleasanter than ... the opposite. Well, life is not lively. Why did you keep me away from Paris? I should have done no harm to anyone ...!

'A politico-social reflection: I fancy it is fairly dangerous to ill-treat a starving dog.'

Busoni might be melancholy, but he could never allow himself to be idle. Preparations were made at once for two recitals in Berlin; in January there were to be three orchestral concerts devoted to his own works. London was to be visited in February, Rome in April. And above all things Busoni desired to play in Paris again; but for various reasons the visit had to be postponed.

The two recitals at Berlin in November resulted in a triumph such as Busoni had never before experienced. It was the first time that he had given a recital in the Philhar-monie, Berlin's largest concert-hall, holding three thousand or more. The hall was full and there was an amazing demonstration of enthusiasm. At the second recital he played Chopin's *Préludes*, the *Hammerklavier* Sonata, and Liszt's Paganini Studies. The audience so far forgot itself as to applaud in the middle of *La Campanella*—a thing unheard of in a Berlin concert-room. One might have been at Naples! An elderly critic apologized sadly to a foreign visitor for the misbehaviour—'nouveaux riches!' After the final applause subsided a voice called out 'Da capo!' Busoni came back to the pianoforte, sat down, and amidst breathless silence looked round, made a face, played a mocking reference to *La Campanella*—

[1] Both Busoni's sons were painters; Benni had taken a studio at Zurich and Lello was studying in Paris.

s

and walked off the platform. 'Such a piece of impertinence!' observed a member of the audience. But it was
impossible to take it in an unfriendly spirit. The impression of the whole programme could never be forgotten,
and the final gesture was thoroughly typical of Busoni.
The audience laughed heartily. Busoni had returned to
Berlin as a conqueror.

A new generation of musicians and music-lovers had
arisen in Berlin, who were more ready to appreciate
Busoni than their predecessors. Busoni's attitude towards
them was sceptical. He loved nothing better than to be
surrounded by the young, and his interest in the younger
generation became strikingly intensified in this later period
of his life. But he still remained critical of their accomplish-
ments, and the helplessly experimental nature of their
music was very evident to a man of his supreme technical
achievement.

'Before the war', he observed to Andreae, 'it was very difficult for
the young and the very young to obtain appreciation or even a
hearing. Now it is impossible to keep them quiet. There is a great
outburst of music which is pieced together at haphazard from Strauss
and Schönberg, utterly without ability or skill (*völlig ungekonnte
Musik*), and people are interested in it. I look back to Strauss's and
Schönberg's youthful works—to my own too—and feel ashamed of
the present age.'

But there were serious musicians among the young and
Busoni was at once ready to recognize their merits.
Towards the end of October his great Concerto was
played by Eduard Erdmann, then a boy of nineteen, who
had prepared it entirely by himself. The critics were
inclined to be supercilious over this ambitious effort;
Busoni made no comment except to say that he was profoundly touched by such enthusiasm and enterprise.

In January he played at Hamburg. His account of
musical conditions at Hamburg is significant.

'Brecher (the conductor) started the rehearsal at nine, by way
of precaution! The orchestra is morally and artistically in a very
bad way; Brecher does not dare say anything to them except with

the most amiable smile. Brecher said that Kapellmeister Pollack would "engage" me for next year. I said to Brecher it was a question whether I should accept an engagement . . .

'Not a soul *loves* and *feels* music. Some make it as a trade, some as time-beaters (*als Taktstriche*), some from vanity. I was very bad-tempered at the rehearsal. Naturally people thought I was playing the "star", although they did not listen. Any way, the "time-beaters" are the ones that deserve most respect, however far away from music they are.'

There were three orchestral concerts devoted to Busoni's own works in January, arranged at Berlin by the newly started musical periodical *Der Anbruch*.[1] The programmes were as follows:

7 January 1921
Lustspielouvertüre (Comedy Overture), Op. 38, *Berceuse Élégiaque*, Op. 42, *Nocturne Symphonique*, *Rondo arlecchinesco*, Op. 46, Violin Concerto, Op. 35 (Emil Telmányi), *Brautwahl* Suite.

13 January 1921
Turandot-Suite, Concertino for clarinet, Op. 48 (Carl Essberger), *Gesang vom Reigen der Geister*, Op. 47 (first performance), *Sarabande* and *Cortège*, Divertimento for Flute (Alfred Liechtenstein), *Tanzwalzer*.

27 January 1921
Konzertstück for Pianoforte and orchestra, Op. 31, *Indian Fantasy*, Op. 44, Concerto for pianoforte, Op. 39 (Pianoforte—Ferruccio Busoni; Conductor—Gustav Brecher).

The first concert did not represent Busoni at his greatest and attracted only a moderate audience. There was a more cordial reception at the second, and, as might be expected, a large and enthusiastic audience for the third, at which Busoni appeared as pianist. Berlin still hesitated to accept him as a composer, but none the less it was clear that a certain body of musicians, including even a few critics, were ready to understand his ideals.

Towards the end of January Busoni decided to abandon

[1] *Der Anbruch* (The Dawn) began as a movement to include literature and all the arts. Its musical organ was at first called *Musikblätter des Anbruch*; this was eventually renamed *Der Anbruch*, under which title it still flourishes.

the projected visit to Paris. He did so with somewhat of a guilty conscience, and it is evident that he was beginning to suffer more and more acutely from overwrought nerves. He would never admit that he was seriously ill, and nothing would induce him to consult a doctor, still less to visit a dentist. Once in America he had complained to Natalie Curtis of toothache. She gave him the obvious advice, which he flatly refused. 'Well then, what do you do when you have toothache?' she asked. 'I thank God for not being sea-sick,' was the grim reply. For years he had suffered from constant minor illnesses such as short attacks of influenza, but as far as possible he had disregarded them; over and over again he had fulfilled his contract to play, whatever his temperature might have been. Such things he regarded as all in the day's work of a travelling virtuoso. Gradually this neglect of health had told upon his constitution, and the anxieties of the years of war had naturally aggravated his condition. He was miserable if he was not working, but the only work which interested him seriously was composition. The older he grew, the more he detested having to play the pianoforte in order to earn a living; and it was the irony of fate that he should achieve his greatest successes as a pianist (to say nothing of the financial success and the more and more pressing need for that) at a time when he would only too willingly have retired completely, as Liszt had done, from the career of a public performer.

With the German currency depreciating daily he could not afford to neglect England, or even those odious provincial tours in England. And every hour that was spent in pianoforte practice, every day spent in travelling and in appearing on a platform, was a moment wasted, a moment that could never be recovered, an apostasy from the mission which he feared he might never live to fulfil.

'This will be a letter that you will think "serious". Do not think that I am mad, ill, or worn out—but I have been working like a horse (or a saint, or an idiot), and when I have finished with Berlin, I have to begin an absurd series of concerts and journeys in England.

I feel neither the energy nor the interest (nor the moral duty) for starting afresh to study programmes, to play them on certain agreed and unalterable dates; what a loss for me, and how deeply I regret it! but I am forced to deny myself Paris this season.

'I know you will think me a criminal. I beseech you to try to understand me. I assure you I can do no more. Be kind and forgiving and I will bless you. Otherwise you will make me unhappy.

'Write to me before the end of this month, when I leave Berlin to go to London. Life is indeed too short.'[1]

He went to England in February, but found life in London depressing. It was a pleasure to meet Sibelius there, and all his old friends were kind and helpful. At Bradford he was delighted to find a conductor who was 'quick of understanding'[2] and gave a good performance of the *Indian Fantasy*. He read Arnold Bennett's *Things that have interested me*, and was amused at his description of an English rehearsal, but could not take him seriously—he was 'knee-deep in Wagner and Strauss!' There was no 'atmosphere' in England, except always the beloved 'Dickens atmosphere' of the streets.

At Manchester he renewed his old friendship with the Brodskys and found Mme Brodsky as 'Russian' as ever. She asked after the two boys. 'Have they become *good* men?' 'I think so,' said Busoni, 'as far as I know.' 'Then they take after Mamma. You are a good artist, but your wife is a good woman.' A young English musician, who had never seen Busoni before, went to hear him play at the Free Trade Hall. 'I shall never forget the shock and the horror of seeing him first come on to the platform; the whole audience seemed to shudder with it. Busoni looked exactly like a corpse.'

In London he played Beethoven's Sonata Op. 111, his own new Toccata and the Sonatina on *Carmen* dedicated to Leonhard Tauber, Chopin's B flat minor Sonata and Liszt's *Venezia e Napoli*. As an encore he played Liszt's

[1] Letter to I. Philipp, January 24, 1921.
[2] Busoni's own words, in English, from a letter to his wife. The conductor was Hamilton Harty.

St. François de Paule. He seemed terribly exhausted; besides that he was embarrassed by a strange pianoforte. He missed his Bechstein sadly, but (as he wrote to a former pupil in Germany) London still refused to permit the appearance of a German instrument on the public platform, although such few as remained in the shops were only too eagerly bought up.

Busoni's interpretations at this time gave the listener a strange sense of perilous adventure. He was no pianist for beginners in the art of listening. He assumed that his audience were as well acquainted with the classics as he was himself; it would be superfluous to tell them what they knew before. Those who went to hear him with a settled idea of how Bach, Beethoven, or Chopin ought to be played came away bewildered, or even infuriated. Yet there was in reality nothing perverse or wilful about his interpretations, and he had long ago laid aside any inclination to exhibit mere mechanical dexterity. Busoni was different from all other pianists because he had an entirely different mental conception of what could be done with the pianoforte. It was only in Vienna, Poland, and Russia, he once said, that there was any tradition of the great pianoforte style. In Italy there had been no one since Clementi. Buonamici had been merely 'a good German pianist', a copy of Hans von Bülow. Sgambati had had more Latin feeling for the instrument. Paris produced only elegant finger-work and lightning precision. Berlin had no understanding whatever for the pianoforte as an instrument in its own right; the German pianists only understood *das Musikalische*, meaning the plain statement of the logical relations between one note and another. The only pianists of recent times whom Busoni could honestly admire were the Liszt pupils of the older generation—Reisenauer, Sauer, and Eugen d'Albert in his prime.

The ordinary amateur generally regards pianoforte technique mainly as a matter of speed and strength, so that it is only natural that the more serious amateur should detest the virtuoso of the conventional type. Busoni undoubtedly could play louder and more rapidly than any one else, whether in single notes, octaves, or chords. Rapidity was for him an accomplishment to be taken for granted, like clear handwriting; strength was equally indispensable, but strictly subject to the condition that the tone must always be beautiful, however loud. And since by the accident of birth Busoni's younger life had been spent in an age of 'monumentality', his conceptions of music in general—until these latest years of his life—were inclined naturally to be 'monumental'. In private life he was a keen collector of engravings and etchings, but as a pianist he regarded the delicate and intimate style preferred in England with resentment or ridicule. There was too much pose of privacy about it; it was a style for amateurs. As an Italian he wanted the pianoforte to sing, and shared Brahms's delight in the combination of *forte* and *dolce*; it was not the function of the pianoforte to whisper or to talk. He had not the least desire to make Bach or Mozart sound as if they were being played on a harpsichord; he knew too much about the harpsichord to have any sentimental illusions about it. For Bach and Mozart the harpsichord had had no more faded fragrance of lavender than his own Bechstein grand pianoforte had for himself. 'Never look back,' he said, and he would play nothing which he could not regard and interpret as prophetic of the future.

Technique was for him merely the servant of expression. Strength and speed were indispensable, in order that what most writers on music call 'passages of display' should take their proper places as decorative backgrounds to the singing melody. He played the first prelude of the *Forty-eight*, and it became a wash of shifting colours, a rainbow over the fountains of the Villa d'Este; he played the fugue, and each voice sang out above the rest like the entries of an Italian chorus, until at the last *stretto* the subject entered like the trumpets of the *Dona nobis* in the Mass in B minor, though in the middle of the keyboard, across a haze of pedal-held sound that was not confusion but blinding clearness.

Most English musicians, and many continental ones too, regard the music of Liszt as an abomination. When Busoni played Liszt in these later years prejudice was irresistibly broken down. Busoni's Liszt was the Liszt of Italy, the Italy of Paganini and Byron, with all the life's experience of Liszt in his old age at Rome. His Chopin was more difficult to accept. The smaller works of Chopin he discarded entirely, as indeed he discarded those of Bach; the French and English Suites were as unsympathetic to him as the Valses and Mazurkas. He played the *Études*, occasionally the Sonatas, more rarely the *Ballades* and a nocturne or two, but most often and most willingly the *Préludes*. The *Préludes*, as he always said, were 'prophetic'. Busoni would have nothing to do with the conventional Chopin of romance, Parisianized Pole and drawing-room consumptive. With Busoni there could be no undertones, no half-statements, no evasions: he was too Italian to allow of anything but the firmest of line and the clearest of colour. Some one said of him that he played the Trio of the Funeral March like a cornet solo; it certainly gave a shock to many a listener. But his attitude towards it was one of severe logic: 'if you honestly believe that the melody is beautiful,' he seemed to say, 'you must sing it with all the fullness of your voice.' He treated the *Ballades* in the same way, and one could only ask oneself whether one honestly believed in them. If they could not be tolerated as Busoni played them, full-blooded and masculine, with never a trace of feminine airs and graces, were they really worth playing at all?

The reader who turns to the list of Busoni's complete repertory will be surprised to find many gaps among the works of Beethoven. Busoni never played the whole of the Sonatas. The reason is easy to guess: as a boy he had to play to audiences which could never have listened to such sonatas as were then within his grasp, as a young man he naturally seized first on the popular favourites of the virtuoso, the *Waldstein* and the *Appassionata*. In later life he played those of the third period, though not all of them. He seems for instance never to have played the Sonata in A major, Op. 101, although one might imagine that it would have been peculiarly well suited to him. A time came when he found it necessary to subject Beethoven to dispassionate criticism, and to admit that there were many works of his which were not on the highest level. In his last years he occasionally played the *Waldstein* and the *Appassionata*, but it was only in the slow movements, and perhaps in the Finale of the *Waldstein*, which he took at an unusually deliberate pace, in order to emphasize its singing quality, that his interpretations had that indescribable dignity and beauty of which he alone, and only in his later life, possessed the secret. He was at his greatest and most prophetic in the *Hammerklavier* Sonata, and in the two last ones, Op. 110 and Op. 111. Never for a moment, even in the most thundering passages or in the intricacies of the fugue, did he lose sight of his unique beauty of tone-quality. To hear him play these sonatas was an almost terrifying experience; dynamic and rhythmical relations were treated with such vast breadth and freedom that one seemed taken up to heights of perilous dizziness and made, as it were, to gaze steadily into the depths until one's vision became serene. The last and loftiest plane of serenity was reached in the *Arietta* and variations of the Sonata in C minor. As he was playing it in London an elderly critic leaned over the shoulder of a younger colleague and remarked in a stage whisper, 'D'you know, I believe the man's *drunk*!'

From London Busoni went on to Rome, where the extent of his appreciation may be measured by the fact that there was conferred upon him the title of Commendatore. Busoni was no little amused by the honour; it made him feel like the old gentleman in *Don Giovanni*. On the return journey he was held up at the Brenner owing to a strike in the Tyrol, and passed the time in a hut surrounded by snow (it was early in May), giving a lesson in strict

261

counterpoint and canon to a young musician whom he had
met in the train.

In May he gave two concerts in Berlin at which he
played six concertos of Mozart. Gustav Brecher was to
have conducted for him, but there was a painful scene at
the rehearsal, Brecher utterly refusing to accept Busoni's
tempi. No self-respecting German conductor of the front
rank could allow a mere pianist to dictate to him the right
pace for a concerto, and Brecher declined to have anything more to do with the concerts. Busoni was quite
unabashed and with Italian indifference to German musical etiquette called upon Otto Marienhagen, the leader of
the orchestra, to take the conductor's place. Marienhagen
was an honest German craftsman of music, who had had
plenty of experience conducting popular symphony concerts to the accompaniment of beer and sausages. Busoni,
it need hardly be said, showed him the respect and consideration which a musician of his type deserved. He
conducted the first concert without rehearsal, and Busoni
was perfectly happy to play under him for the second as
well.

Rehearsals began for *Turandot* and *Arlecchino*. The
State Opera at this time was under the direction of Max
von Schillings and Leo Blech. Despite the fact that they
belonged to the old Wagnerian generation, they both had
a profound respect for Busoni, and since both of them
were musicians entirely free from either vanity or self-
interest, no more fortunate combination could have been
devised for the production of Busoni's operas, or indeed
for the entire conduct of the Berlin opera-house. Busoni
had already hailed with delight their revival of *Così fan tutte*,
a work which had been neglected and misunderstood in
Germany for so many generations that Busoni himself had
never had a chance of seeing it on the stage. It meant
that Berlin had at last come back to value an art that was
limpid and full of delight; Busoni had noticed the same
thing in England too.

The performance of the two operas on May 19 was a

decisive success; with Leo Blech as conductor it need hardly be said that the execution was perfect in every detail. Busoni had indeed been prepared for a thoroughly careful study of his operas, but even he was astonished at the minute accuracy with which every wish of his was carried out by an army of some three or four hundred persons. He expressed his thanks to all concerned in a charming letter to the *Vossische Zeitung*. Of himself and his compositions he said nothing; what he wanted to point out to the opera-going public was the marvellous organization of a great opera-house, and how one single little word of the libretto might set in exactly synchronized movement a whole crowd of collaborators—singers, musicians, scene-shifters, stage hands of every degree. Rehearsals had taught him how much gratitude he owed to numberless obscure people who were doing their duty invisibly, without any share in the public's applause. 'The public takes the most complicated accuracy as a matter of course and coldly criticizes the tiniest hitch. Our benevolent judges —strange figures robed in newspaper, their faces hidden behind a mask of printers' ink—have the power to destroy the constructive labour of years by a single sentence.'

The people at the Opera were already talking of *Doctor Faust* too as if its production was a *fait accompli*. Busoni alone knew how much of it still remained unwritten.

'Each accomplishment of a project is a sort of little death,' he wrote to Philipp on the day after the performance of *Turandot* and *Arlecchino*, 'each fresh beginning a new birth. I always feel depressed when I have completed something. Hope, which is the mainspring of the mental mechanism, runs down and ceases to work—one has to wind it up again by new efforts. *Al lavoro!*'

The summer was spent quietly at work in Berlin. The new opera was by no means the only occupation; Busoni had a wonderful faculty for simultaneous work on a number of plans. He began a transcription for two pianofortes of the *Fantasia Contrappuntistica*; he composed a new movement to form a sequel to the *Concertstück* for pianoforte

263

and orchestra with which he had won the Rubinstein prize thirty years before. Two short pieces were added to an old *Albumblatt* and cadenzas written for Mozart's Concerto in F. Along with composition he was studying the madrigals of Monteverdi recently edited by Hugo Leichtentritt, and was so overcome by their beauty and intensity of expression that he wrote at once to the Minister of Fine Arts at Rome to urge upon him the significance of Monteverdi for modern Italy. Yet *Doctor Faust* was always present to his mind. 'Like a subterranean river, heard but not seen, the music for *Faust* roars and flows on continually in the depths of my aspirations; and I begin to see the moment when it will rise to the surface.' A month later he wrote to Gerda, 'The score (of *Doctor Faust*) goes on by itself; it pulls me along instead of my leading it—just like Giotto!' Towards the end of July he had finished the scene of the students' discussion in the wine-cellar; he thought it was the most skilful piece of craftsmanship that he had yet accomplished for the stage, and he had indeed cause to be proud of it.

The triumphs of London, Rome, and Berlin had restored him to a cheerful frame of mind and the period of workful rest that followed had apparently gone some way to the re-establishment of his health. Gerda was visiting friends in Austria; the young lady who had summoned her so hastily by telephone from Zurich a year before was living close at hand and as usual assumed the functions of an adopted daughter, to Busoni's alternate amusement and despair. Her conversation was unflagging; if Busoni disregarded her, she chattered away with the maid-servant in the same breath. She arrived at breakfast-time to keep him company—when he would much rather have been left alone, and borrowed for him, as a kindly surprise, a 'family edition' of Goethe's plays with illustrations in the 'old German' style of the 1870's, by way of stimulating his inspiration for *Doctor Faust*. Busoni said that Dr. Faust looked like his venerable friend Dr. Kienzl sitting in an old-fashioned wine-room in the Friedrichstrasse, and told her to send the books back to the owner. 'So that's what a brain like hers understands about *Faust*, about me and about art in general!' On Mondays and Thursdays the composition pupils came, clever young men who since then have begun to make a name for themselves—Kurt Weill, Wladimir Vogel, Robert Blum.

In the autumn work was suddenly interrupted by a sharp attack of illness which compelled him at last to place himself in the hands of a doctor. He was able to conduct a concert for his pupil Eduard Weiss, who played the *Indian Fantasy*, in October, and to give a recital for two pianofortes with Petri in November. He was reluctant to admit that he was seriously ill, but confessed it under the seal of the strictest secrecy to Philipp. He was determined to conceal his illness, even at the cost of aggravating his condition, from his wife, in order not to cause her anxiety. He might well think he could conceal it; Gerda was naturally the first person to observe it, though, from the same desire not to cause anxiety to him, she pretended not to be aware of it. He neglected his correspondence, but he continued to work at composition; and in December he startled Berlin by playing six concertos of Mozart.

The illness passed, and he finished the year with a feeling of confidence and hope. He had settled down happily to life in Berlin and was well satisfied with what he had been able to achieve there. *Doctor Faust* was making progress; there remained but one-sixth of it yet to be written. The five composition pupils were a source of genuine happiness to him. Next spring there would be the concerts in London, Paris, and Rome—if only the doctor would make up his mind and come to a definite decision!

The decision was favourable, and in January 1922 Busoni set out for London once more. The English engagements, however fatiguing, had become more and more of an urgent necessity, for the German currency was falling rapidly. In the Dutch restaurant car, as he passed through Holland, Busoni could not resist the temptation

to order a half-bottle of Heidsieck—he always had a
weakness for champagne, though he was never an excessive drinker. When the bill came, he decided to pay for
it in English money; thirteen shillings were more easily
reconciled with his conscience than six hundred and fifty
marks. There were concerts at Glasgow, Manchester, and
Bradford as well as in London, where he gave in addition
a recital with Egon Petri for two pianofortes. The more the
desire deepened in him to retire altogether from the concert platform, the more energy he displayed in his efforts
to make a career for Petri. Busoni had often warned Petri
in earlier years against becoming too much of a scholar
and for having too little ambition as an artist; he thought
that he required perpetual stimulus to make him take any
interest in his own advancement. The London recital for
two pianofortes was given mainly with the object of bringing Petri into notice under the cover of Busoni's more
attractive name. It was Busoni, not Petri, who saw the
practical necessity and value of the step. His own career
was nearing its last end and interested him no longer; but
all his life he had had hard and bitter experience of how
to make a career, and he was determined to use that experience for the benefit of the younger musician. He bom-
barded Philipp with letters about Petri; Petri must make
a decisive success in Paris, and so must that clever young
violinist Josef Szigeti. Busoni made up his mind clearly
and firmly as to who were to be reckoned artists of the
first rank.

London was followed by Paris. Busoni was greeted
with an extraordinary ovation; his very first appearance
on the platform produced a burst of applause which lasted
for ten minutes. Paris gave him the chance of playing
concertos which he could hardly venture to present in
London or Berlin—Mendelssohn's in G minor, and the
E flat of Saint-Saëns.[1] Berlin could never understand
Busoni's veneration of Saint-Saëns. Saint-Saëns interested
him no doubt as having been an intimate disciple of Liszt,

[1] Saint-Saëns died 16 December 1921.

and personal acquaintance (through Ysaye) inevitably brought a sense of friendship, although Busoni's meetings with Saint-Saëns were rare. But there was no doubt about Busoni's sincere admiration for him as a composer. He saw the historic line of his musical ancestry; Gounod, Bizet, and Saint-Saëns were the true heirs of those 'three masters of uncontested greatness', Rossini, Cherubini, and Mendelssohn, the only great masters who could be said to form the school of Mozart. He was not blind to his limitations; but Saint-Saëns, like Anatole France, wisely avoided the problems which were beyond his technique. Saint-Saëns could never be either 'daemonic' or 'mystical'. He was a man of this world; but he was at least 'a *grand seigneur* in the kingdom of music'.

Busoni discussed every detail of his concerts with Philipp, even down to the encores which he proposed to play. Philipp was astonished at his extraordinary memory. He had not looked at the Mendelssohn concerto for twenty-five years, and borrowed a copy from Philipp a day or two before the concert, just to make sure of the entries. One day Philipp suggested that as an encore he should play the *Sposalizio* of Liszt. Busoni suggested a variety of pieces which Philipp did not consider appropriate for Paris. Finally Busoni said he would play something which he had not played for thirty-five years; sat down to the pianoforte then and there and played the C sharp minor Scherzo of Chopin. Philipp said he had never heard Busoni play Chopin like that before. In common with many of Busoni's friends he had always found Busoni's Chopin impossible to accept. But this *impromptu* performance was something quite different. It was not very accurate; it was an impression of the work, almost a transcription; he played it 'as he remembered it, as he felt it'. But before the concert Busoni practised it. The magic of the 'impression' was gone; the work was distorted by over-intellectualization—'he had thought it over'.

Philipp's good advice was only too seldom taken. He was naturally approached by various persons who wished to make Busoni's acquaintance. One of these was a diplomat of high rank, who desired Busoni to play at his own house. Busoni was to name his own fee, he was to play for half an hour and to play whatever he chose; the list of guests was to be submitted to him for his approval, as if he were a member of a royal family. His only answer was 'Jamais!' A more important invitation was that of the President of the Argentine Republic, who was trying to tempt Busoni to Buenos Aires. Philipp introduced him to Busoni after a concert; he was a man of distinguished presence and singular charm of manner and spoke exquisite Italian. Busoni should be his own personal guest; he would have a thoroughly sympathetic audience. He himself would take the responsibility of all the concert arrangements, and Busoni would probably make some two or three million francs. Busoni refused point blank. 'You take me for a commercial traveller for the *Campanella*?'

Philipp refused to accept this answer as definite. He took Busoni and his wife to a restaurant and insisted on discussing the matter seriously. He realized Busoni's state of health better than Busoni did, and foresaw the future with the gravest anxiety. He told Busoni straight out that he must on no account refuse the South American invitation—there were prospects of concerts in Brazil too —because it would be the best possible way of providing for his wife in the event of his death. 'Think of your wife and children!' Gerda burst into tears. That Ferruccio had any sort of duty towards her she would never admit; she had never admitted it to herself for a moment since the day she was married. Her whole life with him had been based on the principle that she claimed no rights and accepted all duties; that was the simple secret of her life's happiness. To hear her husband reminded openly of his duty to herself was more than she could bear. By Busoni Philipp's plain speaking was bitterly resented. He became more and more disagreeable; there was often something strangely devilish about his sarcasm, and on this occasion it became so offensive that the kindly Philipp could tolerate it no longer. He said he would take Mme Busoni home and leave Busoni to himself if he wished.

Busoni might well seem to have become in some ways very like his own father in these last years. The strain of constant over-work and ill-health had begun to tell on his powers of self-control. When one considers the intense and concentrated self-control necessary for such achievements as Busoni's recitals, it is small wonder that self-control should break down utterly in the crises of private life. He had inherited all his father's Tuscan bitterness of tongue and Tuscan genius for the expression of it. After his mother's death he had had a period during which, by some curious form of hallucination, he had often confused Gerda with her, talking to his wife as if she were his mother in moments when he was not fully awake. Gerda had been singularly touched by this unconscious delusion, and felt that it had given her a still deeper and more intimate sense of communion with Ferruccio. And now, in these last years, mother of grown-up sons, she found herself having to be more and more of a mother to her husband as well. If Ferruccio sometimes seemed to grow more and more like Ferdinando, Gerda had more and more need of Anna's gentleness and patience. Anna had spent a life in suffering and in prayer. Gerda's radiant serenity was content to love and to smile.

There was no quarrel; neither Busoni nor Philipp was capable of such a thing. By way of a peace-offering Philipp presented Busoni with Littré's great Dictionary of the French language, and there was no gift that could have given him greater delight. 'What a labour!' he wrote in his letter of thanks; 'one feels modest indeed in face of a work like that!'

On the way back to Berlin he played a concerto of Mozart at Hamburg, and in Berlin he conducted a Philharmonic concert at which Frieda Kwast-Hodapp played the *Concertstück* with the new sequel which Busoni had dedicated to Alfredo Casella. It was hardly suited to her usual massive style—it was sometimes said of her that

269

T

whatever she played she turned to Max Reger! If she made the original *Concertstück* sound like the D minor Concerto of Brahms, as one of Busoni's friends complained, it was hardly surprising, for the influence of Brahms on Busoni showed very conspicuously in this work of over thirty years ago. The new movement was a complete contrast in its exquisite delicacy and its outspokenly Italian melody. Frieda Kwast-Hodapp played it 'like a soap-bubble'—in fact she said so herself. It was difficult to associate her with soap-bubbles, but on this occasion she spoke no more than the truth.

Busoni's one longing, however, was to get back to *Doctor Faust*, and it was always difficult, as he said, to restart the machine after so long an interruption. London and Paris had left him physically exhausted; he thought himself suffering from persistent influenza—*un basso continuo ed ostinato avec quelques variations*. 'The old loves', he added with grim humour, 'which one can never shake off.' But he was always hopeful, and confident in the future. At Paris he had played on a superb pianoforte of Erard's; his fingers still kept the memory of its touch and it seemed to give him the inspiration for some new method of playing which had not yet taken definite shape in his mind. The Hamburg pianoforte had been *bourgeois* as compared to the Erard, but he felt that he had played well and with greater pleasure to himself. And Hamburg itself always pleased him: it seemed like an island separated from the rest of Germany, a pocket edition of London.

Mozart, Saint-Saëns, and the Erard had sown a strange seed, that went on germinating for some months after Busoni returned to Berlin. The new style of pianoforte-playing was constantly in his mind. He finished the *Klavierübung*, taking a malicious delight in basing one of its studies on a theme from the *Faust* of Gounod, which he knew would horrify his German critics. He worked at the fourth Concerto of Saint-Saëns, and composed more cadenzas for concertos of Mozart. He was already thinking about the Erard for his English tour, but feared that it would be useless to him unless he could have it for the provinces as well as for London. No English firm would give him an instrument for the other towns, if he refused to play on it at his London concerts. Busoni knew only too well the psychology of pianoforte-makers.

In May, at the urgent request of the Berlin Philharmonie, he played the E flat Concerto of Beethoven.[1] The result was curious; it was a surprise and a scandal to the critics. Busoni professed himself completely bewildered; he had had no consciousness of any change in his interpretation. But the criticism set him thinking, and gradually the truth began to emerge in his mind. The pianoforte interested him, but not the music written for it. He felt like a man who has amassed immense wealth and does not know how to spend it. As usual, it was to Philipp that he turned for counsel.

'I have devoted myself too much, I think, to Bach, to Mozart, and to Liszt. I wish now that I could emancipate myself from them. Schumann is no use to me any more, Beethoven only with an effort and strict selection. Chopin has attracted and repelled me all my life; and I have *heard* his music too often—prostituted, profaned, vulgarized. He is a little island round which the waters are always rising, until only his two or three peaks stand out—the *Études* and *Préludes* and possibly the *Ballades*. I do not know what to choose for a new repertory!'

Philipp's first suggestions were Alkan and Scriabin. Alkan—Busoni had had his 'period of Alkanism' sixteen years before; he remembered how it had annoyed the Berlin critics. Scriabin—he played through the *Études*, and recalled Scriabin as a boy of eighteen at Moscow in 1890. Moscow—what a nightmare! 'Dreary, mysterious, superficial, ill-natured'—the pupils practising conventional pyrotechnics while their professors spent their nights at the gambling-table, to return to their lessons a couple of hours late, sodden with drink but always with the grand manner of ambassadors, their eternal cigarette only

[1] In the Philharmonie, May 29, 1922. This was Busoni's last appearance in public.

enhancing their pomposity—and Safonov, autocrat of autocrats, summoning them to his chamber like a Chief of Police. Scriabin—'une indigestion de Chopin'.

He left the pianoforte and devoted himself to his composition pupils. They were always an encouragement to him and he looked to them to lead a new campaign against the eccentricities of the 'armistice period'—the 'expressionists' with their 'vaches en aeroplan *et stultitiis similibus*'. People were playing Mozart more and more; that was a sign that dawn was breaking, however slowly.

'Shall I live to see a new dawn? Point of interrogation (much beloved of French authors when they shirk going to the bottom of an argument).

'But I shall always have, when I take my departure, a good conscience of having sought the good and the true in so far as they are within my reach. I do not hold much to the adage "in magnis voluisse sat est"; for me it is a phrase which invites to idleness.

'This Sunday the opera re-opens. It is the end of the summer. Well, I have not wasted my time. I hope you have recovered from your fatigues. One is not yet old, but one is no longer young. The evil is not in growing old, but in being unable to admit it.'

CHAPTER XV

THE CITY OF DARKNESS

THE autumn brought another and a more severe attack of illness, which kept Busoni an invalid for four months. The cause of the trouble was a complaint of very long standing, due to some accidental injury much earlier in life. Busoni had always been mistrustful of doctors and had succeeded fairly well in getting over such illnesses as he had had from time to time, but he now realized that medical advice was urgent. Having once accepted the situation, he placed complete confidence in his physician. Strange as it may seem, he became the most obedient of patients, submitted to every form of treatment, however disagreeable, and established the most friendly relations with his doctor by means of his unfailing sense of humour, which led him to report on the most intimate details of his illness in grotesque verse, unfortunately not suitable for reproduction here. Once when the doctor changed his medicine, the first proving unsatisfactory, he remarked, 'Since you find Czerny no good, we'll try Cramer.'

A perpetual neglect of illnesses and of minor hygienic precautions had weakened the body, and the constant strain of work at high pressure had induced a state in which nervous exhaustion aggravated physical disorder. He had been examined by a Swiss doctor in 1918 and had been told that there was nothing seriously wrong with him. Physicians do not always think it wise to tell their patients the truth. The Berlin doctor knew well enough that the only chance of prolonging Busoni's life lay in complete rest and abstention from work of all kinds, whether composition or pianoforte-playing. It was useless to tell him so: in the first place nothing would have induced Busoni to give up work, as long as he had the strength to go on with it, and even if he had consented, enforced idleness would have made him so unbearably wretched that he

273

might well have been tempted to suicide. Death was not a
theme which he cared to contemplate. Once at Zurich
Andreae had invited him to a performance of Bach's *Actus
Tragicus*.[1] Attracted by the dignity of the title, he went
to hear it, having—strange as it may seem—little or no
acquaintance with Bach's church cantatas; it was a painful
disappointment to him, and he expressed himself bitterly
to Andreae against the German Protestant preoccupation
with death and the morbid desire for it. But he may have
had for some time a premonition that his life would not
be a long one. An English friend, observing how worn
out he looked when he came to London in 1919, had told
him he ought to take a holiday. He looked gravely at the
speaker, and said in an all too significant voice, 'Some day
I shall take a *long holiday*'.[2]

A new interest was given him in the autumn of 1922 by
the foundation at Salzburg of the International Society for
Contemporary Music. He had been consulted in 1921
about the Festival of Contemporary Music organized at
Donaueschingen under the patronage of Prince Fürsten-
berg. Despite all his severe criticism of the younger
composers, he was sincerely desirous of furthering their interests. Max von Schillings had said to him once that now
he was Intendant of the Berlin Opera he meant to seize the
chance of performing *Götterdämmerung* with the absolutely
complete array of brass instruments demanded in Wagner's
original score.[3] Busoni received the idea scoffingly, and
told Schillings that it was much more important to bring
out operas by new and young composers. He was unable
to go to Donaueschingen himself, but he sent his wife to
represent him, and her presence added both charm and
dignity to those enthusiastic little gatherings, at which

[1] *Actus Tragicus* is Bach's own title to the cantata *Gottes Zeit ist die
allerbeste Zeit* ('God's time is the best'); it was the first of the church
cantatas to be published with English words (1873), and its English
popularity was due to the influence of Joseph Barnby.
[2] The words were spoken in English.
[3] Hitherto this had been carried out at Bayreuth alone.

Hindemith, Křenek, van Dieren, and others received acknowledgement almost for the first time. When the news was brought to him of the International Society's inauguration he at once said that as soon as his health permitted it would give him the greatest pleasure to serve the society in any way possible, as pianist, as conductor, or as member of the International Jury.

As long as he was well enough, Busoni was always delighted to have the young musicians round him. Besides the regular composition pupils there was Philipp Jarnach, now settled in Berlin, though compelled to earn a living by the wearisome trade of criticism. Alfredo Casella, whose acquaintance Busoni had made at Rome, was an occasional visitor. Busoni at first mistrusted him. Casella was 'very adroit in conversation, but not so adroit as not to be aware of it'. Busoni appreciated his intellect and his internationalism, but found him rather too much the man of the world for his own taste, until one day he met him with his mother and was able to catch a glimpse of Casella's more human side. And he could sympathize only too well with Casella's thwarted ambitions; no one knew better than Busoni the truth of the saying, *Nemo propheta in patria*.

Not all of the young people were equally welcome. There was a pianist of indefinable nationality, who came and pestered him for a testimonial. She insisted on playing to him, and Busoni was too courteous to refuse a lady's request. She rashly exhibited herself in a work of Albéniz; if there was anything Spanish about it, said Busoni, it must have been the Inquisition. As for the lady, he called her the 'Iron Virgin': she reminded him of that famous instrument of torture in the castle of Nuremberg. 'Physical exhaustion makes me so sweet-tempered,' he wrote, in describing the incident to Philipp.

For some time he had cherished the idea of having some fragments of *Doctor Faust* performed at a concert in Zurich. Andreae cordially supported the plan, but at Christmas 1922 Busoni wrote deciding finally against it. If the fragments made a good impression in the concert-room, they

275

would seem to deny their right to the theatre; if they failed to convince, the performance would only damage the chances of the opera. 'I am not yet sufficiently accredited to run risks of this kind.' The *Sarabande* and *Cortège* had had a cold reception and a hostile press when Furtwängler conducted them at Berlin in February. The opera was still unfinished. Five months had been wasted through illness. But Busoni's head was none the less full of plans for the future. He wrote to Petri in January 1923 suggesting that they should collaborate in bringing out a complete edition of Mozart's pianoforte concertos printed in three pairs of staves—Mozart's original, Busoni's transcription of the solo part, and Petri's pianoforte arrangement of the orchestra. It was a project that was never even begun. The English concerts planned for the following month had to be abandoned; it was a serious sacrifice for Busoni with the German currency falling headlong, but the doctor insisted on absolute rest until March at the earliest. The most unbearable sacrifice was the sacrifice of all those months which might have been devoted to *Doctor Faust*; Busoni's letters to various correspondents show clearly enough that the doctor's judgement was right: the complete abandonment of all work would have been a torture for life.

Convalescence was not without its pleasures. Books were always a consolation to Busoni, and no one could have been more thoughtful and generous than Philipp, who kept him constantly supplied with literature, from Littré's Dictionary and Merimée's novels to those of Anatole France, sometimes in autographed copies, and Jules Verne. He had recently discovered Wilkie Collins, and desired an English friend to obtain him original editions. These were not so easy to procure; eventually Messrs. Chatto & Windus kindly presented him with the collected edition.

The state of affairs in Germany gave him more and more cause for anxiety. Life there was becoming impossible; the financial disaster, which as yet was far from having reached its worst, meant that Germany was not only hampered as to its internal intellectual and artistic life, but was almost as completely cut off from contact with other countries as it had been during the years of war. Busoni began to think of seeking a home elsewhere. Italy refused to receive him; so did Paris. There remained London, where at any rate he knew that he was welcomed with open arms; but he could not help feeling that England was *un pays contre l'art*. And in any case he had neither the strength nor the money to undertake so momentous a move.

All through the early part of the year he was hoping to be able to escape, if only for a short time, to Paris; not to play in public—that was out of the question—but to see his friends and to derive a fresh stimulus from the intellectual and social atmosphere of the city that in these later years exercised so haunting a fascination over him. April came, but still the doctor would not allow him to travel; it was necessary for him to be under constant medical supervision, and it would be too great a risk for him to be treated by a physician who was a stranger to him and who had not followed the course of his illness from the beginning. Busoni obeyed; but patience and resignation, he said, were the most unpalatable of all medicines. He was unable to work in the sense of working at full pressure, but he was not without occupations. He neglected the pianoforte for months, but there were always a number of small matters that helped to pass the time. He wrote three little studies for the pianoforte to illustrate the polyphonic style; they followed suitably on the *Klavierübung*, of which he was correcting the proofs. He began to make a transcription of his *Tanzwalzer* for two pianofortes. But these were trifles; *Doctor Faust* seems to have been laid aside.

Outwardly he was for the most part calm and self-controlled. His natural courtesy, his fundamental kindness of heart, and his unfailing and genuine gratitude for the smallest kindness shown to himself—all these

REMINISCENZA ROSSINIANA

I

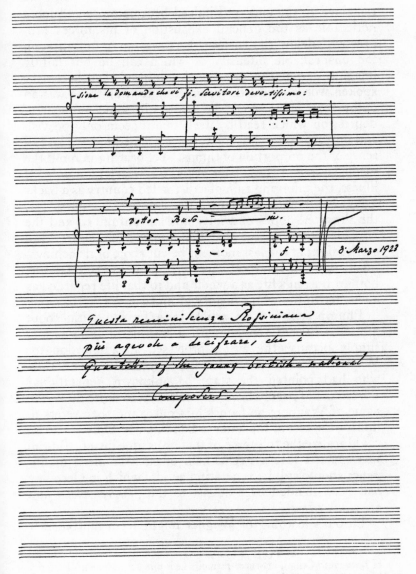

REMINISCENZA ROSSINIANA

II

remained to the end, and indeed became more and more noticeable as the general exhaustion of his forces progressed. Below the surface there was an agony of soul, the unspeakable intensity of which can be but faintly imagined from the occasional glimpses that letters or spoken words revealed. From time to time there was an outburst; a letter would be written in some moment of depression which read by itself might seem only peevish and unreasonable. Busoni at times seemed to have lost all sense of the proportion of things. Yet bearing in mind the whole course of these later years, the weary monotony of illness, the plunging ruin of a distracted country as a background to it, the wandering artist's sense of homelessness, the thwarted hopes of a lofty mission unfulfilled and the horrible dawning fear that the climax of an entire life's work might at the last moment be cut short of its achievement, one can interpret these eruptions in their relation both to Busoni's life as a whole and to that life regarded as a chapter in the whole history of music.

Philipp sent him an article by a French critic about himself. Busoni replied with a torrent of indignation, simply because the writer professed an admiration for Wagner. Was he so blind as not to see that it was Berlioz who had pointed the way for unknown generations? Busoni could hardly bring himself even to write down the name of Wagner; he names him once, and then refers to him for the rest of the letter as Bandinelli![1] Only a Tuscan could realize the full force of that grotesque insult. Busoni was amazed that a Frenchman of such eminent intelligence should still be venerating an idol which in Germany had been handed over at last to the *pauvres vieux* and *nouveaux riches*.

Busoni's loathing of Wagner might seem morbid if it

[1] Baccio Bandinelli (1487–1560), Florentine sculptor, was a great rival of Benvenuto Cellini, in whose memoirs he is often mentioned. 'Posterity has confirmed Cellini's opinion of Bandinelli as an artist; for his works are coarse, pretentious, and incapable of giving pleasure to any person of refined intelligence' (J. A. Symonds).

were judged by this letter alone, but it was a hostility of long standing. Both in private letters and in his published writings he had for several years complained of the burden which Wagner had laid on music during the whole period of his own artistic life. He spoke no more than the truth in saying that Wagner had already been dethroned by the younger generation in Germany. Busoni was not a man who followed fashions, least of all in music; he had abandoned Wagner before most people, with the exception of Nietzsche, whose famous exposure of Wagner was too remote in time to have had any direct influence on the modern attitude. Once past the German enthusiasms of his adolescence, Busoni had turned more and more to the music of his own countrymen. And as the tragedy of his own life deepened, so his aspirations looked ever more and more towards the masters of comedy in music, Mozart, Rossini, Verdi. This accounted for his criticism of Beethoven as well as of Wagner. They had both of them brought ruin upon music, he used to say: Beethoven with his emotional rhetoric (*Pathos*),[1] Wagner with his lasciviousness (*Geilheit*). The imitators of *Tristan and Isolde* had aroused in him an almost moral indignation against the love-scenes of modern opera. After seeing Schreker's *Die Gezeichneten*[2] in 1921 he said that the composer described love entirely from hearsay. 'One *can't* set love to music. The man can't know what love is if he tries to set it to music. The great masters never wrote love-scenes; they originated in the nineteenth century. There are no love-scenes in Mozart.'

In the course of the summer trouble arose in the new International Society. It had been curiously difficult from the first to get a section formed in Italy, and a French musician had even said that it would be utterly impossible,

---

[1] *Pathos* in German does not mean the same as the English *pathos*. *Pathos* in German always implies rhetoric and theatricality, even when such exaggeration may have artistic necessity.

[2] *Die Gezeichneten* was at that time the most extreme example of musical eroticism on the stage.

as the Italians were all much too jealous of each other ever
to form a committee. The first elected jury had recently
published its programmes, in which Italian music was
very scantily represented. Italy in those days was the land
of strikes, and the musicians were true to national type.
They refused to take any part in the Festival to be held
at Salzburg, and said that they would withdraw such
works as had been chosen. As Busoni was known to be
keenly interested in the International Society, and was
obviously the most distinguished musician of modern ten-
dencies with an Italian name, Casella wrote to him to
protest against the unjust treatment of his countrymen.
By a misguided courtesy of intention, he wrote to Busoni
in German, thus at once rousing Busoni's ever-watchful
spirit of criticism, literary as well as musical or moral.
Busoni wrote back to the Italians in plain words. Before
bringing accusations against the foreigner, he said, they
must show a little penitence themselves. In two years the
Russians had made a Russian town of Berlin, simply by
dint of mutual admiration.

'Walischef praises up Karmanzoff, Karmanzoff does the same
by Walischef, and both of them weep tears of admiration for some
other compatriot. The Italians do nothing but speak ill of each
other (*dicono ira di Dio l'un dell' altro*).

'Besides,' he went on, 'a purely Italian school of music at the
present moment simply *does not exist*. One imitates Strauss, another
Debussy, a third toys with Stravinsky, and Wagner remains the
Dalai Lama. Naturally enough foreign countries prefer the
originals to these pale copies.'

When the Italians replied that they were shocked to hear
him speak so poorly of his fellow-countrymen, he re-
joined that that proved him all the more Italian in feeling,
and that his *amour-propre* as an Italian was all the more
sharply wounded by the false situation.

His own *Fantasia Contrappuntistica* had been chosen for
Salzburg, and as he resided in Berlin, the German section
was responsible for its performance. This naturally suggested to the ignorant that Busoni regarded himself as a

German. It had been hoped that he would play it himself
with Petri; but it was quite impossible for him to attempt
it, and it was eventually played by Frieda Kwast-Hodapp
and her husband. There was no offer from Italy to provide
players for it.

'I have been compelled to become a hermit,' he wrote to Baroness
Jella Oppenheimer in July, 'although I feel a powerful impulse towards life, towards sharing life and work with others. And just now
my position in public opinion is such, that I could now accomplish
a great deal more with smaller effort. I trust that an activity on these
lines, an activity of helping things on (*eine fördernde Thätigkeit*)
may yet be granted me.'

In August the warm weather brought a marked im-
provement in his health. 'Warmth is a good doctor,' he
wrote. He was even able to go to Weimar for a few days,
to attend a festival, at which he saw for the first time
Stravinsky's *Histoire du Soldat*. He was completely fascinated by it.

'One had become a child again; one forgot music and literature,
one was simply moved. *There's* something which achieved its aim!
But let us take care not to imitate it!

'One must have much courage and much patience. I have a proof
of that at this moment, for I am beginning to work at the pianoforte
again! ! !

'*Toujours recommencer . . .*'

The financial chaos of Berlin was growing worse. The
trams had ceased running and the mark, normally equal
to a shilling, stood at the billionth part of its value. In
September came the avalanche of the inflation. In October
Busoni and his wife went to Paris for six weeks. Philipp
was appalled at the change which had taken place in
Busoni, and insisted on his being examined by a French
specialist. Busoni resisted for a long time, but was finally
persuaded, as the specialist was an enthusiastic admirer
of him and entirely refused to accept any fee. Unfortunately he was also a keen admirer of Wagner too, and
was rash enough to say so at the interview. He told
Philipp that Busoni was a condemned man. He might live

for a month or less if he continued his present habits; if he gave up all smoking and all alcohol he might live for four or five months more. Nothing would induce Busoni to visit a dentist. Solitude and enforced idleness had begun to make his mind strangely unbalanced, at any rate in contrast with Philipp's unshakable common sense. On any intellectual matter he was perfectly reasonable—there never was the slightest trace of mental derangement or disease; but his emotions were often painfully out of control. He had taken up the pianoforte again, and practised a good deal while in Paris, but he had lost the power of feeling in the tips of his fingers; the sense of touch was entirely gone.

It had been a relief to escape from Berlin, yet Paris had been a disappointment. But the idea of returning to Berlin filled Busoni with increasing anxiety. Before he left Paris he wrote to an English friend: [1]

'. . . I am here since about 6 weeks to recover part of my health, which has been shaken indeed.—But, as everything must have an end, so this bit of peace which I enjoy, comes now to a conclusion. I feel uncomfortable at the idea of returning to Berlin, although there *are* things, which are dear and stimulating to me. But the continuous struggle for mere existence in this late part of my life is disastrouos, and it is threatening to absorbe the energetic faculties of brain and body.—Just yesterday splendid offers has been made to me from America and from Vienna. But I am rather disinclined to visit the first and to settle down in the latter. Italy does not accept Italians, France does not recieve any Strangers.—How do you think that England would reacte, if I decided to make it my Home?'

It was not the first time that he had thought of making England his home. In October 1912 he was in London, and wrote in his diary: 'Seriously considered settling [in London], but the town swallows up the immigrant artist— he creates no more!'

The letter was left unfinished for a fortnight; towards the end of November Busoni resumed it from Berlin.

[1] In English. The letter is here printed with Busoni's original spelling and punctuation.

284

'The first page of this letter was written about two weeks ago in Paris. Today You find me again in Berlin, where difficulties have increased since I left it. Anyway, it gives a certain feeling of comfort, to be surrounded by familiar objects. But, the Home excepted, there is nothing to seek nor to find. . . .

'I have not seen nor heard anything of Music in Paris. There, they move in a *circulus vitiosus*; with a wisdom, which is worse than madness. The town is in a splendid condition. (The return to B. makes the fact more evident.)

'Be kind, and let me hear of you. *Saluti amichevoli.*'

Baroness Jella Oppenheimer was generous of assistance, sending food and other comforts; Austria was in a comparatively sound condition. The mere remembrance of her seemed to have a calming and refreshing influence on him. In earlier days at Vienna he had often felt that she kept him at a certain distance; her letters to him now took on an almost sisterly tone. They brought back to him vividly, in these tedious months of suffering, that old-world Vienna to which she belonged by birth and breeding, that Vienna which had first opened his childish eyes to the splendour of a great and historic city. He read through the novels of Friedrich von Saar, in which the society of Vienna in the 1870's is depicted with all the affectionate detail of personal experience. Those were beautiful days in Döbling, when Busoni had stayed with Frau von Wertheimstein, next-door neighbour of the novelist himself.

'The fresh sting of autumn mornings in the garden! The endless perspectives of life that seemed to be opening out before me!

'I am falling into the habit of old age—reminiscence—and yet I still have something before me to do. I thirst for activity, movement, even for publicity; after all one is a circus horse.' [1]

February brought thoughts of London—there were days pencilled in for him up to the last moment at the Wigmore Hall. During the winter he had started practising for his London recitals. He was going to show London something new this time—Mendelssohn's *Songs without Words*, and the music of an English composer

[1] Letter to Baroness Jella Oppenheimer, February 8, 1924.

U

whom the English themselves had forgotten—Field's *Nocturnes*. They were to represent that new style of pianoforte-playing at which he was aiming: a style for which his old repertory was useless, as he had told Philipp. Field's *Nocturnes* had for him a 'chastity' which Chopin had corrupted; Chopin's, he felt, were too dramatic, too sensual. A copy of Field's lay on his table, annotated with grace notes and cadenzas. But there was no possibility of attempting the journey.

As far as strength allowed, he continued to work at the opera; it was nearing its end. The first signs of spring set him longing for Italy. The thought of Italy recalled Leonardo, 'the skeleton with a torch instead of a skull'. 'I think', he wrote to Baroness Jella Oppenheimer—it was the last letter that he ever wrote—'that even a dead body can still give light on high.' He had begun to realize the hopelessness of his case. The Paris doctor had given him a severe shock; it had taken a long time before his Berlin doctor could restore him to comparative cheerfulness and confidence in himself. His one preoccupation now was *Doctor Faust*; should he be able to finish it before the end came?

The Dresden Opera was waiting anxiously for *Doctor Faust* too; there was no question of its not being accepted for production. Max Slevogt came to see Busoni in May, and his cheery presence brought a fresh stimulus to the invalid. Slevogt, wildest of Wagnerians thirty years before, had made himself the pictorial interpreter of Mozart, both in etchings and on the actual stage.

'What does it matter', he said, 'if the last act of *Doctor Faust* is still unfinished? You ought to have rehearsals put in hand at once. I have often started rehearsals before the last scene was ready, and when the time came it was finished quite safely.' The final scene of the opera was indeed all that remained to be written. But in that very month Busoni became worse, and the work had to be laid aside for ever.

The disease, at first local, had begun gradually to affect

the whole body. There was not the least sign of paralysis or of brain disease, but the general blood-poisoning brought loss of memory and sometimes fits of total unconsciousness. He was an endlessly considerate patient (*ein unendlich liebenswürdiger Patient*), said the doctor. Two nurses had to be engaged. Busoni had a horror of a nurse's uniform; it probably reminded him of the nursing nuns of Italy, perhaps of his father's grotesque death-bed. The nurses were asked not to wear their caps, and he treated them with unfailing courtesy and kindness. One day as he lay in bed, with Gerda, the nurse, and a couple of friends in attendance on him, he laughed and said ironically, 'What a pretty picture for the *Gartenlaube*!'[1] The doctor was singularly touched by Busoni's perpetual gratitude and thoughtfulness towards himself; it was a rare thing to find a patient in so serious a condition constantly remembering his doctor's personal interests, offering him books or other little presents and doing every possible thing that might give him pleasure.

As long as his general strength permitted, his brain remained active; he was keenly interested in all that was going on and took pleasure in seeing visitors. There were frequent performances of music; sometimes a string quartet came to play him a new work by one of his composition pupils. To the younger generation of musicians he was always accessible. There were always the old friends—Michael von Zadora, Philipp Jarnach, and others; and as his illness proceeded the house seemed to be invaded by a strange crowd of new acquaintances. The adoring females were more than ever in evidence. Their discretion was not always equal to their devotion, and Gerda's patience was put to sore trials. But as long as she thought that their company amused Ferruccio she bore with their tactlessness; she was no less concerned to conceal her anxiety from him than he was to conceal his ruin

[1] *Die Gartenlaube*, founded in the days of Mendelssohn and Schumann, with a charming title-page designed by Ludwig Richter, is still the most popular periodical in respectable German family circles.

from her. One of the 'caryatides' came with a story of how Busoni's dead mother had appeared to her in a dream and given her messages for him from another world. Busoni knew perfectly well that the young lady had never seen Anna in her life. Whatever other faculties might have left him, humour and scepticism still remained. He had no illusions as to the fantastic figures that chattered about the house like the *Lemures* who dig the grave of Faust. 'You can see from my *entourage*', he said to Gerda, 'how low I am fallen!'

One day Zadora came to see him. He was the senior of Busoni's pupils in Berlin, having presented himself to Busoni before the days of the Weimar classes. Tall, pale, and thin, with an aquiline profile, he bore—and in earlier years cultivated—a striking resemblance to his fellow-countryman Chopin. He had received his early training in Paris, and Busoni appreciated the exquisite precision of his touch no less than his singular inborn facility for pianoforte-playing. His education had suffered from the hardships of early youth, and a rather naïve want of understanding often made him the butt of Busoni's sarcasms. There had indeed been many episodes of storm between them, but Zadora's loyalty and devotion were proof against the cruellest satire. As often happens with those who have had a hard struggle for existence, it was not always easy to make friends with him; but he had the kindness peculiar to those who have suffered, and it expressed itself in rare moments when he played privately to one or two of his intimate friends, infusing an unexpected warmth and tenderness into the old-fashioned virtuoso pieces of Thalberg or Tausig which so admirably suited his style.

The pianoforte in Busoni's music-room had been silent for many weeks. Suddenly he asked Zadora to play to him. The big doors leading to the music-room were thrown open, and Zadora sat down to the instrument. On the desk lay Mendelssohn's *Songs without Words*. Zadora began to play the 'Venetian Gondola Song'. Venice—

Trieste—was it a last farewell to Italy? Busoni could bear it no longer; he sat up and burst into a paroxysm of tears.

By the end of June he was so weak that he hardly seemed to realize either his surroundings or his own condition. The periods of unconsciousness became more frequent and of longer duration. Gerda could only sit by the bedside and wait for the inevitable end. The house was quiet in these days. A year ago there had been the noise of motor traffic in the street below and the shriek of the tram as it pursued the curve of the little public garden. Now, a sense of ruin hung over Berlin, and the round Viktoria Luise Platz was as silent in the long July twilight as that little round *place* in old Bordeaux where once Busoni had met the reincarnation of Donna Anna.

The stillness was gently broken by the leisurely passing of an old-fashioned cab. Busoni's ear was yet quick enough to catch the sound that came up through the open window. 'Horses' hoofs!' he whispered. 'That reminds me of Helsingfors. Those were wonderful times!' He took Gerda's hand in his. 'Dear Gerda'—the words came slowly—'I thank you for every day that we have been together.' He had thanked her like that every night of their married life. Unconsciousness followed, and lasted for some three or four days. Once the nurse thought she heard him try to utter Gerda's name. He was still unconscious when, at about half-past three on the morning of July 27th, he died.

The Great pianoforte trip

M. Braunwerth Petrov life seemed utterly connected: besides first he was embarrassed by a strange paroxysm.
He raised his head toward the eye he wrote: any former pupil in the new proposition effected to permit the appearance on an ordinary instrument or the public

CHAPTER XVI

'DOCTOR FAUST'

THERE was only one person who understood why Busoni refused the South American invitation, and that was Gerda. 'Let me finish *Doctor Faust* first,' he said to her, 'and when that is over, we can go to South America or anywhere you like.' She knew that it would have been useless to try to explain that to Philipp or to any one else. Busoni knew that Philipp was his truest friend and his wisest counsellor; but Philipp could not help regarding Busoni primarily as a pianist—indeed as the most marvellous pianist that the world had ever seen. About that there could be no doubt whatever; his reputation as a composer could never be so incontestable, even for his most fervent admirers. It was inevitable that musicians, however discerning, should have formed that opinion; Bach and Mozart themselves had in their lifetimes been considered first and foremost as executants. And on the subject of *Doctor Faust* Busoni had become strangely secretive. It was well known that he was composing an opera; the subject was known, the poem had been published as a separate book, the Dresden Opera House had accepted it for production. But he showed the score to no one except Gerda. He became more and more reluctant to talk about it, except to her. She knew every note of it. Ever since their marriage it had always been Gerda to whom he first confided each new project of his whole career. In earlier days he had talked or written freely about his plans and ideas, to Petri, to Robert Freund, to Andreae, and others. *Doctor Faust* belonged to Gerda alone; it belonged to her so intimately and so completely that it would have been impossible to make any one else understand the place which it held in his life, in that life which he had always tried to plan out with such rigorous forethought. For ten years the subject of Faust had been rooted in his mind;

the germ of the idea had been present to him for thirty years and more. The time had come when the work must be completed at all costs; there was no longer anything to which it could be sacrificed, for however short a moment.

In the prologue to *Doctor Faust* Busoni mentions Merlin as one of the dramatic figures which he had at one time considered as the possible subject of an opera. It may be suspected that this idea first occurred to him at Leipzig when he was commissioned to write a Fantasia on Goldmark's opera *Merlin*. There is no trace of his ever having proceeded farther with it. But about 1892 he began to sketch a libretto on the subject of the Wandering Jew (*Ahasvers Ende*). It is a legend which has a certain affinity to the story of Faust.

The few sketches for *Ahasver* that have survived are so fragmentary that one can form no idea of the work as a whole, though it can be seen that the opera was to have its comedy as well as its tragedy. The beginning of the story is lost—perhaps it was never written. There is a sketch for a scene in which Ahasuerus appears as a typical wealthy Jew of Busoni's own time; he is a liberal patron of the fine arts and is entertaining a party which includes various old friends whose acquaintance he made centuries ago—Don Juan, Falstaff, Don Quixote and Sancho Panza. His curse never allowing him to rest, he is obliged perpetually to walk up and down, and excuses himself to his guests on the ground that his doctor has ordered him constant exercise. But the Wandering Jew belongs to the future as well as to the present and past. In another scene we find him as the sole survivor of mankind after the entire human race has been destroyed by the arrival of a new Ice Age. Amid ice and snow Ahasuerus wanders alone under the stars; a bear, last survivor of earth's creatures, seeks in vain for food. He would gladly be its prey, but as he draws near it, the beast drops dead of cold. He attempts to throw himself over a precipice, but a hand holds him back—it is Death himself. Now that the whole earth has been given over to Death, Death's functions are fulfilled;

he is charged to accompany Ahasuerus until the end of all things.

At the beginning of the scene there is a long monologue in which Ahasuerus recalls the whole history of the world as he has witnessed it. He has lost all sense of time; his life has stretched backwards as well as forwards—he is Adam, Moses, David, Solomon, as well as Spinoza. And now he sees himself condemned not merely to wander, but to wander for ever in utter loneliness.

'Knowest thou no pity, thou that callest thyself the God of mercy? Is this thy love towards man? I must acknowledge thy power, but thy goodness I acknowledge not.' Then he repents of his blasphemy and prays for forgiveness, or at least for some sign that he is not alone. An aurora borealis appears in the sky; he begins to hope once more. He would willingly bear his curse to its appointed end if he knew that by so doing he would set thousands of thousands of others free from penance. Apocalyptic portents are seen; the resurrection is at hand. After a prayer of thanksgiving, Ahasuerus, last survivor of humanity, makes himself the advocate of mankind before its judge. The trumpets of the Last Judgement ring out, Ahasuerus is struck dead, the resurrection begins and the curtain falls.

Ahasver was evidently the sort of opera which a young composer sketches but never completes. Berlioz had once sketched a subject almost identical. There is no need to criticize the suitability of Busoni's conception to the practical exigencies of the theatre. What is significant in these fragments is their monodramatic character. They reveal a strange sense of solitude, a sense of solitude perceptible in almost every one of Busoni's works or projects for the stage. Even amidst the merriment of *Die Braut-wahl* we see Edmund Lehsen standing alone before his fresco in Rome; the unwritten Italian operas were to end, the one with Dante sitting alone in the Piazza at Florence, the other with Leonardo deserted by his patrons and protectors. *Arlecchino* ends with Ser Matteo alone with his tailoring and his Dante. Faust dies deserted by man, God, and Devil. *Doctor Faust* was the creation of a solitary, and in a certain sense Busoni had been a solitary all his life.

At some period—the subject is never mentioned in his letters—Busoni had even considered the idea of an opera on Don Juan. We see traces of this idea in the synopsis of the drama that he once planned, exhibiting a hero in three different lives, artist, Don Juan, and millionaire. He speaks of the Don Juan project only in the preface and prologue to *Doctor Faust*. There were other ways of treating the legend besides da Ponte's. Busoni had read Bernard Shaw's *Man and Superman* in July 1909, and it almost looks as if he knew Shadwell's *The Libertine* when he hints at a Don Juan libretto full of monks, inquisitors, subterranean vaults, Moors and Jews and singers of madrigals, ending with the second supper-party at which Don Juan is the guest of the Statue in a ruined chapel. But it was impossible to forget Mozart, and in considering Faust it was impossible to forget Goethe until Busoni determined to go back to the Faust of the early puppet-plays, not only for his subject-matter, but to a large extent for his constructive method as well.

From 1909 to 1914 Busoni kept a sort of diary, in which every three or four days he jotted down a few words—hardly ever a complete sentence. It is not the sort of diary which could be published, but it affords curious revelations of the workings of Busoni's mind. On December 31, 1909, sailing for America on board the *Barbarossa*, he writes:

Rückblick—Ein ereignisreiches Jahr—Abschied von den übrigen 42.
Ein Beginnen.

(Retrospect—an eventful year—farewell to the other forty-two. *A beginning.*)

The name of Faust appears suddenly on October 16, 1910:

Faust—Casperle! besonders ergriffen von drei Studenten. So müsste neues Werk beschaffen sein!

The puppet-play

(Faust—Casperle! singularly moved by the three students.
That is how the new work ought to be made!)

The reference is clearly to the old German puppet-play of
Faust, in which Kasperle, the comic figure—a sort of
German Harlequin—makes a frequent appearance.
  On December 9:

F? Literarisch zu schwer, durch Goethe-Vergleich. Oder es
  müsste etwas ganz Neues sein.
(F[aust]? From a literary point of view too difficult, owing to
  comparison with Goethe. Or else it would have to be something quite new.)

The year 1911 was occupied with *Die Brautwahl*; 1912
was the year of Busoni's conversations with d'Annunzio
on the subject of Leonardo da Vinci. It was in this same
year that he conceived the first inspiration for *Arlecchino*,
as well as being invited to compose music for Wedekind's
parody of *Faust*. In 1913 there are again allusions to
Faust in the diary:

Juli: 20. Faust, Delacroix stets anregend. Translation: 'a gallant
  knight.'
     21. F Musik zum ersten Teil nicht ganz befriedigend.
  Ostergesang, 3 Erzengel, *wie* das machen?
Oktober: Liceo: wie Faust zu Parma Zeit verlierend—'The
  man who could work miracles.'
(July: 20. Faust, Delacroix always suggestive. Translation: *a
  gallant knight*.
     21. Faust music to the First Part not altogether satisfactory.
  Easter Hymn, three Archangels—*how* is that to be done?
October: Liceo: wasting time like Faust at Parma—*The man
  who could work miracles*.)

Busoni was evidently still considering Goethe's *Faust* as
a basis in July; the mention of Parma in October shows
that he had reverted to the puppet-play. A note in the
early part of the following year hints at a reversion to much
older projects:

Februar: 23. Entwurf zu gotischen Theater, Festspiel-
  häusern, Beethovendenkmal. Aladdin, Ahasver tentation.

294

(February: 23. Sketches for Gothic theatre, festival theatres,
Beethoven monument. Aladdin, Wandering Jew temptation.)

Was Busoni in 1913 seriously considering the possibility
of abandoning *Faust* and going back to his youthful idea
of making an opera out of Oehlenschläger's *Aladdin*, or
even of completing *The Wandering Jew*? On September 3,
1914, he writes the three words 'Lionardo: italienischer
Faust'. In November he was considering Goethe's sequel
to *The Magic Flute*; it will be remembered that Busoni's
original idea for Oehlenschläger's *Aladdin* was that it
should be 'something like *The Magic Flute*'. A week later
he notes 'a strange and shuddering Faustus-feeling, when
the new door with the books on it is shut, and the lamp
lighted!' On December 7 comes an allusion to Strindberg
on Luther, and Dr. Faust as Luther's companion. 'Must
remember the Lionardo sheets after the concert.' A recital
was impending; after it was over Busoni began to look for
the sketches of *Leonardo*. What he found, however, were
the sketches for *Faust*.

'Suddenly everything came together like a vision,' he writes in
the diary (December 21). 'Five movements. Monologue about
studies falls out. Assumed that Gretchen episode is all over. During
the pact Easter bells ring! Garden festival at the court of Parma,
the Duchess betrays her love, in a vision appear Herod (Salome)
and John with resemblance: Duke, Faust. Three students from
Cracow, beginning. Night watchman—End. Query, Casperle—
Intermezzi in front of the curtain, without music, or not?'

He bought a new drawing-block the next day to sketch
a scene for the church episode. From that moment the
libretto proceeded without interruption until it was
finished on December 26.

Busoni did not live to complete the music. Up to the
final monologue of Faust the opera was on paper to the
last note; there was no instrumentation of rough sketches
to be done. It had been settled for some time that the
opera was to be brought out at Dresden; Alfred Reucker,
who had recently succeeded Scheidemantel as Intendant,
had been Director of the theatre at Zurich during the years

Theory of Opera

of war and had discussed the production of the opera with
Busoni in detail. The production at Dresden was naturally
delayed by the difficult problem that arose from the
unfinished state of the score. No Italian or German composer of recognized standing could have attempted its
completion with any chance of success; the change of
style would have been too disastrously evident.[1] Most of
Busoni's own composition pupils, gifted as some of them
were, had not yet had time to acquire the necessary experience, an experience intellectual as well as technical.
The only musician who could possibly be seriously proposed for the task was Philipp Jarnach. For a long time
he refused to undertake the responsibility, but finally
yielded to the pressure of Busoni's family and intimate
friends. The opera was staged for the first time at the
Dresden Opera House on May 21, 1925. It was received
with respect rather than with enthusiasm; not more than
four performances were given.[2]

Busoni recorded the history and the theory of his opera
in a prologue in verse which forms part of the printed
libretto and also more fully in a prose preface to the score;
this preface was printed for the first time in *Ausblick*, the
magazine of the Dresden State Theatres, for May 1925.
The second stanza of the prologue in verse admirably
sums up his theory of opera in general:

> Die Bühne zeigt vom Leben die Gebärde,
> Unechtheit steht auf ihrer Stirn geprägt;
> Auf dass sie nicht zum Spiegel-Zerrbild werde,
> Als Zauberspiegel wirk' sie schön und echt;
> Gebt zu, dass sie das Wahre nur entwerte,
> Dem Unglaubhaften wird sie erst gerecht:
> Und wenn ihr sie, als Wirklichkeit, belachtet,
> Zwingt sie zum Ernst, als reines Spiel betrachtet.

(The stage exhibits the gestures of life, but it bears plainly the

---

[1] There was some talk of inviting Arnold Schönberg to compose the
final scene.

[2] Since then *Doctor Faust* has been performed at Berlin, Stuttgart,
Frankfurt, and Hanover.

296

mark of unreality. If it is not to become a distorting mirror, it must act fairly and truly as a magic mirror. Grant that the stage only lowers the values of what is true, it can then do full justice to the incredible, and though you may laugh at drama judging it as reality, it will compel you to seriousness if you regard it as mere play.)

And Busoni ends his prologue with the reminder that his opera is frankly and undisguisedly a puppet-play by origin. It is difficult to define in words what constitutes the puppet-play style—in what way a play for puppets must be planned and written differently from a play for living actors, and in what particular qualities the puppet-play is, or may be, more grimly moving than an ordinary play. Busoni cannot possibly have intended his *Doctor Faust* to be actually performed by puppets, for it can only be given in a large opera-house with every modern technical appliance, not to speak of its vast choral and instrumental requirements. But it has something of the puppet-play in its remoteness from everyday sentiment and sentimentality; the figures in the drama say and do only what is necessary and no more—they have no need and no chance to elaborate their parts with all those 'subtle touches' that on the commercial stage do so much to enhance the private personality of the actor or actress and to appeal thereby to the affections rather than to the intellect of the spectators. The result of this restriction is that *Doctor Faust* may seem lacking in what we might call humanity; but the more nearly it approaches to the manner of the puppet-show, the more it gains in austerity and dignity.

Even in the stage presentation the puppet-show is brought clearly to the notice of the audience. When the main curtain rises, it reveals a second curtain, on which is painted a puppet-theatre, with the characters of the opera ranged in a row before its miniature proscenium. It is but dimly illuminated, and they appear only as suggestions. The orchestral prelude begins; that too is only a vague suggestion, an impressionistic study of distant bells, represented by the orchestra alone without any

actual bells or percussive imitations of them. An actor
rises from a trap in front of the puppet-show and recites
the eighty-two lines of the prologue in verse. He disappears, and at once the first scene is revealed—Faust's
study at Wittenberg, with Faust anxiously watching some
alchemical process at the hearth. Wagner enters and tells
him that three students wish to see him. At first he refuses
to receive them, but relents on hearing that they have
brought him a book with a strange title—*Clavis Astartis
Magica*. As Wagner leaves the room he bursts out into
excited soliloquy: this is the book which will give him
the magic power that he is seeking.

Three young men enter and stand silent; they are
dressed in black, with cabalistic signs on their breasts.

'Who are you?'

'Students from Cracow.'

Cracow! The name recalls Faust's youth, with the
dreams and hopes of his own student days; he welcomes
the students with a sudden kindliness. They hand over to
him a book, a key to unlock it, and a letter which makes it
Faust's property. How shall he reward them? Later, they
answer. He offers hospitality, but they will not stay.

'Then tell me that I shall see you again!'

'Perhaps. Farewell, Faust.'

They go, and a moment later Wagner returns.

'Did you see the students? Are you not going to show
them out?'

'Sir, I saw no one!'

'They left me just now.'

'I saw no one.'

'You have missed them—Ah! Now I know *who* they
were—' and the vessels on the hearth begin to boil and
bubble and steam until the whole scene disappears in the
fumes. Behind the stage voices take up the music of the
first prelude. Are they voices? or are they bells ringing
in the distance? What is the word that we catch now and
then? *Pax*.[1]

---

[1] Busoni wrote this part of the music at Zurich in 1917.

The curtain rises for the second prologue—the scene is the same, at midnight. Faust, the key in his hand, draws a magic circle round him with a sword. The old puppet-plays make him draw the circle with his girdle; Busoni substitutes the sword, as the symbol of protection against danger. He calls on Lucifer to send him his servant, and in the darkness there appear six flames hovering in the air. Question them, says an unknown voice. The first gives his name as Gravis.

'How swift art thou?'

'As the sand in the hourglass.'

Faust dismisses him with contempt; so also he dismisses the next four, Levis, Asmodus, Beelzebub, and Megaeros. Not one is swift enough for him. Megaeros is swift as the storm. That is better, but not enough—'Storm, I blow thee out!'

One flame remains. Faust steps out of the circle; he is disappointed, and thinks it hardly worth while to question the last spirit. The sixth voice calls him.[1] The sixth flame persists, though Faust will not question it. The spirit says that he is swift as human thought. That is more than Faust had hoped. He bids him appear in tangible shape, and Mephistopheles is there. But Faust has stepped out of the magic circle, and instead of being his master, he is his servant. Yet Mephistopheles is willing to serve him—for the present: what is Faust's will? Faust's answer is not that of the conventional Faust; it is characteristic of his new creator's mind:

'Give me for the rest of my life the unconditional fulfilment of every wish; let me embrace the world, the East and the South that call me; let me understand the actions of mankind and extend them; give me Genius! give me its pain too, that I may be happy like no other—make me *free*!'

[1] The scene with the six flames is conceived musically as a set of variations on a theme; the first spirit is a deep bass, and the voices rise progressively, so that the last—Mephistopheles—is a high tenor. Busoni treats him very ruthlessly from a singer's point of view.

And afterwards? Faust must serve Mephistopheles for
ever. Serve! Faust will not serve; rather will he dismiss
Mephistopheles like the rest. But the Devil will not be
dismissed; and he is more practical than Faust:

'Listen, Faust! Your creditors are at the door; you have
deceived them. You have got your girl into trouble; her
brother is after your life. And the priests are after you
too; they smell a rat. Not far wrong either; you'll be burnt
at the stake.'

As he speaks there is a knocking at the door; again it
comes, and more threateningly.

'One word from you,' says Mephistopheles—
'Kill them!'

There is silence. Faust has given way. Still reluctantly
he signs his pact. During part of this scene a chorus of
voices has been heard behind, singing the words of the
Credo and *Gloria*. As the curtain falls they burst into an
Alleluia, and in full force there ring out the Easter bells.[1]

The clamour of the bells dies gradually away, and as the
curtain rises for the *Intermezzo*, the sound of an organ is
heard. The scene is a Romanesque side-chapel in a
cathedral, and the music of the organ dominates the whole
episode. Busoni wanted the organ to be no mere background: it was to fill the whole theatre with its reverbera-
tion. Unfortunately there are few theatres which possess
organs of sufficient power to carry out the composer's
design.

Before a crucifix kneels a soldier in armour; he is
described as 'the girl's brother'. The girl has no part in
the opera; her story was finished long ago. We see only
the brother praying that he may find her seducer and
avenge her ruin. In the doorway Mephistopheles points
him out to Faust. He must be got out of the way, and
Faust lets Mephistopheles see to it. He puts on a monk's
frock and tries to induce the soldier to confess to him. The
soldier refuses; he suspects him for what he is. 'Look to

[1] Busoni had three real bells cast at a bell-foundry in Switzerland; they
are engraved with the names of Gerda, Benvenuto, and Raffaello.

the door,' says Mephistopheles; and an officer with other soldiers enters. He points out the kneeling man as the murderer of their captain; the others fall upon him and slay him, while Mephistopheles in his monk's frock assumes an air of grotesque reprobation. He has killed three birds with one stone: a murder and a sacrilege, and both put down to Faust's account—a good day's business.

Now begins the main action of the play. The Duke of Parma has just married his beautiful Duchess, and the wedding festivity gives occasion for an introductory pageant and ballet, in which Busoni proclaims his devotion to Bizet. The music incorporates the *Cortège* and the *Tanzwalzer* which Busoni composed in the autumn of 1920. There is a procession of huntsmen with trophies, and a fencing display by little pages. The Master of Ceremonies proposes that the Duke and Duchess shall receive the famous Doctor Faust, and he is introduced by Mephistopheles disguised as a Herald. After a chorus of wonder and admiration he begins to display his magic arts by turning light into darkness. He asks the Duchess what she would like to see. Ask the impossible, whispers the Duke in her ear. She asks to see King Solomon, and he appears, playing the harp[1]; in a moment the Queen of Sheba is at his side. The Duke notices that the Queen resembles the Duchess, and that Solomon wears the features of Faust. The Duchess demands more; but this time Faust must guess her desire. He summons up Samson and Delilah; under Delilah's couch huddles a black slave-woman who hands her mistress the fatal shears. Again the Duke notices the resemblance of the figures to Faust and the Duchess. The Duchess tells Faust to choose the next vision himself, and the same faces are seen as Salome and John the Baptist. There is a third figure this time, who resembles the Duke—it is the Executioner.

'At Salome's bidding his head falls,' says Faust.

'He must not die,' the Duchess urges.

[1] Busoni appears to have confused Solomon with David.

Faust knows that she loves him and presses his suit;
she tries vainly to resist. The Duke breaks off the show
and invites Faust to the feast, but Mephistopheles warns
him not to accept: the food is poisoned, the clergy are on
the watch. They leave the stage together. A moment later
the Duchess comes back alone, calling to Faust and seeking
his love. As she goes out singing, the Duke enters with
his chaplain, who breaks the news to him that the Duchess
and Faust have eloped together, riding through the air on
a pair of flaming horses. It would be best to hush the
matter up and marry the Duke of Ferrara's sister for
reasons of state. 'Heaven speaks through you,' says the
kneeling Duke, as the chaplain raises a claw-like hand in
benediction—we recognize Mephistopheles.

Time passes, and Faust is back again at Wittenberg,
discussing philosophy with his students in a tavern. Wine
and metaphysics lead to quarrelling; Faust intervenes.
Nothing is proved, nothing is provable, he says. Let them
follow the good advice of Luther—but before he can
finish his sentence Protestants and Catholics are on the
way to a fight. Faust manages to quell them and quote
Luther's famous words, on which they start to sing the
praise of wine and woman, the Catholics in Latin and the
Protestants in German. A musical scene worthy of Berlioz
develops in which the tune of *Ein' feste Burg* becomes
prominent. Faust sits absorbed in dreams. A student
asks him to tell them about his adventures with women.
There was a woman once—a Duchess—in Italy—on her
wedding-day—hardly a year ago, though it seems an
eternity. Does she ever think of him?

A courier hurries in—it is Mephistopheles.

'Don't let me disturb you! The Duchess of Parma is
dead and buried: sends you this for a memento.'

It is the corpse of a new-born child. Is it? No, it is
only a bundle of straw. Mephistopheles sets it on fire, and
in the smoke there appears Helen of Troy. Faust is left
alone with the vision, but just as he is about to grasp it
it vanishes. Three dark figures stand in the shadow; they

are the three students from Cracow, come to demand
the return of the book, the key, and the letter. It is too
late; Faust has destroyed them. His time is up at midnight, they say. He dismisses them with contempt. 'Go
thy ways, Faust!' Their voices die away in the distance.
Faust views the moment not with fear, but with relief.
All is over at last; the way is free; the evening's end is
welcome.

The last scene shows a street in Wittenberg; snow is on
the ground, and the night-watchman's high grating voice
announces ten o'clock. A party of students are congratu-
lating Wagner on his inaugural speech; he has succeeded
Faust as Rector of the University. It was a discourse
worthy of his great predecessor, says one. That was an
unfortunate remark. Dr. Wagner is a genuine German
professor: 'Faust? well, Faust was—a visionary—more
than that. As a man of learning by no means infallible;
and—Lord have mercy upon us—his way of life was
deplorable. Good night, gentlemen.'

He retires; the students sing a serenade, interrupted by
the Watchman, who puts them to flight. Faust enters, and
looks up at Wagner's house that once was his own. On
the doorstep sits a beggar-woman with a child at the
breast. In the church opposite they are singing the *Dies
Irae*. Faust turns to give something to the beggar-woman
and recognizes the Duchess. She hands him the child;
it is dead. She vanishes; Faust, aware of evil spirits,
moves towards the church, but the soldier stands in the
doorway and bars his entrance with his sword. But Faust
is still master of spirits, and bids this one vanish too. He
kneels before the crucifix at the side of the church door.
He would pray, but he can remember no prayer, only
magical incantations. As he kneels the Watchman passes
by and raises his lantern; the light reveals the figure not
of Christ but of Helen. Faust turns away in horror, then
controls himself and sets about his last final effort of will.

It is at this point that Busoni's manuscript ends and
Jarnach's completion begins.

Faust lays the corpse of the child on the ground before him and covers it with his cloak; then he throws his girdle on the ground and steps within its magic circle. By the supreme effort of will and longing Faust transfers to the child his own personality. In the child he will continue his own existence and his own activity; what he built askew the child shall make straight; he shall carry out what Faust neglected and unite Faust, as an Eternal Will, with all generations that are to come. He dies; then, as the Watchman is heard announcing the stroke of midnight, the dead body sinks and there rises a naked youth holding a green twig in his hand. With arms uplifted he strides gaily through the snow into the town. Over Faust's body the Watchman lifts his lantern. Has this man met with an accident? he asks. It is Mephistopheles; he picks up the body and carries it off as the curtain falls.

One cannot apply to *Doctor Faust* the ordinary standards of operatic criticism. It moves on a plane of spiritual experience far beyond that of even the greatest of musical works for the stage. On its first production a German critic said of it that it could be compared only with *Parsifal*; it may be doubted whether the comparison would altogether have pleased Busoni. The poem by itself is a literary work of extraordinary power and imagination. It shows clearly how much Busoni owed to the lifelong study of Goethe; it is not Goethe's portrait of Faust, but it is written in Goethe's language. It combines the simplicity of the puppet-plays with something of the concentrated agony of Marlowe.

Busoni's prose preface (*On the Possibilities of Opera*) cannot be summarized shortly. Its argument is directed against a traditional prejudice, still even now perhaps current in Germany, that opera is an inferior form of musical art, and that the loftiest ideal of music is to be found only in the symphony. Busoni takes Mozart's view, that the music of an opera must form a complete musical whole in itself, independently of words or actions, and he further points out what is well known to any serious student of musical history, that most of the language of what is called absolute music is historically derived from the music of opera. An opera must have musical form, just as much as a symphony, and *Doctor Faust* is divided up into a number of separate musical forms—a plan which has been followed by various later composers of opera. And opera, Busoni contends, is the one form into which the musician can throw everything that he has to say; there is no style of music which it necessarily excludes. But there is much that has to be excluded when we come to consider the drama and its words, for an opera should deal only with such subjects as are incomplete without music; Busoni stands in direct opposition to the 'music-drama' of Bayreuth. And he will have no using of music to describe what can be seen upon the stage by the eye, just as Mozart in *The Magic Flute* makes no attempt to describe musically the fire and the water; in that scene the music represents only the sound of the magic flute itself and the general sense of solemnity and awe.

Thus the stage demands a purer standard of music than the symphony; it demands a type of music in which expression is concentrated to its utmost. Thanks to the conditions of the theatre, the extremest and most painful intensities of expression are accepted there without hesitation. There must necessarily follow a decline in the productivity of operatic composers, for Busoni conceives as an ideal an opera in which a truly creative composer should give expression to everything of which his imagination is capable—'a musical Dante, a musical *Divine Comedy*!'

Busoni was resolved to put 'everything' into *Doctor Faust*. It is the summing-up of his life's work and experience. Each of his larger compositions is surrounded by a number of small satellites, and *Doctor Faust* takes up and develops ideas from various shorter works that had preceded it, such as the *Nocturne Symphonique* and the Second Sonatina. The *Sarabande and Cortège* had been written definitely as studies for the opera; to what extent Faust may have been in Busoni's thoughts when he composed the other works cannot be said. But in any case they help to explain the opera and the opera helps to explain them. That most mysterious of all Busoni's compositions, the Second Sonatina, becomes clear when we hear its themes associated with the three students from Cracow. It is not that the Sonatina in any way 'represents' the figures of the opera; it is simply that the sound of the orchestra in the theatre makes clear what was obscure and even unpleasant on the pianoforte.

Musicians, in so far as they have thought over the philosophical problems of music at all, have been divided in their opinions as to its ultimate nature. Some have taken the view that the only music which exists is that which has been made by men, the actual sounds produced by actual instruments, a number of actual identifiable works composed by various persons at various periods of history. Busoni took the other view—that music exists as an ideal, of which our most venerated masterpieces are merely fragments often inadequately overheard in the composer's imagination, and inadequately reproduced there in audible sounds. Still more inadequately are these fragments committed to notation on paper. This philosophy was the basis of Busoni's attitude to the classics that he interpreted at the pianoforte. We see it far back in the letter to the Belgian critic Marcel Rémy, about 1902,[1] in which he defends his 'modernizations'.

Busoni, even then, was one of the most remarkable pianists living, but he was only at the beginning of his own career as a pianist and as a musician. Regarding him as a pianist alone, his life was a perpetual series of 'new beginnings', and all these new beginnings were necessary to him, because his ever widening experience of life and of music made him discontented with the pianoforte as he himself commanded it. There was no limit, it seemed, to the problems of pianoforte technique, in order to master the infinite resources of the instrument—resources hitherto undiscovered—for the interpretation of that ideal music

[1] See Chapter VI.

which a life's experience revealed, and a lifetime's wisdom gradually discarded. The *Fantasia Contrappuntistica* was planned for no instrument; it is music and nothing else.

We have seen already how both in his pianoforte-playing and in his composition Busoni was constantly striving towards that state of music which he called *Auflösung*, a state in which one should be conscious of it not as made up of single notes or phrases but as a direct spiritual experience. It is in *Doctor Faust* that he reaches the farthest heights of spirituality, and it is this mystical quality which makes *Doctor Faust* unique among all operas. But it is a hard task for humbler mortals to follow Busoni's path, and we cannot hope to attain understanding of his vision until we have pursued it along his own track, sharing the successive experiences that each of his earlier works recorded.

Faust is the seeker after experience. The nature of that experience has varied with that of the poets who have portrayed him: there is the Faust of Marlowe, of Goethe, and also of Gounod. Busoni's Faust is his own. The outline of the story remains the same, but magic and the devil are mere symbols for things perhaps impossible to express in words. Every poet has to paint in Faust the portrait of himself, whether it be that self which the world sees, or that other self which the poet may perhaps never have been able to realize in life.

> Der dritte meiner Reih' ist nicht geringer,
> Ein trotz'ger Geist, ein Einzelner, auch er:
> Ein Tiefbelesener, ein Höllenzwinger,
> Vieldeutiger zumal, und sonst auch mehr;
> Ein schwacher Mensch und doch ein starker Ringer,
> Den Zweifel tragen hin und wider her;
> Herr des Gedankens, Diener dem Instinkt,
> Dem das Erschöpfen keine Lösung bringt.

> The third of my series[1] is no lesser:
> a spirit of defiance, a solitary too;

---

[1] i.e. Merlin, Don Giovanni, Faust; 'the others' in line 4 are the first two names.

> a man deep-read, a constrainer of Hell,
> more mysterious than the others, and more than that;
> a weak man, yet a stout wrestler,
> whom doubts drive hither and thither;
> master of thought, slave to instinct,
> exhausting all things, finding no answer.

If the stanza does not quite accurately describe Busoni as his friends knew him, it may well describe him as he inwardly felt himself to be. And from the first moment of the drama to the end we are constantly made to feel that Faust speaks with Busoni's own voice. 'Life rolls ever faster, and—no longer upwards. I may not give so much time to others.' It is Busoni composing his *Doctor Faust* and wondering if he will ever live to finish it. 'Oh my old beloved Cracow! Your shapes recall my youth. Dreams, ambitions! How greatly have I hoped!' One recalls the scene in the restaurant at Hamburg in 1912 and that strange cry of 'Klagenfurt!' Even the tiny touch of the hospitality and courtesy offered by Faust to the mysterious students from Cracow at once reminds one of Busoni himself; in the opera it is so small a thing that one wonders why it should be there at all unless it was a subconscious expression of his own personality.

The pact with Mephistopheles—'Give me Genius'—is a new interpretation of Faust's desires. 'Genius, with all its sufferings, that I may be happy as no other.' And then, at the moment when Faust signs the bond, as the unseen chorus sings:

Et iterum venturus est cum gloria judicare vivos et mortuos,

Faust's despairing and defiant cry:

'There is no mercy, no eternal blessedness, no forgiveness. There! When my time runs out we shall see; perhaps thou yet wilt be the loser—am I not thy master?'

Faust as the magician, with his visions of Solomon, Samson, and John the Baptist, each bearing his own features; is it not Busoni, most miraculous of interpreters, yet always, in the vision of Bach, Mozart or Beethoven,

presenting himself? Faust among the students at Wittenberg; one remembers Busoni, always surrounded by the
young, provoking them by terrifyingly critical observations
on all that they had been taught blindly to revere. 'You
will never be happy,' said Philipp to Busoni once; 'you are
Faust and Mephistopheles in one.' It was true enough;
Faust, the seeker after truth, was always accompanied by
Mephistopheles, the eternal sceptic. And this Faust is
not merely a philosopher; he is a man who can enter
joyously into all the pleasures of life and share them with
others.

It is Busoni again who speaks to us after the vision of
Helen has eluded his grasp:

'Man is not able to attain perfection. Then let him strive according to his measure and strew good around him, as he has received
it. I, wise fool, hesitator and waster, have accomplished nothing;
all must be begun afresh; I feel as if I were drawing near to childhood again.

'I look far out into the distance; there lie young fields, unculti-
vated hills that swell and call to new ascent. Life smiles with
promise.'

How many times in Busoni's life had he spoken and
written of 'a new beginning'! 'Never look back'—the
words recur perpetually in his letters.

The students return and demand the book; Faust
dismisses them 'with the commanding gesture of a *grand
seigneur*'. One sees Busoni in the flesh.

The last scene of all—Faust with the dead child. The
child, Busoni tells us in his preface, is a symbol. Faust's
union with the Duchess was an act of impulse, with no
sense of deliberate purpose towards an ultimate end. The
appearance of Mephistopheles with the dead child is meant
to convey to Faust a warning of this ultimate purpose, but
Faust does not understand it, and Mephistopheles leads
him further astray by conjuring up the vision of Helen.
From the body of the dead child the 'Ideal' is to arise, but
Faust finds this 'Ideal' false and deceptive. He renounces
all hope of it, and renounces magic too by destroying

the magical book. It is only when he meets the Duchess again in the last scene that he grasps the significance of the child, and it is only after his last attempt at an approach to God has proved vain and futile that he can perform the mystic rite by which he transfers his own personality to the oncoming generation, thereby renewing his own exhausted life in the life of the future.

Busoni had been brought up in an atmosphere of Catholic piety, but he had already reacted against the doctrines of the Church when he was a young man, and although he never altogether lost a certain affection for the picturesque aspect of Catholicism, he never again returned to the Christian faith. Writing to the Swiss poet Hans Reinhart—a keen enthusiast for Wagner—in 1917, he says:

'Wagnerism and Christianity as well are nothing to me, and my feeling is that it is time to sweep away these two beliefs altogether, or at least to leave them in peace and not to poke about in them any more.'

To the same correspondent he wrote again in May 1923, thanking him for a book, to which he alludes in the first sentence here quoted:

'I suspect that your "New Life" becomes a dream-vision in other forms of what previously was hostile to life. It has always affected me unpleasantly from childhood to note how South German art makes eyes at death and treats death as its perpetual motive. Against that my Latin blood rebels. Our Latin inability to preoccupy ourselves with death is seen at its best in Verdi's *Requiem* and Rossini's *Stabat Mater*, in which life departed is irradiated by the life of the present. Even Dante's *Inferno* is retrospective, and concerns itself exclusively with the acts committed by the damned during their lives. In Orcagna's *Dance of Death*[1] living people walk past coffins, holding their noses.

'Nowhere in my life did I hear so much talk about death as in Switzerland, where people (to speak honestly) are unusually careful and concerned for their earthly existence. Those of Latin origin will exchange life for an idea without any longing for death; they do so rather from a longing to enrich their lives.'

---

[1] Busoni refers to the frescoes in the Campo Santo at Pisa.

Experience

Faust at his last end is conscious of being liberated from God and Devil alike; he will set mankind free from the eternal quarrel which has been handed on from generation to generation. It is to the new world of youth that he looks forward. That new generation which he loved—and often chastised so ruthlessly—is already learning to carry on those ideals to which all his life he had aspired.

'Habe nun, ach! Philosophie, Juristerei und Medizin—'

Faust is the seeker after experience. There are many people who value their experiences, but few who value experience. They are only too often afraid of pursuing experience beyond those single experiences that they have valued, because they are afraid that new experience may destroy for them the value of the old. Busoni's life had been crowded with experiences in endless profusion and variety. Setting aside what he had traversed in fifty years of professional life as a musician, he had enriched his personality with an astonishing knowledge of literature, painting, and architecture. In his travels over almost all Europe and North America he had stored up the memory of landscape in all its diversities; in every country he had sought the knowledge of human beings of all conceivable types. He had known the struggles and the glories of the virtuoso, the inward concentration of the composer, the self-dedication of the teacher; he had won the love and devotion of pupils and friends, he had experienced what perhaps was to him the most precious experience of all in his life—thirty years and more of unclouded sympathy and happiness in marriage.

Busoni had the courage not only to pursue experience, but to discard without hesitation or regret those fruits of earlier experience which in the course of time had come to lose their savour. We can trace his musical progress in his pianoforte repertory;[1] we can watch him gradually discarding one composer after another, as they fail to satisfy

[1] See Appendix.

311

his ever soaring standard. That keen critical sense which he applied so rigorously to himself, both as pianist and as composer, gave him the reputation among the more traditional-minded of being nothing but an iconoclast and a destroyer. To timid souls it was certainly frightening to hear him speak of Schubert as 'a gifted amateur',[1] to listen to his grotesque mockery of Schumann and his titles to the movements of *Carneval*, to read that Chopin did not understand how to write for the pianoforte and that Beethoven did not possess the technique to express his emotions. In those last years, when he wrote to Philipp that he felt himself forced to abandon the whole of his former repertory, he might well seem, for the moment, to be no more than a world-weary cynic hurling forth his last gesture of surfeit and despair. But despair was an emotion entirely outside Busoni's experience. 'Dear Gerda, let us hope for the future,' he had written to his wife at a moment when fortune looked blackest. Whatever he discarded he left behind him in the spirit of the snake that casts its skin. It had been precious while it lasted; one has only to turn back to his earlier writings or recall the memory of earlier conversations to see that he discarded nothing until he had completely exhausted all that there was to be learned from it. Even the ruin remained sometimes as a memorial; if younger friends attempted in their haste to overtake his startling judgements, they were reminded that they had no right to discard these things until they too had gone through all the experience of understanding them.

The greatest, the most apparently inexhaustible, of the masters were but transitory; this fact one must recognize without trembling. Even the score of *Figaro*, he found, had its weak places. All must come to an end in its time, but each end was a new beginning—a new beginning not for his own development alone, but for the whole art of music. Music was infinite: its past was as nothing to its future. If he was forced to recognize the limitations of

[1] Recorded by Wilhelm Kienzl.

human life, there was always a new music to come, far beyond the boundaries of his own personal knowledge. In the endless history of the art, what could be the achievement of any one man, be he Bach, Mozart, or Beethoven? They were all 'beginners', each the beginner of a new era, prophet of a new vision of music's infinity.

APPENDIX I

BUSONI'S LAST ILLNESS

AT the time of Busoni's death and for some years previously so
many unfounded rumours were in circulation as to his alleged intemperance that it is necessary to give a medical account of his last
illness on the authority of his physician, Dr. Hans Meyer of Berlin.
It was commonly reported in Switzerland that Busoni was taken
home every night from the station restaurant at Zurich in a state of
complete intoxication. Directly after his death Italian papers asserted
that he had died of *delirium tremens* in an inebriates' home. It cannot
be too emphatically stated that these stories were utterly untrue. At
the same time it is not difficult to guess the gradual process by which
they came into existence.

Busoni was an Italian by birth and breeding; he was naturally
brought up from infancy to regard wine as his normal beverage. He
was always fond of wine and appreciated wines of fine quality, but
he never drank to excess at any time of his life. It is obvious that he
could never have carried out the programmes that he played if he
had been an habitual drunkard. There are several letters of his in
which he expresses a horror of drunkenness, and Max Reger's
letters to Busoni, as well as the fact that he destroyed Busoni's
letters to him, point clearly to the conclusion that Busoni warned
him very seriously against habits of intemperance.

No one ever saw Busoni the worse for liquor, but it must be
frankly admitted that strangers might sometimes have supposed
him to have drunk more than was good for him. Busoni loved
cheerful company, and often became very exuberant in manner
when enjoying the society of congenial friends. He was entirely
free from hypocrisy and given to expressing himself very openly; if
he was happy, he made no secret of the fact, and his volcanic laughter
may well have shocked the ears of conventional people when they
heard it in a public restaurant. At the end of a social evening the
empty bottles would generally be ranged in front of Busoni, and
it was naturally supposed that he had drunk the contents of all of
them.

Wherever Busoni went he was regarded as rather eccentric, and
his biting remarks often made him enemies. It was only natural
that such people should spread malicious gossip about his private

life, and gossip of that type is quickly exaggerated and willingly believed by many ordinary people when an artist, especially a famous one, is the subject of it. In countries where beer is the normal drink, an habitual wine-drinker is always accused of extravagant living, even though he confine himself, as Busoni normally did, to the lightest and cheapest types of wine. It must be added that Busoni never touched spirits in any form. Medical examination showed no trace whatever of alcoholic poisoning.

The disease of which Busoni died was chronic inflammation of the kidneys together with chronic inflammation of the muscles of the heart. It was of long standing and probably due to some accidental injury received much earlier in life. It was often asserted that Busoni was an excessively heavy smoker, but medical examination showed no trace of serious poisoning by nicotine. He certainly smoked a good many cigars, but only the light ones commonly smoked in Germany.

It must be borne in mind that a concert performer cannot possibly live the life of an ordinary citizen. All virtuosi, instrumental as well as vocal, are obliged to go on to the platform fasting. It is well known that the pangs of hunger can be temporarily assuaged by tobacco and the illusion of a full meal created. This accounted for a good many of Busoni's cigars. To a man who undertook such programmes as Busoni played, often under conditions of severe strain due to the fatigue of travelling, as well as to occasional illness, certain stimulants were an absolute necessity. At his later recitals in London and elsewhere a bottle of champagne was often provided for him, but he hardly ever drank more than a single glass of it. In spite of the other complications induced by the kidney trouble his digestion functioned well until they became too serious for it not to be affected.

APPENDIX II

FERRUCCIO BUSONI'S PIANOFORTE REPERTORY

THE following list gives the works played by Busoni with the date and place of first performance by him, as far as it has been possible to ascertain from programmes and criticisms, but it is probably far from complete. It does not include chamber works which Busoni played with other performers, nor does it include a large number of his own youthful compositions which he played in earlier years. Some of them have disappeared and many were never printed. Only those works of Busoni are given here which are included in the catalogue of his works printed as Appendix IV. In the early programmes it is often impossible to identify the exact work played since pieces are put down in them merely as 'Fugue' or 'Minuet' with no indication of key.

Transcriptions are entered under the names of the original composers.

ALKAN, CHARLES VALENTIN

Étude en rythme molossique, Op. 35	Berlin, 1901
Étude (Andantino) in G major, Op. 35	" "
Étude (Allegro barbaro), Op. 35	" "
Le Tambour bat aux champs, Op. 50	" "
Étude in D major, Op. 35	" 1902
Étude in E major, Op. 35	" "
Cantique des cantiques, Op. 31	" "
Capriccio alla soldatesca, Op. 50	" 1903
Fantasia for the left hand	" 1908

AUBER-LISZT

Tarantelle from *La Muette de Portici*	Hamburg, 1887

BACH, JOHANN SEBASTIAN

Prelude and Fugue	Trieste, 1875
Fugue	" "
Prelude in F major	Venice (Lido), 1875
Fugue in C major	" "
Fugue	Gmunden, 1876
Minuet	" "

317

x

Fugue	Ischl, 1876
Invention in C minor	Gmunden, 1876
Fugue in A minor	„ 1877
Chromatic Fantasia and Fugue	Baden,[1] 1878
Fugue in A minor	„ „
Préambule in G major	„ „
Sarabande in A minor	„ „
Rondeau in C minor	„ „
Gigue in G major	„ „
Prelude and Fugue in A minor	Graz, 1878
Sarabande in B minor	„ „
Prelude and Fugue in C minor	Cilli, 1879
Prelude and Fugue in G major	Neuhaus, 1879
Prelude and Fugue on the name 'Bach' in B flat	Graz, 1880
Gavotte in G minor	Bologna, 1883
Preludes and Fugues from the *Wohltem-periertes Klavier*	Helsingfors, 1888
Concerto in D minor	„ 1898
Six Preludes from the *W. K.*: A minor (II), C sharp major (I), B flat minor (I), F sharp major (I), F sharp minor (II), D major (II)	Zurich, 1916

BACH-BUSONI

Prelude and Fugue in D major for organ	Leipzig, 1888
Prelude and Fugue in E flat major for organ	Helsingfors, 1890
Chaconne for violin	Boston, 1893
Toccata, Adagio and Fugue in C major	Manchester, 1899
Toccata and Fugue in D minor for organ	Berlin, 1901
Chorale-Preludes for organ: *Wachet auf* and *In Dir ist Freude*	London, 1901
Chorale-Preludes for organ: *Ich ruf zu Dir* and *Nun freut euch*	Berlin, 1902
Chromatic Fantasia	London, 1902
Preludio, Fuga e Fuga figurata (study after the *W. K.*)	„ 1909
Adagio and Fugue in C major for organ	„ 1913
Capriccio sopra la lontananza del fratello dilet-tissimo	Berlin, 1914

[1] i.e. Baden near Vienna, not Baden-Baden.

318

Prelude, Fugue and Allegro in E flat major for the Lautenklavier	Berlin, 1914
Goldberg Variations	„ „
Chorale-Prelude for organ: *Komm Gott Schöpfer*	Zurich, 1916
Concerto in D minor	„ 1919

BACH-LISZT

Fantasia and Fugue in G minor for organ	Hamburg, 1887

BACH-TAUSIG

Toccata and Fugue in D minor for organ	Trieste, 1885

BEETHOVEN, LUDWIG van

Sonata in C major, Op. 53	Bozen, 1879
Sonata in D minor, Op. 31, No. 2	Graz, 1880
Sonata in C minor, Op. 111	„ 1881
Sonata in F minor, Op. 57	Bologna, 1882
32 Variations in C minor	„ 1883
Sonata in F minor, Op. 2, No. 1	Trieste, 1885
Variations in E flat (*Eroica*), Op. 35	Helsingfors, 1888
Concerto in E flat major, Op. 73	Leipzig, 1890
Sonata in E major, Op. 109	Helsingfors, 1890
Concerto in G major, Op. 50	Boston, 1890
Sonata in B flat major, Op. 106	„ 1892
Rondo a capriccio, Op. 129	„ 1893
Variations on a Waltz of Diabelli, Op. 120	Berlin, 1895
Choral Fantasia, Op. 80	Düsseldorf, 1896
Sonata in E flat major, Op. 81a	Trieste, 1897
Sonata in F sharp major, Op. 78	London, 1897
Six Bagatelles, Op. 126	„ 1899
Sonata in C sharp minor, Op. 27, No. 2	„ „
Sonata in A flat major, Op. 26	Berlin, 1901
Sonata (*Pathétique*) in C minor, Op. 13	„ 1903
Sonata in A flat major, Op. 110	„ „
Concerto in C minor, Op. 37	„ 1906
Concerto in C major, Op. 15	Zurich, 1919

BEETHOVEN-BUSONI

Écossaises	Helsingfors, 1888

BEETHOVEN-LISZT

Fantasia on *The Ruins of Athens*	Helsingfors, 1891

Ninth Symphony for 2 pianofortes (with José   Weimar, 1900
  Vianna da Motta)
Adelaïde   Manchester, 1904
Busslied   Berlin, 1906

BELLINI-LISZT
Fantasia on *Norma*   Berlin, 1894
Grande Fantaisie sur *La Sonnambula*   „   1905
Réminiscences de *Norma* (for 2 pianofortes,   Basle, 1918
  with Ernst Lochbrunner)

BRAHMS, JOHANNES
Variations on a theme of Handel, Op. 24   Vienna, 1884
Sonata in F minor, Op. 5   „   „
Concerto in D minor, Op. 15   „   1897
Variations on a theme of Paganini, Op. 35   Berlin, 1900

BRAHMS-BUSONI
Four Chorale-Preludes for organ, Op. 122   Berlin, 1903

BUSONI, FERRUCCIO
Five Pieces (Op. 3): *Preludio, Menuetto,*   Vienna and
  Gavotta, Étude, Gigue   Baden, 1878
Fugue in C minor, Op. 21   Baden, 1878
Gavotte in F major, Op. 25   Vöslau, 1878
Prelude in A minor, Op. 37, No. 2   Graz, 1880
Gigue in C minor, Op. 10 or 11?   „   „
Gavotte in F minor, Op. 70   Trieste, 1881
Prelude and Fugue in C minor, Op. 36   „   „
Prelude and Fugue in C major, Op. 21   Milan, 1881
Preludes in G major and E major, Op. 37   „   „
Minuet in C major, Op. 61   „   „
Preludes in A minor and B major, Op. 37   „   „
Una festa di villaggio, Op. 9   Bergamo, 1882
Preludes (D flat major, E flat minor, B flat   Bologna, 1882
  major), Op. 37
Prelude and Fugue, Op. 36   „   „
Tre pezzi nello stile antico, Op. 10   „   „
Danza Notturna, Op. 13   „   „
Prelude in C major, Op. 5?   „   1883
Racconti fantastici, Op. 10   „   „
Macchiette Medioevali   „   „

Marcia di paesani e contadine, Op. 32	Trieste, 1883
Scène de Ballet, Op. 6	Vienna, 1884
Prelude and Fugue, Op. 5	„ „
Étude en forme de variations, Op. 17	„ „
Prelude in C sharp minor, Op. 37	Trieste, 1884
Étude in B minor, Op. 16	„ „
Deuxième Scène de Ballet, Op. 20	Gorizia, 1884
Bourrée, Op. 11, No. 4	Vienna, 1884
Six *Études*, Op. 16	„ „
Variations and Fugue on Chopin's Prelude in C minor, Op. 22	„ 1885
Kleiner Tanz, Op. 30	Frohnleiten, 1885
Concert Fantasia (with orchestra) Op. 29 (not printed)	Leipzig, 1890
Preludes (C major and F sharp minor) Op. 37	Helsingfors,1890
Dritte Ballettszene, Op. 30	„ 1891
Contrapunktischer Tanz, Op. 30	„ „
Konzertstück (with orchestra), Op. 31a	New York, 1892
Concerto, Op. 39	Berlin, 1904
Six Elegies	„ 1908
Fantasia on Bach's *Christ Du bist der helle Tag* (In memoriam Ferdinando Busoni)	London, 1909
Fantasia Contrappuntistica	Basle, 1910
First Sonatina	„ „
Second Sonatina	Milan, 1913
Berceuse	„ „
Vierte Ballettszene (new edition)	„ „
Indian Fantasy, Op. 44 (with orchestra)	Berlin, 1914
Zwei Tanzstücke, Op. 30a: *Waffentanz*, *Friedenstanz*	„ „
Sonatina *ad usum infantis*	Zurich, 1917
Indianisches Tagebuch	„ „
Improvisation on Bach's Chorale *Wie wohl ist mir* for 2 pianofortes (with Ernst Lochbrunner)	„ „
Fourth Sonatina *In diem Nativitatis Christi MCMXVII*	„ 1920
Sonatina super *Carmen*	London, 1920
Toccata	Berlin, 1920
Fantasia Contrappuntistica (version for 2 pianofortes, with Egon Petri)	„ 1921

Drei Albumblätter	London, 1922
Concertino, Op. 54 (with orchestra)	Paris, 1922

See also BACH, BEETHOVEN, BRAHMS, GOUNOD, LISZT, MOZART, PAGANINI, WAGNER.

CHOPIN, FRÉDÉRIC[1]

Fantaisie-Impromptu, Op. 66	Trent, 1878
Études, Op. 10:	
F minor	Cilli, 1879
G flat major	Berlin, 1894
12 *Études* complete	„ 1902
Études, Op. 25:	
C sharp minor and A minor	Trieste, 1884
12 *Études* complete	Berlin, 1896
Valse in A minor, Op. 34, No. 2	Cilli, 1879
Tarantella, Op. 43	Neuhaus, 1879
Polonaise	„ „
Ballade in A flat major, Op. 47	Graz, 1879
Ballade in F minor, Op. 52	Trieste, 1885
The 4 Ballades complete	London, 1899
Berceuse, Op. 57	Graz, 1879
Valse in A flat major	Bologna, 1882
Polonaise brillante in E flat major, Op. 22	„ „
Andante spianato, Op. 22	Modena, 1883
Polonaise	„ „
Prelude in D minor, Op. 28, No. 24	Bologna, 1883
24 Preludes complete	Zurich, 1906
Nocturne in C minor, Op. 48, No. 1	Trieste, 1884
Polonaise in B flat major, Op. 71, No. 2	„ „
Polonaise in A flat major, Op. 53	„ „
Sonata in B flat minor, Op. 35:	
Marche funèbre	„ „
The complete sonata	Trieste, 1885
Fantaisie-Polonaise, Op. 61	„ „
Nocturne in D flat major, Op. 27, No. 2	Hamburg, 1887

[1] Many of Chopin's works (Polonaises, Mazurkas, Impromptus, Nocturnes, and Scherzos) appear in Busoni's programmes, even as late as 1920, without any indication of key or opus number. Busoni was in the habit of making his final choice on the very evening of the concert.

Up to 1890 these unidentified works are given in this list; after 1890 only those are mentioned which can be identified.

Polonaise in C sharp minor, Op. 26, No. 1	Helsingfors, 1889
Nocturne in F sharp major, Op. 15, No. 2	,, ,,
Nocturne in C sharp minor, Op. 27, No. 1	,, ,,
Barcarolle, Op. 60	,, 1891
Impromptu in F sharp major, Op. 36	Boston, 1892
Sonata in B minor, Op. 58:	
Last movement only	Berlin, 1894
Complete	,, 1899
Scherzo in B flat minor, Op. 31	,, 1895
Nocturne in E flat major	London, 1897
Concerto in E minor, Op. 11	Berlin, 1898
Polonaise in F sharp minor, Op. 44	,, 1900
Nocturne in F major, Op. 15, No. 1	London, 1905
Polonaise in A flat major, Op. 40, No. 1	,, ,,
Nocturne in E flat major, Op. 55, No. 2	Berlin, 1906
Scherzo in C sharp minor, Op. 39	Eastbourne, 1912
See also LISZT (Hexameron)	

CHOPIN-LISZT

Chants polonais, Nos. 1, 3, 4, 5	Bologna, 1883

CLEMENTI, MUZIO

Sonatina in F major, No. 4	Trieste, 1873

CZERNY, CARL. See LISZT (Hexameron)

DONIZETTI-LISZT

Réminiscences de *Lucrezia Borgia*	Trieste, 1885
Valse à capriccio sur deux motifs de *Lucia* et *Parisina*	,, 1899
Grande paraphrase sur la marche de Donizetti	Berlin, 1908

FRANCK, CÉSAR

Prélude, Choral et Fugue	Berlin, 1902
Prélude, Aria et Final	,, 1908

FUMAGALLI, ANTONIO

Rêverie, Op. 100	Graz, 1881
Souvenir, Melodie	Milan, 1882
Carnevale di Venezia	Empoli, 1882
See also GORDIGIANI-FUMAGALLI	

GOLDMARK, CARL

Prelude and Fugue, Op. 29	Vienna, 1884

GOLINELLI, STEFANO
Studio in C major   Bologna, 1882
Allegria, Tempo di Valz   "   1883

GORDIGIANI-FUMAGALLI
Preghiera alla Madonna (O santissima Vergine Maria)   Trieste, 1881

GOTTSCHALK, FERDINAND
Le bananier, chanson des nègres, Op. 5   Vienna, 1884

GOUNOD-LISZT
Faust-Walzer   Milan, 1882

GOUNOD-LISZT-BUSONI
Faust-Walzer   New York, 1910

GRIEG, EDVARD
Concerto in A minor, Op. 16   Copenhagen, 1896

HANDEL, GEORGE FREDERIC
Two Fugues in C major   Trieste, 1874
Air and Variations in E major from the   Gmunden, 1877
   Fifth Suite
Gavotta variata   Graz, 1880

HAYDN, JOSEPH
Variations in D major (from the Sonata in   Hamburg, 1887
   D major)

HENSELT, ADOLPHE
Concerto in F minor, Op. 16   Berlin, 1898

HERZ, HENRI. See LISZT (Hexameron)

HUMMEL, JOHANN NEPOMUK
Tema con variazioni   Trieste, 1874
Rondo mignon   "   1875
Bagatelle in B flat minor   "   "
Bagatelles   Gmunden, 1876
Concerto in B minor, Op. 89   Berlin, 1898

LIAPUNOV, SERGIUS
Concerto   ? 1911-1913?

324

LISZT, FRANZ

Douze Études d'exécution transcendante:

Eroica	Trieste, 1881
Mazeppa	Berlin, 1899
Feux-Follets	,, 1901
Harmonies du soir	,, ,,
Complete	Berlin, 1903

Années de Pèlerinage: Italie

Venezia e Napoli, Canzone	Empoli, 1882
Venezia e Napoli, complete	Bologna, 1883
Lo Sposalizio	Boston, 1891
Après une lecture de Dante	Berlin, 1896
Complete	,, 1900

Années de Pèlerinage: Suisse

Au bord d'une source	
Vallée d'Obermann	
Le mal du pays	Berlin, 1903
Complete	,, 1909

Années de Pèlerinage: Troisième Année

Les jeux d'eau à la Villa d'Este	,, 1903
Complete	,, 1909

Hungarian March	Bologna, 1883
Mélodies Hongroises, No. 1	Trieste, 1884
Polonaise No. 2 in E major	Helsingfors, 1890
Waldesrauschen, Étude	,, 1891
Mephisto-Walzer, No. 1	,, ,,
Les Préludes (for 2 pianofortes, with José Vianna da Motta)	,, 1891
Fantasia and Fugue on the name 'Bach'	Boston, 1893
Deux Légendes	,, ,,
Concerto in A major	Berlin, 1894
Ballade	,, 1895
Hexameron (Variations on the March from *I Puritani* by Liszt, Thalberg, Pixis, Herz, Czerny, and Chopin)	,, ,,
Hungarian Rhapsody No. 12	,, ,,
Variations on *Weinen, Klagen* (Bach)	,, ,,
Bénédiction de Dieu dans la solitude	Helsingfors, 1895
Polonaise No. 1 in C minor	London, 1899
Sonata in B minor	Berlin, 1900

Faust-Symphony (for 2 pianofortes, with José   Weimar, 1900
  Vianna da Motta)
Rhapsodie Héroïde-Élégiaque   Berlin, 1901
Hungarian Rhapsodies, Nos. 6 and 13   ,,   ,,
Concerto in E flat major   London, 1901
Gnomenreigen, Étude   ,,   ,,
Todtentanz   Aachen, 1903
Apparitions, No. 1   Berlin, 1905
Ballade, No. 2   ,,   ,,
Valse mélancolique (Caprices-Valses, No. 2)   ,,   ,,
Concerto pathétique for 2 pianofortes (with   Amsterdam, 1905
  Egon Petri)
Venezia e Napoli (unpublished first version)   Berlin, 1908
Hungarian Rhapsody (unpublished) "No. 20"   ,,   ,,
Valse oubliée   ,,   1911
Die Zelle in Nonnenwerth   ,,   ,,
Galop chromatique   ,,   ,,
Valse oubliée, No. 2   Milan, 1913
Hungarian Rhapsody No. 19   Berlin, 1914
Der Weihnachtsbaum   Basle, 1918
Todtentanz (first version)   Zurich, 1919

See also AUBER, BACH, BEETHOVEN, BELLINI,
    CHOPIN, DONIZETTI, GOUNOD, MENDELS-
    SOHN, MEYERBEER, MOZART, PAGANINI,
    ROSSINI, SCHUBERT, SCHUMANN, VERDI,
    WAGNER.

LISZT-BUSONI

Spanische Rhapsodie (with orchestra)   Hamburg, 1894
Fantasia and Fugue on *Ad nos, ad salutarem*   Berlin, 1897
  undam (from *Le Prophète*)
Mephisto-Walzer   ,,   1901
See also MOZART

MENDELSSOHN BARTHOLDY, FELIX

Presto in E minor (Op. 16, No. 2?)   Trieste, 1875
Rondo capriccioso, Op. 14   Baden, 1878
Variations sérieuses, Op. 54   Klagenfurt, 1879
Spinnerlied, Op. 67, No. 4   Cilli, 1879
Minuet from the Sonata in E major, Op. 6   Neuhaus, 1879
Volkslied, Op. 53, No. 5   ,,   ,,
Presto in F sharp minor   Bologna, 1883

Lied ohne Worte	Bologna, 1883
Concerto in G minor, Op. 25	Berlin, 1898

MENDELSSOHN-LISZT

Wedding March and Fairies' Dance from *A Midsummer Night's Dream*	Bergamo, 1882

MEYERBEER-LISZT

Réminiscences de *Robert le Diable*	Berlin, 1899

MOZART, W. A.

Sonata in C major (first movement)	Trieste, 1873
Concerto in C minor (K. 491)	„ 1875
Rondo in A minor	„ „
Rondo	Vienna, 1876
Sonata in C major (K. 309), Finale	Gmunden, 1876
Rondo alla Turca from Sonata (K. 331)	Hamburg, 1887
Gigue (K. 574)	„ „
Concerto in A major (K. 488)	Berlin, 1898
Concerto in D minor (K. 466)	Lausanne, 1908
Sonata for 2 Pianofortes (K. 448 with Ernst Lochbrunner)	Zurich, 1917
[1]Concerto in D minor (K. 466)	„ 1918
[1]Concerto in C minor (K. 491)	St. Gallen, 1919
[1]Concerto in A major (K. 488)	Zurich, 1919
[1]Concerto in E flat major (K. 271)	Liverpool, 1921
[1]Concerto in E flat major (K. 482)	London, 1921
[1]Sonata for 2 Pianofortes (K. 448 with Egon Petri)	Berlin, 1921
[1]Concerto in G major (K. 453)	„ „
[1]Concerto in C major (K. 467)	„ „
[1]Concerto in C major (K. 503)	„ „

MOZART-BUSONI

Giga, Bolero e Variazioni	London, 1909
Andantino from Concerto in E flat major (K. 271) for pianoforte solo	Liverpool, 1913
Duettino concertante (after the Finale of the Concerto in E flat major, K. 271) for 2 pianofortes (with Egon Petri)	Berlin, 1921
Fantasia in F minor for a mechanical organ (for 2 pianofortes, with Egon Petri)	London, 1922

[1] First performance with Cadenzas by Busoni.

327

Busoni's Repertory

MOZART-LISZT
Réminiscences de *Don Juan*	Trieste, 1884
Réminiscences de *Don Juan* (for 2 piano-fortes, with Egon Petri)	Berlin, 1908

MOZART-LISZT-BUSONI
Figaro-Fantasie	Berlin, 1911

NOVÁČEK, OTTOKAR
Concerto	Copenhagen, 1896
Toccata in E flat major	„ „

PAGANINI-BUSONI
Introduzione e Capriccio	London, 1909

PAGANINI-LISZT
Six Études
?	Graz, 1881
?	Milan, 1881
E major and E flat major	Bologna, 1882
La Campanella	St. Petersburg, 1890
Complete	Boston, 1892

PERGOLESI-THALBERG
Aria	Vienna, 1885

PIXIS, PETER. See LISZT (Hexameron)

PORPORA, NICCOLO
Fugue in B flat major	Trieste, 1875

RAMEAU, JEAN-PHILIPPE
Gavotte variée in A minor	Trieste, 1875

ROSSINI-LISZT
La Serenata e l'Orgia	Berlin, 1901

RUBINSTEIN, ANTON
Étude in F major, Op. 23, No. 1	Trieste, 1884
Concerto in D minor, Op. 70	Helsingfors, 1889
Concert in E flat major, Op. 94	Vienna, 1896
Variations in G major, Op. 88	Brussels, 1900
Étude in G major	London, 1901
Étude	„ „

328

SAINT-SAËNS, CAMILLE

Variations on a theme of Beethoven for | Helsingfors, 1891
2 pianofortes (with William Dayas)
Concerto in F major, Op. 103 — Hanover, 1902
Scherzo for 2 pianofortes, Op. 87 (with — Zurich, 1917
Ernst Lochbrunner)

SCARLATTI, DOMENICO

Preludio (G major)	Trieste, 1875
Capriccio in A major	Trent, 1878
Allegro in G major	Graz, 1880
Presto in G major	Trieste, 1881
Gigue	Bologna, 1882
Pastorale	Trieste, 1884
Sonata di Concerto	„ „

SCHLÖSSER, ADOLPH

Concert *Étude* — Boston, 1893

SCHUBERT, FRANZ

March (perhaps *Moment musical* in F minor?)	Graz, 1878
Minuet from Sonata in G major, Op. 78	„ „
Impromptu in E flat major, Op. 90, No. 2	„ „
Impromptu, Op. 90, No. 4	London, 1897
Four Impromptus, Op. 90	Berlin, 1903

SCHUBERT-LISZT

Valse-Caprice	Trent, 1878
Valse	Modena, 1883
Erlkönig	Trieste, 1885
Hungarian March	Boston, 1892
Wanderer-Fantasie, Op. 15	„ 1893
Soirée de Vienne	Trieste, 1897
Soirée de Vienne, No. 3	Berlin, 1897
Wanderer-Fantasie (with orchestra)	London, 1898
Der Lindenbaum	Vienna, 1898
Auf dem Wasser zu singen	Manchester, 1899
Die Forelle	Berlin, 1911

SCHUMANN, ROBERT

Armes Waisenkind⎱ (*Album für die Jugend*,	Trieste, 1873
Soldatenmarsch ⎰ Op. 68)	
Knecht Ruprecht „	„ 1874

329

Busoni's Repertory

Aufschwung (*Phantasiestücke*, Op. 12, No. 2)	Vienna, 1878
Grillen (*Phantasiestücke*, Op. 12, No. 4)	Baden, 1878
Fabel (*Phantasiestücke*, Op. 12, No. 6)	Vöslau, 1878
Ende vom Lied (*Phantasiestücke*, Op. 12, No. 8)	Graz, 1879
Phantasiestücke, complete	Milan, 1913
Andante and Variations for 2 pianofortes, Op. 46 (with Anna Busoni)	Graz, 1878
Novellette in D major, from Op. 21	Cilli, 1879
Concerto in A minor, Op. 54	Graz, 1881
Études Symphoniques, Op. 13	Bologna, 1882
5 Posthumous *Études Symphoniques*	„ 1883
Novellette	„ „
Toccata, Op. 7	„ „
Scherzino from *Faschingsschwank*, Op. 26	Graz, 1883
Kreisleriana, Op. 16	Vienna, 1884
Variations on the name 'Abegg', Op. 1	Boston, 1892

SCHUMANN-LISZT
Widmung	? 1879

SILAS, EDOUARD
Bourrée	Milan, 1881

STRAUSS-TAUSIG
Walzer	Hamburg, 1887
Nachtfalter-Walzer	„ „
Man lebt nur einmal (Walzer)	Graz, 1888

THALBERG, SIGISMUND. See LISZT (Hexameron) and PERGOLESI

TCHAIKOVSKY, PETER ILITCH
Concerto in B flat minor	London, 1900

VERDI-LISZT
Fantaisie sur *Rigoletto*	Boston, 1894
Fantaisie sur *Le Troubadour*	Berlin, 1911

WAGNER-BUSONI
Trauermarsch from *Götterdämmerung*	Trieste, 1884

WAGNER-LISZT
March from *Tannhäuser*	Trieste, 1884
Overture to *Tannhäuser*	Berlin, 1895

WAGNER-TAUSIG
Walkürenritt   Vienna, 1884

WEBER, CARL MARIA von
Rondeau brillant, Op. 62   Gmunden, 1877
Sonata in A flat major, Op. 39   Trieste, 1884
Concertstück, Op. 79   Hamburg, 1894
Perpetuum mobile (finale of the Sonata in   1887
    C major, Op. 24)   „
Sonata in C major, complete   Berlin, 1897
Sonata in D minor, Op. 49   Weimar, 1901

APPENDIX III

PROGRAMMES OF FERRUCCIO BUSONI'S TWELVE ORCHESTRAL CONCERTS IN BERLIN, 1902–9

I. BEETHOVEN-SAAL, 8 November 1902.
1. Edward Elgar, Prelude and 'Angel's Farewell' from *The Dream of Gerontius*, Op. 38.
(First performance in Berlin.)
2. J. Guy Ropartz, *Pêcheur d'Islande*, musique pour le drame de MM. Pierre Loti et L. Tiercelin, fragments symphoniques.
(First performance in Germany.)
3. Giuseppe Tartini, Concerto for violin and orchestra. (Solo violin: César Thomson.)
4. Camille Saint-Saëns, Ouverture *Les Barbares*.
(First performance in Germany.)
5. Arcangelo Corelli, Dodicesima Sonata *La follia* per violino e pianoforte (César Thomson).
6. Christian Sinding, Rondo infinito, Op. 42.
(First performance in Germany).

II. BEETHOVEN-SAAL, 15 November 1902.
1. Ed. von Mihalovich, *Pans Tod*, symphonische Dichtung.
(First performance in Germany.)
2. Jean Sibelius, *En saga* (conducted by the composer).
(First performance in Germany.)
3. Théophyle Ysaye, Concerto pour piano et orchestre. (Solo pianoforte: the composer.)
(First performance in Germany.)
4. Frederick Delius, *Paris*, a nocturne.
(First performance.)
5. Franz Liszt, Zweiter Mephisto-Walzer.

III. BEETHOVEN-SAAL, 5 November 1903.
1. Vincent D'Indy, *L'Étranger*, introduction symphonique du 2º acte.
(First performance in Germany.)
2. Claude Debussy, Prélude à *L'Après-midi d'un Faune*.
(First performance in Berlin.)

332

3. Hector Berlioz, *Marche troyenne* ('La Prise de Troie').
   (First performance in Berlin.)
4. César Franck, *Les Djinns*. (Solo pianoforte: José Vianna
   da Motta).
   (First performance in Berlin.)
5. Carl Nielsen, *Die vier Temperamente*, Op. 16.
   (First performance in Germany.)
6. Heinrich Schenker, *Syrische Tänze*, instrumentiert von
   Arnold Schönberg.
   (First performance.)

IV. BEETHOVEN-SAAL, 17 December 1903 (announced but postponed).

   BEETHOVEN-SAAL, 10 November 1904.
1. W. A. Mozart, Overture to *Die Entführung*, with concert-
   ending by Ferruccio Busoni.
   (First performance.)
2. Ottokar Nováček, *Hymnus*, from the posthumous String
   Quartet, Op. 13, played by the stringed orchestra.
   (First performance in Germany.)
3. Ferruccio Busoni, Concerto for pianoforte, orchestra and
   male chorus, Op. xxxix. (Solo pianoforte: the composer.
   Conductor: Dr. Karl Muck.)
   (First performance.)

V. BEETHOVEN-SAAL, 1 December 1904.
1. Rudolf Nováček, Sinfonietta for eight wind instruments.
   (Conducted by the composer.)
   (First performance in Germany.)
2. César Franck, *Le Chasseur maudit*.
3. Claude Debussy, *Nuages* and *Fêtes*, nocturnes.
   (First performance in Germany.)
4. Ferruccio Busoni, *Geharnischte Suite*, Op. 34a.
   (First performance.)

VI. BEETHOVEN-SAAL, 12 January 1905.
1. Alberic Magnard, Troisième Symphonie. (Conducted by
   the composer.)
   (First performance in Germany.)

333

Y

2. Hans Pfitzner, Scherzo. (Conducted by the composer.)
3. Jean Sibelius, Second Symphony. (Conducted by the composer.)
      (First performance in Germany.)

VII. Beethoven-Saal, 21 October 1905.
   1. César Franck, Prélude, Choral et Fugue, orchestré par Gabriel Pierné.
         (First performance in Germany.)
   2. Otto Singer, Concerto in A major for pianoforte and orchestra, Op. 8. (Solo pianoforte: José Vianna da Motta; conducted by the composer.)
         (First performance.)
   3. Hector Berlioz, *Les Nuits d'Été* for voice and small orchestra. (Singer: Ida Ekman.)
         (First performance of the complete work in Germany.)
   4. Ferruccio Busoni, *Turandot Suite*, Op. 41.
         (First performance.)

VIII. Beethoven-Saal, 9 December 1905 (announced but postponed).
      Sing-Akademie, 18 January 1906.
   1. J. S. Bach, Organ Sonata in E flat, No. 1, arranged for orchestra by H. H. Wetzler. (Conducted by Wetzler.)
         (First performance.)
   2. Eduard Behm, *Frühling*, Tonstück für Orchester. (Conducted by the composer.)
         (First performance.)
   3. N. Rimsky-Korsakov, Fantaisie de Concert pour violon et orchestre sur des thèmes russes, Op. 33. (Solo violin: Michael Press.)
   4. Vincent D'Indy, Suite en Ré dans le style ancien, Op. 24.
         (First performance in Germany.)
   5. Eugène Ysaye, *Rêve d'enfant* and *Poëme élégiaque* for violin and orchestra. (Solo violin: Michael Press; conducted by the composer.)
         (First performance in Germany.)
   6. Louis F. Delune, Symphony in C major. (Conducted by the composer.)
         (First performance in Germany.)

IX. BEETHOVEN-SAAL, 8 November 1906.

1. Vincent d'Indy, Symphony in B flat, Op. 57.
2. Vincent d'Indy, Symphonie sur un chant montagnard pour piano et orchestre, Op. 25. (Solo pianoforte: Rudolph Ganz; conducted by the composer.)
3. Beethoven, First movement from the Pianoforte Concerto in C minor, with Cadenza by C. V. Alkan. (Solo pianoforte: Rudolph Ganz.)
4. Gabriel Fauré, Suite for orchestra *Pelléas et Mélisande.*
(Berlioz's Overture *Les Francs-Juges* and Debussy's *Danse sacrée et danse profane* were in the original programme, but they were cut out to make room for Vincent d'Indy's Symphony in B flat.)
(All first performances in Germany.)

X. BEETHOVEN-SAAL, 11 January 1907.

1. Ferruccio Busoni, *Comedy* Overture.
(First performance.)
2. Hermann Behr, Adagio molto and Scherzo from a Symphony in E minor. (Conducted by the composer.)
(First performance.)
3. Johan Wagenaar, *Saul und David,* Tondichtung nach Rembrandts Gemälde. (Conducted by the composer.)
(First performance in Berlin.)
4. Hugo Kaun, *Es war einmal* Phantasiestück für Violine und Orchester. (Solo violin: Michael Press.)
(First performance in Berlin.)
5. F. Liszt, Zwei Episoden aus Lenaus *Faust* (*Nächtlicher Zug* und *Der Tanz in der Dorfschenke*).

XI. BEETHOVEN-SAAL, 3 January 1908.

1. Jean Sibelius, *Pohjolas Tochter,* Sinfonische Fantasie.
(First performance.)
2. Ferruccio Busoni, Concerto for violin, Op. 35a. (Solo violin: Emile Sauret.)
3. F. Liszt, *Tre Sonetti di Petrarca*: (1) *Pace non trovo,* orchestrated by Ferruccio Busoni. (Singer: Felix Senius.)
(First performance.)

335

Orchestral Concerts

4. Paul Ertel, Bacchanal (third movement of the *Harald-Symphonie*, Op. 2).
   (First performance.)
5. F. Liszt, *Tre Sonetti di Petrarca*: (2) and (3) with pianoforte accompaniment (Felix Senius). (Accompanist: Busoni.)
6. F. Liszt, *Mazeppa*.

XII. BEETHOVEN-SAAL, 2 January 1909.

1. César Franck, Symphony in D minor.
2. W. A. Mozart, Overture to *Don Giovanni*, with concert-ending by Ferruccio Busoni.
   (First performance.)
3. F. Schubert, Introduction and Rondo for violin and pianoforte, arranged for violin and orchestra by Alexander Z. Birnbaum. (Solo violin: Birnbaum.)
4. Béla Bartók, Scherzo for orchestra from a Suite. (Conducted by the composer.)
   (First performance in Germany.)
5. F. Liszt, *Salve Polonia*, interlude from the oratorio *Stanislaus*.

CATALOGUE OF THE WORKS OF FERRUCCIO BUSONI

SHORTLY before his death Busoni prepared a catalogue of all his works that he considered worthy of record. This catalogue was printed by Breitkopf & Härtel soon after his death, together with another catalogue drawn up by themselves on a different system of classification. Neither catalogue is strictly complete and free from errors. Busoni's is interesting as the expression of his own criticism of his works, but it is evident that in drawing it up his memory was often at fault. The catalogue here printed is based on a careful collation of both the above lists with the title-pages of the original editions made by Dr. Friedrich Schnapp. In the grouping it follows Busoni's catalogue, but it includes all those works of his which were printed, with the names of the original publishers. Some works were transferred later to other publishers; the publications of Lucca (Milan) were taken over in 1888 by Ricordi. All titles are given here in their original languages; dedications have been reduced to the names alone.

Busoni's opus numbers are very confusing. As a boy he numbered each work as he wrote it, whether it was published or not. After reaching Op. 40 at the age of 17 he gave the numbers of unpublished *juvenilia* to new works; later he started again at Op. 30, adding an *a* to Op. 30–6. The Pianoforte Concerto he numbered in roman figures as Op. xxxix. From Op. 41 onwards the numbering proceeds regularly, though some works appeared without opus number.

OPERAS

Die Brautwahl, musikalisch-fantastische Komödie nach E. T. A. Hoffmanns Erzählung (The Bridal Choice), Opera in 3 acts. Libretto by F.B. after E. T. A. Hoffmann. DED. Gustav Brecher. COMP. 1908–11. First performed at Hamburg, 12 April 1912. FULL SCORE, Harmonie-Verlag, Berlin, 1914; VOCAL SCORE (Pf. arr. by Egon Petri), B. & H., 1914.

Turandot, eine chinesische Fabel (a Chinese tale), Opera in 2 acts. Libretto by F.B. after Carlo Gozzi. DED. Arturo Toscanini. COMP. 1917. First performed at Zürich, 11 May 1917. VOCAL SCORE (Pf. arr. by Philipp Jarnach), B. & H., 1918; FULL SCORE, B. & H., 1919.

337

Busoni's Works

Arlecchino, oder Die Fenster, ein theatralisches Capriccio (Harlequin, or The Windows, a theatrical capriccio) in 1 act. Libretto by F.B. DED. Arthur Bodanzky. COMP. 1914–16. First performed at Zürich, 11 May 1917. VOCAL SCORE (Pf. arr. by Philipp Jarnach), B. & H., 1917; FULL SCORE, B. & H., 1918.

Doktor Faust (Doctor Faust). Libretto by F.B. COMP. 1916–24. Left unfinished at Busoni's death and completed by Philipp Jarnach. First performed at Dresden, 21 May 1925. VOCAL SCORE (Pf. arr. by Egon Petri and Michael von Zadora), B. & H., 1926; FULL SCORE, MS.

WORKS FOR ORCHESTRA

FOUR SUITES

OP. 25. Symphonische Suite for orchestra: (1) Präludium, (2) Gavotte, (3) Gigue, (4) Langsames Intermezzo, (5) Alla breve (Allegro fugato). DED. Hans Richter. FULL SCORE, C. F. Kahnt, Leipzig, 1888. Gavotte arr. for Pf., B. & H., 1888.

OP. 34 *a*. Zweite Orchester-Suite (Geharnischte Suite) (Suite in Armour): (1) Vorspiel (to Jean Sibelius), (2) Kriegstanz (to Adolf Paul), (3) Grabdenkmal (to Armas Järnefelt), (4) Ansturm (to Eero Järnefelt). COMP. 1895, REVISED 1903. DED. to the 'four friends of Lesko at Helsingfors (1889)'. FULL SCORE, B. & H., 1905.

OP. 41. Orchester-Suite aus der Musik zu Gozzis *Turandot* (*Turandot* Suite): (1) Die Hinrichtung, das Stadttor, der Abschied (aus der Musik zum I. Akt), (2) Truffaldino (Introduzione e marcia grottesca), (3) Altoum (Marsch), (4) Turandot (Marsch), (5) Das Frauengemach, Einleitung zum III. Akt, (6) Tanz und Gesang, (7) Nächtlicher Walzer (aus der Musik zum IV. Akt), (8) In modo di marcia funebre e finale alla turca (aus dem V. Akt). DED. Dr. Karl Muck. COMP. 1904. FULL SCORE, B. & H., 1906. Appendix I: Verzweiflung und Ergebung. Appendix 2: Altoums Warnung. COMP. 1911. FULL SCORE, B. & H. 1911.

OP. 45. Orchester-Suite *Die Brautwahl*: (1) Spukhaftes, (2) Lyrisches, (3) Mystisches, (4) Hebräisches, (5) Heiteres. DED. Curt Sobernheim. FULL SCORE, B. & H., 1917.

SIX ELEGIES

OP. 42. Berceuse élégiaque—*Des Mannes Wiegenlied am Sarge seiner Mutter* (The man's lullaby at his mother's coffin), poem for orchestra. In memoriam Anna Busoni *née* Weiss, ob. 3 October 1909. FULL SCORE, B. & H., 1910. Arr. for Pf. solo.

OP. 43. Nocturne Symphonique for orchestra. DED. Oskar Fried. COMP. 1912. FULL SCORE, B. & H., 1914.

338

Op. 46. Rondo Arlecchinesco for orchestra. DED. F. A. Stock, Chicago. COMP. 1915. FULL SCORE, B. & H., 1916.

Op. 47. Indianisches Tagebuch. Zweites Buch. *Gesang vom Reigen der Geister* (Song of the Spirits' Dance), second book of the Indian Diary: study for small orchestra. DED. Charles Martin Loeffler. COMP. 1915. FULL SCORE, B. & H., 1916.

Op. 51. *Sarabande* and *Cortège*, two studies for *Doktor Faust* for orchestra. DED. Volkmar Andreae. COMP. 1918–19. FULL SCORE, B. & H., 1922.

MISCELLANEOUS ORCHESTRAL WORKS

Op. 32 *a*. Symphonisches Tongedicht (Symphonic Poem) for orchestra. DED. Arthur Nikisch. COMP. as Konzert-Fantasie for Pf. and orch. 1888–9 (unpublished); REVISED as orchestral work, 1893. FULL SCORE, B. & H., 1894.

Op. 38. Lustspielouvertüre (Comedy Overture) for orchestra. DED. Wilhelm Gericke. COMP. 1897, REVISED 1904. FULL SCORE, B. & H., 1904.

Op. 53. Tanzwalzer (Waltzes) for orchestra.. To the memory of Johann Strauss. COMP. 1920. FULL SCORE, B. & H., 1922. Pf. arr. by M. von Zadora (revised by F.B.), 1922.

FOR PIANOFORTE AND ORCHESTRA

Op. 31 *a*. Konzertstück (Introduction and Allegro) for Pf. and orchestra. DED. Anton Rubinstein. COMP. 1890. Awarded the Rubinstein Prize for composition, 1890. FULL SCORE, B. & H., 1892.

Op. 39. Concerto per un Pianoforte principale e diversi strumenti ad arco fiato ed a percussione. Aggiuntovi un coro finale per voci d'uomini a sei parti. Le parole alemanne del poeta Oehlenschlaeger, danese. (Concerto for Pf. and orchestra with chorus of male voices, words by Oehlenschlaeger.) (1) Prologo ed Introito, (2) Pezzo giocoso, (3) Pezzo serioso, (4) All'Italiana, (5) Cantico. COMP. 1903–4. FULL SCORE, B. & H., 1906. Arr. for 2 Pfs. (Egon Petri), 1909. Extended Cadenza to the fourth movement, 1909. Version without final chorus (MS.).

Op. 44. *Indianische Fantasie* (Indian Fantasy), on themes from the music of the North American Indians: Fantasia—Canzone—Finale. DED. Natalie Curtis. COMP. 1913. FULL SCORE, B. & H., 1915.

Op. 54. Romanza e Scherzoso for Pf. and orchestra. DED. Alfredo Casella. COMP. 1921. FULL SCORE, B. & H., 1922. Performed along with the Konzertstück, Op. 31 *a*, under the title of Concertino.

TRANSCRIPTIONS AND ARRANGEMENTS FOR PIANO-FORTE AND ORCHESTRA

J. S. BACH, Concerto in D minor. Konzert D Moll für Klavier und Streichorchester, freie Bearbeitung von F.B. DED. Victor Bendix, 1899.

Busoni's Works

F. LISZT, *Spanish Rhapsody*, arranged as a concert piece for Pf. and orchestra by F.B. DED. Arthur Friedheim. PUB. C. F. W. Siegel, 1894.

W. A. MOZART, Rondo concertante after the Finale of the Concerto for Pf. in E flat major (K. 482) for Pf. and orchestra. COMP. 1919. PUB. B. & H., 1922.

SOLO INSTRUMENTS AND ORCHESTRA

OP. 35 *a*. Konzert D-dur für die Violine. DED. Henri Petri. COMP. 1896–7. FULL SCORE, B. & H., 1899.

OP. 48. Concertino for clarinet and small orchestra. DED. Edmondo Allegra. FULL SCORE, B. & H., 1919.

OP. 52. Divertimento for flute and orchestra. DED. Philippe Gaubert. COMP. 1920. FULL SCORE, B. & H., 1922.

VOCAL WORKS WITH ORCHESTRA

OP. 35. *Ave Maria* for Baritone and orchestra. DED. Niccola Bezzi. FULL SCORE and Pf. arr., Lucca, 1882.

OP. 40. *Primavera, Estate, Autunno, Inverno* (The Four Seasons), 4 poems by Dall'Ongaro for male voices (soli and chorus) with orchestra or Pf. DED. Pietro Bini. FULL SCORE, Lucca, 1882.

OP. 49. Zwei Gesänge (Two Songs) for baritone with small orchestra: (1) Altoum's Prayer (*Turandot*), *Konfutse, dir hab' ich geschworen.* (2) Mephistopheles' Song (Goethe's *Faust*), *Es war einmal ein König.* No. 2, COMP. 1918. FULL SCORE, B. & H., 1919.

Unter der Linden (Under the lime-tree), Song for soprano and orchestra: words by Walther von der Vogelweide. DED. Amélie Nikisch. FULL SCORE, MS. with Pf. acc., Kistner & Siegel, 1885. Arranged for orch. 1893.

Il Sabato del Villaggio (The Village Saturday), Cantata for Soli, Chorus and orchestra: poem by Leopardi. DED. Luigi Mancinelli. COMP. 1882. FULL SCORE and vocal score, MS. (unpublished).

OP. 55, II. Zigeunerlied (Gipsy Song): *Im Nebelgeriesel, im tiefen Schnee* (Goethe), for baritone and orchestra. COMP. 1923. FULL SCORE and Pf. arr., B. & H., 1924. (There is no Op. 55, I.) First pub. as suppl. to *Die Musik*, Jahrg. xv. Heft 8, with Pf. acc., May 1923.

Grausige Geschichte vom Münzjuden Lippold (The horrible history of the Jew coiner Lippold) from *Die Brautwahl*, arranged for concert performance by F.B. 16 Feb. 1923. FULL SCORE, MS. unpublished.

FOR PIANOFORTE

OP. 3. Cinq Pièces pour Piano: Preludio, Menuetto, Gavotta, Étude, and Gigue. COMP. 1877. PUB. Spina, Vienna, 1877 (out of print).

340

Op. 4, 5, 6. Trois morceaux: Scherzo, Prelude and Fugue, Scène de Ballet (out of print). DED. Mme Betty de Preleuthner. PUB. Emil Wetzler, Vienna, 1884.

Op. 8. Scherzo (tratto dalla sonata Op. 8 in mi maggiore). DED. Filippo Filippi. COMP. 1877. PUB. Lucca, 1880 (at latest).

Op. 9. *Una Festa di Villaggio, sei pezzi caratteristici* (Village Festival): (1) Preparazione alla Festa, (2) Marcia trionfale, (3) In Chiesa, (4) La Fiera, (5) Danza, (6) Notte. DED. Angelo e Fanny Speckel. PUB. Lucca, 1882.

Op. 10. Tre pezzi nello stile antico: Minuetto, Sonatina e Gigue. DED. (1) Ernesto Colombani, (2) G. Gaiani, (3) Alessandro Busi. PUB. Lucca, 1882.

Op. 11. *Danze Antiche* (Old Dances): Minuetto, Gavotta, Gigue, Bourrée (wrongly numbered Op. 10 on title: Op. 11 on first page of music). DED. (1) Riccardo Eckhel, (2) Giulio Fumagalli, (3) Giuseppe Sinico, (4) Antonio Zampieri. PUB. Lucca, 1882.

Op. 12. *Racconti fantastici* (Fantastic tales). 3 Pezzi caratteristici. DED. Stefano Golinelli. No. 1. Duello. No. 2. Klein Zaches (vedi la novella fantastica di E. T. A. Hoffmann). No. 3. La Caverna di Steenfoll (vedi il racconto fantastico di G. Hauff). COMP. 1878. PUB. Trebbi, Bologna, 1882.

Op. 13. *Danza Notturna* (Nocturnal dance) per Pianoforte. PUB. Trebbi, Bologna, 1882.
Macchiette medioevali (Medieval figures): (1) Dama, (2) Cavaliere, (3) Paggio, (4) Guerriero, (5) Astrologo, (6) Trovatore. PUB. Trebbi, Bologna, 1883.

Op. 14. Minuetto. DED. Paula Flamm. COMP. 1878. PUB. Lucca, at latest 1880.

Op. 16. Six Études for Pf. DED. Johannes Brahms. COMP. 1883. PUB. Albert J. Gutmann, Vienna, 1883.
Étude 15. En forme d'Adagio d'une Sonate (in D flat). COMP. probably 1883. Evidently intended for Op. 16. It contains the theme of the slow movement of the Concerto, Op. 39. Unpublished. The MS. bears the note in pencil 'An Gussy Cottlow 1892', which suggests that Busoni had some intention of publishing it.
Two more Études intended for Op. 16 exist in MS.: Étude 16. Nocturne in B flat minor; Studio 18 in F minor. COMP. 1883.

Sonata in F minor. DED. Anton Rubinstein. COMP. 1883. MS. unpublished.

Op. 17. Étude en forme de Variations. DED. Johannes Brahms. COMP.? PUB. Albert J. Gutmann, 1884.

Op. 20. Zweite Ballettszene (in F major). DED. Anna Weiss-Busoni. PUB. B. & H., 1885.

Busoni's Works

Op. 21. Preludio e Fuga in stile libero in Do minore. DED. L. F. Casa-morata. COMP. 1878. PUB. Lucca, 1880.

Op. 22. Variationen und Fuge in freier Form über Fr. Chopins c-moll Präludium (Op. 28, No. 20). DED. Carl Reinecke. COMP. 1884. PUB. 1885. See Klavierübung.

Op. 25. Gavotta for Pf. DED. Paula Flamm. COMP. 1878. This is not from the Symph. Suite Op. 25. PUB. Lucca, 1880 at latest.

Op. 30. (1) Kontrapunktisches Tanzstück. (2) Kleine Ballettszene III. (Third Scène de Ballet). Awarded the Rubinstein Prize for composition in 1890. PUB. B. & H., 1891 (out of print).
Revised in 1914 as Op. 30 a. Zwei Tanzstücke for Pf.: (1) *Waffentanz* (War Dance), (2) *Friedenstanz* (Peace Dance). PUB. D. Rahter, Hamburg, 1914.

Op. 32. *Marcia di paesani e contadine* (Peasants' March—composed as addition to *Una Festa di Villaggio*). PUB. Lucca, 1883.

Op. 33. Vierte Ballett-Scene in Form eines Concert-Walzers. DED. Carl Stasny. PUB. 1894 (out of print). Revised in 1913 as Op. 33 a. Vierte Ballett-Szene, Walzer und Galopp (1892–1913). PUB. B. & H., 1913.

Op. 33 b. Stücke für Pianoforte: Series I: (1) Schwermuth, (2) Frohsinn, (3) Scherzino. DED. Max Reger. Series II: (4) Fantasia in modo antico, (5) Finnische Ballade, (6) *Exeunt Omnes*. DED. Mrs. Isabella S. Gardner, Boston. PUB. Peters, 1896.

Op. 36. Preludio e Fuga. DED. Alfredo Catalani. PUB. Lucca, 1882.

Op. 37. 24 Préludes. DED. Louis Cimoso. COMP. 1879–80. PUB. Lucca, 1882.

Op. 61. Menuetto capriccioso, pub. together with Op. 70 in one book. DED. Frau Josefine von Wertheimstein. COMP. 1879. PUB. Spina, Vienna, 1880.

Op. 70. Gavotte. DED. Frau Baronin Sophie von Todesco. COMP. 1880. PUB. Cranz, 1880. See Op. 61.

Elegien. 6 neue Klavierstücke (Elegies: (seven) new pieces for Pf.): (1) *Nach der Wendung* (Recueillement). DED. Gottfried Galston. (2) *All'Italia* (in modo napoletano). DED. Egon Petri. (3) *Meine Seele bangt und hofft zu dir* (Chorale-Prelude). DED. Gregor Beklemischeff. (4) *Turandots Frauengemach* (Intermezzo). DED. Michael von Zadora. (5) *Die Nächtlichen* (Waltzer). DED. O'Neil Phillips. (6) *Erscheinung* (*Notturno*). DED. Leo Kestenberg. (7) *Berceuse* (arrangement of Berceuse Élégiaque). DED. Johan Wysman. COMP. 1907. No. 7 was published separately and then added to the Elegies. PUB. B. & H., 1908–9.

An die Jugend, a series of pieces for Pf.: (1) Preludio, Fughetta ed Esercizio. DED. Josef Turczyński. (2) Preludio, Fuga e Fuga figurata (study

342

after Bach's *W. K.*). DED. Louis Theodor Gruenberg. (3) Giga, Bolero e Variazione (study after Mozart). DED. Leo Sirota. (4) Introduzione e Capriccio (Paganinesco) (DED. Louis Closson). Epilogo. DED. Émile R. Blanchet. Two pieces under one number. No. 1 is a first version of the First Sonatina. PUB. Zimmermann, 1909, afterwards transferred to B. & H.

Nuit de Noël, Esquisse. DED. Frida Kindler. PUB. Durand, Paris, 1909.

Indianisches Tagebuch (Indian Diary), Book I: Four studies for Pf. on motives of the Redskins of North America. DED. Helen Luise Birch. COMP. 1915. PUB. B. & H., 1916.

Drei Albumblätter for Pf.: (1) (Zürich.) DED. Albert Biolley. (2) (Roma.) DED. Francesco Ticciati. (3) (Berlin.) In the style of a Chorale-Prelude. DED. Felice Boghen. No. 1. Also arranged by F.B. for flute and Pf. COMP. (1) B. & H., 1917, (2 & 3) 1921. PUB. 1921.

Toccata: Preludio, Fantasia, Ciaccona. DED. I. Philipp. First pub., as *Notenbeilage zu Musikblätter des Anbruchs, Sonderheft Ferruccio Busoni*, Jänner, 1921 Universal-Edition. 'Zweite Ausgabe'. PUB. B. & H., 1922.

Ten Variations on a Prelude of Chopin in C minor for Pf. DED. Gino Tagliapietra. Revised version of Op. 22 (1922). PUB. B. & H., 1922.

Fünf kurze Stücke zur Pflege des polyphonen Spiels (Five short pieces for the study of part-playing). DED. Edwin Fischer. PUB. B. & H.,1923.

WORKS BASED ON J. S. BACH

Fantasia after J. S. Bach. 'Alla memoria di mio padre Ferdinando Busoni, morto il 12 maggio 1909.' PUB. B. & H., 1909.

Fantasia Contrappuntistica. Four versions: (1) Grosse Fuge—Kontrapunktische Fantasie über Joh. Seb. Bachs letztes unvollendetes Werk für Klavier ausgeführt von F.B. DED. Wilhelm Middelschulte. COMP. 1910. PUB. Schirmer, New York (numbered edition), 1910. This version does not include the Chorale Prelude. (2) Fantasia Contrappuntistica. Preludio al Corale 'Gloria al Signore nei Cieli' e fuga a quattro soggetti obbligati sopra un frammento di Bach. Edizione definitiva, Giugno, 1910. PUB. B. & H., 1910. (3) Preludio al Corale e fuga sopra un frammento di Bach (edizione minore della 'Fantasia Contrappuntistica'). DED. Richard Buhlig. COMP. 1912. PUB. B. & H. 1912. (4) Arrangement for 2 Pfs.

Zwei Kontrapunkt-Studien für Klavier nach Joh. Seb. Bach. (Two contrapuntal studies after J. S. Bach.) (1) Fantasia and Fugue in A minor, (2) Canonic Variations and Fugue on the theme of Frederick the Great (from the *Musikalisches Opfer*). PUB. B. & H., 1917.

343

SIX SONATINAS

(First) Sonatina. DED. Rudolph Ganz. COMP. 1910. PUB. Julius Heinrich Zimmermann, Leipzig, 1910.

Sonatina Seconda. DED. Mark Hambourg. COMP. 1912. PUB. B. & H., 1912.

Sonatina (third) ad usum infantis pro clavicembalo composita. DED. Madeline M.* Americanae. PUB. B. & H., 1916.

Sonatina (Fourth) in diem Nativitatis Christi MCMXVII. DED. Benvenuto [Busoni]. COMP. 1917. PUB. B. & H., 1918.

Sonatina (Fifth) brevis. In Signo Joannis Sebastiani Magni. Free transcription of Bach's small Fantasia and Fugue in D minor. DED. Philipp Jarnach. PUB. B. & H., 1919.

Sonatina (Sixth) super *Carmen* (Kammerfantasie über Bizet's *Carmen*) for Pf. DED. Leonhard Tauber (Paris). COMP. 1920. PUB. B. & H., 1921.

Klavierübung.

First edition in 5 parts: (1) Sechs Klavierübungen und Präludien. DED. An die Musikschule und das Konservatorium in Basel. COMP. 1917. PUB. 1918. (2) Drei Klavierübungen und Präludien. Same ded. COMP. 1917–18. PUB. 1919. (3) Lo Staccato, with preface dated Zürich, Juli 1920. PUB. 1921. Same ded. (4) Acht Etüden von Cramer (see Cramer). (5) Zehn Variationen über ein Präludium von Chopin. DED. Gino Tagliapietra. Perpetuum mobile. DED. Cella Delavrancea. Tonleitern. COMP. 1922 and PUB. 1922.

Second edition: Klavierübung in zehn Büchern von F.B., zweite umgearbeitete und bereicherte Ausgabe: (1) Tonleitern, (2) Von Tonleitern abgeleitete Formen, (3) Akkordisches, (4) *A trois mains*, (5) Triller, (6) Lo Staccato, (7) Acht Étuden nach Cramer, (8) Variationen und Varienten zu Chopin, (9) Sieben kurze Stücke zur Pflege des Polyphonen Spiels, (10) Étuden nach Paganini-Liszt.[1] PUB. 1925.

FOR PIANOFORTE (FOUR HANDS)

OP. 27. *Finnländische Volksweisen* (Finnish Folk-Tunes). DED. Fräulein Anna Lindelöf. PUB. Peters, 1889.

FOR TWO PIANOFORTES (FOUR HANDS)

Improvisation on Bach's Chorale *Wie wohl ist mir, O Freund der Seele*. DED. Marchese Silvio della Valle di Casanova. COMP. San Remigio im Juni 1916; Zürich im August 1916. PUB. B. & H., 1917.

[1] Anhang zu 10. Introduzione e Capriccio (Paganinesco) (from *An die Jugend*). Paganini-Busoni.

W. A. Mozart; Duettino Concertante after the Finale of the Pf. Concerto in F major (K. 459). COMP. 1919. PUB. B. & H., 1921.

Fantasia Contrappuntistica, Choral-Variation über *Allein Gott in der Höh' sei Ehr'*, gefolgt von einer Quadrupel-Fuge über ein Bach'sches Fragment. DED. James Kwast and Frieda Kwast-Hodapp. Preface and drawing of the architectural plan by F.B. PUB. B. & H., 1922.

FOR ORGAN

OP. 7. Prelude (on a ground bass) and Fugue (double fugue on a chorale). DED. Dr. Wilhelm Mayer. PUB. Cranz, 1881. Appeared originally as Op. 76. Printed at B.'s own expense—'Eigenthum des Componisten'.

CHAMBER MUSIC

OP. 19. String Quartet in C major. DED. Julius Heller (Trieste). COMP. 1880–1. PUB. Score and parts, Kistner & Siegel, 1886.

OP. 23. Kleine Suite for Violoncello and Pf. DED. Alwin Schröder. PUB. B. & H., 1886.

OP. 26. Second String Quartet in D minor. DED. Henri Petri. PUB. Score and Parts, B. & H., 1889.

OP. 28. Bagatelles for Violin and Pf. (Easy violin pieces for Egon Petri at the age of seven). PUB. Peters, 1888.

OP. 29. (First) Sonata for violin and Pf. Awarded the Rubinstein Prize for composition in 1890. DED. Adolf Brodsky. PUB. D. Rahter, Hamburg, 1891.

OP. 34. Serenata for violoncello and Pf. DED. Francesco Serato. PUB. Lucca, 1882 at earliest.

OP. 36 *a*. Second Sonata for violin and Pf. in E minor. DED. Ottokar Nováček. COMP. 1898. PUB. B. & H., 1901.

Kultaselle: ten variations on a Finnish folk-song for Violoncello and Pf. DED. Alfred von Glehn (Moscow). PUB. Rudolf Dietrich, Leipzig, 1891? The same theme is treated in Op. 33 *b*.

Albumblatt for flute (or muted violin) and Pf. DED. Albert Biolley. PUB. B. & H., 1917. The original version of the first Albumblatt for Pf.

Elegy for clarinet and Pf. DED. Edmondo Allegra. PUB. B. & H., 1921.

SONGS WITH PIANOFORTE

OP. 1. Song, *Ave Maria*. DED. Angelo Masini. COMP. 1877. PUB. Cranz, 1878.

OP. 2. Song, *Ave Maria,* for contralto. DED. Princesse Marie Stcherbatoff. COMP. 1878. PUB. Cranz, 1879.

OP. 15. Two songs (Byron): (1) *Ich sah die Träne* (I saw thee weep),

(2) *An Babylons Wassern* (By the waters of Babel). DED. Frau Caroline Gomperz-Bettelheim. PUB. Albert J. Gutmann, 1884.

By the waters of Babel for a man's voice and piano. Words by Lord Byron. DED. Oliver Clark. Revised version of Op. 15, No. 2, made in London, February 1901. Completed from the original MS. by Egon Petri, 1930. Unpublished.

OP. 18. Zwei altdeutsche Lieder ('Two old German songs): (1) *Wohlauf! Der kühle Winter ist vergangen* (Neidhard von Reuenthal), (2) *Unter der Linden* (Walther von der Vogelweide). DED. Pia von Sicherer. PUB. Kistner & Siegel, 1885.

OP. 24. Two songs for a low voice: (1) Lied des Monmouth *Es zieht sich eine blut'ge Spur* (Th. Fontane), (2) *Es ist bestimmt in Gottes Rath* (E. von Feuchtersleben). DED. Melanie Mayer ((2) only). COMP. 1879. PUB. Kahnt, 1886.

OP. Two Songs: (1) *Wer hat das erste Lied erdacht?* (V. Blüthgen). CCMP. 1880. (2) *Bin ein fahrender Gesell* (R. Baumbach). PUB. 1884, in commissione presso M. V. Vicentini, Trieste.

OP. 30. Album Vocale: (1) *Il fiore del pensiero* (Ferd. Busoni). (2) *L'ultimo sonno* (Michele Busoni). COMP. 1879. (3) *Un organetto suona per la via* (L. Stecchetti). (4) Ballatella, *Luna fedel ti chiamo* (Arrigo Boito). PUB. (Schmidl) 1884, in commissione M. V. Vicentini, Trieste, 1884.

OP. 38. *Lied der Klage* (Song of Mourning) (O. von Kapff) for contralto. DED. Elise Polko. COMP. 1878. PUB. Spina (Cranz), ? 1879.

OP. 39. *Des Sängers Fluch* (Uhland), ballad for contralto voice and Pf. DED. Albin von Vogel. COMP. 1879. Eigenthum des Componisten, 1879.

Two poems by Goethe for baritone and Pf.: (1) Lied des Unmuts *Keinen Reimer wird man finden,* (2) Lied des Mephistopheles *Es war einmal ein König.* DED. Dr. Augustus Milner. PUB. B. & H., 1919.

Song, *Die Bekehrte* (Goethe) for mezzo-soprano. DED. Frl. Artôt de Padilla. COMP. 1921. MS.

Song, *Schlechter Trost* (Goethe) with orchestra or pianoforte. COMP. 1924. PUB. 1924 (with pf.) in *Navigare necesse est,* Festschrift for Anton Kippenberg, Insel-Verlag, Leipzig, 1924.

ARRANGEMENTS AND TRANSCRIPTIONS FOR PIANO-FORTE SOLO

J. S. BACH:

There are two separate collections of J. S. Bach's works edited by Busoni: the *Busoni-Ausgabe* (Busoni Edition) of the Pianoforte works in 25 books, edited by Busoni in collaboration with Egon Petri and Bruno Mugellini, and the *Bach-Busoni gesammelte Ausgabe* (Collected Edition of Bach-Busoni) which includes the two annotated volumes of the *Wohl-temperiertes Klavier* and five more volumes of collected transcriptions, arrangements, and free compositions after Bach.

Bach-Busoni, complete Edition

This edition assembles in 7 volumes the works named below with the dates of their first publication.

BAND I. *Bearbeitungen* (Arrangements) I. Lehrstücke (Teaching pieces).
Widmung (Dedication) on the theme BACH with that of the *W.K.* Book I. Fugue 1. COMP. 27 July 1914.
18 short preludes and Fughetta. Bologna, May 1914. Copyright 1916.
Inventions in two parts (DED. Musik-Institut in Helsingfors). PUB. B. & H., 1892. 2nd ed. 1914. Inventions in three parts (DED. Musik-Institut in Helsingfors). PUB. B. & H., 1892. 2nd ed. 1914.
Four Duets. PUB. B. & H., 1915.
Prelude, Fugue, and Allegro in E flat major. PUB. B. & H., 1915.

BAND II. *Bearbeitungen* (Arrangements) II. Meisterstücke (Master Works).
Chromatic Fantasia, transcription for Pf. PUB. B. & H., 1911; orig. Simrock, date ?
Clavier Concerto in D minor.
Aria and 30 Variations (Goldberg-Variations). DED. I. Philipp. ARR. 1914. PUB. B. & H., 1915.

BAND III. *Uebertragungen* (Transcriptions).
Prelude and Fugue for organ in D major. DED. Kathi Petri. COMP. 1888. First published about 1890, B. & H., 2nd ed. 1902.
Prelude and Fugue for organ in E flat major. DED. William H. Dayas. PUB. D. Rahter, Hamburg, 1890; 2nd ed. B. & H.
Toccata for organ in D minor. DED. Robert Freund. PUB. B. & H., 1900.
Toccata for organ in C major. DED. Robert Freund. PUB. B. & H., 1900, together with Toccata in D minor.
Ten Chorale Preludes for organ. Two books. DED. José Vianna da Motta. PUB. B. & H., 1st ed. 1898; 2nd ed. Book I, 1907, Book II, 1909.
Chaconne for violin solo. DED. Eugen D'Albert. PUB. B. & H., 1897?

BAND IV. *Compositionen und Nachdichtungen* (Compositions and Free Transcriptions).
Fantasia alla memoria di mio padre (Fantasia in memory of my father). See *ante* (Works for Pianoforte solo).
Preludio, Fuga e fuga figurata, see *An die Jugend*, No. 2.
Capriccio sopra la lontananza del fratello dilettissimo. DED. Arthur Schnabel. Preface dated July 1914. PUB. B. & H., 1915.

347

Busoni's Works

Fantasia, Adagio e Fuga, completed and transcribed. DED. Moritz Moszkowski. PUB. B. & H., 1915.

Fantasia Contrappuntistica (edizione minore), third version. See *ante*.

Fantasia Contrappuntistica, second version.

BAND V. *Das Wohltemperierte Klavier* (Book I). Arranged and explained with examples and directions for the study of modern pianoforte technique in connexion with it, together with an Appendix on the transcription of Bach's Organ works for the Pianoforte. Dated New York, January 1894.

Prelude and Fugue for organ in E minor, transcription for Pf. (Appendix to the *W.K.*, Book I.)

BAND VI. *Das Wohltemperierte Klavier* (Book II) with notes and studies. Dated New York, March 1915. PUB. 1916.

BAND VII. *Nachträge zu* (Supplement to) *Band I–IV*.

(a) *Bearbeitungen* (Arrangements): Toccatas in E minor, G minor, G major. Dated Zürich. Copyright 1920.

Fantasia and Fugue in A minor. DED. Dr. Hugo Leichtentritt.

Fantasia, Fugue, Andante and Scherzo. Copyright 1920.

Transcriptions: Chromatic Fantasia and Fugue, transcribed for violoncello and Pf. DED. Hans Kindler. PUB. B. & H., 1917.

Improvisation on the Chorale *Wie wohl ist mir* for 2 Pfs. See *ante*.

Canonic Variations and Fugue on the theme of Frederick the Great from the *Musikalisches Opfer*. DED. Dr. H. Huber. PUB. Zürich, Sept. 1916.

Sonatina Brevis in Signo Joannis Sebastiani Magni. See *ante* (Sonatina).

Versuch einer organischen Klavier-Notenschrift (Attempt at an organic notation for the Pianoforte). PUB. 1910. The complete edition was published Christmas 1920.

The Busoni-Ausgabe (Busoni Edition) of J. S. Bach's Clavier Works in 25 volumes, edited by Busoni, Egon Petri, and Bruno Mugellini, includes the following works edited by Busoni, in addition to those included in the 'Bach-Busoni' Editions:

VOL. XVI. *Sarabande con Partite* in C major; *Aria variata alla maniera italiana* in A minor.

Revised editions in one volume, 1907. Sechs Tonstücke. Klavier-Übertragung. Neue durchgesehene Ausgabe. (1) Prelude and Fugue for organ in D major, (2) Four Chorale Preludes for organ, (3) Chaconne for violin solo.

BEETHOVEN:

Benedictus from the Mass in D major, transcribed for violin and orchestra. PUB. B. & H., 1916.

Écossaises, arranged for concert performance. DED. Gerda Sjöstrand. PUB. B. & H., 1889.

Three Cadenzas by F.B. for the Violin Concerto, Op. 61, for solo violin, strings and drums. COMP. 1914. DED. Arrigo Serato.

(Beethoven's) Cadenzas to the Pianoforte Concertos in C major, C minor, and G major, arranged by F.B. DATED Weimar, 1900. PUB. Heinrichshofen, Magdeburg, 1901.

Two Cadenzas by F.B. for the Pianoforte Concerto in G major, awarded Rubinstein Prize for comp. 1890. PUB. Rahter, 1891.

Analysis of the Fugue from the Sonata, Op. 106. (Appendix to the *W.K.*, Book I.)

BIZET:

Sonatina super *Carmen*. See above.

BRAHMS:

Six Chorale Preludes for the organ, Op. 122, transcribed for Pf.:
(1) *Herzlich thut mich erfreuen*, (2) *Schmücke dich, o liebe Seele*, (3) *Es ist ein' Ros' entsprungen*, (4) *Herzlich thut mich verlangen*, (5) *Herzlich thut mich verlangen*, (6) *O Welt, ich muss dich lassen*. PUB. B. & H., 1902.

Cadenza by F.B. for the Violin Concerto, Op. 77, for violin solo and drums. DED. Arrigo Serato. PUB. Simrock, 1914.

CHOPIN:

Polonaise in A flat major, Op. 53, edited by F.B. PUB. Schmidl, Trieste, 1909.

Variationen und Varianten über Chopin. See *ante* (Klavierübung).

CORNELIUS:

Fantasia for Pf. on themes from *The Barber of Bagdad*. PUB. Kahnt, 1886.

J. B. CRAMER:

Eight Études, edited by F.B. DED. Carl Lütschg (St. Petersburg). PUB. Schlesinger, Berlin, 1897. See *ante* (Klavierübung).

N. W. GADE:

Novelletten (Pf. Trio), Op. 29, arranged for 2 Pfs. by F.B. PUB. 1889.

GOLDMARK:

Merlin, vocal score with Pf. accompaniment by F.B. PUB. 1889.

Trascrizione di Concerto sopra motivi dell'Opera *Merlino* del Maestro C. Goldmark. Lucca, 1888, transferred to Ricordi.

LISZT:

For Pianoforte Solo:

Complete Études, edited by F.B. for the Franz Liszt-Stiftung, three volumes. PUB. B. & H., 1910–11.

Select Pf. works edited by F.B. for the Franz Liszt-Stiftung. *Harmonies du Soir, La Campanella, Ronde des lutins*, Étude de Concert in D flat major, *Murmures du bois*. PUB. B. & H., 1917.

Six Paganini Études, edited by F.B. PUB. B. & H., 1912.

349

Busoni's Works

Six Paganini Études, transcribed by F.B. for study and for concert. Étude 6. Theme with Variations. DED. Ignaz Friedmann. COMP. 1913. PUB. 1914. Étude 3. *La Campanella.* DED. Leopold Godowsky. PUB. 1916. Étude 2. Andantino Capriccioso. PUB. 1917, with 3 and 6. Étude 4. Arpeggio. PUB. 1923. Étude 1. Tremolo, Étude 5. *La Chasse.* PUB. with 2, 3, 4, 6. 1923 or 1924.

Fantasia and Fugue for organ on the Chorale *Ad nos, ad salutarem undam,* transcribed by F.B. for Pf. DED. Josef Sattler. PUB. B. & H., 1897.

Fantasia on two motives from Mozart's *Figaro.* Completed from the almost complete original MS. DED. Moriz Rosenthal. PUB. 1912.

Réminiscences de 'Don Juan', edited by F.B. Grosse kritisch-instruktive Ausgabe. DED. Ernest Lochbrunner. Preface dated Zürich, June 1917. PUB. B. & H., 1918.

Heroischer Marsch in ungarischem Styl. Edited by F.B. DED. Egon Petri. PUB. Schlesinger, 1905.

Hungarian Rhapsody, No. 19, freely arranged for concert use by F.B. PUB. B. & H., 1920.

Hungarian Rhapsody, No. 20. After a copy in the Liszt Museum at Weimar. About 1900. MS. unpublished.

Mephisto-Walzer, newly arranged for Pf. from the orchestral score by F.B. DED. Count Rozwadowski. PUB. New York, Schirmer, 1904.

Polonaise No. 2 in E major for Pf. with final cadenza by F.B. DED. George Boyle. PUB. Simrock, 1909.

Légendes. Nouvelle édition rédigée et commentée par F.B. (1) *St. François d'Assise: la prédication aux oiseaux.* MS. unpublished. March 1910.

With orchestra:

Spanish Rhapsody. See above.

Totentanz for Pf. and orchestra, original version edited from the autograph MS. (1849) in possession of Marchese Casanova. First published by B. & H., 1919. Preface dated Zürich, 20 Mar. 1918. With notes by Philipp Jarnach.

Pace non trovo (I find no peace), Sonnet 104 of Petrarch: Liszt's original Pf. accompaniment transcribed for orchestra by F.B. DED. Felix Senius. FULL SCORE, Schirmer, New York, 1911.

Instrumental Music:

Valse Oubliée for Pf. arranged for violoncello and Pf. by F.B. PUB. B. & H., 1917.

MOZART:

For Pianoforte Solo:

Cadenzas by F.B. for the Pianoforte Concertos: E flat major (K. 271). DED. José Vianna da Motta. PUB. 1916. G major (K. 453). DED. Alicja Simon. PUB. 1922. F major (K. 459). COMP. 1920. PUB. 1922. D minor (K. 466) (two versions). DED. Richard Faltin. PUB. 1907.

350

C major (K. 467). DED. Marcelle Herrnschmidt. PUB. 1922.
E flat major (K. 482). COMP. 1919. A major (K. 488). PUB. 1919.
C minor (K. 491). PUB. 1919. C major (K. 503). COMP. 1922.
Symphonies in D major (K. 202), G major (K. 318), and G major
(K. 444), arranged for Pf. by F.B. 1888.
Andantino from the Pf. Concerto in E flat major (K. 271) freely ar-
ranged for Pf. solo with a cadenza by F.B. DED. Eduard Steuermann.
PUB. B. & H., 1914.

For two Pianofortes:
Duettino Concertante. See *ante*.
Fantasia in F minor for a mechanical organ (K. 608) arranged for
2 Pfs. DED. Rosamond Ley and Ursula Creighton. COMP. 1922.
PUB. B. & H., 1923.
Overture to *The Magic Flute* arranged for 2 Pfs. COMP. 1923. PUB.
B. & H., 1923.
Sonata for 2 Pfs. in D major (K. 448) arranged with a Cadenza by
F.B. COMP. 1921. MS. unpublished.

For and with Orchestra:
Overture to *Don Giovanni* for orchestra with concert-ending by F.B.
COMP. 1908. FULL SCORE, Schirmer, 1911.
Overture to *Die Entführung aus dem Serail* for orchestra with concert-
ending by F.B. FULL SCORE AND PARTS, B. & H., 1904.
Concert Suite from *Idomeneo* arranged for orchestra by F.B.: Overture,
Sacrifice Scene, and Festal March. DED. Othmar Schoeck. PUB.
B. & H., 1919.
Rondo Concertante for Pf. and orchestra. See above.
Adagio from the Clarinet Concerto (K. 622) for clarinet and orchestra
with a Cadenza by F.B. DED. Edmondo Allegra. FULL SCORE and
parts, B. & H., 1922.
Cadenza istrumentata for the slow movement of the Flute Concerto
in G major (K. 313). DED. Albert Biolley. COMP. 1919. FULL SCORE,
MS. unpublished.
Cadenza istrumentata for the slow movement of the Flute Concerto in
D major (K. 314). DED. Albert Biolley. COMP. 1919. FULL SCORE,
MS. unpublished.

For Pianola:
Overture to *The Magic Flute* arranged for the pianola. MS. in possession
of Egon Petri.

OTTOKAR NOVÁČEK:
Scherzo from the First String Quartet arranged for Pf. DED. Ragnhild
Lund. PUB. E. W. Fritzsch, Leipzig, 1893.

ARNOLD SCHÖNBERG:
Pf. piece Op. 11. No. 2: concert interpretation by F.B. ARR. 1909.
PUB. Universal Edition, 1910.

Busoni's Works

F. SCHUBERT:

Overture, *Der Teufel als Hydraulicus*, Overture in D major, Overture in B flat major, Five Minuets with six Trios and Minuet, Five 'Deutsche' with coda and seven Trios. Arranged for Pf. PUB. B. & H., 1888.

Overture in D major, Overture in E minor, Overture in D major in the Italian style, Overture in C major in the Italian style Op. 170. Arranged for Pf. PUB. B. & H., 1889.

R. SCHUMANN:

Concert Allegro with Introduction in D minor, Op. 134, arranged for 2 Pfs. PUB. B. & H., 1888.

R. WAGNER:

Funeral March for Siegfried's Death from *Götterdämmerung* arranged for Pf. Alla memoria di Luigi Cimoso. PUB. Lucca, 1883.

C. M. VON WEBER:

Clarinet Concerto, newly arranged with Cadenzas by F.B. DED. Edmondo Allegra. COMP. 1920. FULL SCORE, MS. unpublished.

LITERARY WORKS

Entwurf einer neuen Aesthetik der Tonkunst. First edition, Schmidl, Trieste, 1907. American translation by T. S. Baker, 'Sketch of a new Esthetic of Music', Schirmer, 1911. Second Edition, Insel-Verlag, 1910.

Der mächtige Zauberer (The Mighty Magician), Libretto from a short story by Gobineau. DED. Gerda [Busoni]. Written 1905; PUB. Schmidl, 1907.

Die Brautwahl (The Bridal Choice), Libretto after a story by E. T. A. Hoffmann. PUB. Schmidl, 1907.

Turandot, Libretto after Gozzi's play. PUB. B. & H., 1919.

Arlecchino, Libretto. PUB. B. & H., 1919.

Der Arlecchineide Fortsetzung und Ende (Continuation and end of the Harlequinade), Libretto. MS. unpublished.

Doktor Faust (Doctor Faust), Libretto. PUB. G. Kiepenheuer, 1920.

Das Geheimnis (The Secret), Libretto: three scenes after Villiers de l'Isle-Adam. PUB. Blätter der Staatsoper, Berlin, Nov. 1924.

Die Götterbraut (The Bride of the Gods), Libretto written for L. T. Gruenberg.

Das Wandbild (The Picture on the Wall), Libretto. DED. Philipp Jarnach. Set to music by Othmar Schoeck. PUB. B. & H., 1920.

Gesammelte Aufsätze: Von der Einheit der Musik (Collected Papers: On the Unity of Music). PUB. Max Hesse, 1922.

Lehre von der Übertragung von Orgelwerken auf das Klavier (Method for the transcription of organ works for the pianoforte). Appendix to the *W.K.*, Book I.

Versuch einer organischen Klavier-Notenschrift (Attempt at an organic notation for the Pf.). PUB. Breitkopf & Härtel, 1910.

INDEX

353

Index

355

Index

Index

Index

servatoire, 77; influence on F.B.,
82; concerts at, 106, 114; F.B. as conductor, 130; Riga compared with,
198; F.B.'s last thoughts of, 289
Henselt, Adolphe, work played by
F.B.: Concerto in F minor, 112
Herrmann, Hans, 252
Herzog, Wilhelm, 137
Hess, Sarah, 96
Hess, Willy, 122
Hindemith, Paul, 275
Hofmann, Joseph, 221
Hoffmann, E. T. A., *Cardillac*, 141;
Die Brautwahl, 170; account of H.,
170 ff.; influence of H. on F.B.'s
mind, 171; episodes suggesting H.:
at Birmingham, 172 ff.; at Verona,
178 ff.; at Bordeaux, 179; in London, 243
Hollmann, Joseph, 123
Hugo, Victor, 179. *See also* Busoni,
Ferruccio, compositions, *Espère,
enfant*
Hummel, J. N., works played by
F.B.: Theme with Variations, 17,
22; *Rondo mignon*, 19; Concerto in
B minor, 112

I Promessi Sposi, 50
Ibsen, Henrik, 180, 189
Improvisation, by F.B., 29 ff., 33, 42,
71 ff.
Indipendente, L', 44, 48, 57 ff., 155 ff.
Innsbruck, 155
International Society for Contemporary Music, 274 ff., 281 ff.
Italy and Italians: Italian women, 51,
189; German views on Italian
music, 54, 135 ff.; F.B.'s ambitions
for I., 79, 154, 165, 178, 188, 206,
212, 221, 244; I. views of marriage,
84, 188; I. publishers' indifference
to Bach, 103; I. and the romantic
movement, 115; F.B. on Italian
music in 19th cent., 116; Liszt as I.
composer, 117, 151, 168; I. composers writing German music, 118;
F.B.'s pleasure in talking I., 119;
characteristic fauna of I., 119;
conductors, 136; Bartolini's restaurant, 137; *bersaglieri's* song, 139;

life in, 153; Comedy of Masks, 170;
Hoffmann a link with I., 171;
Die Brautwahl, 174; 'the Italian
Faust', *ibid.*; 'an end in Italy', 153,
175; disappointment in I., 177;
fascination of, *ibid.*; symbol of
F.B.'s aspirations, 184; a villa in
Tuscany, 190, 194, 209; I. musicians at San Francisco, 195; I. architecture at Moscow, 198; 'Sono le
sedie!', 205; impressions of I., 209,
213, 245; I. and war, 221, 223;
I. musicians on strike, 282; farewell
to I, 289

Jadassohn, Salomon, 68
Jarnach, Philipp, 237, 275, 287, 296
Joachim, Joseph, 80, 103, 122
Joseffy, Raphael, 221
Journal de Genève, 232
Journal de Liége, 109

Kahnt, C. F., 66
Kajanus, Robert, 77
Kalbeck, Max, 56, 160
Kampf um Rom, Ein (Felix Dahn), 179
Kansas City, 193 ff
Kapff, Otto von, meets F.B., 27 ff.;
correspondence with F.B., 31 ff.;
negotiations, 35; K. and F.B.'s
love-affair, 61 ff.; marriage, 122;
calls on F.B. at Vienna, 165; a
'Hamlet' type, 227; helped by
F.B. and Baroness Oppenheimer,
239
Kardorff, Konrad von, 137
Keller, Gottfried, 56, 189
Kestenberg, Leo, 149, 247
Kienzl, Wilhelm, 27; collects money
for F.B., 33; reviews, 36; pupil of
W. Mayer, 37; Dr. K. and Dr.
Faust, 264; records F.B. on Schubert, 312 *note*
Kircher, Athanasius, 153
Kistner, C. F., 60
Klagenfurt, 29 ff., 33 ff., 246
Klengel, Julius, 81
'Knights of Columbus', 240
Koch von Langentreu, Hofrat Adolf,
164
Kreisler, Fritz, 152, 211, 222

361

Index

363

Index

ment of, 145; F.B.'s *Klavierübung*, 239; technique, 259; Erard p. at Paris, 270; resources of the, 306 ff.

Pianoforte-playing: Anna Busoni's, 6, 9; Ferdinando B.'s, 16; Ferruccio B.'s, in 1875, 19; in 1885, 54; at Hamburg and Trieste in 1887, 71; at Hamburg in 1889, 82; reproduction of organ tone, *ibid.*; virtuosity, 100; influence of Rubinstein, 102 ff.; monumental style, 103; F.B.'s in 1894, 108; impressionism, 109, 145 ff., 210, 307; at Brussels (1902), 109; F.B.'s playing of Liszt, 146; sensitive young men, 159 ff.; examinations in, 217; F.B.'s playing in 1921, 258 ff.; F.B. on great pianists, 258; F.B. aiming at a new style, 270

Picello (Harlequin), 195

Pisa, 40, 42, 310

Pitt, Percy, 136, 173 *note*

Pizzetti, Ildebrando ('Ildebrando da Parma'), 203

Podrecca, Guido, 119

Poe, Edgar Allan, 171, 188 ff.

Polko, Elise, 32

Prague, 36, 114, 207 *note*

Prelinger, Frau Dr. (*née* Mayer), 39, 49 ff., 55, 65, 73, 165 ff.

Presse Musicale, La, 9

Programmes, F.B.'s: Trieste (1873-4), 17; proposed for Graz (1879), 33; Graz (1881), 40; Empoli (1882), 42; Vienna (1883), 46; Hamburg (1887), 71; Graz (1888), 72; Helsingfors (1888), 77; *ibid.* (1889), 85; Berlin (1898), 112; Berlin (Liszt recitals 1904), 150; Vienna (privately 1908), 166; America (1910), 191; Berlin (1920), 253; Berlin (orchestral concerts of F.B.'s works, 1921), 255; London (1921), 257

Proske's *Musica Divina*, 60

Protestantism, effects of, 98, 274

Puccini, Giacomo, 115, 160 ff., 182, 198

Pugno, Raoul, 136

Puppet-theatre, at Trieste, 14; F.B. on *Die Brautwahl*, 183; Bergamo resembling, 213; *Teatro dei Piccoli*,

230; puppet-play of *Faust*, 293 ff.; puppet-play style, 297

Rameau, J. Ph., work played by F.B.: Gavotte with Variations, 19

Recoaro, 11

Reinecke, Carl, 54, 80

Reinhardt, Max, 153

Reinhart, Hans, 310

Reisenauer, Alfred, 258

Rémy, Marcel, 110 ff., 306

Rémy, W. A. (*pseud.*), *see* Mayer

Reuenthal, Neidhard von, 51

Reucker, Alfred, 295 ff.

Reznicek, E. N. von, 37

Ricci, Luigi, 6

Richter, Hans, not at home, 44; on Italian and English composers, *ibid.*; absent from F.B.'s concert, 46; postpones F.B.'s suite, 48; tries suite, 51; buries his mother-in-law, 65; in London at Gambrinus, 123; on Mahler, *ibid.*; on *Die Brautwahl*, 182

Richter, Ludwig, 118, 287 *note*

Ricordi, Tito, 182, 204

Riemann, Hugo, 75

Riga, 198

Roland von Berlin, 135

Rome, Anna Busoni plays at, 7; Trieste compared with, 153; F.B.'s first success in, 196; *Teatro dei Piccoli*, 230; F.B.'s sympathetic reception at, 230

Rosé, Arnold, 51

Rosegger, Peter, 64

Rossi, Arnaldo, 195

Rossini, G., F.B. improvises on theme from, 30; R. at Bologna, 207; his wig, 214, 216; opera performed by puppets, 230; R. of the school of Mozart, 267; *Reminiscenza Rossiniana*, 278 ff.; *Stabat Mater*, 310

Rotterdam, 70

Rovereto, 30

Rubinstein, Anton, F.B. meets, 20; fiery style, 24; testimonial to F.B., 26 ff.; advice to F.B., 31; concert at Vienna, 47; lesson from, 59; at Helsingfors, 78; R. Prize, 94, 124;

365

2A

Index

Index

PLATE I

THERESIA WEISS

1778

JOSEF WEISS

GIUSEPPE WEISS
1799–1892

CAROLINA WEISS
née DE CANDIDO

PLATE II

ANNA BUSONI
née BINI *about* 1860

FERDINANDO BUSONI
1872

ANNA WEISS
1855

ANNA WEISS
about 1860

PLATE II

THE HOUSE AT EMPOLI IN WHICH FERRUCCIO BUSONI
WAS BORN

PLATE IV

SALZBURG, 1868

GRAZ, 1871

GMUNDEN, 1876

VIENNA, 1878

FERRUCCIO BUSONI

ANNA BUSONI and FERRUCCIO BUSONI

LAIBACH, 1883

FERRUCCIO BUSONI

MILAN, 1881

LATE VI

FERRUCCIO BUSONI   HELMI SJÖSTRAND
GERDA BUSONI   CARL AENEAS SJÖSTRAND
née SJÖSTRAND

MOSCOW, 1890

FERRUCCIO BUSONI and LESKO
LEIPZIG, 1888

PLATE VII

ANNA BUSONI

TRIESTE, 1897

FERDINANDO BUSONI

PLATE VIII

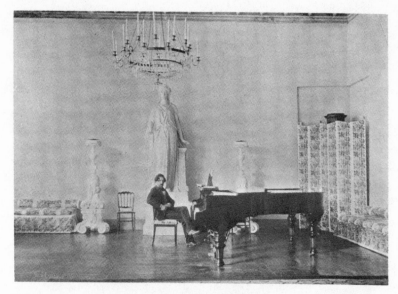

THE TEMPELHERRENHAUS, WEIMAR

THE *MEISTERKLASSE* AT WEIMAR, 1900

PLATE IX

FERRUCCIO BUSONI
LONDON, 1901

PLATE X

RAFFAELLO, GERDA, and BENVENUTO BUSONI
BERLIN, 1902

BENVENUTO and FERRUCCIO BUSONI
BERLIN, 1904

PLATE X

FERRUCCIO BUSONI

LONDON, 1905

PLATE XII

FERRUCCIO and GERDA BUSONI

BERLIN, 1908

PLATE XIII

THE MEISTERKLASSE AT VIENNA, 1908

PLATE XIV

TRIESTE, 1907

FERDINANDO BUSONI
TRIESTE, 1901

PLATE XV

GERDA BUSONI
NEW YORK, 1911

FERRUCCIO BUSONI
after a concert in the Beethoven-Saal
BERLIN, 1912

PLATE XVI

FERRUCCIO BUSONI and GIOTTO
ZÜRICH, 1918

PLATE XVII

FERRUCCIO BUSONI
ZÜRICH, 1918

PLATE XVIII

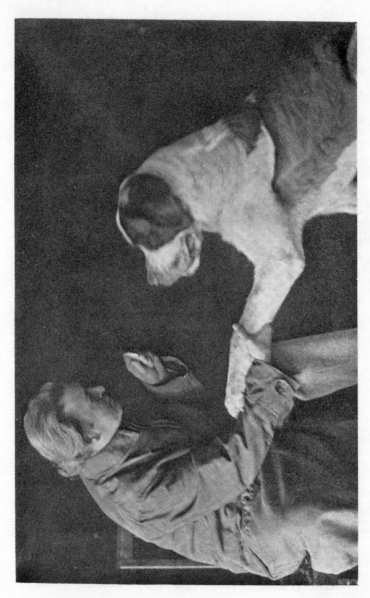

FERRUCCIO BUSONI and GIOTTO
ZÜRICH, 1918

PLATE XIX

RICCARDO RIPAMONTI, MARCHESE SILVIO CASANOVA,
FERRUCCIO BUSONI, UMBERTO BOCCIONI

UMBERTO BOCCIONI and FERRUCCIO BUSONI

SAN REMIGIO, PALLANZA, 1916

PLATE XX

FERRUCCIO BUSONI and JEAN SIBELIUS

FERRUCCIO and GERDA BUSONI

LONDON, 1921

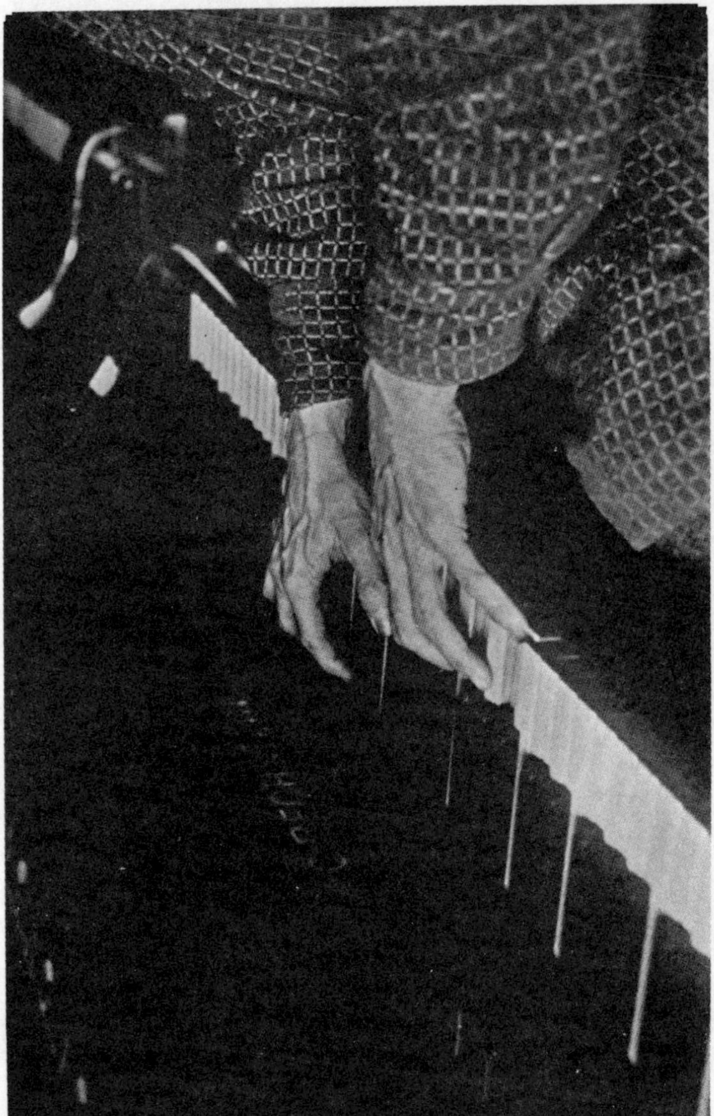

PLATE XXI

FERRUCCIO BUSONI'S HANDS

BERLIN, 1922

FERRUCCIO BUSONI

PLATE XXII

PARIS, 1923

PLATE XXIII

BUSONI PLAYING BEETHOVEN

A drawing by KAPP